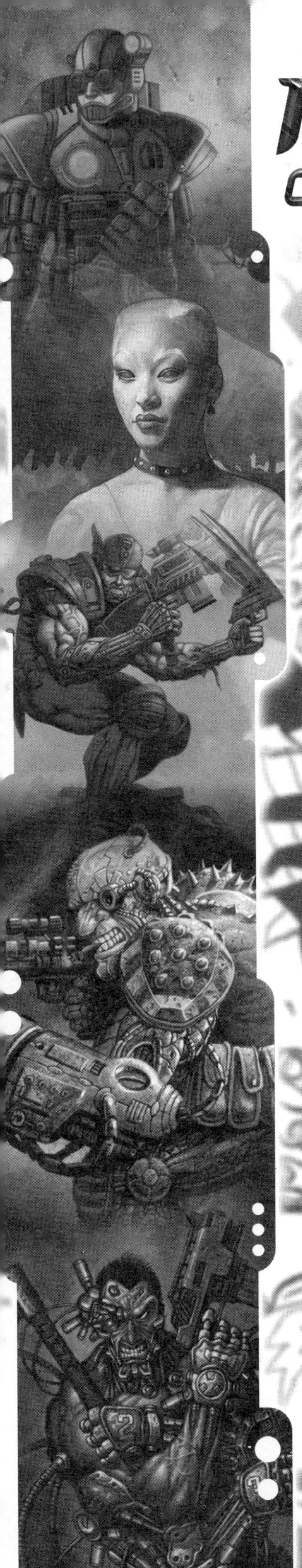

TM

TABLE OF CONTENTS

INTRODUCTION	**6**
Developer's Say	**6**
Updating Your Characters	**7**
CYBERTECHNOLOGY	**8**
Cyberware Defined	**8**
Implanting	**10**
Grades of Cyberware	**10**
Cyberware Classifications	**11**
Power Sources	**11**
The Power Players	**12**
The Big Player: Yamatetsu	**12**
The Second Tier	**12**
The Specialists	**12**
On the Bench	**13**
Cyberware Equipment	**13**
Senseware	**13**
Communications	**18**
Brainware	**19**
Riggerware	**23**
Bodyware	**25**
Cyberlimbs	**32**
Cyberware Compatability	**32**
Bonuses	**33**
Strength	**33**
Quickness	**34**
Multiple Cyberlimb Enhancements	**35**
Armor	**35**
Concealment	**35**
Equipment Capacity	**35**
CYBERLIMB ACCESSORIES	**36**
Cyberweapons	**41**
General Cyberware Rules	**42**
BattleTac Systems	**44**
Cyberware and Critters	**44**
Eyes	**44**
Cyberware Grades	**44**
Cyberware and Hacking Pool	**45**
Effects of Increased Reflexes	**45**
Interconnectivity	**46**
Cyberware and Magic	**47**
Protocols	**47**
Cyberware and Signature	**47**
Small Unit Tactics Skill	**47**
Cyberware and Social Interaction	**48**
Task Pool	**48**
Cyberware Triggers	**48**
Vision System Use	**48**
CYBERMANCY	**50**
Defining Cybermancy	**50**
How Cybermancy Works	**50**
Advantages of Cybermancy	**52**
Drawbacks to Cybermancy	**52**
Where to Find It	**53**
The Megacorps	**53**
The Others	**54**
Cybermancy Rules	**54**
Access to Cybermancy	**54**
Ground Rules	**54**
Less Than Zero	**55**
Cybermantic Magic	**55**

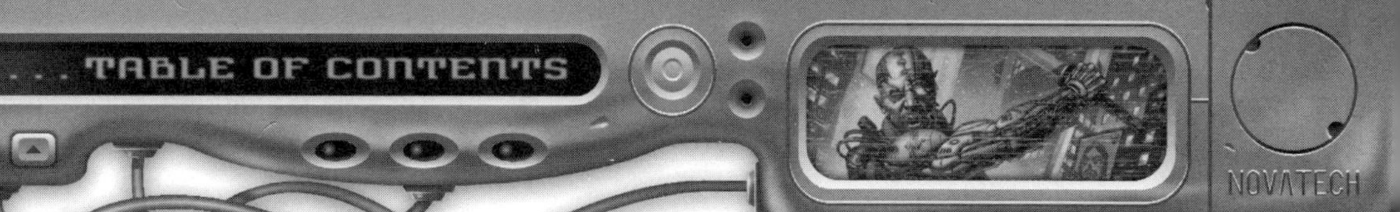

Side Effects 56
Better Off Dead 56
Magical Resistance 56
Dual Nature 57
Karma Hazing 57
Changes to Reaction/Perception 57
Lost in the Details 58
Changes to Willpower 58
Invoked Memory Stimulator 58
Social and Karma Penalties 58
Long-Term Effects 59
Chronic Dissociation Syndrome 59
Cancer 59
BIOTECHNOLOGY 60
Bioware Defined 60
Implanting 60
Bioware Grades 62
Bioware Drawbacks 62
Bioware and the Awakened 62
Biosystem Overstress 62
The Power Players 62
The Implant Kings 62
The Second Tier 63
Others to Watch 63
The Harvesters 63
Bioware 63
Basic Bioware 63
Cultured Bioware 72
Cosmetic Bioware 76
Bioware Rules 76
Bioware Grades 76
Effects of Installing Bioware 77
Bioware Drawbacks 77
Bioware and the Awakened 78
Excessive Bioware Drawbacks 78
Bioware Compatability 78
Bioware and Magic Effects 79
Bioware and Critters 79
NANOTECHNOLOGY 80
Nanotechnology 101 80
Inside the Arcology 80
Outside the Arcology 82
The Nanomachine Explained 82
Construction 82
Power Sources 83
Self-Replication 83
Autonomy 83
Uses of Nanotech 83
Humanity—Caught In the Gears 83
Heavy Industry and Manufacture 85
Space—The Deep Black 85
Computers 85
What It Can't Do 85
Who's Doing What to Whom 86
The Big Three 86
Lean and Mean 87
Sitting in the Nano-Dust 89
Nanotech Gear 90
Nano-Implants 90
Nanoware 91
Nanogear 95
Nanotech Rules 96
Nanotech and Its Uses 96
Nanodrones 96
Nanoware 98
Acquiring Nanoware 98
Installation 99
Nanite Loss 99
Thermographic Detection 100
Nanoware Detection 100
CHEMISTRY 101
The Basics 101
Applied Industrial Chemistry 101
In the Shadows 102
Pharmaceuticals 102
Categories 102
Use of Pharmaceuticals 102
Chemistry and Alchemy 104
Radicals and Orichalcum 104
Magical Compounds 104
The Power Players 104
Neck and Neck: S-K and Z-IC 104
Second Tier 104
Specialists 105
Drug Rules 105
Dosage 105
Drug Attributes 105
Drug Effects 105
Working with Chemicals 107
Chemical Tools 107
Making Controlled Substances 108
Substance Abuse 108
Becoming Addicted 108
Getting a Fix 109
Acquiring a Tolerance 109
Addiction Effects 109
Kicking the Habit 109
Applied Chemtech Compounds 111
Chemtech Application Gear 113
Pharmaceutical Compounds 117
Magical Compounds 122
DAMAGE AND HEALING 124
Stress Points 124
Stress Level 126
Stress Test 126
Wound Effects 126
Determining Wound Effects 126
Cybersystem Damage 127
Cyberware Failure 128
Bioware Damage 128
Bioware Failure 128
Attribute Damage 129
Attribute Failure 129
Stress Maintenance 130

Cyberware Stress Repair 130
Bioware Stress Repair 130
Attribute Stress Repair 131
Using Stress 131
Consciousness 131
Reviving Unconscious Characters 131
Effects of Retaining Consciousness 132
Scars 132
Dermal Armor Damage 133
Optional Rules 133
Expanded First Aid Modifiers 133
Expanded Doctoring 133
Healing Physical Damage 134
Called Shots and Wound Effects 134
Deadlier Over-Damage and Wound Effects 134
SURGERY 135
Surgical Skills 135
Active Skills 135
Knowledge Skills 136
Medical Gear 136
Medkits 136
Medical Shops (Clinics) 138
Medical Facilities (Hospitals) 138
Mobile Medical Shops 138
Medical Telepresence Gear 139
Body Parts 139
Finding Treatment 140
Medical Providers 140
Finding Emergency Medical Care 142
Non-emergency Medical Care 143
Getting In the Door 143
Surgery Overview 144
Diagnosis and Profiling 144
Detecting Implants 145
Surgical Planning and Preparation 145
Options 145
Creating A Procedure 145
Surgical Tests 146
Cosmetic Tests 146

Implant Surgery 146
Therapeutic Surgery 147
Transimplant Surgery 147
Trauma Surgery 148
Surgical Options 148
Negative Options 149
Positive Options 150
Surgery Damage 151
Paying the Price 151

Man & Machine Credits

Writing
Robert Boyle
Martin Gotthard
Eleanor Holmes
Michael Mulvihill
Sebastian Wiers

Product Development
Michael Mulvihill
Robert Boyle

Project Editing
Jean Rabe
Robert Boyle
Sharon Turner Mulvihill
Paolo Marcucci

Shadowrun Line Developer
Michael Mulvihill

Editorial Staff
Editorial Director
Donna Ippolito
Managing Editor
Sharon Turner Mulvihill
Associate Editor
Robert Boyle
Assistant Editor
Davidson Cole

Art Staff
Art Director
Jim Nelson
Assistant Art Director
Fred Hooper
Cover Art
Marc Sasso
Back Cover Art
Paul Bonner
Jim Nelson
Marc Sasso
Matt Wilson
Cover Design
Fred Hooper
Layout
Fred Hooper
Jim Nelson
Illustration
Janet Aulisio
Tom Baxa
Paul Bonner
Tom Fowler
Fred Hooper
Dave Martin
Kevin McCann
Jim Nelson
Steve Prescott
Marc Sasso
Ron Spencer
Shane White
Matt Wilson

Playtesting, Spot Writing and All-Around Help
Robert Barker, Michael S. Bobroff, Duane Brickler, Perry Fawcett, Patrick Goodman, Jeremy Guillemette, J. Keith Henry (to whom I owe a personal thanks for writing one heck of a paragraph that put many things into perspective for me), John Hollar, Joanna Hurley, Jeff Jones, Steve Kenson, Gregory B. Lusby, Paolo Marcucci, Rich Osterhout, John Reid, Brent Smith, Jon Szeto, Myron Thompson, James Vaughan; The Whatevers (Edie Bell, Robert Boyle, Berianne Bramman, Tim Curtin, Anara Gesserit, William Gold, Chris Shaffer, Jeff Smith, Sebastien Wiers); and, of course, The Mysterious Dvixen.

Dedication

This book is dedicated to a guy who has helped me since the very first stages of SR3 were barely conceived. He has worked in some way on every *Shadowrun* product for more than a year, and each time I forget to credit or thank him. It's ironic that I would choose to dedicate this book to him, because he never plays characters with cyberware (he prefers magic)—and yet I did so because I think it will mean that much more. Heck, he compiled all the equipment tables for this book! So, thank you, Flake, for helping out and not complaining too much when I forgot that you did!

—MM

Corrected Fourth Printing

Published by FASA Corporation • 1100 W. Cermak Road • Suite B305 • Chicago, IL 60608

FASA Corporation can be reached on America OnLine (e-mail—FASAInfo (BattleTech, Shadowrun, General Information) or FASA Art (Art Comments) in the Online Gaming area (Keyword "Gaming"). Via InterNet use <AOL Account Name>@AOL.COM, but please, no list or server subscriptions. Thanks!

Visit FASA on the World Wide Web at
http://www.FASA.com

INTRODUCTION

Man & Machine is the advanced cyberware and implant sourcebook for the *Shadowrun* game system.

This book offers new gear, new technology, new concepts and new options for game play, expanding what was offered in previous *Shadowrun* material.

In addition to containing a significant percentage of new material, *Man & Machine* represents a compilation of material originally published in various *Shadowrun* books that are now out of print or were based on previous editions of the *Shadowrun* rules: information presented in *Shadowtech, Cybertechnology, Neo-Anarchist's Guide to Real Life, Corporate Security Handbook, Cyberpirates, Lone Star, Renraku Arcology: Shutdown* and *California Free State* has been revised and updated for use with *SR3*. Any references in this book to the *Shadowrun* rules refer to the third edition of the rules.

Man & Machine begins with *Cybertechnology,* the science (or perhaps art) of blending flesh and metal to expand a metahuman's capabilities. The overview covers the essentials of cyberware, from why there is Essence loss to how pieces of cyberware talk to each other and who are the power players in the cybernetic community—including which megacorporations work which sides of the shadows. The cyberware gear section offers nearly a hundred pieces of cyberware; some familiar, some new and cutting-edge. This chapter also includes rules for cyberlimb enhancements and for stacking gear in a limb at no Essence loss, plus rules for integrating all this new cyber into your game and for magic and cyber compatibility.

Cybermancy provides an overview of the mysterious technique of keeping a metahuman alive without Essence, describing who does it and how and providing rules for its use in game play. *Biotechnology* involves replacing flesh parts with enhanced and improved flesh parts. The overview describes the advantages and drawbacks of this equipment, followed by bioware gear and rules for implanting it and for its limitations.

The newest science for use by shadowrunners is *Nanotechnology*—the science of implanting nanites into your body to achieve increasingly efficient and fantastic effects. The overview explains the technology and how it works, followed by more than twenty pieces of gear and rules for making nanoware compatible with bio- and cyberware.

Chemistry offers information about various drugs, gases, chemical weapons and gear, including spray and squirt cannons and guns. Poisons and toxins, as well as the rules for addiction and explosives, are presented here. The section ends with a discussion of magical compounds, herbal concoctions derived from Awakened flora.

Damage and Healing provides all the information characters need to know about taking damage and the long-term effects on cyber- and bioware as well as on their physical Attributes. The concept of Stress damage, used to indicate the condition of a piece of gear or Attribute, is included, as are the effects of such Stress on each type of gear. Advanced and optional damage, healing, doctoring and first aid rules are also included in this section.

Surgery covers everything from implantation to significant repair, including how to get trauma care and hospitalization. This chapter also discusses surgical skills and facilities, introduces the specialized mobile medical shops, and covers finding the best doctor, rules for trauma surgery and exactly what services DocWagon performs.

DEVELOPER'S SAY

Don't get me wrong, revising the entire *Shadowrun* magic system was hard … very, very hard.

But updating the gear and associated rules for *Man & Machine* made the revision of the magic system feel like a picnic. You hold in your hands the most difficult-to-produce book ever published for *Shadowrun.*

Why, you may ask, was this so hard? Simply put, we can make up stuff about magic, and as long as we are consistent, everyone is happy. You can't just make up stuff about the human body, or about chemistry or biology, or how people heal or how they die. That stuff, unfortunately, is pretty well-established. Therefore, we have to create fictional stuff that fits with what even the most science-ignorant already know. Then we have to make sure it works in the rules of *Shadowrun.*

So, to see the process, let's begin with Essence loss—a pure game mechanic that needs a scientific basis to work.

Essence is not scientific; it is the realm of magic and mana. But it plays an important part in the existence and maintenance of the flesh body and must be addressed in any discussion of implant parts.

We need to *really* define what Essence loss represents, but it's never been fully explained. For example, does a person lose Essence when they lose a limb, or have a pin put in to fuse a bone or even implant a pacemaker? How about when they transplant a liver or, in *Shadowrun,* a cloned body part? None of those things have ever been described in terms of Essence.

We do know you can lose Essence when you take a deadly wound, receive incompetent medical care or suffer an addiction. We also know that adding cyberware immediately removes Essence and that different grades of cyberware remove different amounts of Essence.

So our first distinction is that Essence loss doesn't happen just because a person is cut open or something is damaged and needs to be removed. Nor is it lost when something the body already has is replaced with the same type of item (liver for liver, lung for lung, flesh limb for flesh limb).

This limits Essence loss to something that happens when foreign elements are implanted in the body.

But again, this sweeping statement fails because pins, hip replacements and pacemakers shouldn't cause you to lose Essence. So what is it about cyberware that causes Essence loss?

Cyberware needs to be implanted and connected to the neuropathways, unlike pins and pacemakers, which have no need to talk to the brain. So the unique thing about cyberware is that it's a non-natural implant that talks to the brain.

So this machine—metal, ceramic, polymers and other future-tech stuff—must be connected to the ol' fleshy gray matter. This is how cyberware differs from all other implants, and it is here that Essence is lost.

Basic brain research (if it can be called that) confirms that the brain isn't too keen on being rewired to accept new things, especially things it identifies as foreign objects. So how would the brain feel about accepting a machine as flesh? My guess is (and here's the sci-fi part of it all) not that good. In fact, I'm willing to state that the brain's acceptance of a machine as flesh (and the constant nanotech upgrade to maintain that connection) is where Essence loss begins.

Not only do I state it here—that's the rule.

By the act of implanting cyberware, the brain has been changed in a very fundamental way that moves it away from mana and toward machine.

With our most difficult decision made, we now had to apply that criterion to every piece of gear. Bioware, because it is a flesh implant (enhanced flesh, but flesh nonetheless), imposes no Essence loss. Chemical addiction (as well as trauma and surgery) creates fundamental changes to the body that force the brain to adjust itself to functioning out of attunement with mana, and therefore creates a loss of Essence. Nanites don't change much of the flesh's connection with the brain, so they don't cause Essence loss.

***

You will note that, at this point, we really haven't even begun to discuss cyberware, bioware or any specific gear-related issue.

Welcome to working on *Man & Machine.*

For each piece of gear, from chemical compounds to datajacks, we had to measure the concept against multiple yardsticks, everything from how it works (or would work) in the real world (using real science) to how it functions in the game mechanics.

Sure, we made stuff up—and lots of it—but no matter what we did, we always had to go back to whatever scientific reality existed. We had to resist the temptation to make cyberware something it wasn't. We needed to make sure that the rules for cyberware did not turn tech into magic (as happened in *Cybertechnology*), and that magic didn't devolve into genetic mumbo jumbo (as described in *Shadowtech*).

We wanted to take the science part of sci-fi/fantasy and give it the spotlight. *Man & Machine* is gear and tech and toys in all their glory, ready-made for you to use and abuse.

UPDATING YOUR CHARACTERS

One of the most important answers you'll want answered is, how do I update my *SR2* cybered characters to *SR3?* Basically, only a few pieces of cyberware were changed. The tactical computer, encephalon and a few others that had multiple operations for a single unit were completely reconfigured; some were broken down into smaller, more useful devices.

One of the big differences many of you will find is that your characters have more Essence to play with—that's right, more! Cyberlimbs now have the space to carry multiple attachments at no additional Essence cost!

For those characters riding the ragged edge of life due to an excess of cyberimplants, read the new descriptions of the gear that you already carry and note the changes to those pieces of gear, adjusting your Essence accordingly.

For those characters with bioware, there is no Essence loss, but there are plenty of drawbacks, for both mundanes and magicians. Read through the entire bioware section to determine how the system has changed. The primary change is that the rules in *Man & Machine* limit bioware to a maximum of 9 points. Because the penalties for having more bioware than Essence are quite severe, the easiest solution is to simply choose certain items and declare that they will cease to work, bringing the bioware points cost to 9 or less.

All the other sections are either completely new or offer new game applications, so you should read all about going under the knife and healing your wounds before you head back out into the shadows.

Here's my advice to you: first, determine the "man" part—that's the part that's fleshy and soft and has a tendency to bleed. Most likely, you'll know of a real kick-butt "machine" part that you can't wait to have installed. Now if the surgeon (Biotech Skill 2) would stop drinking the synthalcohol and clean up his shop (Rating 2) and install the piece of betaware in you before you need trauma surgery, then you'll be ready for biz ...

As always,

Have Fun!
Play Games!
And try not to bleed on the nurse!

Mike Mulvihill

In 2061, survival in the shadows makes demands on the metahuman body that it was not designed to meet, such as protecting internal organs from bullets or interfacing directly with a computer. Moving at lightning speed is not something an ordinary metahuman normally needs to do, but such an ability is considered necessary in many walks of life. Fortunately for those who feel the need, scientific advances now allow the metahuman body to surpass its limitations by merging man with machine, a process called cybertechnology. This process takes metahumanity into territory where the body was never intended to go.

While magic might be considered metahumanity's greatest gift, cyberware is metahumanity's greatest cheat. While only a privileged few can use magic, anyone can use cyberware.

CYBERWARE DEFINED

Cyberware, at its simplest, is an implanted technological device that can be manipulated by the metahuman body. Cyberware covers everything from enhancements such as datajacks, bone lacing and move-by-wire systems to devices that compensate for disabilities or damage that would otherwise be crippling.

Cyberware comes in many forms and consists of many components, such as plastic derivatives, ceramics and non-corrosive (as well as nonmagnetic and even non-conductive) metal, insulated microfiberoptic lines, microelectronics, microcomputers, microoptical processors, microgyroscopes and engines, electronically stimulated polymers and other myomers.

Direct Neural Interface

Most cyberware is either connected directly to the brain or wired into the nervous system, creating a direct neural link that allows the implant to be controlled by mental commands, usually a physiological impulse of some kind. In other words, the act of extending a retractable handblade is as easy and unconscious as flexing a muscle; the user does not need to mentally issue an "open" command to the handblade.

85
ACCESS
FURY
IAMS-2
PUP
PRESCOTT

Many devices installed in cyberlimbs and body compartments, however, are not equipped to be hardwired to the body; for example, it is just not practical to cybernetically control a lockpick gun (p. 27). Likewise, many devices classified as headware (for example, a tactical computer), when installed in a cyberlimb, are not automatically connected to the brain or nervous system. Such items require a direct neural interface (DNI), a translator that allows the device to interact with and be controlled by the brain (see p. 39).

Interconnectivity

To get the most from your cyberware, it is often necessary for various devices to communicate with each other. For example, if you have an eye camera and headware memory, the eye camera should be connected to the headware memory in such a way that the pictures you take can be stored there.

Cyberware devices can be linked to each other using an input/output transfer device, which allows the cyberware to exchange data. Both datajacks (p. 298, *SR3*) and routers (p. 22) fulfill this role. Such devices can also transfer data to and from external devices linked via a datajack or DNI connection.

For more information on interconnectivity, see p. 46.

IMPLANTING

As the Universal Omnitech advertisement states: "If you can imagine it, we can implant it."

Though the natural metahuman body is incapable of meeting the demands of the twenty-first century, it still represents a marvel of construction and performance. Using the machine that is cyberware to tamper with the machine that is the body by adding to, removing from or otherwise altering it is guaranteed to make the original machine run or look different. Even installing something as unobtrusive as a datajack means the metahuman head actually has a hole in it—a small piece of skull has been removed, and the human brain has been exposed. The skull's purpose is to protect the brain, but metahumanity is willing to compromise that function for the ability to process computer images that much faster and better. Even though the hole is quite small, the fact remains that the skull's role has been circumvented.

Cyberware radically alters the original flesh body, and such alterations take a toll. You might consider it "just a datajack," but that relatively unobtrusive piece of cyberware changes how the brain operates and how the body protects itself.

Essence

Cyberware can do more than bioware (p. 60) or flesh replacement parts (p. 139), and it is diverse enough in design to work on everything from the brain to limbs to internal organs and the nervous system—for all practical purposes, its applications are unlimited. The one limit to implanting cyberware is created by the nature of the metahuman body: for each piece of cyberware implanted, the metahuman loses Essence—that element which separates the living from the nonliving. In *SR3*, Essence is defined as a body's life force, its wholeness, its cohesive and holistic strength. Cyberware cuts through that like a hot knife through butter.

Essence loss is not simply a result of removing flesh: people who lose limbs or organs but do not replace them with cyberware do not lose Essence. The loss of Essence is a result of connecting a machine to the nervous system using microsurgery and nanotechnology. By doing so, you have changed the fundamental nature of your body—you gain an operational advantage, but you are no longer whole.

A point exists at which the brain can no longer accept additional machine elements as part of the body, if those parts are installed in the standard way. Every metahuman possesses six points of Essence that can be traded for cyberware; this appears to be a limit science alone cannot surpass. As a result, cyberware research developed simultaneously in two directions. One avenue sought to make the interface between the man and the machine less catastrophic to the body, i.e., reduce the Essence cost. This resulted in improving grades of cyberware. The other direction looked for a way to trick the body into accepting more cyberware than it had Essence to replace using specialized magical means. This created cybermancy (p. 50).

GRADES OF CYBERWARE

Cyberware is available in four grades. From lowest to highest grade, they are: basic, alphaware, betaware and deltaware. The better the grade, the lower the Essence loss and the higher quality the components.

The most common cyberware is basic cyberware. Not exactly Essence-friendly, it is constructed for the mass market and readily available. Any surgeon or street doctor can implant basic cyberware. It has the advantages of being relatively inexpensive, easy to obtain and simple to install. The disadvantage is that it cannot be customized to an individual or a specific purpose—what you see is what you get.

Alphaware is better-constructed than basic cyberware. The materials have higher quality control, and the devices receive more rigorous testing. In general, alphaware must be ordered, though it is beginning to be available as a stock item. It is as readily available as basic cyberware, but it costs twice as much and also reduces Essence loss.

Betaware is custom-fitted and adjusted to the user's physiology. Betaware must be special-ordered, and the client must undergo tests to analyze their body's condition and submit to chemical tests and DNA screening. Betaware replaces many of the gyros and microengines used in basic cyberware and alphaware with myomers. Betaware implants cost four times as much as basic cyberware. It is less easily available and takes longer to produce. Betaware implants cost less Essence than basic or alphaware and are difficult to acquire on the street.

The rarest grade of cyberware (and perhaps the ultimate in cybernetic enhancement) is deltaware. Deltaware is always custom-built for each user as part of the surgical process. Constructed of the highest-grade metals, plastics and ceramics, deltaware borders on art—the electronics are wired as the implant is put into the body to ensure perfect compatibility and flawless construction. Deltaware generally wires the myomers directly to the body's electrical impulses, so surgeons must be trained in both microelectronics and medicine. Deltaware is not available on the street, and the people capable of creating and implanting it are buried so deeply in the corporations that their names and locations are rarely even whispered in the shadows. Deltaware-capable clinics often offer access to cybermancy (p. 50), even if they cannot perform it themselves. Deltaware implants, parts and tools cost eight times as much as basic cyberware.

Basic, alpha and beta cyberware is available used. The quality of this cyberware must be considered suspect, but it is cheap and will still do the job for which it was designed. Used deltaware cannot be purchased, but if you can otherwise acquire it, you can have it installed as if it were betaware.

Rules for cyberware grades appear on p. 44.

CYBERWARE CLASSIFICATIONS

Cyberware is divided into three classifications, based on location and use: headware, bodyware and cyberlimbs.

One of the many advantages that cyberware offers metahumanity is that each piece can dramatically expand the role of a metahuman body part. For all that metahumanity's primary characteristic and advantage is its adaptability, the truth is that a flesh eye has a specific and singular function. Cyberware manufacturers now offer replacement parts that can perform multiple functions. For example, a cybereye offers more than twenty-five options, not including option packages and stackable operations.

Headware

It is easy to determine which items fall into the headware classification. Any cyberware that is implanted in the head is considered headware, which ranges from the exotic (cyberskulls) to the mundane (datajacks). Perhaps the most useful of all cyberware, headware's proximity to the brain also makes it some of the most dangerous to install. The fact that pieces of the skull need to be removed or drilled through in order to install headware allows the body's most important organ to be exposed and, in some cases, damaged. This risk has in no way diminished the popularity of datajacks, radios, additional memory and other accessories.

Headware is subdivided by function into senseware, matrixware, riggerware, communications and brainware.

Senseware consists of eye, ear and nasal modifications as well as chemical analyzers and weapons confined to sensory orifices. This type of cyberware implantation is popular because it allows multiple options to be added in a single procedure. Senseware can improve existing senses and add new ones.

Matrixware is the narrowest branch of headware, but the most commonly implanted, consisting primarily of datajacks and cerebral cyberdecks.

Riggerware consists of a rigger remote control deck and access installed in a cranial interface.

Communications headware is a very common enhancement. No one thinks twice about having a radio, telephone or other communications device implanted into their skull. The shadow community's increased use of headware communications and the value of a rigger's detection devices mean the next advancement in headware communications is most likely to involve the ability to jam another's communications.

Brainware is the catchall category for headware and includes such items as headware memory, advanced-function processors such as the tactical computer, tooth compartments and even cortex bombs. The brainware classification originally described only headware designed to enhance (and even outperform) the brain, but the proliferation of unique pieces of gear that were difficult to categorize expanded the scope of this classification.

Bodyware

Bodyware covers all cyberware not implanted in the head. Any devices that use the central nervous system to deliver messages to the brain are considered bodyware, as are move-by-wire systems and high-end wired reflexes that bypass the normal nervous system routing, as are bone restructuring, body plating and even cybertorsos. Bodyware also includes any devices that can be built into cyberlimbs, such as hand blades or smartgun links.

Cyberlimbs

Once a subclassification of bodyware, cyberlimbs have evolved into a unique classification as a result of advances in the number of objects that can be incorporated into a single limb. Cyberlimb owners can now customize their limbs as easily as their cybereyes, even including storage compartments. Cyberlimbs have a high Essence cost because of the number of neural pathways that must remain open to the brain.

POWER SOURCES

Early efforts in cyberware required battery packs and recharging to power the devices, but like the dodo and the honest corporate official, they are things of the past. By reinforcing the natural myolinear sheath interfacing that connects the nervous system pathways using superconductive and macroconductive materials that are constantly repaired and reconnected via nanotechnology, cyberware can be powered from within the body. Cyberware now runs on the natural neural bioelectricity that powers the flesh body.

Even items that would seem to use more energy than the body can produce, such as cyberlimbs or wired reflexes, can perform at the levels they do because these superconductive pathways pick up bioelectric current from other parts of the body and instantaneously feed it to the areas that need the power. The process used to redistribute neural bioelectricity alters the body's biochemistry. Some researchers believe that this base physiological change may also reduce Essence, which could explain why there have been no further breakthroughs since the development of deltaware.

THE POWER PLAYERS

So, who's on the cutting edge of cyberware? The real question is, who isn't? Cyberware is so pervasive that every megacorporation and most AA and A corps are involved in its manufacture, distribution or implantation at some level.

THE BIG PLAYER: YAMATETSU

Yamatetsu stands alone on top of the heap of companies, big and small, that work and play in cybernetics. Yamatetsu does not specialize; it does it all. They have developments in every type and classification of cyberware; they have conducted extensive research into Essence loss; they offer versions of cyberware for all metahuman types; they rank as the number one manufacturer and distributor of metahuman cyberlimbs, torsos and skulls; their CrashCart subsidiary offers implantation; and they have all grades of cyberware available.

THE SECOND TIER

The following corporations have their hands in many aspects of cybernetics, but they do not try to do it all.

Cross Applied Technologies

Cross focuses on headware, particularly research, though Leonard Aurelius has recently allocated more resources to manufacturing. Their spies are hidden deep in research companies around the globe, allowing them to acquire various lines of research and discoveries and put them in the hands of their scientists, who are consistently able to make leaps of logic that elude those focused solely on their own methods. They then sell back parts of the completed research to the corps from whom they stole it.

They have access to all grades of cyberware but must obtain it through second and third parties.

Renraku

Say what you will about their fall from the top and their various internal and external problems, their cybernetic divisions took no real hits. The technology that was pushing them to the top of the AAA platform is still cutting-edge. Their focus has been mainly on matrix- and other headware research and manufacturing. The Renraku subsidiary Iris Firmware creates microelectronics specific to the cybernetic field that are used in everything from cyberlimbs to cybereyes.

Renraku does very little implantation work.

Shiawase

Shiawase Biotech, an entire division dedicated to cybertechnology and related fields such as bio- and nanotechnology, is credited with so many research breakthroughs in nearly every cybernetic field that many consider them the developers of the first working deltagrade cyberware. The focus of this company in recent years has been on nanotechnology and biotechnology. Their manufacturing arm produces only the highest-end goods, and they own a few exclusive, private implant clinics.

THE SPECIALISTS

The following megacorporations work on only one aspect of cybertechnology or specialize in one field of cyberware. Their success in a narrow sphere of influence has allowed them to make a name for themselves in both the corporate world and in the shadows.

Ares Macrotechnology

As their name states, Ares is involved in macroelectronics rather than micro. Their research and manufacturing focus on smartgun links and other cyberware that incorporates or assists weaponry, such as cyberguns, oral and optical weapons and articulated arms.

Aztechnology

Aztechnology provides various versions of basic-grade cyberware worldwide. To boost their research and manufacturing capabilities, they have formed a strategic alliance with Universal Omnitech.

Mitsuhama Computer Technologies

Any cybernetic breakthrough made by MCT is a result of their manufacturing capability in microelectronics and specialized materials for their robotic and drone divisions, and is related to those areas. They manufacture cyberware according to the same stringent and efficient guidelines they use for manufacturing drones, and this crossover in manufacturing techniques is responsible for the current widespread availability of alphaware.

Mitsuhama does very little implantation for the public, but they supply most of the microelectronic tools and raw materials for those who do.

Transys Neuronet

Best known for its research and design of matrixware, Transys Neuronet is no longer a one-trick pony with its expansion into skillwires and chipjacks. Together with R&D, their manufacturing capabilities produce the best headware memory devices on the market, and their credits include move-by-wire systems and the innovative cybernetic routers. This AA corp shows no signs of allowing anyone else into the niche market it has cornered.

Universal Omnitech

This AA corporation is involved in nearly every aspect of cybertechnology, but its main claim to fame is that nearly every doctor capable of alpha or better cybernetic surgery techniques was trained at a Universal Omnitech medical facility.

ON THE BENCH

These corps also work with cybertechnology, though their primary focus lies in other areas.

DocWagon

By volume, the number-one company in the world for implanting and repairing cybernetics, DocWagon medics do a passable job with basic- and alpha-grade cyberware. They employ only a few doctors and technicians capable of dealing with beta- or delta-grade goods, and those only at specific locations.

Novatech

Novatech has been fighting to stay alive, which has meant a drop in research and manufacturing resources dedicated to cybernetics. They represent the sleeping giant of cybertechnology: as Fuchi, they commanded the top cybernetic spot, and they retained many scientists in the shakeup. Currently, however, they lack the facilities and deep pockets needed to conduct pure research successfully. They have put more and more of their nuyen into matrixware and cyberdecks in order to produce revenue, but doing so has soaked up research capital. They still have a few aces in the hole—including a deltaware manufacturing, research and implanting clinic.

Saeder-Krupp

Saeder-Krupp's involvement covers all aspects of cyberware, naturally, but it has lagged behind in research of late. They were the first corporation to introduce circuitry to bypass the central nervous system, and thus became the number-one manufacturer of skillwires and wired reflexes. Others have subsequently duplicated these early efforts.

Wuxing

Involved in cybertechnology only through investments and their position in the Pacific Prosperity Group, Wuxing falls far behind the other megas in cybernetics.

CYBERWARE EQUIPMENT

SENSEWARE

BALANCE AUGMENTER

The balance augmenter enhances the inner ear's natural balance mechanism. It works so well that new users must often retrain themselves to be able to fall down intentionally.

Game Effects

This device reduces the target numbers by –2 for any skill tests involving balance, such as climbing, walking across a narrow platform, landing after a jump, and so on. It also reduces by 2 the target number to avoid Knockdown (see p. 124, *SR3*). The character must make a Willpower (4) Test to intentionally fall down.

CHEMICAL ANALYZER AND GAS SPECTROMETER

These two items basically function the same way.

The chemical analyzer is usually implanted in the tongue or in a finger tip. Its components include a contact surface (micropads distributed over the finger tip, tongue or other body part), the analyzer device and an optional chemical reference program. When placed in contact with a small sample of a compound, the analyzer can determine its chemical composition. The sample may be in any solid or liquid form (powder, liquid, aqueous solution and so on).

Housed in the main sinus chambers, a gas spectrometer is used to provide an analysis of the chemical composition of gases. Only a small sample is needed for analysis; usually a quick sniff will suffice.

On its own, the chemical analyzer/gas spectrometer will provide only the raw chemical breakdown or composition. In conjunction with a chemical reference program, it can provide common and/or industrial compound names and will prepare a short description of the application and properties of the material in question. The reference program can be built into the analyzer or accessed through headware memory, a chipjack or even through a datajack to a computer running the program.

A display link, image link or datajack is required to output the information provided.

Game Effects

The analyzer/spectrometer functions with a Chemistry Skill of 2 plus the rating of the chemical reference program. For example, a chemical analyzer/gas spectrometer with a built-in Rating 4 reference program performs at Chemistry Skill 6 to determine a compound's composition. If the character also possesses Chemistry Skill, it may be used as a Complementary Skill for the analyzer/spectrometer test. The target number for analyzing most compounds is 4 (6 or higher for rare or complicated chemicals); the number of successes determines the amount of information learned. (General guidelines for revealing information to characters appear on pp. 231–32, *SR3*.)

Only one reference program may be used at a time. The program has a size multiplier of 3.

Unless the compound is extremely caustic or lethal (for example, acid or mustard gas), the amount required for analysis is not enough to inflict damage or harm to the appendage or user (subject to gamemaster discretion).

EYE DATAJACK

The eye datajack is a dataport located behind the iris of the cybereye. When slight pressure is applied to the corner of the eye, it pops open to reveal a standard datajack. This datajack is practically invisible to a visual scan when not in use. An eye datajack in use, however, is very obvious. The eye cannot be used when the datajack is in use.

Game Effects

Eye datajacks have a Concealability of 10 when not in use. They function as standard datajacks (p. 298, *SR3*).

This device can only be used as a cybereye accessory.

EYE LASER SYSTEMS

Eye laser systems have a number of uses, depending on power, range and frequency. Basic eye laser units offer three power levels: low, medium and high. Modifications and accessories are available for these systems, some of which have minimum power requirements. Common uses for eye lasers include target designators, laser microphones, optical scanning links and tool lasers.

Basic Eye Laser System

This is the basic unit, including only the laser. Because this system is contained within a cybereye, it functions as a microlaser system, low in power compared with normal lasers. The power of the unit determines its effective range.

Game Effects: Eye lasers can only be used with cybereyes.

This system can be used to temporarily blind someone with whom the user is in eye contact. The target must be in range and looking at the character. The character uses a Complex Action and makes an Opposed Quickness Test, with the user gaining additional dice per the Laser Table. Each net success adds a +1 modifier to all actions by the target, up to a maximum of +8. Flare compensation reduces this modifier by –2. Because this effect wears off fairly quickly, reduce the target number modifier by –2 per Combat Turn.

Eye lasers rely on LOS and so do not have a Flux Rating.

Batteries cost 150 nuyen. They must be recharged according to usage per the Laser Table. Replacing batteries requires a Biotech (6) Test with a base time of 10 minutes.

LASER TABLE

Laser Power	Effective Range	Additional Dice for Blinding Targets	Batteries
Low	5 m	+1	100 minutes
Medium	50 m	+2	50 minutes
High	500 m	+3	25 minutes

Laser Designators

A laser designator marks a target with reflected laser light so that a weapon with an appropriate tracker/seeker head can home in on the reflected light.

Game Effects: Only high-powered eye lasers can be used as laser designators.

The character makes a ranged weapons Attack Test to "lock on" to the target, using the Launch Weapons (Spotter) Skill (see p. 114, *Cannon Companion*, for laser designator ranges). Combat Pool may be used; however, if the act of spotting occurs for longer than one Combat Turn, dice spent on the Spotting Test do not refresh until the turn after the character finishes spotting. The spotter must maintain laser contact with the target until the indirect fire strikes the target; spotters suffer +2 to other tests during this time. To resolve indirect fire, make a standard Attack Test, using extra dice equal to the successes achieved when locking on to the target.

For more information on indirect fire, see p. 99, *Cannon Companion*.

Laser Microphone

Similar to external laser microphones, this unit allows you to read the laser reflection from a windowpane and translate the vibrations to "hear" sound from the other side.

Game Effects: Eye laser microphones must be medium- or high-powered. They work in a similar fashion to the ones described on p. 290, *SR3*. The output of the microphone must be linked to an ear recorder, subdermal speakers, an external speaker or similar equipment to be "heard," or it can be recorded in headware memory or externally.

Optical Scanning Link

The optical scanning (optiscan) link allows two users to communicate via laser beam. The communicators must be within line of sight (and within range). The beam is secure because it is difficult to intercept and is not susceptible to jamming, as are radios. However, smoke and bad weather can disrupt communication.

The optical scanning link has two components, an infrared laser emitter unit and a data receptor. Users of these systems establish the communications link by staring into each other's eyes. The system must be linked to a transducer (p. 19) to translate thoughts into laser signals for transmitting; when receiving, signals must be processed via a display link or transducer.

An external optiscan plug-in link is also available for electronic devices equipped with a datajack port, allowing the user to communicate with the device. A linked transducer does not work for such connections; a linked datajack is necessary to access the device.

Game Effects: Anything that obscures line of sight (heavy smoke, an intervening object or anything imposing a Perception modifier of +4 or more) disrupts communication between the datajack and remote. External devices must be DNI-equipped (see p. 39) to be accessed or manipulated using this system.

Cyberware	Essence	Cost	Availability	Street Index	Legality
Balance Augmenter	.4	14,000¥	8/2 wks	2	Legal
Chemical Analyzer and Gas Spectrometer	.2	2,500¥	4/6 days	1	Legal
Built-in Program	—	Mp x 200¥	4/6 days	1	Legal
External Program	—	Mp x 150¥	5/4 days	1.25	Legal
Eye Datajack	.25	2,200¥	6/48 hrs	2	4P–N

It is nearly impossible to communicate with this system while moving. For this reason, many characters also install the RAS override (p. 22) to turn their body off while using the laser link.

Laser signal bandwidth is not strong enough to handle simsense connections, so it cannot be used for rigging or decking.

Both the eye unit and the remote adaptor have a Concealability of 10.

Tool Laser

This modification is useful for cutting through thin objects or creating small welds. Due to its low power, it has minimal use as a weapon.

Game Effects: The tool laser can cut a 5 centimeter line through material with a Barrier Rating of 10 or less per Combat Turn. Only high-powered eye lasers can be used as laser tools, but they use the ranges for low-powered lasers.

If the laser tool is used as a weapon, use a Complex Action to make an Attack Test using the character's Laser Weapons Skill. Apply a +1 modifier per meter of range. The Damage Code of the attack is 4L. Modify the Power by –1 against targets up to 2 meters away, and by –2 against targets up to 4 meters away. The laser tool will not penetrate reflective metals or silvered glass, but it can cut mirrored plastics.

EYE LIGHT SYSTEMS

This light system mounts high-powered, low-heat lights in the cybereye that channel a tight, polarized beam outward along a path parallel to the optical center of the eye. An amount of light sufficient to see by using standard low-light eyes falls wherever the user is looking. The tight beam and polarization minimize the beam's scatter, so the light can't be seen unless the user is staring directly at another person.

The Brightlight accessory is a powerful flash system similar in effect to the standard flash-pak, but with an even stronger punch. When loaded with superflash bulbs, it creates a flash bright enough to overload optic nerves, blinding and stunning opponents. The superflash is visible for up to 3 kilometers if line of sight is not blocked, and it may be visible through barriers at the gamemaster's discretion.

Game Effects

The eye light system reduces darkness modifiers by –4 (–6 if the user also has low light vision). This system has a range of 100 meters; reduce the bonus by 1 per 10 meters if attempting to see anything beyond that distance.

Brightlight units affect targets in the same way as a flash-pak (p. 283, *SR3*). Brightlight units burn out after three uses and the bulb and battery must be replaced at a cost of 150 nuyen. Performing the replacement requires a Biotech (6) Test with a base time of 10 minutes.

The high-powered superflash works against any targets facing the user. (If the facing of a target cannot be clearly determined, make an Opposed Reaction Test between the user and target. Targets who achieve fewer successes than the user are affected.) Victims must make a Damage Resistance Test against 12M Stun damage. Reduce the Power of the flash attack by –1 per meter and by –2 for targets with flare compensation. Each damage box taken also imposes a +1 modifier for tests involving vision (including combat). This effect fades at the rate of 1 damage box (and the associated +1 modifier) per minute. For example, if the character takes 5 boxes of Stun damage, they suffer a +5 modifier to all tests requiring vision. As the effect fades, the first box of Stun damage healed also reduces the modifier by 1.

The superflash is so overwhelming that even targets not facing or behind the user (including allies) may be affected by light reflected off walls and other large surfaces. Apply the *Blast in a Confined Space* rules (p. 119, *SR3*) to determine the effect, reducing the Power by –1 per meter.

Whenever a character uses the superflash unit, roll 2D6. On a result of 2 or 3, the character's cybereyes are overloaded and burnt out. The character is blind until they are repaired.

Superflashes are one-use only. Replacement batteries and bulbs cost 10 nuyen each.

EYE WEAPONS

Only two types of eye weapons are available: a dart-shooter and a gun. For both weapons, a single ammo load sits in the eye and is fired through a hole running parallel to the optical axis. When the weapon fires, a sheer covering tears away and reveals the barrel. The eye dart fires narcoject or toxin rounds; the eye gun fires microbullets.

Cyberware	Essence	Cost	Availability	Street Index	Legality
Eye Laser System					
Low Power	.2	3,000¥	8/72 hrs	2	5P–N
Medium Power	.3	5,000¥	8/1 wk	2	5P–N
High Power	.5	8,000¥	8/2 wks	2	5P–N
Laser Designator	.1	6,000¥	12/1 mo	3	5P–R
Laser Microphone	.1	2,000¥ x Rating	Rating/72 hrs	2	5P–N
Optiscan Link	.15	2,500¥	8/72 hrs	3	3P–N
Optiscan Remote Adaptor	—	2,000¥	8/2 wks	2	3P–N
Tool Laser	.15	3,000¥	8/1 wk	2	5P–N
Eye Light Systems	.2	1,200¥	4/72 hrs	1.5	Legal
Brightlight Feature	.2	2,200¥	8/2 wks	3	7P–Q
Superflash	—	+500¥	8/2 wks	3	7P–Q

Eye weapons have at least two disadvantages. Using them tends to leave you partially blind for a short time and inflicts a nasty recoil shock.

Game Effects

Eye weapons must be installed in cybereyes. Each eye can hold only one weapon. Each weapon holds only one shot; reloading requires a Biotech (6) Test with a base time of 10 Combat Turns.

Firing an eye weapon requires the Active Skill Eye Gun, which is linked to Quickness. Eye weapons cannot be used with any aim enhancers or accessories including smartlinks.

Each shot fired causes 1 point of Stress to the cybereye.

Eye Dart: This weapon fires half-Power (round up) narcoject/toxin rounds in the same way as a hold-out pistol, with one-half range (round down). After firing, a character must apply a +2 modifier to all visual tests for a period of (4 – unaugmented Body) Combat Turns (minimum 1 Combat Turn).

Eye ammo rounds cost four times the normal price. See *Chemistry*, p. 101, for details on narcoject and toxin rounds.

Eye Gun: Treat as a hold-out pistol with one-half range (round down) and a +1 recoil modifier. After firing, a character must apply a +2 modifier to all visual tests for a period of (6 – unaugmented Body) Combat Turns (minimum 2 Combat Turns).

Eye gun rounds cost five times the normal price.

INDEPENDENT CYBEREYES

Cybereyes can be installed almost anywhere on the body: in the palm, in the back of the head, smack in the middle of the forehead and so on. These can be installed individually or in pairs.

Visual input from independent cybereyes is spliced directly into the optic nerve. This mismatched imaging is confusing to the brain and tends to disorient the user.

Game Effects

Use the *Single Cybereyes* rules, p. 44, for accessorizing independent cybereyes, but use the installation costs below.

Anytime more than one set (either an independent eye or a pair of eyes, either natural or cyber) of cybereyes is used simultaneously, apply a +1 modifier to all of the user's target numbers for each set beyond the first. Closed eyes do not count toward this effect.

Apply a +4 target number modifier when making ranged attacks using only an independent cybereye (doing so forces the brain to process information in an unfamiliar way). Add a +2 target number modifier when making any tests requiring the user to judge distance.

See also *Cyberware and Social Interaction,* p. 48.

INTERNAL GPS

This implanted global positioning system receives and cross-references data from numerous satellites and can calculate the user's position and coordinates to within 2 meters. This cyberware is most commonly used in conjunction with the orientation system (p. 18).

Game Effects

This device is an internal version of the Nav-Dat GPS (p. 294, *SR3*), except that it does not come equipped with map data.

MICROSCOPIC VISION

Using optical lenses to magnify the visual image of small objects near the user's eyes, this system functions as a built-in microscope.

Game Effects

Objects being scrutinized must be within 15 centimeters of the eye; they can be magnified up to 1,000 times their normal size, and the system can zoom in and out. When undertaking an action that involves fine manipulation of small or microsized objects (such as electronics or computer repair), microscopic vision modifies target numbers by –2.

Microscopic vision implants can be installed in cybereyes or as retinal modifications.

OLFACTORY BOOSTER

An olfactory booster is a combination of a number of small receptors implanted into the nasal passages and the back of the mouth that provide increased sensitivity to smells. Olfactory boosters contain high-level cut-offs to prevent discomfort and distraction from intense odors.

Game Effects

Each level of olfactory booster adds 1 die to any Perception Tests to identify or detect a smell. Because the olfactory booster makes many odors obvious to the user, the gamemaster may also choose to modify the target number for such tests by –4 (per the Perception Test Modifiers Table, p. 232, *SR3*).

Because taste is associated with smell, every 3 levels (round up) of olfactory booster will also add 1 die to Perception Tests for taste.

ORAL DART AND ORAL GUN

Oral weapons are useful for surprising opponents. The oral dart and oral gun are similar to the eye versions and are concealed in the roof of the mouth. Each weapon stores a few rounds of ammo, and each has a safety that keeps them from firing unless the user's mouth is open. The dart fires toxin rounds, the gun microbullets.

Game Effects

Firing these weapons requires the Active Skill Oral Gun, which is linked to Quickness. No aim enhancers or other accessories can be used.

The gamemaster may impose penalties on characters equipped with oral darts or guns when such characters make Perception Tests using their innate sense of smell, because such cyberware may interfere with the normal functions of the sinuses.

Oral Dart: This weapon fires narcoject/toxin rounds at the same ranges as hold-out pistols. Reloading requires a Biotech (4) Test and a base time of 10 Combat Turns. Double the cost of ammo for this weapon (see *Chemistry,* p. 101, for details on narcoject and toxin rounds).

Oral Gun: Treat as a hold-out pistol with an ammo capacity of four shots. Reloading requires a Biotech (4) Test and a base time of 10 Combat Turns. Triple the cost of ammo for this weapon.

ORAL SLASHER

The oral slasher is a spring-loaded extendable baton with a blade on the tip, stored underneath the tongue. When triggered, it shoots directly outward, impaling any close target, then retracts into the mouth.

Game Effects

The oral slasher has a range of 1 meter. Using this weapon requires the Active Skill Oral Strike, which is linked to Quickness. If the user rolls more 1s than successes on his Attack Test or the target dodges, the user may damage himself, in the same manner as if using a monofilament whip (p. 275, *SR3*).

Cyberware	Essence	Conceal	Ammo	Mode	Damage	Cost	Availability	St. Index	Legality
Eye Dart	.25	10	1	SS	Special	4,200¥	8/2 wks	2	7P–Q
Eye Gun	.4	9	1	SS	3L	6,400¥	6/1 wk	3	6P–Q
Independent Cybereyes									
Pair	.5	—	—	—	—	15,000¥	6/72 hrs	2	Legal
Single	.3	—	—	—	—	10,000¥	6/72 hrs	2	Legal
Internal GPS	.1	—	—	—	—	2,000¥	5/6 days	1.5	Legal
Microscopic Vision	.1	—	—	—	—	5,000¥	5/48 hrs	1	Legal
Olfactory Booster	.2	—	—	—	—	1,000¥/level	6/8 days	1	Legal
Oral Dart	.25	10	3	SS	Special	3,600¥	6/1 wks	2	6P–Q
Oral Gun	.4	9	4	SS	4L	5,600¥	6/72 hrs	3	6P–Q
Oral Slasher	.25	10	—	—	6M	10,500¥	8/1 wk	2.5	6P–Q

ORIENTATION SYSTEM

The orientation system is a mapping unit designed to interface with map data, positioning input and imaging software. The orientation system can take data from a GPS unit (linked internally, through a datajack or even via radio) and/or mapsofts (linked via chipjack, headware memory or a datajack) and render an impressive three-dimensional display. The constructed image can be displayed through an image link or output through a datajack. The user's exact positioning is indicated, as well as elevation relative to sea or street level. Input from other GPS units and tracking devices can be integrated into the display as well. Distances between points of reference and icons are also calculated and shown as a background feature.

Game Effects

Depending on the input information and map detail, a character using an orientation system should be able to determine his position, navigate a course, easily tail targets fitted with a tracking signal, find the nearest exit and so on, subject to gamemaster discretion.

Map datasofts vary in size and price, depending on completeness and complexity. A basic city street map can cost as little as 25 nuyen (basic autonav routes), while a detailed city block map (including sewage, gas and electricity maintenance accessways) could cost as much as 1,000 nuyen. There is a thriving black market in purloined maps of corporate facilities, sewer systems and so on; gamemasters should increase the availability and street index of mapsofts as they see fit.

Orientation systems can also be used to create maps, assuming they have some sort of sensory input (for example, GPS or ultrasound sight readings), and storage memory (headware or datajack-linked) is available.

SPATIAL RECOGNIZER

The spatial recognizer improves on the ear's natural ability to pinpoint the direction from which a sound is coming. Useful when trying to find a hidden enemy that you can hear, it's especially handy in situations where your natural ability might be confused by echoes.

Game Effects

This cyberear accessory reduces the target numbers by 2 for Perception Tests based primarily on sound location whenever a character attempts to track something by listening for movement. If the user also has high-frequency hearing, which is directional, apply an additional –1 modifier.

If the user also possesses the orientation system, which provides a headware map of an area, increase the target number modifiers by half. For example, if a character has a spatial recognizer and the orientation system, the target number modifier for Perception Tests based primarily on sound would be –3.

ULTRASOUND VISION

Ultrasound vision systems have three components: an emitter, a receiver and a processor. The emitter device installed in one eye sends out continuous ultrasonic pulses, sweeping forward from side to side. The receiver installed in the other eye (creating a necessary angle of deflection) receives the echoes of these pulses and converts them to electrical signals, which are fed to the processor. The processor (also built into the eyes) builds a topographic image from these signals, showing depth, forms and texture as depicted by the echoes.

When activated, the ultrasound "map" overlays the user's vision (in much the same way that thermographic vision overlays natural sight; see p. 49). Shapes and forms are outlined and textured, allowing the user to distinguish objects that other vision systems can't detect.

Game Effects

Ultrasound vision reduces visibility modifiers (p. 232, *SR3*) by half (round up). If installed with high-frequency hearing modification, reduce the ultrasound vision cost and Essence Cost by 20 percent.

Because this system builds images from sound and transforms them into visual input, indirect illusion spells that affect sight do not affect this system. For example, a character cloaked by an invisibility spell would be visible to a character with ultrasound vision as an outline and faintly textured image. However, because the character is not being viewed directly, they cannot be targeted with magic. Modify by +4 the target numbers for any other actions directed at characters "visible" only through ultrasound.

Indirect illusion spells that affect sound will affect ultrasound vision, however. The silence spell affects ultrasound sight in the same way that invisibility affects normal vision. Characters cloaked using a silence spell do not show up as ultrasound images, and may not be located by an empty space in the ultrasound map image.

White noise also affects ultrasound vision. Add a number equal to the rating of the white noise generator to the target numbers for any actions performed using ultrasound vision.

Cybernetic ultrasound sight is affected by mana-based indirect illusion spells (in addition to physical spells), because it has been purchased with Essence.

COMMUNICATIONS

INTERNAL VOICE MASK

The internal voice mask creates a resonating frequency that distorts the pitch and timbre of the user's voice and makes it unrecognizable. High- and low-frequency modulator accessories allow the user to "speak" at high or low frequencies that are inaudible to most metahumans.

Cyberware	Essence	Cost	Availability	Street Index	Legality
Orientation System	.25	15,000¥	5/6 days	1.5	Legal
Spatial Recognizer	.2	1,200¥	4/48 hrs	2	Legal
Ultrasound Vision	.5	10,000¥	6/48 hrs	2	Legal

Game Effects

This device works in the same way as the external voice mask (p. 291, *SR3*). This device cannot be used to imitate a voice.

The frequency modulators, combined with high- or low-frequency hearing cyberware, can be useful for covert communications. Characters speaking via infrasound (low frequency) cannot communicate as much information as quickly as normal speaking; speaking a single word/short phrase takes a Simple Action, and a full sentence requires a Complex Action. Infrasound travels farther, however, and penetrates barriers better than normal sound.

SUBDERMAL SPEAKERS

Usually implanted under the skin just behind the ear, these tiny speakers vibrate various bones in the ear to transmit sound.

Game Effects

Sound transmitted through subdermal speakers cannot be overheard. Communications headware such as radios and telephones already include such implants; this system's primary stand-alone function is to accommodate datajack-linked communications gear.

TRANSDUCER

The transducer is a device that is wired directly into the brain and translates nonvocalized mental impulses into words and vice versa. An external version of this device also exists, creating the same effect when linked between a datajack and a radio.

In addition to being useful for clandestine communications between shadowrunners, the transducer has revolutionized the lives of people who were born unable to vocalize or who have suffered severe damage to their vocal cords.

Game Effects

When linked to a radio, telephone or other communications device through either a datajack or a router, the user can send and receive communications without speaking aloud. There is no visible or audible external evidence of this system's use. This unit can also convert spoken words into text for a display link or other linked device.

If two characters with transducers connect to each other via datajack, they can effectively communicate mind to mind.

BRAINWARE

ASIST CONVERTER

An ASIST converter converts simsense signals (transferred through a datajack) into something the metahuman brain can understand, and vice versa. All simdecks, cyberdecks, remote control decks and other direct neural interface devices contain this technology.

Game Effects

Otaku who wish to jack into the Matrix without a cyberdeck need an ASIST converter to translate data to and from their datajack. ASIST converters come as external plug-in modules or as an integral datajack modification (which costs no extra Essence).

CHIPJACK EXPERT DRIVER

This device improves a chipjack so that skillsofts may be interpreted and processed more efficiently. Essentially, it allows the user to apply the skills and knowledge of a skillsoft with greater effect. The expert driver can boost the effectiveness of any skillsoft, from tai chi to Italian cooking.

Game Effects

A chipjack expert driver grants a Task Pool, equal to its rating, to be used with the skill encoded on a chip (see *Task Pool*, p. 48).

This accessory must be purchased separately for each chipjack.

CRANIAL CYBERDECKS

Cyberdecks may be installed as a cranial interface, popular because they have a high concealability and easy mobility and are generally very convenient.

Game Effects

These cranial cyberdecks use the standard rules for cyberdecks. The cranial cyberdeck cost does include the external datajack.

Memory: In twentieth-century terms, active memory serves as implanted RAM. It cannot be used for any other purpose than for active utilities.

Cyberware	Essence	Cost	Availability	Street Index	Legality
Internal Voice Mask	.1	4,000¥ x Rating	6/48 hrs	1	6P–Q
High-freq. Modulator	—	8,000¥	6/48 hrs	1.25	6P–Q
Low-freq. Modulator	—	8,000¥	6/48 hrs	1.25	6P–Q
Subdermal Speakers	.1	650¥	4/72 hrs	2	Legal
Transducer	.1	2,000¥	4/1 wk	1.5	Legal
External Transducer	—	1,000¥	3/72 hrs	1	Legal
ASIST Converter					
External Plug-in	—	50¥	4/24 hrs	1	Legal
Datajack Accessory	—	1,000¥	6/36 hrs	1.5	Legal
Chipjack Expert Driver	.1/Rating	5,000¥ x Rating	4/48 hrs	1	Legal

Headware memory (p. 298, *SR3*) can be used for both active and storage memory. Other linked memory sources may also be used for storage memory (but not active memory). Active and storage memory costs are not included in the costs shown below and must be purchased separately.

DATA COMPACTOR

Compactor logic circuitry is an accessory to headware memory. It increases data-storage capacity by using advanced data-compression algorithms. Stored data is compressed, then uncompressed automatically when needed.

Game Effects

A data compactor decreases the size of data downloaded into headware memory by 20 percent per rating. For example, a Rating 3 compactor would decrease a 100 Mp file by 60 percent; the file would effectively take up only 40 Mp of headware memory. A character with this accessory can choose to not compress a file when placing it in headware memory.

Accessing or transferring data to and from headware memory normally requires a Simple Action. Compressed data takes a bit longer to access, depending on how tightly the data is packed. Accessing data from Rating 1 and 2 compactors still requires only a Simple Action; accessing data from Rating 3 and 4 compactors requires a Complex Action.

Compressed data must be uncompressed in order to be read (this can also be done by a decker with a compressor utility).

Compactor cyberware can be integrated with a data lock (p. 298, *SR3*) and installed as a joint package. Reduce the compactor's cost and Essence cost by 50 percent when installed with a data lock.

DATA FILTER

The data filter, when activated, blocks the flow of information from short- to long-term memory. The user cannot later recall or remember anything that happened while the data filter was active. This device is popular with influential people who need to have aides or secretaries present during confidential proceedings; such employees are fitted with a data filter that can be remotely activated.

The drawback to data filters is that the user is distracted while it is activated and cannot remember anything for more than a few minutes.

Data filters are also implanted within the "hosts" and "hostesses" of underworld bunraku parlors. The data filter ensures privacy, while a personafix chip turns the host(ess) into whomever the client desires.

Game Effects

While active, a character with a data filter suffers a +2 perception modifier and will not remember anything that occurred later. Data filters can be set to deactivate after a certain length of time (the subject will not remember to turn it off). They are also designed to receive a simple radio signal, transmitted from a hand-held remote (Flux 0) operated by the character's "handler."

A data filter only prevents the retention of memory received by the user's own senses. It does not block the functioning of ear recorders, simrigs, eye cameras or other cyberware recording devices.

ENCEPHALON

This expert-system microcomputer is hardwired directly into the user's brain and uses its processing power to augment the user's own information-processing abilities. The encephalon expands the brain's neural network, taking over minor and redundant "background" processes and freeing up the brain's processing power for more important cognitive tasks. While more powerful encephalons are possible, they are pointless because they exceed the threshold at which the brain can interpret and manipulate data.

Game Effects

Encephalons provide a Task Pool equal to their rating for Intelligence-linked skills (see *Task Pool*, p. 48).

Encephalons help deckers process information more quickly; add the encephalon rating directly to the Hacking Pool

Cyberware	Essence	Cost	Availability	St. Index	Legality
Cranial Cyberdeck					
Allegiance Sigma	1.9	14,000¥	4/1 wk	.8	4P–S
Sony CT–360–D	2.5	75,000¥	6/2 wks	1	4P–S
Novatech Hyperdeck-6	2.7	150,000¥	6/2 wks	1	4P–S
CMT Avatar	2.8	300,000¥	8/2 wks	1	4P–S
Renraku Kraftwerk-8	2.9	450,000¥	10/1 mo	1	4P–S
Transys Highlander	3.0	700,000¥	14/1 mo	1	4P–S
Novatech Slimcase-10	3.2	1,500,000¥	18/1 mo	1	4P–S
Fairlight Excalibur	3.5	2,000,000¥	24/2 mo	1	4P–S
Data Compactor					
Rating 1	.1	9,500¥	6/60 hrs	1	Legal
Rating 2	.15	19,000¥	6/60 hrs	1	Legal
Rating 3	.2	28,500¥	6/60 hrs	1	Legal
Rating 4	.25	38,000¥	6/60 hrs	1	Legal
Data Filter	.3	5,000¥	6/36 hrs	1.5	Legal

(see *Cyberware and Hacking Pool,* p. 45). When a character is decking, they do not receive the Task Pool bonus, only the Hacking Pool.

Encephalons allow a character to learn more quickly. Add the encephalon rating to Intelligence when determining the cost of new skills.

The encephalon does not boost magical ability and does not aid any use of magic, magical perception or Magical Skills.

INDUCTION DATAJACK

The induction datajack is implanted under the skin. To use it, the character must attach a magnetic induction adaptor to the jack cable. This positions the cable against the datajack, and information is transferred optically through the skin.

Game Effects

Induction datajacks work the same way as standard datajacks (p. 298, *SR3*). They are invisible to visual scans and have a Concealability of 10 against physical searches. Apply a +1 target number modifier to cyber-scans that may detect such a datajack.

INVOKED MEMORY STIMULATOR

The invoked memory stimulator (IMS) periodically dredges up and triggers various memories. The character hears voices, sees faces, remembers people long dead or long forgotten, remembers good times and bad times and so on. The memories are so vivid that the character may occasionally confuse memory with reality.

Invoked memory stimulators are used primarily by people who have undergone cybermancy (see p. 58). The memory flashes help keep the human part of cyberzombies from drifting away.

Game Effects

The IMS and the memories it provokes have no specific game effects, but the gamemaster should use invoked memories as a roleplaying or storytelling tool. The IMS cannot be used to create memories, only to recall them.

MATH SPU

A math subprocessor unit (SPU) amplifies the host's mathematical abilities by enhancing math calculations as a background neural process. As a side benefit, the subprocessor also functions as a stopwatch, an alarm clock and an extremely accurate chronometer.

Game Effects

The math subprocessor adds twice its rating as a Complementary Math Skill to any math-related skill tests. The SPU also provides deckers with a Hacking Pool bonus equal to its rating.

MULTI-SLOT CHIPJACKS

These systems incorporate several chipjacks into one. They feature multiple chip slots, allowing more than one soft to be used simultaneously.

Game Effects

Each chip slot acts as an independent chipjack (see p. 298, *SR3*).

RAS OVERRIDE

The reticular activation system (RAS) override is a device built into every simdeck, cyberdeck and remote control deck. It impedes the user's natural senses such as sight and sound, so that the real world does not interfere with the simsense being experienced. Stimuli such as pain are not overridden, however, so a character who takes damage or feels the heat of a burning building around him will be aware of it. The RAS also restricts the body's muscle activation mechanism, which keeps the user from moving in response to the simsense. The RAS filters through just enough minor muscle activity to keep the user from cramping up.

Though built into simrigs, cranial cyberdecks and cranial remote control decks, the RAS override is also available as an independent implant. Favored by users of optiscan links, some penal institutions have also been known to use remotely activated RAS override implants in conjunction with simsense systems to hinder troublesome inmates.

Game Effects

When active, the RAS override inhibits the user's natural sensory input and muscle control; modify by +8 all Perception Tests and actions involving the real world.

Some sims have a built-in RAS override disabler that incapacitates this implant and allows the user to experience the sim

Cyberware	Essence	Cost	Availability	Street Index	Legality
Encephalon					
Rating 1	.75	40,000¥	6/12 days	2	Legal
Rating 2	1.5	115,000¥	6/12 days	2	Legal
Induction Datajack	.3	3,000¥	5/4 days	2	Legal
Induction Adaptor	—	100¥	4/48 hrs	1.5	Legal
Invoked Memory Stimulator	.25	100,000¥	10/2 mo	4	3P–Q
Math SPU					
Rating 1	.1	2,000¥	6/60 hrs	1	Legal
Rating 2	.15	5,000¥	6/60 hrs	1	Legal
Rating 3	.2	11,000¥	6/60 hrs	1	Legal

and real world simultaneously. Depending upon the sim, such a user may experience up to a +4 modifier to all target numbers to account for the effects of experiencing two realities simultaneously.

ROUTER

The router is a junction device that acts as an input/output conduit between cyberware devices. Like a datajack, each router has a direct neural interface, allowing the user to monitor and manipulate transfers between devices. Devices are connected to the routers through various assigned ports; cyberware that is not headware must be connected using expensive nanite-constructed microfilament fiberoptic cables.

Game Effects

Routers allow cyberware devices to communicate with and transfer data to each other, as described in *Interconnectivity* (p. 46). If connected to a datajack, all devices linked to the datajack and router (including external devices) may communicate/transfer data.

Each device connected to the router must have a dedicated port. The direct neural connection to the brain does not take up a port; connecting to a datajack or other router does take up a port (on both devices).

Routers cannot be used to connect to devices within a cyberlimb; they require a DNI connection (p. 39). A cyberlimb DNI may be linked to a router as if it were headware.

Routers do not allow a device to be cybernetically controlled; they merely allow the device to communicate with or through other implants. To be cybernetically controlled, the device needs a DNI connection.

Routers have a maximum of ten ports (not including the brain).

TACTICAL COMPUTER

A tactical computer is a dedicated expert system designed to integrate data input from numerous "senses," analyze it and enhance the user's overall "feel" for a combat situation.

The base tactical computer model features one input port linked to each of the user's five basic human senses (metahuman senses such as low-light vision are not included). Additional ports may be installed for additional sensory input. Each port must be either dedicated to a specific sense upon installation or installed as a "generic" port. Any "sense" may be linked to the computer, including natural senses (dwarf thermographic vision), cyber-sense implants (low-frequency hearing) or even externally connected sensor devices (a surveillance camera on a drone, transmitting images through the user's headware radio, linked through a router).

The tactical computer uses the sense feeds to track targets and motion, predict movements, compute trajectories and otherwise anticipate events and outcomes. Appropriate responses are calculated and fed back to the user as subconscious impulses.

This implant can be used as a stand-alone device, or it can act as the master unit for a cybernetic BattleTac system, if linked to a radio.

Game Effects

When installed, each port must be designated as dedicated to a specific sense (the port can only receive input from that sense) or a generic port. Generic ports may be assigned to receive input from different senses as needed. However, a specific tactical program for the sense being used must be run in order for the tactical computer to understand and analyze the sense's data. This program can be run from a chip, headware memory, or any other linked device.

When installed, the basic senses of normal sight, hearing, taste, touch and smell are automatically hooked up to tactical computer ports.

Each tactical sense program requires 50 Mp.

Even if a sense is connected to the tactical computer, that input is only relevant if the computer can use the data the sense is providing. For example, the sight of a character with normal vision operating in near or complete darkness would be useless. Senses such as touch and taste would rarely be useful in a combat situation. Gamemasters should carefully weigh which senses actually apply to a given situation.

Every 2 senses that are applicable to the current combat situation give the tactical computer 1 rating point. Each rating point provides 1 additional die to the user's Combat Pool (maximum bonus of 4), adds +1 to the user's Small Unit Tactics Skill and allows the character to use 25 percent (cumulative, maximum 100 percent) of his Combat Pool for Surprise Tests. These bonuses apply for both ranged and melee combat. If the user does not have the Small Unit Tactics Skill, use the bonus as the character's skill rating. Tactical computer bonuses do not assist in rigging or decking.

For information on using the Small Unit Tactics special Active Skill, see p. 47.

If sensory input is received through a radio, each sense takes up a radio channel.

Cyberware	Essence	Cost	Availability	Street Index	Legality
Multi-slot Chipjacks					
2 Slots	.25	2,000¥	3/72 hrs	.9	Legal
3 Slots	.3	3,000¥	3/72 hrs	.9	Legal
4 Slots	.35	4,000¥	3/72 hrs	.9	Legal
RAS Override	.05	1,000¥	4/48 hrs	1	Legal
Router	.1	1,000¥	Always	1	Legal
Each Port	.01	200¥/500¥*	Always	1	Legal

* Ports connected to headware cost 200¥; ports connected to non-headware cyberware cost 500¥.

Orientation systems (p. 18) are extremely useful to tactical computer users. If linked to a tactical computer port, an orientation system counts as two senses.

All system functions are background tasks, requiring no actions to call up or perform.

BattleTac System Modification: A tactical computer can be easily integrated with teams using the BattleTac system (see p. 44). If linked to a radio, a tactical computer modified for BattleTac protocols can act as a BattleTac master unit. The tactical computer can transmit constant battlefield data to BattleTac receiver units (both cybernetic and external), allowing small units to respond more quickly and effectively.

BattleTac Cyberlink: This implant is the cybernetic model of the BattleTac receiver unit. When linked to a radio, this headware receives the BattleTac data and uses it to build a tactical map, which can be displayed through the user's image link or output via datajack to another display device. In game terms, the user of this implant uses the Small Unit Tactics Skill more effectively and can take advantage of other BattleTac features such as indirect fire.

The BattleTac cyberlink can also translate cybernetic sensory systems that are linked to it into BattleTac protocols, which can then be transmitted via linked radio to the BattleTac master unit, where it can be used as sensory input.

If installed with an orientation system, the BattleTac cyberlink is purchased at half its cost and Essence cost.

TACTICAL COMPUTER BONUSES

Rating	Combat Pool Bonus	Pool Usable for Surprise Test	Small Unit Tactics Skill Bonus
1	1	25%	+1
2	2	50%	+2
3	3	75%	+3
4	4	100%	+4

RIGGERWARE

Rigger remote control decks and accessories can be installed in a cranial interface. Implanted components can be used with linked external decks.

BATTLETAC™ FDDM MASTER UNIT

A variant of the BattleTac™ system for remote control networks, the Fire Direction Data Manager system (FDDM) enables one drone to act as a spotter, relaying targeting data to other drones via the remote control network. This allows drones that cannot "see" the target to fire on it.

Game Effects

The BattleTac FDDM system allows one drone to fire its weapons at a target detected by another drone. The remote control deck must carry the master unit as an accessory. Both the spotting drone and the firing drone must be adapted for the BattleTac FDDM. For more information, see *Indirect Fire,* p. 60, *Rigger 2.*

BATTLETAC™ IVIS MASTER UNIT

A variant of the BattleTac™ system for remote control networks, IVIS stands for Inter-Vehicle Information System. The system enhances the data-sharing capabilities between the remote control deck and drones. By improving information-sharing, these systems enable drones to execute more complex and sophisticated tactics to accomplish their assigned tasks.

Game Effects

IVIS enables a rigger to assign a complex mission to a group of drones. Only drones whose pilots have been modified to interact with BattleTac IVIS receive the benefit of this system.

When the rigger issues the command, he makes a Small Unit Tactics (Vehicle Tactics) Test against Target Number 5. Successes from this test can be divided between two uses: providing extra dice for the drone group's Comprehension Test or creating a dice pool for the drone group known as the IVIS Pool. The IVIS Pool dice are shared by the drones in the group and can be used for any tests made by the drones. The IVIS Pool functions like other dice pools, and it lasts until the drone group completes its task or is given a new one. IVIS Pool dice are not available to drones that a rigger has jumped into.

CRANIAL REMOTE DECKS

Cranial remote decks (CRD) incorporate computer and microtronic advances that allow riggers to control drones through a remote deck in their head. This offers the rigger greater mobility and reduces the number of external devices he must manage.

Game Effects

Cranial remote decks use the standard rules for a remote control deck, except that its small size limits a CRD to a Flux

Cyberware	Essence	Cost	Availability	Street Index	Legality
Tactical Computer	1.5	400,000¥	12/60 days	4	2P–R
Each Dedicated Port	.1	10,000¥	12/60 days	4	2P–R
Each Generic Port	.1	5,000¥	12/60 days	4	2P–R
Tac. Sense Program	—	5,000¥	8/1 mo	4	6P–R
BattleTac Modification	—	+10,000¥	+6/—	4	2P–R
BattleTac Cyberlink	.2	30,000¥	12/30 days	4	2P–R

Rating of 0. If a rigger wishes to increase a CRD's transmission power, he must connect the CRD to an external or cyberlimb signal booster (see p. 40).

Riggers with CRD may use linked headware memory as remote control storage memory.

REMOTE CONTROL ECCM

This system of electronic counter-countermeasures protects a cranial remote control deck's network from outside noise, whether from excessive solar activity or jamming.

Game Effects

Rules for ECCM appear on p. 138, *SR3* and p. 98, *Rigger 2.*

REMOTE CONTROL ENCRYPTION MODULE (RCEM)

The nature of mobile subscriber simsense technology (MSST) protocols prevents remote control networks from using broadcast encryption like other transmitters. However, the digital encoding and spread-spectrum routines provided by the RCEM are specially designed for remote control network security. This implant encodes and decodes remote control signal transmissions for a cranial remote deck, making them indecipherable to intruders who intercept a remote control channel.

Game Effects

Remote control encryption modules are available in ratings of 1 through 10. They are incompatible with standard broadcast encryption techniques. Likewise, normal broadcast decryption programs (p. 289, *SR3*) are ineffective against RCEM encryption; only rigger decryption modules can break the encryption of RCEMs. For more information on using RCEMs, see *Signal Interception,* p. 68, *Rigger 2.*

RIGGER DECRYPTION MODULE

A diagnostics tool used by security riggers, the rigger decryption module's firmware cryptographic routines can be used to decrypt control network signals encoded by an RCEM as well as encrypted rigged security systems.

Game Effects

The rigger decryption module decodes encryption routines used by the RCEM or by CCSS security systems. The higher-rated the module, the more protocols are programmed into its firmware, up to a maximum rating of 10. It does not decrypt standard broadcast or data encryption.

To decrypt RCEM signals, use the rules on defeating deck encryption, p. 69, *Rigger 2*. For defeating CCSS encryption, see p. 80, *Rigger 2*.

RIGGER PROTOCOL EMULATION MODULE

The rigger protocol emulation module allows a rigger's cranial deck to emulate many of the protocols used on contemporary rigged security systems and drones. This system is required for infiltrating and "hijacking" a rigged security system and is also used for conducting meaconing, intrusion and interference attempts against a remote control network.

Game Effects

The higher-rated the module, the more protocols are programmed into its firmware, up to a maximum rating of 10. For more information on using these modules, see p. 89, *Rigger 2*.

BODYWARE

AUTO-INJECTOR

An auto-injector is an implanted device that dispenses medication or compounds. Auto-injectors have many uses, from diabetics who need regular insulin doses to psychiatric patients taking medication to ward off depression. Prisons, governments and corporations are also known to use auto-injectors to ensure compliance or maintain control.

Auto-injectors dispense just about any drug or chemical known to metahumanity directly into the bearer's bloodstream. Each auto-injector carries one dose; expanded models are also available that can hold up to 5 total doses.

Auto-injectors come in two styles, reusable and one-shot. Reusable units feature an external port through which they can be refilled and are usually implanted just below the skin's surface in a location offering convenient access. These models can be connected directly to an IV to provide a constant dose. One-shot units are usually implanted in such a way that they cannot be detected by a visual scan and, as the name implies, are good for one use only. They are commonly used to introduce deadly substances into an unwilling victim.

Game Effects

Auto-injectors are merely a delivery device; the substances within them, however, will produce varying effects (see *Chemistry*, p. 101).

The auto-injector has some type of trigger that releases its contents into the bloodstream; this may be a built-in clock or timer; a signal from a linked radio unit; datajack or other source; the presence of specified chemicals in the bloodstream; and so on. This trigger must be chosen when the auto-injector is purchased.

BALANCE TAIL

Grafted to the base of the spine, this weighted cybernetic tail extends for slightly more than one meter. Connected to an expert system balance processor, the tail adjusts to keep the user's center of gravity balanced. The tail is not under conscious control and tends to twitch and sway randomly as the user moves.

People equipped with a balance tail must have their clothes customized to accommodate the extra limb.

Game Effects

The balance tail reduces the target number by –2 of any tests involving balance, including climbing, walking a ledge, jumping, falling, Knockdown and so on. If combined with balance augmentation earware, the cumulative modifier is –3. See *Cyberware and Social Interaction*, p. 48, for other effects.

BIOMONITOR SYSTEM

Implanted biomonitors measure the user's vital signs and body functions, including heart rate, blood pressure, respiratory rate, temperature, blood-sugar and -alcohol level, blood-

Cyberware	Essence	Cost	Availability	St. Index	Legality
BattleTac FDDM	.15	200,000¥	10/21 days	3	5P–R
BattleTac IVIS	.15	150,000¥	8/14 days	3	5P–R
Remote Control Deck	.3	25,000¥ x Rating	4/72 hrs	2	Legal
Remote Control ECCM					
Ratings 1–3	.2	Rating x 15,000¥	4/7 days	2	Legal
Ratings 4–6	.3	Rating x 35,000¥	6/14 days	3	6P–Q
Ratings 7–9	.4	Rating x 75,000¥	12/28 days	4	5P–R
Rating 10	.45	900,000¥	18/45 days	5	4P–R
RC Encryption Module	.2	Rating x 10,000¥	(Rating)/(Rating) days	3	8P–W
Rigger Decryption Module	.2	Rating x 17,500¥	(Rating + 2)/(Rating) days	3	8P–W
Protocol Emulation Module	.2	Rating x 5,000¥	(Rating + 2)/(Rating) days	2	Legal
Auto-injector					
Reusable	.1	1,000¥ + contents	4/72 hrs	1.5	6P–N
One-shot	.05	1,500¥ + contents	4/72 hrs	1.5	4P–Q
Extra Dose Capacity	—	+500¥ per dose	4/72 hrs	1.5	As above
Balance Tail	.5	10,000¥	8/1 wk	2	Legal

cell counts and so on. Information from this device can be output through linked devices such as display links or datajacked medkits, but usually it is transferred to an implanted diagnosis processor.

The diagnosis processor is an expert-system computer that uses biomonitor information to diagnose any anomalies or medical problems. It is similar to the computer included in external medkits and can suggest remedies, antidotes and medical procedures. Typically, the prognosis, health warnings and medical suggestions are output to a linked subdermal display monitor, but they can also be output through other linked devices. The processor is typically programmed to alert the user to certain dangerous conditions (poisoning, low bloodsugar level, erratic pulse, nitrogen narcosis and so on); other alert conditions and actions may be specified by the user, such as contacting DocWagon (using a linked telephone) if the user's life is in danger.

The subdermal display unit is implanted on the lower arm (usually the left), under the skin. The unit displays text in a color that can be seen through the user's skin; in effect, it looks like the arm is a display screen. Subdermal pressure buttons allow the user to scroll the text, switch to other windows, make queries and so on. If the user's health is threatened, a warning display will flash on the screen (this option can be muted if circumstances require stealth or concealment). Medical response teams are trained to check a victim for biomonitor displays immediately upon arrival.

Game Effects

The three components of this system can be implanted as a pre-linked whole or used piecemeal.

Biomonitor: Installed in the chest, this device monitors the body's systems and outputs the information.

Diagnosis Processor: Like a medkit, this device can make Biotech Skill Tests to identify health threats and determine a course of action. It has a Biotech Skill of 5. It can be programmed to trigger display warnings or be linked to autoinjectors, communication devices, internal air tanks and so on.

Subdermal Display: When inactive, this device has a Concealability of 10.

BODY COMPARTMENTS

In addition to the finger tips and teeth, other places on the body can be hollowed out or replaced with compartments to hide small objects and devices. Typically, creating such compartments requires removing a small section of bone and replacing it with a plasteel case. Placement options are limited but include rib sections, toe compartments, hollow kneecaps and so on. More esoteric compartments are also possible, such as a small one located behind the navel.

Body compartments are primarily used to conceal items, though such objects must be quite small. They can also be used to conceal the existence of a datajack or chipjack, though a thorough cyberscan is still likely to detect their existence. If you connect a datajack to the compartment, you can also control any DNI-equipped device you store in the compartment.

Some common compartment-stored devices include drug injectors, lockpicks and lockpick guns, micro-transceivers and so on. A recent development is a synthetic finger tip that can mimic a fingerprint pattern downloaded from a print-scanner accessory. The scanner can be used to "read" a print directly from a hand (assuming the owner of the limb is alive or recently dead), or it can scan a readable print recently left by the owner on an appropriate surface.

Game Effects

Body compartments may only be placed in areas of the body that could reasonably be hollowed out or replaced (the gamemaster has final say). These compartments are quite small; as a general rule, only devices with a Concealability of 9 or higher can be stored in such compartments, with a limit of one per compartment.

Rules for tooth, finger-tip and toe-tip compartments can be found on p. 299 and p. 301, respectively, of *SR3*. All other compartments use the following rules.

Body compartments cannot be detected by a visual scan, and they have a Concealability of 10 against physical searches. Add +1 to the target number for cyberware detection scans made against them.

In general, using a weapon or item installed in a body compartment in combat requires the use of the Cyber-Implant Weaponry Skill. Monowhips require the use of the Whips Skill instead.

Injector: Holds one dose of any chemical, poison, toxin or other appropriate compound. The needle has a Damage Code of (STR + 3)L, but the maximum damage that can be caused is a Moderate wound, and the needle will not pierce hardened armor. The target must take damage to be injected. Replacing the dose takes 2 minutes.

Lockpicks: Lockpicks are used against key-and-tumbler locks (though outdated by the standard of modern maglocks, they remain inexpensive and effective). Most key-and-tumbler locks have a Rating of 4 or 5, depending on their complexity. Picking them requires use of the special Active Skill Lockpicking (linked to Quickness). Lockpicking requires both hands, with the pick in one and a torque wrench (external or implanted) in the other, and a base time of 20 seconds x the lock rating.

Lockpick Gun: This device simultaneously "rakes" the lock's tumblers with a motorized, expert-system-driven pick and applies torque to turn the lock. Each lockpick gun has Lockpicking Skill equal to its rating (maximum 10).

Synthetic Fingerprint: To use this system, a fingerprint must first be obtained using a portable print-scanner. The scanner is then jacked into the synthetic finger tip and the print's pattern downloaded. When being used to deceive a fingerprint scanner, make an Opposed Test between the synthetic print system's rating and the scanner's rating. If the scanner achieves any net successes, it detects the fake and triggers an alert. If the results are a tie, it asks to repeat the scan. Otherwise, the fake print deceives the scanner.

BONE LACING

Two new bone-lacing methods are available, supplementing the existing plastic, aluminum and titanium models. Ceramic bone lacing augments bones with a sturdy, impact-resistant poly-ceramic coating. Kevlar™ bone lacing weaves a protective ballistic mesh around the user's bones and joints.

Game Effects

Ceramic and Kevlar bone lacing are similar to the bone lacing described on p. 300, *SR3*. Armor provided is cumulative with worn armor. Neither type of bone lacing can be seen by a metal detector. A character may install only one type of bone lacing.

Ceramic Bone Lacing: This treatment adds +1 to the character's Body Attribute and provides 2 points of impact armor. It imposes the same encumbrance as titanium (+15 kg) and has an effective Barrier Rating of 8. Unarmed attacks by a character with ceramic lacing inflict (STR + 3)M damage.

Kevlar Bone Lacing: Kevlar lacing adds +1 to the character's Body Attribute and provides 1 point of ballistic armor. It imposes the same encumbrance as plastic bone lacing (+5 kg) and has an effective Barrier Rating of 5. It provides no bonus to unarmed attacks.

CYBERFINS

Cyberfins consist of retractable spurs and webbing implanted in the hands and feet. When extended, they allow the user to swim as if using ordinary swim fins.

Cyberware	Essence	Cost	Availability	St. Index	Legality
Biomonitor	.3	5,000¥	6/72 hrs	2	Legal
Diagnosis Processor	.2	2,500¥	6/72 hrs	2	Legal
Subdermal Display	.1	500¥	4/48 hrs	1	Legal
Body Compartment	.2	5,000¥	4/48 hrs	1	Legal
Injector	—	500¥ + contents	4/72 hrs	1.5	6P–N
Lockpicks	—	500¥	8/2 wks	3	6P–Q
Lockpick Gun	—	Rating x 250¥	8/2 wks	3	6P–Q
Synthetic Fingerprint	—	Rating x 2,000¥	(Rating x 2)/1 wk	3	4P–Q
Scanner Accessory	—	Rating x 500¥	Rating/72 hrs	3	6P–V
Bone Lacing					
Ceramic	1.5	40,000Y	6/21 days	2	6P–Q
Kevlar	1	20,000¥	6/21 days	2	6P–N

Game Effects

Characters using cyberfins can swim at half their normal walking or running rate (see p. 47, *SR Companion*). In addition, the wearer can use cyberfins to attack (treat as hand razors with –1 Power). Cyberfins are not compatible with standard swim fins or any type of gloves.

CYBERSKULL

A cyberskull uses a plasteel framework to protect against fatal head shots and other brain damage. The synthetic version requires replacing some parts of the skull and reinforcing others. The obvious model involves removing the skin and hair and constructing a protective structure around the skull.

Game Effects

Cyberskulls protect headware from being damaged. If a character with a cyberskull takes damage to headware (see p. 127), reduce the Stress incurred by –2. If the Stress is reduced to 0 or less, the headware is not damaged.

Cyberskulls also reduce the Damage Level of called shots to the head by one level (in effect, they cancel out the called-shot Damage Level bonus).

Obvious cyberskulls are frightening to behold and tend to provoke hostile responses from strangers. A character with an obvious cyberskull suffers a +4 penalty to all Charisma and Social Skill Tests. However, such characters receive a +3 bonus for open-ended Intimidation Tests.

See p. 35 for armor rules and p. 36 for equipment capacity rules.

CYBERTORSO

Like the cyberskull, the cybertorso is a protective covering that surrounds the chest and abdomen. Ribs and muscles are reinforced or replaced, and the entire section of the body is layered with a shell.

Game Effects

The cybertorso adds +1 to the character's Body Attribute and protects internal bodyware in the same way that a cyberskull protects headware. The cybertorso also reduces by half (round up) the additional Essence cost of cyberlimb Strength or Quickness enhancements beyond 3 points (see *Cyberlimbs*, p. 33).

See p. 35 for armor rules and p. 36 for equipment capacity rules.

DERMAL SHEATH

Dermal sheathing combines the latest advances in dermal plating technology with a semi-synthetic skin sheath. The result is protection that is smoother and less bulky than standard dermal plating, with greater self-regenerative capability.

Some dermal sheaths use a technology derived from ruthenium polymers, allowing the sheath to change across a wide array of colors through a low-level electric charge. The color display is facilitated by built-in expert logic circuitry. It can use input from imaging scanners to match the sheath to its owner's surroundings for a camouflage effect, or it can display text or images input from linked sources such as headware memory.

Game Effects

The dermal sheath boosts the character's Body Attribute by a number of points equal to the sheath's rating plus 1; for example, Rating 2 sheathing adds 3 points. It also provides impact armor equal to one-half the rating, rounded up.

Sheaths composed of ruthenium work exactly as described under ruthenium polymers (p. 114). The logic circuits are DNI-equipped, so coloration can change with a mental command (this requires a Simple Action). Words and images from a linked source can also be displayed, in the event a character wishes to make a statement with his skin. Imaging scanners can be implanted or worn externally and linked by datajack.

FLEX HANDS

This modification replaces most of the bones in the hands with a type of memory plastic that deforms under continuous pressure and then returns to its normal shape. This allows the user to squeeze his hand out of handcuffs and other restraining devices.

Cyberware	Essence	Conceal	Cost	Availability	St. Index	Legality
Cyberfins	0.3	—	10,500¥	5/48 hrs	1.25	3P–N
Cyberskull						
Obvious	.75	—	35,000¥	6/4 days	1	Legal
Synthetic	.75	10	55,000¥	6/4 days	1	Legal
Cybertorso						
Obvious	1.5	—	90,000¥	6/4 days	1	Legal
Synthetic	1.5	8	120,000¥	6/4 days	1	Legal
Dermal Sheath						
Rating 1	.7	—	24,000¥	6/14 days	1.5	6P–N
Rating 2	1.4	—	60,000¥	6/14 days	1.5	6P–N
Rating 3	2.1	—	120,000¥	8/14 days	1.5	5P–N
Ruthenium	+.2	—	+150,000¥	+2/+4 days	+.25	4P–N
Image Scanner (each)	+.05	—	+8,000¥	—	—	—

Game Effects

A character with flex hands receives –2 to target numbers for any tests using the Escape Artist skill, as well as any other tests that involve hand contortions. Flex hands are not compatible with bone lacing, and can be turned on and off.

FOOT ANCHOR

This retractable, spring-loaded, heavy-duty spur shoots down through the heel of the foot, anchoring the user to the ground or impaling a target. Primarily intended for use in cyberfeet, when installed in ordinary feet they require extensive ankle and shin bracing so that the bones don't snap off near the blade when pressure is applied.

Game Effects

The foot anchor cannot penetrate materials with a Barrier Rating higher than 10 (most pavement has a Barrier Rating 8). Each foot anchored increases the amount of weight a character can hold up or hang on to by a maximum of 50 kilograms. If the foot anchor is set into a material with a Barrier Rating of less than 10, each Barrier Rating point below 10 reduces the amount of weight by 5 kilograms.

As a weapon, the foot anchor inflicts (STR – 1)M damage. With a foot anchor extended for use as a weapon, the user's movement rate is reduced to half their Quickness (round down), and they modify the Dodge Test by +1.

Anchored users receive 1 point of Recoil Reduction per foot anchor, and their target number to resist Knockdown is reduced by 1 per anchor. Only one anchor can be installed in a foot.

HYDRAULIC JACKS

Hydraulic jacks require extensive and obvious modifications to the legs, making them most common among those with cyberlegs. Hydraulic jacks greatly increase the maximum distance (both vertical and horizontal) the user can jump, increase running speed and absorb impact from falls.

Game Effects

A character equipped with hydraulic jacks adds rating x 20 percent to his maximum jump distance (see p. 47, *SRComp*). Each rating point also adds an extra die for Athletics (Running) Tests. Add a number of dice equal to the jacks' rating to Athletics (Jumping) Tests.

If a character can manage to land on his feet, hydraulic jacks can also absorb some of the impact of a fall. (Landing on one's feet requires a successful Quickness (5) Test for a height of 5 meters or less, +1 to the target number for every additional 4 meters.) Reduce the Power level of the fall by the jacks' rating.

Hydraulic jacks have a maximum rating of 5.

INTERNAL AIR TANK

The internal air tank is an independent air source implanted below a lung (and requiring partial removal of that lung). The user can breathe from the tank, making her immune to any airborne toxin or other compound.

Air tanks are pressurized to allow greater air storage. They may also be filled with other gaseous compounds. A tracheal vent accessory is also available that allows the contents to be exhaled without the substance passing through the user's trachea.

Game Effects

Internal tanks hold approximately 75 minutes worth of air, though the amount of air consumed may vary depending on underwater depth, lung capacity and activity. Refilling it (through an intake valve placed just under the rib cage) takes 5 minutes.

If a character is using an internal air tank for underwater operations, modify by –1 tests for treading water or floating (p. 48, *SRComp*).

Because air tanks are pressurized, a breach (for example, from damage) may cause an explosion. Whenever an air tank takes Stress (see *Cybersystem Damage*, p. 127), roll 1D6. On a result of 1, the tank explodes. An exploding air tank inflicts 10S damage on the owner; external armor (worn armor, dermal plating or sheaths and so on) does not protect the character, though bone lacing and other internalized impact armor do. Nearby characters may also be damaged; reduce the Power of the explosion by –2 per meter, and subtract from the Power any external impact armor the character is wearing.

The tracheal vent allows the tank's contents to be released without passing through the owner's respiratory system. Characters releasing a noxious gas through a tracheal vent, however, must still protect themselves from inhaling the poison using a respirator or another air tank. To determine the effects of a released gas, use the rules for gas delivery systems given on p. 90 of *SRComp*.

JOLT-ALERT

This device, attached to the spinal cord at the base of the neck, sends a shock through the user's nervous system via a small electric pulse that jolts the user instantly awake. The jolt-alert must be linked to a triggering mechanism, such as a retinal clock, headware telephone or even a datajack-linked external alarm system.

Cyberware	Essence	Cost	Availability	Street Index	Legality
Flex Hands	.4	8,000¥	6/72 hrs	2	7P–N
Foot Anchor	.4	14,000¥	6/7 days	2	Legal
Hydraulic Jacks	.75 + (.25 per Rating)	Rating x 5,000¥	5/6 days	1	Legal
Internal Air Tank	.25	1,200¥	4/5 days	1.5	Legal
Tracheal Vent	.1	750¥	4/5 days	1.5	Legal

Game Effects

When the jolt-alert is triggered, the user instantly jerks awake. Users with Deadly Stun damage cannot be roused to consciousness with this device.

MAGNETIC SYSTEM

This system consists of a series of electromagnets mounted along the length of a limb (for example, foot, shin and knee). When the system is activated, the user can hold on to or cling to ferrous-metal objects more strongly.

Note that in 2061, most metals are nonferrous, semi-metallic polymer compounds, including those used in weapons and cyberware. Ferrous metals are still used in heavy vehicles (big cars and trucks), building support structures (railings, beams, cables) and so on. Ferrous metal can also be added to devices such as gun grips to take advantage of a magnetic system (it practically guarantees that you won't drop the gun).

The magnetic field produced by this system is not strong enough to interfere with electronics or computers, which are primarily optical-based.

Game Effects

Each magnetic system adds +4 to a user's Strength for purposes of holding or clinging to metallic items. Only one magnetic system can be installed in a limb.

Each limb system can only hold about 25 kilograms on its own (so a person weighing 75 kilograms would need at least three magnet systems to cling to an object through magnetic force alone). Multiple systems are cumulative.

MOVE-BY-WIRE SYSTEM

Move-by-wire systems are based on similar systems used for aircraft and vehicle maneuverability. The system puts the body in a constant state of seizure, so that it wishes to move in all directions simultaneously. An implanted expert computer monitors the seizure and counteracts its effects until the user wishes to move. At that point, it channels the effects of the seizure along the motion path desired. When the user moves, she does so with unnatural smoothness.

Move-by-wire users frequently suffer from slight but uncontrollable muscle tremors in specific muscle groups when they are at rest, mostly due to errors in the system's seizure compensation. Other side effects, such as temporal lobe epilepsy with complications (TLE–x), are possible, but less common.

Higher-rating move-by-wire systems take speed to a new level. Users of such systems are able to act repeatedly before others manage to move even once.

Game Effects

The move-by-wire system provides a number of bonuses, as shown in the Move-by-Wire Bonuses Table. The Quickness bonus does not count when calculating the character's Reaction Attribute.

MOVE-BY-WIRE BONUSES TABLE

Rating 1: +1 Quickness, +2 Reaction, +1D6 Initiative, +1 die for Athletics and Stealth Tests
Rating 2: +2 Quickness, +4 Reaction, +2D6 Initiative, +2 dice for Athletics and Stealth Tests
Rating 3: +3 Quickness, +6 Reaction, +3D6 Initiative, +3 dice for Athletics and Stealth Tests
Rating 4: +4 Quickness, +8 Reaction, +4D6 Initiative, +4 dice for Athletics and Stealth Tests

In addition, a character with a Rating 3 move-by-wire system must take an extra action at the end of the first Initiative Pass every Combat Turn. Likewise, a character with a Rating 4 system must take an extra action at the end of both the first and second Initiative Passes in the turn. The character must take these extra actions (they can be held, but they are lost at the beginning of the character's next Combat Phase) and must recalculate his next Initiative Pass normally after doing so (subtract 10 from Initiative).

This system is not compatible with any other Reaction- or Initiative-enhancing cyber- or bioware. Move-by-wire systems may not be fitted with a reflex trigger (see p. 301, *SR3*) or otherwise turned on and off.

Stress

Because move-by-wire systems put the central nervous system into a constant state of seizure, the character automatically racks up Stress Points (p. 124), as shown in the Automatic Stress Table, and must make a Stress Test. Apply the Stress to both Quickness and Reaction. The Stress can only be removed by therapeutic surgery (p. 147).

Each time the character takes Stress, he must make an unaugmented Willpower (move-by-wire rating x 2) Test. If he fails the test, he develops TLE–x and is plagued by feelings of alienation and loss of his sense of self. These feelings make his social responses subtly inappropriate, so he suffers a –1 penalty to Charisma and all Charisma-based skills in important social situations.

The character also suffers distorted perceptions, and judging spatial relationships and coordinating perceptions and actions become difficult. In circumstances that the gamemaster deems dangerous or tactically crucial—such as whether an individual notices a needed clue—apply a +2 penalty to the target numbers for Perception Tests, reduce Initiative by 2, and reduce Reaction by 1D6.

TLE–x can be corrected with brain surgery, but because the procedure involves cutting away a small area of brain tissue that has become chronically dysfunctional, it can only be done twice. The is a Correct Failure procedure for therapeutic surgery with a base target number of 8. Add a +2 modifier to the target number for the second surgery; after that, the condition becomes permanent. In chronic cases, the epilepsy can spread and cause afflictions such as impotence and incontinence. In such cases, the gamemaster may decrease Social Skills and Charisma appropriately.

An individual with TLE-x may also suffer acute seizures. If such a character suffers a Moderate (or worse) wound and is engaged in combat or some other type of conflict, the player must make a Willpower (6) Test. If the test fails, the character collapses in an epileptic seizure and suffers 6M damage. Roll 1D6 and multiply the result by 10 to determine the number of Combat Turns the seizure lasts. At the end of that time, roll 1D6 again and multiply the result by 10. This number represents the number of minutes the character remains unconscious.

If the move-by-wire system fails (or Quickness or Reaction fail in part due to incurred Stress), the character must succeed in an unaugmented Willpower (move-by-wire rating x 2) Test or suffer a breakdown of brain functions known as catastrophic clonic seizure syndrome (CCSS). Involuntary functions such as breathing continue to work normally, but the affected character is incapable of voluntary action and is barely aware of what is happening around him. He experiences the world as a terrifying, whirling chaos of nightmarish sensations and intense pain. CCSS renders a victim's move-by-wire system permanently dysfunctional, and it must be removed. Additionally, the character may suffer long-term damage such as reduced Quickness, Intelligence and/or Willpower, at the gamemaster's discretion. CCSS victims can recover fully, but there is also a chance that the victim will only possess the awareness and quality of life of a family pet.

AUTOMATIC STRESS TABLE

System Rating	Accumulate 1 Stress Point every:
1	6 months
2	4 months
3	2 months
4	1 month

OXSYS CYBERGILL

The OXSYS cybergill draws in water and filters out oxygen through forced osmosis, allowing users to breathe underwater. Carbon dioxide and water gases are absorbed into the water through reverse osmosis and expelled. Unlike the external version, the oxygen is delivered via solution directly into the bloodstream, averting the danger of oxygen toxicity.

The gills are implanted on both sides of the neck adjacent to the thyroid gland. A cutoff valve must also be installed in the lower trachea to prevent lung action during operation, and pulmonary bypasses must be inserted in the heart to reroute blood flowing toward the lungs up into the gills.

Game Effects

Divers using cybergills are immune to oxygen toxicity; however, they remain vulnerable to nitrogen narcosis and decompression sickness from the residual amount of nitrogen trapped in the lungs.

As a matter of common practice, divers who choose cybergill implantation also install an internal air tank (p. 29) containing pure helium that they use to flush residual nitrogen out of their lungs.

Cybergills allow a user to stay underwater indefinitely, though the system must be replaced after approximately 1,000 hours of use (this varies depending on diving depth, lung capacity and activity). Replacing filters requires cyberware repair surgery, and costs about 1,500 nuyen total.

RETRACTABLE CLIMBING CLAWS

Similar to retractable hand razors, climbing claws extend from the finger tips and assist in climbing.

Game Effects

Reduce by –2 the target number for all Climbing or Clinging Tests for characters with climbing claws. Characters who use their climbing claws to make an attack have a Damage Code of (STR – 1)L.

SMARTLINK-2

An advanced version of the basic smartlink unit, the smartlink-2 provides better targeting abilities and more accurate calculation of indirect firing arcs.

Game Effects

Smartlink-2 systems operate in the same way as standard smartlink systems (p. 301, *SR3*). When using a smartlink-2, apply only a +2 Called Shot modifier (rather than the usual +4). Also apply a –1 modifier for linked weapons such as under-barrel grenade launchers, grenade guns, rocket launchers and similar systems.

Missile launchers and other systems with an inherent Intelligence Rating cannot benefit from the smartlink system.

Smartlink-2 systems only work with guns that are smartlink-2-equipped.

Cyberware	Essence	Cost	Availability	Street Index	Legality
Jolt-alert	.1	1,500¥	4/48 hrs	1.5	Legal
Magnetic System	.3	2,800¥	6/7 days	2	Legal
Move-by-Wire					
Rating 1	2.5	250,000¥	8/10 days	2.5	3P–R
Rating 2	4	500,000¥	12/20 days	3	3P–R
Rating 3	5.5	1,000,000¥	18/30 days	3	3P–R
Rating 4	7	2,000,000¥	20/45 days	3.5	3P–R
OXSYS Cybergill	.75	12,500¥	5/72 hrs	1.75	Legal
Retractable Climbing Claws	.3	10,000¥	5/72 hrs	1.5	6P–N

SMARTLINK SUBSYSTEMS AND ACCESSORIES

The smartgun link system breaks down into four components: an I/O device (typically a subdermal palm induction pad that syncs with the smartgun's system), an eye display, a ballistics processor and a limited simsense rig (for body posture/gun position sensing). Some users may not want the whole package. For example, a user with an image link doesn't need the eye display, he just needs to connect his existing cyberware to the smartlink system. Some users may wish to avoid the palm pads (detectable by touch), preferring to jack a smartlinked gun through a datajack instead.

Two accessories for the smartlink system are available: the range finder and the personalized smartlink safety.

Range Finder: This smartlink accessory indicates the current range to the target or whatever the smartgun is pointed at. The distance is listed under the smartgun link's targeting icon in the field of vision.

Personalized Smartlink Safety (PSS): A smartgun equipped with this modification has the safety permanently engaged unless it is in contact with a smartlink system that carries the proper (encrypted) serial number.

Game Effects

For a smartlink system to function, the basic four components or an appropriate substitute must be present. An image link or smart goggles serve as appropriate replacements for the eye display. The palm pads can be exchanged for a direct datajack connection. A simrig can be substituted for the limited simsense rig. Either a standard or smartlink-2 ballistics processor can be used.

If a smartlink system is not entirely cybernetic (any non-implant substitutions are made), the smartlink provides only a –1 bonus to ranged combat.

Smartlinks only work with guns that are smartlink-equipped (or smartlink-2-equipped, as appropriate).

Note that smartlinks do *not* act as a camera; they merely provide a visual indication of where the weapon is pointed. Smartlinks also cannot distinguish between friends and enemies.

If a smartlink system user wishes to use smartlink weapons in his second hand, he need only install a second induction pad and link it to the system already in place.

Range Finder: The range finder can only be used with a smartlink. When used with a smartlink-2, it provides a –1 modifier to targets at long range and –2 to targets at extreme range. These modifiers are not cumulative with range modifiers provided by image magnification accessories.

When used with a smartlinked grenade launcher and air-timed mini-grenades, the range finder can auto-set the grenades to explode at a certain distance; reduce the scatter dice from 3D6 to 1D6.

PSS: A smartgun with a personalized safety feature only works for the user possessing the specific smartlink system for which it was programmed. The gun is just a chunk of metal to anyone else. A gun can be programmed to operate for more than one smartlink system (for example, it can work for all members of a team). The serial number's Encryption Rating is 8.

STEPPED REFLEX TRIGGER MODIFICATION

Rather than completely turning off their wired reflexes, some users prefer to turn them down. This modification to the reflex trigger allows users to operate their wired reflexes at a lower level than the level at which they were purchased.

Game Effects

A reflex trigger that is modified for stepped functioning allows a user to spend a Simple Action to turn his reflexes on and off, or switch to a lower or higher level of wired reflexes (but not higher than their actual level; see p. 302, *SR3*).

CYBERLIMBS

Cyberlimbs represent the replacement of any limb or part of a limb with a cyberware substitute. Where noted, cybertorsos and cyberskulls count as limb replacements.

Cyberlimbs must be designated as either obvious or synthetic when purchased (see p. 301, *SR3*).

GENERAL RULES

Each cyberlimb has a Strength and Quickness independent of the user's Attributes. Cyberlimbs can also have increased Armor Values and provide bonuses to Body and Power. Synthetic cyberlimbs have a Concealability Rating, which defines how real (or unreal) they appear to observers.

CYBERWARE COMPATIBILITY

Bone lacing, dermal armor, dermal sheaths, muscle augmentation, muscle replacement and orthoskin are not compatible with cyberlimbs, though they can be used to enhance the durability of the remaining natural parts of a person's body. If installed in a character with cyberlimbs, reduce cost and Essence cost of these items by 10 percent per cyberlimb (5 percent per partial limb) to reflect the fact that some necessary systems have already been implanted.

Cyberware	Essence	Cost	Availability	Street Index	Legality
Retractable Climbing Claws	.3	10,000¥	5/72 hrs	1.5	6P–N
Smartlink-2	.5	3,500¥	6/48 hrs	2	5P–N

Gear	Mount	Conceal	Weight	Cost	Availability	St. Index	Legality
Smartlink-2 Modifications							
External	Top/under	–2	.75	800¥	6/48 hrs	2	4P–N
Internal	—	—	.25	x150%	As weapon	As weapon	4P–N
Smart Goggles	—	0	.1	3,500¥	4/36 hrs	2	4P–N

The more replacement parts a character has, the less bonus he receives from protective implants, because there is less flesh to protect. As a rule of thumb, characters can receive two complete cyber replacements and still gain the armor or Body bonuses from any of the cyberware listed in this section. For characters with three cyber replacements, subtract 1 from the armor/Body bonuses of each item; for characters with four replacements, subtract 2 from the armor/Body bonuses. A character with more than four replacements receives no armor/Body bonuses from the cyberware listed in this section. (For purposes of determining how many limbs have been replaced, count one limb and the torso as a single replacement and the skull and a partial limb as a single replacement.)

Gorgon the street monster samurai has plastic bone lacing (+1 Body) and dermal plating 3 (+3 Body). After an unusually nasty series of street fights, he finds himself with two cyberarms and a cyberleg. This reduces his Body bonus from each cyberware item by 1, leaving him with only +2 Body. Because he has two cyberarms, however, he gets an additional +1 Body. A month later, he gets a cybertorso (yes, all his cyberware is alphaware), reducing his cyberware Body bonuses down to +1 (offset by the +1 Body the cybertorso gives him).

BONUSES

Multiple cyberlimbs make a character less vulnerable to damage. A pair of cyberarms adds +1 to a character's Body; a pair of cyberlegs adds +2 to Body. These modifiers are cumulative. Partial replacement limbs, and cyberhands and -feet, do not add to a character's Body.

Likewise, unarmed attacks made with cyberlimbs are more powerful. A character with one cyberlimb or two partial cyberlimbs adds +1 Power; a character with two cyberlimbs adds +2 Power. Additional limbs beyond two provide no additional bonus, and the total Power bonus cannot exceed +2.

Cyberhands and -feet do not provide attack bonuses.

STRENGTH

Cyberlimbs have a base Strength Attribute slightly higher than the racial average of the owner. Cyberlimbs for humans and elves are built with a base Strength of 4, for orks and dwarfs with a base Strength of 6, and for trolls with a base Strength of 8. For metavariants, use the Strength Attribute of the race from which the variant derives (for example, minotaurs use the troll Strength).

Cyberskulls and -torsos do not have Strength Attributes.

Limitations

Each cyberlimb can be enhanced to have a higher Strength, though enhancing a limb by more than 3 points requires additional Essence loss and nuyen because the arm's mountings must be reinforced.

Because the body must be structurally modified to accommodate enhanced cyberlimbs, a character may not possess a cyberlimb with a Strength Rating higher than twice his Body, or Body + 4, whichever is lower. For example, a character with Body 3 can have a cyberlimb with a Strength Rating no greater than 6; a character with Body 9 can have a cyberlimb with Strength no greater than 13.

Partial Cyberlimb Strength

Characters may boost the inherent Strength of cyberhands and -feet, but the boosted Strength does not add to the Power of unarmed combat attacks. Such enhancements cost 20,000 nuyen per point of additional hand or foot Strength, to a maximum of +3, and cost no additional Essence. Increased hand Strength can only be applied to gripping.

Lower cyberarms and -legs use the same Strength enhancement rules as for cyberhands and -feet, but they cost 35,000 nuyen per point.

Unbalanced Strength

Cyberlimb-equipped characters with more than one cyberlimb or cyberlimbs with Strength enhancements may have different Strength Ratings for different limbs.

A character with limbs of different Strength Ratings may not be able to take full advantage of a limb's Strength in every situation. As a broad guideline, assume that if the character can apply a limb properly in a situation, that limb's full Strength Rating can be used. For example, a character trying to pull up someone who has fallen over the edge of a building can use the Strength Rating for the cyberarm that is actually supporting the fallen person. In this same situation, the character cannot use the Strength Ratings of his other limbs unless he manages to get proper leverage or succesfully brace the limb. If a character manages to use more than one limb to its full advantage in a given situation, use the

Cyberware	Essence	Cost	Availability	Street Index	Legality
Smartlink Subsystems					
Induction Pad	.1	200¥	4/48 hrs	1.5	5P–N
Eye Display	.1	300¥	4/48 hrs	1.5	Legal
Ltd. Simsense Rig	.1	1,000¥	4/48 hrs	1.5	5P–N
Standard Processor	.2	1,000¥	4/48 hrs	1.5	5P–N
Smartlink-2 Proc.	.2	2,000¥	6/48 hrs	2	5P–N
Range Finder	.1	2,000¥	8/48 hrs	1.5	5P–N
Personalized Safety	—	200¥	4/48 hrs	1.5	Legal
Stepped Reflex Trigger	—	+25%	As wired	As wired	4P–Q

Gear	Mount	Conceal.	Weight	Cost	Availability	St. index	Legality
Pers. Safety Modification	—	—	.1	1,000¥	3/36 hrs	1.5	Legal

average of the Strength Ratings (round down) for those limbs.

In situations such as unarmed or armed combat, it is impossible to tell for certain when and how a particular limb is being used, so the player must choose one of the following alternatives.

The player's character may use the average Strength Rating of all four limbs as the Strength Rating for melee combat. If the character also has Strength-enhancing cyberware such as muscle replacement or muscle augmentation, the appropriate Strength bonuses from such cyberware apply to all natural limbs equally and should be added to the Strength of each natural limb.

Alternatively, the character can lead his attack with any limb he chooses (within reason; leading with a cyberleg when attacking with an ax makes no sense). He then uses the Strength Rating of only that limb for the attack. Attacks made with a lead limb receive a maximum melee Power bonus of +1.

Chris's character has a natural Strength of 5, muscle replacement 2, a cyberarm (Strength 8) and a cyberleg (Strength 9). When engaged in melee combat, Chris has two options. The first is to use an averaged Strength Rating for all melee-related tests. The average Strength of this character is 7 (7 + 7 (one arm and one leg of natural flesh with muscle replacement) + 8 (cyberarm) + 9 (cyberleg) = 31; 31 ÷ 4 = 7.75, rounded down to 7), and he receives a +2 bonus to the Power of his attacks for having two cyberlimbs.

However, if the character is striking with his cyberarm or kicking with his cyberleg, Chris may want to use the second option and lead with the appropriate limb. Leading with the cyberarm would use Strength 8; leading with the cyberleg would use Strength 9. In either case, because the character was leading with one cyberlimb, he receives only a +1 Power bonus.

QUICKNESS

A cyberlimb has a base Quickness of 4.

Quickness enhancements to cyberarms or cyberlegs should be the same for both limbs in a pair. If a character has two cyberarms or two cyberlegs, and one of the pair has a higher or lower Quickness Rating, the player character must apply a modifier equal to the difference between the limbs' Quickness Ratings to the target numbers for all tests involving movement or coordination. Modifiers from arm and leg pairs are cumulative.

Unbalanced Quickness

Determine the average Quickness of multiple enhanced limbs as for Strength enhancements. Use this average Quickness when calculating Combat Pool, Reaction and Initiative.

Cyberskulls and torsos do not have unique Quickness Attributes.

The street samurai sample character in SR3 (p. 75) has two cyberarms, neither of which has Quickness enhancements. They are balanced against each other, with a Quickness of 4, so he is not penalized with target number modifiers for movement and coordination. However, his cyberarms' Quickness 4 does not match the Quickness 6 of his natural legs. The average Quickness of all limbs is 5 (4 + 4 + 6 + 6 = 20, divided by 4), to be used when calculat-

ing Combat Pool, Reaction and Initiative. The Man and Machine *rules give this sample character a Combat Pool of 5, a Reaction of 5 (10) and an Initiative of 5 (10) + 3D6.*

Simply adding Quickness enhancements (p. 40) to each cyberarm would balance the character's limbs again. This would cost no Essence but would cost the character 60,000 nuyen per limb (plus 10 percent, per Multiple Cyberlimb Enhancements).

Limitations

As with Strength enhancements, any single cyberlimb can accept only up to 3 points of Quickness enhancement before a player character must spend additional Essence and nuyen to modify the body to handle the extra stress of the enhancements.

A character can enhance the Quickness of a cyberlimb to twice his natural Quickness or Quickness + 4, whichever is lower. For example, a character with Quickness 2 can have a cyberlimb with an enhanced Quickness Rating of no greater than 4; a character with Quickness 10 can have a cyberlimb with enhanced Quickness no greater than 14.

MULTIPLE CYBERLIMB ENHANCEMENTS

The requirements and modifications for one type of enhancement are often at odds with those of another, so when adding multiple enhancements (Strength, Quickness or Integrity) to the same limb, add 10 percent to the purchase price of any enhancements beyond the first. For example, a character who has a Strength enhancement in one cyberarm must pay 110 percent of the cost of a Quickness or Integrity enhancement to add that enhancement. If the character chooses to add both the Quickness and Integrity enhancements at the same time, he must pay an additional 10 percent of the cost of each enhancement.

ARMOR

Armor, called body plating (see p. 37), can be added to cyberlimbs, -torsos and -skulls. Determine the body's overall coverage by averaging all body plating values. Player characters who want complete protection must acquire armor for each of five possible hit locations: arms, legs, head, front torso and back torso. To find the overall Armor Rating, add up the ratings of the individual pieces of armor and average the result, rounding down.

When a called shot is made against a character, or a specific limb or area is otherwise targeted or damaged, use only the Armor Rating for that location.

Cyberlimb body plating is cumulative with worn armor. The bonus it provides does not count toward layering armor, but the average body plating ballistic Armor Rating does count toward determining the Quickness modifier (see p. 285, *SR3*).

The hotshot street samurai Razor has 4 points of ballistic armor on his chest, 2 points covering his back, 2 points covering his legs, 2 points on his arms and 1 point protecting his head. This gives him a total of 11 points of ballistic armor plating distributed around his body. To find the average, divide the sum (11) by 5 (total possible hit locations). The result is 2.2, rounded down to 2, so Razor has an overall ballistic Armor Rating of 2.

CONCEALMENT

Synthetic cyberlimbs have a base Concealability of 8, modified by any limb modifications or added implants. Higher-grade cyberware is more concealable than basic cyberware: raise the Concealability by +2 per grade (10 for alphaware, 12 for betaware and 14 for deltaware). This bonus also applies to the Concealability of any devices built into the limb.

As a general rule, each device implanted in a cyberlimb that doesn't have a Concealability modifier listed on the Equipment Capacity Cost Table, p. 36, reduces the synthetic limb's Concealability by –1 per unit of equipment capacity space it occupies. Gamemasters may modify this as appropriate for the item in question.

Synthetic cyberlimbs are more likely to be noticed if the onlooker spends a long period of time in proximity to the owner. Even synthetic cyberlimbs don't move quite as naturally as the real thing, and after a while the onlooker will notice the replacement. A cyberlimb becomes even more obvious if a character is under the influence of alcohol or drugs; the artificial limb does not flail around with quite the right degree of abandon. After a reasonable period of interaction, apply a –2 modifier to an onlooker's Perception Test to determine if a character has a cyberlimb (for example, spending an entire evening at a bar in the company of the character). Depending on the duration, frequency and continuity of observation, the gamemaster may increase the modifier to a maximum of –4.

EQUIPMENT CAPACITY

Replacement limbs offer a certain amount of space that can be used to accommodate additional equipment. The amount of space available depends on the limb and is different for obvious cyberlimbs and for synthetic. The space is measured in units of equipment capacity. Each unit offers roughly 50 cubic centimeters of space.

The Equipment Capacity Table lists the number of equipment capacity units (ECU) in various cyber replacement parts. The Equipment Capacity Cost Table lists the number of equipment capacity units various implants and devices require in order to be installed in cyber replacements.

Most additional equipment can be installed in cyberlimbs without Essence cost. Equipment that must interface with other, non-cyber parts of the body, however, does cost additional Essence, as shown on the Equipment Capacity Cost Table.

For equipment not listed on the table, the gamemaster can establish an equipment capacity unit cost based on the gear's approximate size, using the Equipment Capacity Units Table.

Unless the equipment description includes it, most devices installed in a cyberlimb do not have a direct neural connection to the brain. In order for the user to cybernetically control such a device, it must be installed with a direct neural interface (see p. 39). These items are marked with an asterisk under Essence Cost on the Equipment Capacity Cost Table.

Cyberskulls and -torsos: These rules only apply to implants placed into the structural frame of cyberskulls and cybertorsos. For example, headware placed inside the head would not take up cyberskull equipment capacity units, but retractable horns built into the cyberskull would.

EQUIPMENT CAPACITY COST TABLE

Implant	Equipment Capacity Units	Essence Cost	Concealability Modifier
Chemical analyzer	.5	—	–.5
Cyberdecks			
Custom	5	—*	–4
Stock	4	—*	–3
Cyberfins (per hand/foot)	.25	—	–.5
Cyberguns			
Holdout pistol	1	—*	–1
Light pistol	1.5	—*	–1
Machine pistol	2	—*	–2
Heavy pistol	2.5	—*	–2
Submachine gun	3	—*	–3
Shotgun	3.5	—*	–2
External clip port	.25	—*	–1
Laser sight	.25	—	–.5
Silencer	.5	—	–1
Sound suppresser	1	—	–2
Cybersquirt	2	—*	–2
Cyber taser	1	—*	–.5
Datajack	.5	.2	–1
Finger tip compartment	.25	—*	—
Foot anchor	4	—	–1
Gas spectrometer	.5	—	–.5
Handblade	.5	—	–5
Retractable	1	—	–.5
Hand razors	.25	—	–3
Retractable	.5	—	–.5
Horns (cyberskull only)	.5	—	–3
Retractable	1	.1	–2
Hydraulic jacks	4 + .5/rating	.25	–3
Independent cybereyes			
Pair	2	.2	–2
Single	1	.1	–1
Magnetic system	3	—	–1
Orientation system	1	—*	–.5
Remote control deck	5	—*	–4
BattleTac FDDM	.25	—	—
BattleTac IVIS	.5	—	–.5
Remote control ECCM	.5	—	–1
RC encryption module	.25	—	—
Rigger decryption module	.25	—	—
Rigger protocol emulation	.25	—	—
Retractable climbing claws	1	—	–.5
Shock hand	1	—	–.5
Smartlink system	.5	.25	—
Induction pad	.25	—	—
Spur	.5	—	–4
Retractable	1	—	–.5
Strength Enhancement			
Each point up to 3	—	—	–1
Each point over 3	1	.4	–2
Subdermal display (biomonitor)	.5	—	–.5
Tactical computer	4	.5	–4
Each additional sense port	.5	.1	—
Venom sack (per 2 doses)	.25	—	—

* These items are not cybernetically controlled unless they are connected to a direct neural interface (see p. 39).

Cyberware Grade: Higher-grade cyberware offers less equipment capacity because the implants are more streamlined and ergonomic and are therefore smaller and have less space available. Reduce the number of equipment capacity units available in a limb by 10 percent for alphaware, 20 percent for betaware and 25 percent for deltaware. Round fractions to the nearest .25.

CYBERLIMB ACCESSORIES

BODY PLATING

This ceramic and hybrid-polymer plating can be installed on the outer casing of cyberlimbs, -skulls and -torsos. Intended primarily as protection for obvious cyberlimbs, this bulky armor can also be used in limited amounts on synthetic parts. In addition to standard impact and ballistic protection, ablative armor is also available. Ablative armor absorbs kinetic energy from attacks and then vaporizes.

Game Effects

Each point of ballistic or impact armor is purchased separately. This armor is cumulative with worn armor. For rules on calculating overall protection, see *Armor,* p. 35.

Each point of ablative armor adds 2 to both the cyberlimb's Ballistic and Impact Armor Ratings. When struck by an attack with a Power greater than [3 x (points of ablative armor)], reduce the bonus to ballistic and impact armor by 1. Ablative armor panels can be replaced, requiring an appropriate B/R (5) Skill Test and a base time of 5 minutes per point.

Body plating on cybertorsos must be designated for either the front or rear torso.

No more than 10 points of ballistic and 10 points of impact armor (including ablative bonuses) may be added to a single cyberlimb (front and rear torso are counted separately).

CYBERARM GYROMOUNT

A street samurai favorite, the cyberarm gyromount provides better balance and reduced recoil for improved firing capability. This system is concealed when not in use, but when activated, counterweights pop out of the owner's wrist and begin to spin.

Game Effects

This piece of cyberware works like a standard gyromount and provides 3 points of recoil reduction. It can be used with any weapon of a size up to and including a light machine gun. It can only be installed in a full cyberarm or articulated arm.

Unactivated, this system reduces Concealability by 1; when activated, reduce Concealability by 6.

EQUIPMENT CAPACITY TABLE

Cyber Replacement	Max. Equipment Capacity (in units) Obvious	Synthetic
Hand/foot	2	1
Full arm	10	5
Full leg	20	10
Upper arm	6	3
Lower arm	4	2
Upper leg	12	6
Lower leg	8	4
Skull	2	1
Torso	7	3

CYBERHAND SAFETY

Similar to the smartlink and biometric safety systems, this system mounts a pass-chip in a cyberhand. The grips of the user's weapons are modified with a specialized chip reader attached to the weapon's internal safety. When a person picks up the weapon, the reader scans the cyberhand's chip. If the codes encoded in both systems match, the weapon's safety is shut off. If the systems don't match, the safety remains active, rendering the weapon harmless.

Game Effects

The encryption of the cyberhand chip's embedded pass-code has a rating of 8.

To change ownership of a weapon, the character must burn in a new firmware optical chip. Blank chips cost 50 nuyen and can be programmed using a computer repair shop or facility.

CYBER HOLSTER

Installed in a cyberlimb, this built-in holster conceals a pistol until the user cybernetically triggers it to open. Pneumatic pistons pop the holster out and slide the weapon into position for an easy draw.

Game Effects

Cyber holsters may only hold pistols, but they can hold any kind, from holdout to heavy, and including machine pistols and tasers. The specially designed compartment also conceals the pistol from weapon detectors; add +2 to attempts to detect the holstered weapon.

Cyber holsters may only be installed in cyberlimbs. Readying or quick-drawing a cyber-holstered weapon requires a Simple Action, per the standard rules (p. 107, *SR3*).

The Equipment Capacity Units includes space for the holstered gun.

"KID STEALTH" CYBERLEGS

These obviously non-metahumanoid cyberlegs are shaped like the hind legs of a quadruped animal, such as a dog. The feet can be hoof-shaped, paw-shaped or splayed like the feet of a bird. The shape of these legs allows the user to run more quickly and increases the power of kicking attacks. Characters may also install toe razors or retractable blades.

Game Effects

All "Kid Stealth" legs are obvious. Both legs must be the same.

A character with these legs adds a +1 running multiplier; for example, a human with Kid Stealth legs runs at a rate of Quickness x 4. Add +2 to the Power of any kicking attacks made with these legs. Add 1 die to Athletics Tests involving jumping (p. 47, *SRComp*).

To add toe razors or blades, use the rules for hand razors or blades, but attacks with these weapons add +2 to the Power of the attack.

Kid Stealth cyberlegs have an equipment capacity of 10 units each.

EQUIPMENT CAPACITY UNITS TABLE

Equipment Capacity Units	Approximate Size	Examples
.5	Micro	Pen, microflare, skillsoft chip, razor blade, lockpicks
1	Small	Knife, holdout pistol, cellphone, GPS, lockpick gun
3	Medium	Heavy pistol, computer, signal locator, grapple gun
5	Large	Jammer, cyberdeck, simdeck, medkit

Cyberware	Essence	ECU	Cost	Conceal	Availability	St. Index	Legality
Body Plating							
Ballistic Armor (per point)	—	.5	2,500¥	–.5	8/2 wks	1	Legal
Impact Armor (per point)	—	.5	4,000¥	–.5	8/2 wks	1	Legal
Ablative Armor (per point)	—	1	7,000¥	–1	12/3 wks	2	4P–Q
Cyberarm Gyromount	—	4	40,000¥	–1/–6	10/3 wks	2	4P–R
Cyberhand Safety	—	.5	800¥	—	3/36 hrs	1.5	Legal

Gear	Mount	Weight	Cost	Conceal	Availability	St. Index	Legality
Cyberhand Safety Modification	—	.1	1,000¥	—	3/36 hrs	1.5	Legal

CYBERSKATES

Cyberfeet equipped with in-line roller skates allow quick movement for those adept at skating on blades. Retractable models are available.

Game Effects

Cyberskates can only be installed in cyberfeet. Cyberskates allow the user to skate with a movement rate of Quickness x 2 (walking) or Quickness x 6 (running). Skating characters receive normal movement modifiers, with an additional +1 to difficult ground modifiers. A skating character also receives a +1 target number modifier for any Dodge Tests.

In restricted combat conditions or crowded terrain, cyberskate users must succeed in an Athletics (Skating) (5) Test at the end of each Combat Turn they move, or else fall prone.

Extending or retracting cyberskates requires a Complex Action.

DIRECT NEURAL INTERFACE (DNI)

Direct neural interface (DNI) is a device that links a user's brain to a specially modified piece of equipment in order for that equipment to be cybernetically controlled. Commonly used for equipment installed in cyberlimbs or body compartments, DNI allows the user to issue mental commands to operate that equipment.

Output from the equipment must be viewed through a display link (text), image link (images) or other translation gear (for example, simsense signals could be experienced through a simrig).

Game Effects

Simply put, a DNI is a dedicated datajack connection to a specially modified piece of equipment. Any external device that is DNI-modified can be controlled via datajack.

Only devices that have been adapted for DNI control may be manipulated through DNI. Most headware implants that are instead installed in cyberlimbs are already DNI-adapted; they require only a DNI implant to connect them to the brain. For example, if a cyberdeck is installed in a cyberlimb, the user must still externally jack into it (by connecting a cable between the datajack and the deck's jackport), unless it has been connected to the user via DNI.

HOOK HAND

This hand replacement offers no frills or cyber-enhancements. The hook hand consists of a plate attached to the wrist stump and various hand attachments that connect to the plate. The device is only sophisticated enough for the brain to manipulate various servomotors to accomplish simple tasks. Most hook hands consist of a hooked weapon or knife.

Game Effects

Players and gamemasters can choose any attachments for a hook hand, provided that the weight of the attachment is no greater than the character's Strength divided by 10. For example, a character with Strength 5 can have a hook hand that weighs up to .5 kg.

The base damage inflicted by a hook hand in melee combat is (STR + 1)M. This should be adjusted appropriately for a knife or spur attachment, using the standard knife or spur Damage Codes. Hook hands can be removed (voluntarily or otherwise).

Hook hands are available only in standard grade.

INTEGRITY ENHANCEMENT

Cyberlimbs can be designed to incorporate stronger structural integrity and protection for internal components. Reinforcing cyberlimbs in this way increases bulk and cost, but it also reduces stress to the limb and interior damage.

Game Effects

Cyberlimb integrity enhancements have a maximum of 3 points per cyberlimb. Each point of integrity reduces by –1 the target number for cyberlimb Stress Tests (p. 126). This bonus also applies to any equipment built into the limb.

Integrity enhancements also help protect the cyberlimb against damage. Whenever a cyberlimb with integrity enhancements (or anything built into the cyberlimb) is targeted by a called shot, add a number of Body dice equal to the cyberlimb's integrity enhancement to the Resistance Test.

PARTIAL CYBERLIMBS

In the same way that a cyberarm requires extensive shoulder and torso modification and a cyberleg requires substantial hip bracing, partial cyberlimbs (forearm, hand, foot, lower leg) require the rest of the limb to be reinforced to compensate for the additional weight and strength.

Cyberhands and cyberfeet can be designed for easy removal and substitution, giving the owner flexibility in available features. Such replacement parts simply require a quick-release attachment available at an increased cost.

Game Effects

Use the standard cyberlimb rules for partial cyberlimbs, with the exceptions noted in those rules.

Replacement Limbs: Attaching/removing a replacement part requires a free hand and a Complex Action.

PEG LEG

The peg leg retains the classic styling seen in old pirate movies; a plate attached to the knee or hip, with a peg made of wood or some other material fastened to the plate. The advantage of modern peg legs is that the owner now has minimal motor control over the attachment.

Game Effects

Peg legs do not confer any Body or Strength modifiers. Because a peg leg does not function like a natural leg or a cyberleg, reduce the character's Quickness when determining movement rate by –1 for the knee-length peg leg and by –2 for the hip-length leg. A person with a peg leg cannot walk normally; a successful Perception (5) Test allows an observer to notice that the individual has a peg leg.

Modifications or other cyberware cannot be added to peg legs, though the leg can be hollowed out as a place to keep documents, jewels, keys or other items no larger than the character's fist in diameter and no longer than the character's forearm.

Peg legs can be removed from their attachment plate, and many people have a variety of peg legs for different occasions. A character may sharpen the point of the peg leg and use it as a weapon with the statistics and Damage Code of standard hand spurs. The gamemaster determines whether the character loses his or her balance when using a peg leg as a weapon, depending on the situation.

Peg legs only come in standard grade.

Cyberware	Essence	ECU	Cost	Conceal	Availability	St. Index	Legality
Cyber Holster	.1	4	5,000¥	10	4/48 hrs	1	5P–N
Cyberskates	—	2	1,000¥	–5	3/24 hrs	1	Legal
Retractable	—	4	2,500¥	–2	4/48 hrs	1	Legal
Kid Stealth Legs (ea.)	1	—	100,000¥	—	6/2 wks	2	Legal
Direct Neural Interface	.1	.25	4,500¥	—	4/6 days	1	5P–Q
DNI Adaptation	—	—	x 150% of cost of device	—	—	—	Per device
Hook Hand	.1	—	30¥	—	1/6 hrs	1	Legal
Integrity Enhancement (per point)	—	1	30,000¥	–1	6/4 days	1.5	6P–N
Partial Cyberlimb							
Cyberhand/cyberfoot							
Obvious	.35	—	20,000¥	—	3/4 days	1	Legal
Synthetic	.35	—	25,000¥	10	3/4 days	1	Legal
Cyber forearm/lower leg							
Obvious	.65	—	40,000¥	—	4/4 days	1	Legal
Synthetic	.65	—	50,000¥	9	4/4 days	1	Legal
Replacement Modification	—	1	+10%	—	+2/+2 days	2	Legal

QUICKNESS ENHANCEMENTS

Major upgrades to the motion servos can improve a cyberlimb's movement speed. Typically, this speed is fine-tuned to correspond to the user's natural speed and reflexes or to other cyberlimbs.

Game Effects

Each cyberlimb has a base Quickness of 4. See *Quickness,* p. 34, for additional rules on Quickness modifications.

SIGNAL BOOSTER

Cyberlimb signal boosters consist of high-powered relays and signal amplifiers installed inside a cyberlimb. They amplify the signals of transmitters such as headware radios and cranial remote decks, thus increasing the transmitter's effective range and resistance to electronic warfare.

Game Effects

Cyberlimb signal boosters increase the Flux Rating of a cranial remote deck, headware radio or other linked transmitter by the booster's rating.

Signal boosters are available in ratings from 1 to 10. Only one device can draw power from the signal booster at a time. Signal boosters function for 50 hours before they need recharging.

TELESCOPING CYBERLIMBS

Cyberlimbs built with this feature can extend outward like an antenna. Telescoping cyberlegs elevate the user, allowing him to reach higher. Telescoping cyberarms allow the user to reach farther than their normal ability. Extended limbs are not flexible and can be clumsy to move with or use.

Game Effects

Only full cyberlimbs, or lower leg or lower arm cyberlimbs, can be modified with the telescoping feature. Telescoping cyberlimbs require a Simple Action to pop out or retract. Such cyberlimbs increase the user's height or reach by 1 meter. Telescoping cyberarms can be used to negate an opponent's Reach bonus by –1, but they do not add any Reach bonus to the user. Because of their awkwardness, the gamemaster may apply a +1 target number to tests involving the telescoped limb where limited flexibility is a factor.

WEAPON MOUNTS

A variety of weapon mounts exist for the street samurai who chooses to literally bristle with weapons.

External Mount: This is a simple mounting point, similar to a hardpoint, that allows a weapon to be used while keeping the hands free.

Tracking Mount: This mount features a motorized pivoting system. If linked to a target designator system, it can track targets automatically without effort by the user.

Articulated Arm: The articulated arm is a separate articulated tracking mount, usually anchored to a cybertorso in the middle of the back. This mount extends out over the user's shoulder or out to the side for a clear field of fire; it has a full range of motion except for a dead spot behind the user's head.

See *Cyberware and Social Interaction,* p. 48, for information on social penalties for obvious cyberware.

Game Effects

Weapon mounts may only be mounted on a cyberlimb or cybertorso. The gun must be connected to the user with a DNI implant (see p. 39) or manually triggered. To take advantage of a smartgun link, the gun must be smartgun-equipped and the mount must be linked (via router) to a smartgun link. Only one gun can be attached to each mount.

Retractable mounts require a Simple Action to pop out or retract.

For 10 nuyen (plus ammo costs), player characters can buy external ammo pods that store 50 rounds of ammunition. Only one pod can be mounted at any given time.

External Mount: Attaching or detaching a weapon from this mount requires a Complex Action. The external mount supports light, heavy or machine pistols and submachine guns. If the weapon is not mounted in a location where it can be intuitively aimed (for example, on the shoulder facing to the rear), add a +2 modifier to the target number when firing it. This mount offers no recoil compensation bonuses.

Tracking Mount: This mount functions the same as an external mount. If it is linked to a target designator system, it can be fired at marked targets (add laser sight bonuses for such shots, but not smartlink bonuses). It can support the same weapons as the external mount and provides no recoil compensation.

Articulated Arm: This mount works like a tracking mount but has a full range of motion and covers a 360-degree firing area. The articulated arm can support all light weapons up to a

Cyberware	Essence	ECU	Cost	Conceal	Availability	St. Index	Legality
Peg Leg							
Knee Length	.2	—	50¥	—	1/6 hrs	1	Legal
Hip Length	.4	—	120¥	—	1/6 hrs	1	Legal
Quickness Enhancement							
1–3 points (per limb)	—	—	30,000¥	–.5/point	8/4 days	1.5	6P–Q
4+ points (per limb)	.3/point	1/point	45,000¥	–1/point	8/4 days	1.5	6P–Q
Signal Booster	—	4	Rating x 15,000¥	–1	6/72 hrs	1.5	Legal
Telescoping Cyberlimb	—	3	10,000¥	–1	6/72 hrs	1.5	Legal

light machine gun. The system gives users 3 points of Recoil Reduction, plus the modifiers for a laser sight.

CYBERWEAPONS

In order for a cyberweapon to be fired reflexively, it must be equipped with a DNI connection (see p. 39). Otherwise, it must be triggered manually.

In order to use a smartgun link, a weapon must be smartlink-equipped and connected (via a router) to a smartlink system.

CYBER DARTGUN

Modeled on the popular narcoject series of dartguns, this implanted pistol can deliver a dart that efficiently penetrates most armor and delivers a single dose of whatever compound it contains.

Game Effects

Treat the cyber dartgun as a light pistol. The darts can be loaded with one dose of a compound (beginning on p. 111).

Resolve attacks with this weapon using the standard ranged combat rules. See *Drug Effects*, p. 105, for determining the effect of the injected drug.

CYBERGUNS

Though designed to be installed in cyberarms, cyberguns may also be implanted in natural limbs. Typically, the gun is placed along the forearm bone and fires through a port at the base of the palm. All cyberguns have an internal magazine ammunition load and can be reloaded through a slot in the arm. An external clip port can also be installed, though it makes the presence of the gun quite obvious.

Cyberguns can be equipped with a smartlink, a laser sight or even a silencer or sound suppresser.

Game Effects

The number before the slash under *Ammo* is the weapon's built-in ammo capacity; the number after the slash is for external clips.

The Concealability listed represents how hidden the weapon is inside a natural arm. The weapon is obvious when it is being fired or when using an external clip.

The laser sight, silencer and sound suppresser accessories function as described on p. 281, *SR3*. The silencer may only be used on the light and heavy pistols, and the sound suppresser can only be used on the machine pistol and SMG.

Cyberguns may not be fitted with recoil compensation or any other accessories not described here.

CYBERSQUIRT

The cybersquirt is an implant version of the popular, non-lethal Ares SuperSquirt II (see p. 115). This weapon uses two reservoirs, one holding DMSO gel (dimethyl sulfoxide, see p. 112) and the other holding the chemical of choice. When fired, the DMSO and the chemical are mixed and sprayed at the target via silent and recoilless compressed air. The DMSO essentially forces the skin of the target to absorb the delivered chemical/biological agent. Armor offers little protection from this weapon, as the spray quickly soaks through and reaches the skin.

The cybersquirt is mounted along the forearm, with a spray nozzle port in the base of the palm. External reservoir clip ports may also be installed (one each for the gel and chemical).

Game Effects

The cybersquirt holds 10 chemical rounds and the gel

Cyberware	Essence	ECU	Cost	Conceal	Availability	St. Index	Legality
External Mount	—	3	5,000¥	–5	6/4 days	2	3P–R
Retractable	—	5	15,000¥	–2/–5	6/4 days	2	3P–R
Tracking Mount	—	5	25,000¥	–6	8/7 days	2	3P–R
Retractable	—	7	40,000¥	–3/–6	8/7 days	2	3P–R
Articulated Arm	—	7	110,000¥	—	12/24 days	2	2P–R
Retractable	1	7	200,000¥	–5/—	12/24 days	2	2P–R

	Essence	Conceal	Ammo	Mode	Damage	Cost	Availability	St. Index	Legality
Cyber Dartgun	.3	10	5(m)	SA	—	1,000¥	8/7 days	2	6P–Q
Fichetti Brand Cyberguns									
Holdout Pistol	.15	12	2(m)/6(c)	SS	4L	250¥	8/7 days	2	8P–Q
Light Pistol	.35	10	12(m)/12(c)	SA	6L	650¥	8/7 days	2	6P–Q
Machine Pistol	.4	8	12(m)/35(c)	SA/BF	6L	900¥	8/7 days	2	4P–Q
Heavy Pistol	.6	8	10(m)/10(c)	SA	9M	800¥	8/7 days	2	4P–Q
Submachine Gun	1	6	12(m)/24(c)	SA/BF	7M	1,800¥	8/7 days	2	3P–Q
Shotgun	1.1	6	10(m)/10(c)	SA	8S	1,200¥	8/7 days	2	4P–Q
External Clip Port	.1	–1	—	—	—	100¥	8/7 days	2	As gun
Laser Sight	.1	–1	—	—	—	700¥	8/7 days	2	Legal
Silencer	.2	–2	—	—	—	1,000¥	8/7 days	2	As gun
Sound Suppresser	.3	–3	—	—	—	1,500¥	8/7 days	2	As gun

reservoir holds enough gel for up to 10 shots. See *Applied Chemtech Compounds*, p. 111, for examples of chemicals that can be used in this weapon.

Porous armor, such as armor clothing and Kevlar weaves, offers no protection against DMSO. For characters wearing such armor, reduce the Power of the chemical by half the target's Impact Armor Rating (round up). Only individuals in fully sealed rigid armor or wearing suits specifically designed to protect against chemical/biological agents are immune to the penetrating effects of DMSO (see *Drug Effects*, p. 105).

The compressed CO_2 canister that forcibly ejects the spray must be replaced or recharged every 50 shots, at a cost of 50 nuyen.

Each time the cybersquirt takes Stress, roll 1D6. On a result of 1 or 6, the reservoirs begin to leak. The owner suffers the effects of the chemical per the rules in *Chemistry*, p. 101.

Cybersquirts can be equipped with a smartlink or with the laser sight described under cyberguns, but they cannot have any other accessories. The cybersquirt has the same firing range as light pistols.

CYBER TASER

Designed to be implanted in a cyberarm/hand, this weapon is also commonly implanted in the base of the palm on natural hands. It operates in the same way as a standard taser pistol, firing standard taser darts connected through 15-meter wires to a capacitor implanted in the palm.

Game Effects

The cyber taser does 10S damage, but it can fire only two shots. After two shots, it must be "reloaded" by installing new darts and wires. The battery must be recharged after ten uses. The cyber taser has the same range as the standard taser.

Cyber tasers can be equipped with a smartlink or with the laser sight described under cyberguns, but they cannot have any other accessories.

FANG IMPLANTS

Enlarged canines, anchored for support and sharpened for penetration, are available in standard or extendable models.

Game Effects

Fang attacks suffer a –1 Reach modifier. The extendable model looks like normal canines until they are triggered.

HORN IMPLANTS

Synthetic horns come in a wide array of shapes and sizes, from curled troll horns to devil horns to single rhinoceros-style horns. Horns are usually installed in the skull, but some users implant rows of horns to form a "bone crest" along the head, neck and/or back. All horn implants are structurally braced for use in combat.

Retractable "telescoping" models are also available to give users the advantage of surprise.

Game Effects

Horn attacks suffer a –1 Reach penalty. Each two minor horns (similar to those of a goat) count as one implant, as do single larger horns (such as those of a rhinoceros or ram).

SHOCK HAND

This system consists of shock pads built into the knuckles or palm of the hand that inflict a nasty electric shock to anything with which they are in contact when activated. They are designed to be mounted in cyberlimbs; ceramic ridges and insulation protect the user if installed in natural hands.

Game Effects

The shock hand must be recharged after 12 uses. This device may also be implanted in a foot, elbow and other extremities.

VENOM SACK

A small reservoir containing a toxin or other compound can be implanted as an accessory to a cyber-implant blade or dart weapon. The weapon itself is hollowed out or otherwise modified so that the compound coats the blade or dart and any targets struck are dosed.

Game Effects

Venom sacks come in 2-dose increments. Only one dose can be used on a blade or dart at a time, and the dose is used up when the weapon strikes a target. See *Drug Effects*, p. 105 in *Chemistry*, for rules on resolving such attacks.

The cost for the venom sack does not include the toxin or compound it contains. Refilling a venom sack requires a Biotech (6) Test with a base time of 10 minutes.

GENERAL CYBERWARE RULES

As with all *Shadowrun* game mechanics, the rules for cyberware can only approximate real life. The concepts of cybertechnology, while rooted in real science, offer too many possibilities and potential problems to be realistically simulated by even the most comprehensive rules. As a result, gamemasters must allow latitude for situations that don't fit the rules and even occasionally bend the rules or create house rules for the sake of good game play. The important thing is to keep the game moving and to have fun—don't get bogged down in the details.

The following rules flesh out several aspects of cyberware not covered in the equipment descriptions or equipment-specific rules.

BATTLETAC SYSTEMS

The BattleTac system integrates tactical communications and data transfer into a battlefield information exchange network. In effect, each BattleTac system has at least two parts, a master component and a receiver component. A master component receives data from a number of linked sources, usually a unit of soldiers with cybernetic or external sensory gear and drones.

The master component uses input data to build a comprehensive picture of the tactical situation. This includes mapping features, enemy identification and positioning, current status of

individuals and drones, targeting data, tactical requests and commands, video feeds and other factors. This data is continuously updated and fed back to receiver components. Characters equipped with receiver components can consult them for tactical information and suggestions.

Both master components and receiver components can be purchased as external models or as cybernetic implants (see *Tactical Computer* and *BattleTac Cyberlink*, p. 23).

BattleTac Game Effects

BattleTac systems have several game effects. First, they can increase a user's Small Unit Tactics Skill (see p. 47) and thus boost the unit's Initiative. Second, they allow members of a unit to use indirect fire against designated targets (see p. 60, *Rigger 2*). Third, they allow a unit to share quickly a wide range of information. Any piece of information known to one member of the BattleTac network can be fed to the rest of the network; this requires a Simple Action, though linked sensory information is

	Essence	Conceal	Ammo	Mode	Damage	Cost	Availability	St. Index	Legality
Cybersquirt	.4	8	10/10(c)	SA	Special	1,400¥	8/6 days	2	5P–Q
External Clip Port	.1	–1	—	—	—	100¥	8/7 days	2	As gun
Cyber Taser	.3	10	2	SA	10S Stun	2,000¥	6/4 days	1.5	5P–Q

Cyberware	Essence	Conceal	Damage	Cost	Availability	St. Index	Legality
Fangs	.1	5	(STR +1)L	5,000¥	4/48 hrs	1	Legal
Extendable	.15	9	(STR + 1)L	8,000¥	5/48 hrs	1	5P–N
Horns	.1	—	(STR)M	12,000¥	4/48 hrs	1	Legal
Retractable	.25	8	(STR)M	16,000¥	5/48 hrs	1	5P–N
Shock Hand	.25	5	8S Stun	1,300¥	6/4 days	2	4P–Q
Venom Sack (2 doses)	.05	—	—	500¥	4/48 hrs	2	4P–Q

automatically fed to the network. Once input, this data can be accessed by anyone else in the network; accessing is automatic for characters with cyberlinks (or the tactical computer), accessing data from a receiver component takes a Simple Action. This allows a unit to move in a coordinated manner and act upon data input from other unit members.

BattleTac and Drone Networks

Rigger remote-control networks can mimic BattleTac networks through use of the BattleTac IVIS system (see p. 23). A rigger with a remote control deck equipped with an IVIS master component can use the advanced information-sharing capabilities to issue more complex orders to IVIS-equipped drones.

An IVIS-equipped remote control network can also be integrated with a BattleTac network. In such cases, the rigger and remote control deck act as a node between the BattleTac master component and the rigger's drones. In other words, the BattleTac master component conveys data to the rigger, which then transmits it to the drones (and vice versa, for sensory feeds). The rigger must have a BattleTac cyberlink or a receiver component connected to his remote control deck (or a BattleTac master component, if the rigger is the BattleTac network's focal point). Additionally, one of the rigger's RCD ports must be dedicated to communicating with the BattleTac master component and network.

This setup allows the rigger and drones to exchange data, as described in *BattleTac Game Effects*. It also allows the rigger to receive Initiative bonuses from the Small Unit Tactics Skill (and thus his drones as well).

A drone network cannot take advantage of a BattleTac network's indirect fire capability unless the network is equipped with BattleTac FDDM (see p. 23). If the remote control deck and drones are so equipped, they may act as spotters for each other and others in the BattleTac network, and vice versa.

CYBERWARE AND CRITTERS

Critters do not cope well with cyberware implants, which tend to impede their mental faculties and act as a source of unnatural irritation. Rules for cybered critters appear on p. 6 of the *Critters* book.

Awakened creatures especially do not handle cyberware well, because it reduces their Essence and diminishes the power of their abilities. The cyberware of creatures that are transformed by the human-metahuman vampiric virus (HMHVV) breaks during the transformation process, as described under *Infection*, p. 33, *SRComp*.

Creatures with the regeneration power can only bear to have implants for a short time. They tend to find implants incredibly painful and quickly purge such devices from their bodies.

EYES

Cybereyes and accessories are described on p. 299, *SR3*.

Unless stated otherwise, any eye modification can be purchased as a retinal modification for natural eyes or as a cyber modification to cybereyes.

Single Cybereyes

Though cybereyes are usually purchased in pairs, they can be purchased singly. A single cybereye costs 60 percent of the standard purchase price, takes up .1 Essence and accepts accessories worth only .25 points of Essence before increasing the total Essence cost for the eye. Cybereye accessories that require a pair in order to function at their optimum level, such as low-light amplification, thermographic vision and eyelight systems, are less effective in a single eye. The gamemaster may need to determine the exact loss of efficiency, but in general such systems operate about half as well in one eye as they do in two. If purchasing such systems for a single eye, reduce their cost and Essence Cost by 25 percent.

There is no disadvantage to purchasing a single-eye enhancement for only one eye. Vision magnification systems can provide proper magnification with only one eye, but they eliminate depth perception in the cybereye. While the vision magnification is active, apply a +2 modifier to the target number for any tests involving distance, including ranged attack tests.

Single-eye Accessories: The following accessories are single-eye enhancements: Camera, Display Link, Eye Datajack, Eye Laser Systems, Eye Weapon System, Image Link, Opticam, Retinal Clock.

Eye Modification Limits

The small size of the metahuman eye socket represents a built-in limitation to the number of accessories that can be installed in a cybereye. Player characters cannot walk around with guns, darts, lasers, cameras and a variety of other accessories packed into such a confined space. To reflect this, characters may have accessories worth a maximum of 1.2 Essence points installed in a pair of cybereyes, and only one accessory per eye may be a laser, an opticam or a weapon system.

CYBERWARE GRADES

Cyberware comes in various grades, each defining a level of cyberware quality. There are four grades of cyberware: basic, alphaware, betaware and deltaware. Used cyberware (commonly advertised as "thriftware" to make it more palatable) is available in all grades except delta.

Alpha, beta and delta grades represent various levels of quality and sophistication beyond standard, off-the-shelf cyberware. Each grade is an exponential improvement over the next lower grade.

If basic cyberware is comparable to a mass-produced home computer system bought in any store, alphaware represents a computer constructed specifically for the user from chosen components. Likewise, betaware would represent a factory-ordered customized computer with all the bells and whistles, including top-of-the-line software, loads of memory and just-released peripherals. Deltaware would be like owning your own maxed-out supercomputer, ergonomically designed and customized for every use you can think of and more.

Only standard and alpha-grade cyberware are mass-produced. Beta-grade and delta-grade cyberware are custom-made for an individual, which makes them Essence-friendly but also prohibitively expensive. Medical costs and repair times for delta-grade cyberware are exponentially higher than those for standard equipment.

Used cyberware is less reliable than new cyberware of the same grade.

Essence reductions and cost multipliers for alpha, beta, and delta-grade and used cyberware appear on the Cyberware Grades Table. The grade can also affect the equipment capacity and Concealability Rating of cyberlimbs (see p. 35).

CYBERWARE GRADES TABLE

Grade	Essence Cost Reduction	Cost Multiplier	Availability
Alpha	–20% (x .8)	2	Standard
Beta	–40% (x .6)	4	+5/x 1.5
Delta	–50% (x .5)	8	+9/x 3
Used	By grade	.5	Standard

Essence Reduction

Reduce the Base Essence Cost by the percentage listed (or use the multiplier given in parentheses). Round all numbers up. Essence Cost may never be reduced below .01 in this manner.

Cost Multiplier

Multiply the cost for the cyberware by the number indicated. This represents *only* the cost for the piece of cyberware and does not include doctors' fees and hospitalization. See *Surgery,* p. 135, for details on implantation costs and options.

Availability

Player characters can receive basic, alpha- and often even beta-grade custom cyberware at most shadow clinics. Alphaware is as available as basic cyberware, but betaware typically has an Availability equal to the normal rating + 5, with 1.5 times the time period. Betaware is not available to starting characters.

Delta-grade cyberware is far more difficult to acquire. Joe Shadowrunner is extremely unlikely to stumble across a delta-grade cyberware clinic. Some corps run such clinics, but a player character cannot just call up and make an appointment to go in for a lube job. The corp has to *want* the character at the clinic (and if the corp wants someone, there's got to be a reason). At the least, deltaware Availability should be +9/x 3 that of basic cyberware.

Used cyberware is as easy to find as basic cyberware, though the sources that provide it are usually questionable. Obtaining used cyberware involves dealing with organleggers or ghouls at the worst and shady and unprincipled clinics at the best.

See *Finding Treatment,* p. 140, for information on finding a clinic.

Accessories and Systems

Accessories to a device that is alpha-, beta- or delta-grade must also be of the same grade. Likewise, if components of a system are bought separately, such as the various elements of a smartlink system, they must all be of the same grade. Devices that are installed within a cyberlimb or body compartment do not need to be the same grade as the limb/compartment.

Used Cyberware Drawbacks

Used cyberware is usually not as polished and well-maintained as new cyberware, and it has its share of kinks and flaws. Each used cyberware item comes with 1D3 *permanent* Stress Points. These Stress Points can never be removed, and they are cumulative with any Stress Points incurred through use (see *Damage and Healing,* p. 124).

CYBERWARE AND HACKING POOL

The following rules replace the *Cyberware and the Pool* section on p. 19 of *VR2.*

Only two cyberware devices affect the Hacking Pool: the encephalon and the math SPU. Both add their rating in dice to the decker's Hacking Pool; these bonuses are cumulative. For example, a decker with a Rating 2 encephalon and a Rating 3 math SPU would add 5 dice to her Hacking Pool. These extra dice act like other Hacking Pool dice for all purposes (see p. 44, *SR3*).

EFFECTS OF INCREASED REFLEXES

Characters with wired reflexes or any other kind of cybernetic reflex enhancements are prone to react without thinking because they are constantly on edge. At the gamemaster's discretion, such a character tends to react reflexively in situations where a perceived threat exists, regardless of whether that threat is real. The unexpected appearance of a stranger or dangerous-looking people, a sudden threatening move or action and a violent motion in a crowd all might set off a wired character. In such situations, have the character make a Perception Test (p. 231, *SR3*). Apply a +1 modifier to the target number per +1D6 Initiative bonus the character possesses. This modifier represents the character's tendency to react before fully analyzing the situation.

If the character fails the Perception Test, they instinctively react in whatever way the gamemaster deems appropriate. They may dive for cover, push the suddenly moving person down, or even draw and fire a gun. If the action is particularly destructive, the character may make a Willpower Test against the unmodified target number for the Perception Test to avoid performing the action.

The gamemaster should use this rule sparingly, as an occasional reminder of what it's like to live on the edge. Constantly forcing the character to acknowledge the danger his enhancements represent will turn him into a hyperactive nervous wreck and won't be much fun for the player. Reserve this mental torture for appropriate situations—potentially threatening crowds, lonely dark streets and particularly tense encounters.

INTERCONNECTIVITY

Characters may wish to establish a datalink between two (or more) pieces of cyberware that don't normally "talk" to each other. For example, a headware telephone isn't normally datalinked to a chemical analyzer, but if they were, the user could send data from the analyzer to the telephone, which could then fax it somewhere. To establish such a datalink, the devices must be connected through a router (p. 22) or a datajack.

Routers and datajacks facilitate the flow of information between linked cyberware devices much like a computer network. To be part of this network, the device must be linked to a dedicated port on the datajack or router. Each datajack and router has a defined number of ports that different devices can be plugged into. The standard *SR3* datajack has five integral ports: one providing a direct neural connection to the brain, one represented by the surface "jack" into which external devices may be plugged, and three others that can be used as dedicated connections to other pieces of cyberware. With the exception of the external jackpoint and brain connection, all ports must be dedicated (hardwired) to a specific piece of cyberware. Any that are left unassigned can be connected to new implants at a later time.

Any device connected to a datajack or router port can exchange data with any other device so connected. For example, if you have an image link and headware memory connected through your datajack's port, you can display image files from your headware memory on your image link. If any such linked device is also connected to another in some way, any devices that are part of the "chain" may communicate. For example, if your headware memory is linked to your datajack and you're also jacked into a cyberdeck and connected through the Matrix to a security camera, you could download pictures from the camera (through the deck and the datajack) to your headware memory.

A device only needs to be hooked up to a datajack or router port if the user wishes the device to communicate with other devices with which it does not normally exchange data. There is no point in connecting bone lacing cyberware to such a network, as bone lacing does not exchange information with other devices. Devices that are considered accessories to another device do not need to be linked in this way, as they are already integrally connected to the device to which they are an accessory. For example, thermographic vision does not need to be linked to a cybereye, nor does an ear recorder need to be linked to a cyberear.

Likewise, components of a particular "system" do not need to be linked via router or datajack because they are integrally linked to the system of which they are a part. The various components of the smartlink system (p. 32) are automatically linked to one another; however, if an image link was used instead of the standard smartlink eye display, the image link and the smartlink system would need to be linked via datajack or router.

Note that cyberware grade is not a factor when linking between devices. Two items of different grade may be linked, and the grade of the router or datajack is not an issue.

I/O Speed (Optional Rule)

Given the advanced data transmission rates of the 2060s, transferring data from cyberware device to cyberware device is incredibly fast. As a general rule, any data transfer between two devices takes a mere Simple Action, no matter the size.

In some cases, however, the players may desire or need to know the exact speed of transmission. As an optional rule to cover such instances, consider data transfers between datajacks, routers and other cyberware or external devices to occur at a rate of 1,000 Mp per Combat Turn. For data that is encrypted or compressed, double its normal Mp size for determining transfer speed; such data is more complex and requires more error-checking.

Mental Access

Just because a cyberware device is linked to a datajack or router (and thus to the brain) doesn't mean the data it produces is "readable" by the brain; in most cases it isn't. Depending on the data format, it must be channeled through a display link (text), image link (images), knowsoft link (skillsoft), ear recorder (sound), simrig (simsense) or some other device to be understandable.

CYBERWARE AND MAGIC

Because cyberware is paid for with Essence, it is considered an integral part of the body's organic system. This means that spells cannot target cyberware separately from the whole body. Combat spells such as Wreck and Ram cannot target cyberware, detection spells such as Catalog or Analyze Device cannot detect cyberware, and a manipulation spell such as Fix cannot repair cyberware. Likewise, a transformation manipulation such as Shapechange transforms cyberware as well; such cyberware cannot be used in the new form.

If cyberware is removed from the body, it can be targeted like any other device.

The same restrictions apply to adept powers. Cyberware cannot be targeted separately by powers such as distance strike or smashing blow; the victim's body must be targeted.

It is possible to enchant cyberware devices (see *Enchanting*, p. 39, *MITS*), but this must be done before the item is implanted. For example, a combat mage could have his spur blades enchanted into a weapon focus. Even though such enchanted implants are hidden from visual detection, they are still visible via astral perception and are vulnerable to astral attack.

PROTOCOLS

Data comes in many forms: raw text files, images, sound files, simsense and more. Though data may be easily transferred between devices, the destination device may not be able to do anything with it, depending on its purpose. For example, a simsense signal recorded into headware memory from rigging a drone would be useless if transferred to a display or image link; neither is capable of displaying or playing back simsense. If sent to a simrig, however, the recording could be played back.

Likewise, several cyberware devices allow a user to broadcast over radio frequencies. While most transmissions (including cellphone calls) fall under the coverage of standard radio operations and protocols, there are two notable distinctions. Because of the large amount of bandwidth and the multiple frequencies required for simsense transmissions, only simlinks and remote control decks can transmit and receive simsense signals. Additionally, remote control decks use a specific protocol system for rigger remote control networks, which is different from standard simsense broadcasts.

The gamemaster has the final word regarding what protocols a particular piece of data or broadcast uses and whether a device can use or translate it.

Broadcast Encryption/Decryption

All standard radio and simsense broadcasts can be encrypted or decrypted using the *Broadcast Encryption* rules, p. 289, *SR3*. Rigger remote control networks may be encrypted and decrypted through the use of rigger protocol emulation and decryption modules (see p. 25).

Jamming

Standard radio and simsense transmissions are also subject to interference and jamming, as described in *ECCM*, p. 289, *SR3*. Rigger remote control networks follow the rules given in *SR3* and *Rigger 2*.

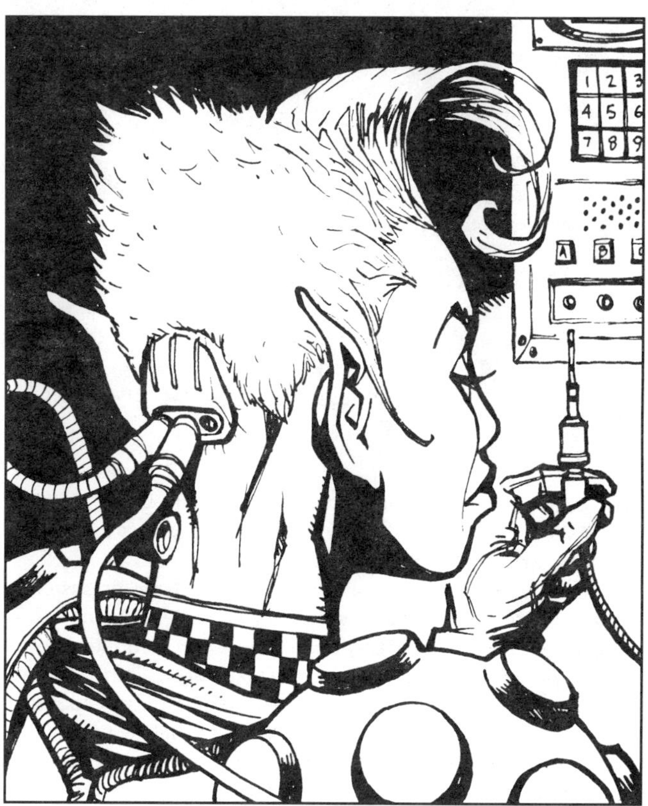

CYBERWARE AND SIGNATURE

Normally, metahumans have a Signature of 6 (5 for trolls) for the purposes of Sensor Tests and sensor-enhanced Gunnery Tests. A significant amount of cyberware may decrease this rating, making the character more visible to sensors. A character with an Essence of between 0 and 3 must subtract 1 from their Signature. A cyberzombie must subtract an additional 1 for each 2 points of negative Essence.

SMALL UNIT TACTICS SKILL

Small Unit Tactics is a special Active Skill that is linked to Intelligence. It represents a character's ability to perceive and analyze the tactical nature of a combat situation and to exploit it to her advantage. Small Unit Tactics has three specializations: BattleTac Systems, Vehicle Tactics and Matrix Tactics.

Characters with this skill can gain an Initiative bonus for their teammates (and themselves) under certain conditions by communicating orders and suggestions based on their tactical assessment.

To use the skill, the character must convey their analysis/orders on their last action of a Combat Turn. It takes a Complex Action to communicate in this way to team members. The success of their tactical aid is represented by a Small Unit Tactics Test that is applied to team members receiving the communication. Only one skill test is made, but individual team members may have different target numbers. The base target numbers and modifiers are represented on the Small Unit Tactics Test Table. The maximum number of team members who can receive an Initiative boost is equal to the character's Small

SMALL UNIT TACTICS TEST TABLE

Situation	Base TN
Character in direct (face-to-face or close LOS) contact with team member	4
Character in radio communication with team member	6
Character in LOS with team member, but no audio communication (i.e., hand gestures)	8
	Modifiers
Character linked to team member via BattleTac cyberlink	–2
Character linked to team member via BattleTac receiver component	–1
Character wounded	+/– Damage modifiers
Team member has Perception modifiers	+/– Perception modifiers

Unit Tactics Skill (not including the character himself).

If the skill is only being used for the character's own benefit, no Complex Action is necessary to communicate.

If this skill is used in conjunction with a BattleTac system, tactical information is more efficiently conveyed. A character using a cybernetic master component (a tactical computer modified for BattleTac, see p. 22) needs to take only a Simple Action to convey orders. A character using a BattleTac master component may also receive a bonus to their Small Unit Tactics Skill.

Every 2 successes achieved against the target number gives that team member a +1 bonus to their Initiative during the next Combat Turn. This Initiative bonus may not exceed the character's Reaction (for example, if the character's Reaction is 4, the highest bonus they can receive is +4).

If more than one character is attempting to improve a team member's bonus in this way, only the highest bonus achieved is used, at –1 for conflicting orders. For example, if a team member receives a +3 bonus from one character and a +5 bonus from another, they would use +4 (highest 5, minus 1).

If this skill is used in preparation for an ambush (by either the ambusher or ambushee), it may also add dice (one for every 2 successes) to the Reaction/Surprise Tests.

CYBERWARE AND SOCIAL INTERACTION

As described in *Cyberware and Social Interaction,* p. 93, *SR3,* characters with large quantities of obvious cyberware suffer some disadvantages in social situations. In cases where the character's cyberware is extremely odd or downright scary, additional modifiers should be applied. For example, a character with an obvious cyberskull or cybertorso, independent cybereyes, "Kid Stealth" legs, articulated arm weapon mounts and even a balance tail comes across to most people as a grade-A freak. Characters sporting such weird or menacing implants should suffer an additional +1 or +2 to all Charisma or Charisma-linked Skill Tests. Because the cyberware also makes the character more intimidating, the same modifier should also apply as a bonus to Intimidation or Interrogation Open Tests.

TASK POOL

The Task Pool is a special pool of dice that grants extra dice for the use of skills when the device is activated.

Some devices add the Task Pool to all skills (see expert driver, p. 19); others, such as the encephalon (p. 21), only add the Task Pool to the following Intelligence-linked skills: Technical, Build/Repair, Knowledge and Language. This Intelligence bonus does not affect Perception Tests or the calculation of Reaction or any dice pools.

The Task Pool uses the standard dice pool rules (p. 43, *SR3*).

CYBERWARE TRIGGERS

Unless otherwise stated, cyberware that is capable of being activated or deactivated can be done so with a mental impulse. This is because the cyberware has been attached to the user's nervous system, so it can be used in the same way the user would move a finger or flex a muscle. Typically, when a cyberware device is installed, the user must spend some time adjusting to this new ability and will doubtlessly trigger the device accidentally a few times. Activating or deactivating cyberware is a Free Action.

If the gamemaster allows it, methods of manually triggering a cyberware device may also be used, such as a subdermal switch. Such triggers incur no extra cost. They can be both a drawback (if enemies find out about them) and an advantage (if friends know about them). Triggering cyberware manually requires a Simple Action.

VISION SYSTEM USE

The following information elaborates on the fundamental characteristics and capabilities of natural and cybernetic low-light and thermographic vision and the use of multiple vision systems. This section also provides an updated Visibility Modifiers Table, expanding on the table that appears on p. 112, *SR3.*

Low-light Vision

Also known as night sight, night vision or light amplification, low-light vision works by amplifying even the tiniest amount of available light. If any light is present, even in such faint quantities as moonlight leaking through low cloud cover or traces of a streetlight flickering into an abandoned basement, then low-light vision has something to amplify. If no light is available, low-light vision is useless. The gamemaster has the final say on whether there is sufficient light for low-light vision to function.

VISIBILITY MODIFIERS TABLE

	Normal	Normal w/Eyelights	Low Light	Low Light w/Eyelights	Thermo	Ultrasound
Full Darkness	+8	+4	+8/+8	+2/+2	+4/+2	+4
Minimal Light	+6	+2	+4/+2	—/—	+4/+2	+3
Partial Light	+2	—	+1/—	—/—	+2/+1	+1
Glare	+2	+2	+4/+2	+4/+2	+4/+2	+1
Mist	+2	+2	+2/—	+2/—	—/—	+1
Light Smoke/Fog/Rain	+4	+4	+4/+2	+4/+2	—/—	+2
Heavy Smoke/Fog/Rain	+6	+6	+6/+4	+6/+4	+1/—	+3
Thermal Smoke	+4	+4	+4/+4	+4/+4	+8/+6	+2
White Noise	—	—	—/—	—/—	—/—	+Rating

Note: When modifiers are separated by a slash, the first number applies to cybernetic vision, the second to natural vision.

Characters with low-light vision can carry their own light source, generating enough light to be able to see. For example, the tiny glow from a penlight, which cannot be seen from more than a few meters away, could illuminate a map, sign or similar small object or area enough for a low-light-equipped character to see. Likewise, a directional flashlight could subtly illuminate the area ahead of the user, allowing them to see and move using low-light vision.

Natural low-light vision is always operating, providing vision enhancements automatically as needed.

Thermographic Vision

Thermographic vision reads the heat (infrared energy) emitted by a target. Aside from heat, little other detail is provided, but this does allow the viewer to navigate and distinguish between objects. Cybernetic and external thermographic systems superimpose this image over a basic, amplified low-light display for greater detail. Natural thermographic vision is always operating, and also superimposes the thermographic display over normal vision. For example, a troll sees exactly what humans see, except that every object and person is tinged with the heat it radiates.

Different heat levels are represented by different colors. Hot objects (an engine block or pot of boiling water) show as white, while cool objects (room temperature) show as black, with every temperature difference in between displayed as shades of red or green. "Hot" and "cold" are determined in relation to the local air or room temperature. For example, thermographic vision used outside in the winter easily spots a person or vehicle, because they appear hot compared with the air temperature. On the other hand, little difference exists between the ambient temperature of a South American rain forest and the radiated heat of a metahuman, making thermographic vision almost useless for differentiating between forest and person.

When characters are using thermographic vision, the gamemaster should consider the relative temperature of objects against the ambient temperature to determine if the target is differentiated from the surroundings, and apply any appropriate modifiers.

Multiple Vision Systems

Dwarfs and trolls, who have natural thermographic vision, see both the normal visible spectrum and heat patterns (translated from the infrared spectrum). The thermovision is "layered" over the normal vision, so that the heat pattern of an object is integrated into its visible appearance.

Similarly, characters with more than one vision system (low-light, eyelights, ultrasound and thermographic) may use such systems simultaneously (along with normal vision). However, cybernetic vision users also have the option of turning one of their vision systems off, should it be necessary (avoiding thermographic heat glare, for example). Note that this will not save a character from suffering from flash or glare modifiers once they have been affected; even if the character switches from one system to another, the eyes have still been affected, and modifiers will apply.

Visibility Modifiers

A character with more than one vision system in use at once receives the lowest modifiers applicable to his vision. For example, a character with cybernetic low-light and thermographic vision would suffer only a +1 visibility modifier in heavy smoke or fog.

The Visibility Modifiers Table shows the various modifiers for certain situations, including how they affect the eyelight and ultrasound systems described in this book.

In the world of *Shadowrun,* the concepts that allow cybermancy to exist remain locked away in black corporate clinics. In the shadows, cybermancy is mostly a rumor, a tall tale used to scare other runners or embellish a story told over drinks. Stories of dead-eyed cyberzombies rank alongside the yarn about the shadowrunning dragon or the spirit of the Matrix. Very few know the true facts, and even fewer understand the implications.

DEFINING CYBERMANCY

Cybermancy is a multidisciplinary science that combines aspects of biology, cybernetics and the magical healing arts. Where cybertechnology deals with constructing implants and installing them in the body, cybermancy travels further down this road and explores the complex relations between body, spirit and machine more thoroughly.

As discussed in *Cybertechnology,* p. 8, the advantages of cyberware implantation are limited by the metahuman body itself. Each implant reduces the body's Essence, cutting away a portion of the person's life force. Each body also has a specific limit of just how much Essence it can lose before it dies. Though higher grades of cyberware help reduce the impact on Essence, even deltaware cannot allow a body to exceed the Essence limit.

Seeking to push the envelope even further, many talented minds were set to the task of how to keep the body alive when the Essence limit was breached. Artificial life-support systems were clearly impractical, but some experts were convinced that the body could somehow be kept alive after it should be dead. The answer to this problem was not found in science, but in magic. By adding ritual sorcery to the process, the body's spirit could be trapped within the flesh, and the subject could be kept alive even though the amount of machine exceeded the measure of man. And so the art of cybermancy was born.

HOW CYBERMANCY WORKS

Under normal circumstances, when a person's Essence is reduced to 0 or less, the spirit slips away and the body dies. Cybermancy uses advanced techno-magical techniques to fool the spirit into remaining and convincing the body that it is still alive.

Exactly how this process works is a closely guarded secret. Numerous theories, research, hints and guesses have provided some framework, but most details remain vague or unknown. It is suspected that an array of scientific techniques are used to keep the body functioning, including implanted auto-injectors with reservoirs of necessary drugs and nutrients, nanites that continuously update the subject's DNA sequence and cybernetic stimulation of memory centers to ground the subject's awareness.

On the arcane level, a magical ritual that binds the spirit to the flesh is performed simultaneously with the surgical process. Though several different versions of the ritual exist, they have common characteristics. The ritual takes several days to complete and includes a major, difficult astral quest. Some versions of the ritual are said to involve coerced or bribed spirits of man, blood spirits or other powerful spirits who sacrifice portions of their energy to anchor the subject's life force. The drain from this ritual is staggering even to advanced initiates, and some practitioners are said to use sacrificial magic to counteract this effect.

Even though cybermancy allows a person's Essence to be reduced to less than 0, the process still has its limits. Complications occur regularly because the procedure is incredibly complicated, dangerous and difficult; it is not uncommon for it to fail. The procedure cannot be made permanent, and the recipient's handlers must exercise constant vigilance and maintenance to keep the subject's life force from drifting away.

ADVANTAGES OF CYBERMANCY

The most obvious advantage of cybermancy is that it allows more cyberware to be implanted in the subject than is normally possible. In effect, the person's abilities can be boosted to unimaginable levels, guaranteeing that they will be one of the most feared combat monsters on the streets. Realistically, the subject has crossed the line and can no longer be considered fully metahuman; they have been transformed into something else entirely, more machine than metahuman. Cybermantic subjects represent the first cyborgs.

A beneficial side effect of the cybermantic process is that the subject becomes more resistant to spells. The synchronization between the subject's body and aura is warped, making it more difficult to channel mana into the subject.

DRAWBACKS TO CYBERMANCY

The negative aspects of cybermancy far outweigh the positive aspects. The research continues, though undoubtedly many cybermantic subjects are unwilling or lack the power to choose otherwise; such is the price of corporate servitude.

First on the list of drawbacks is the simple fact that the body must be kept alive artificially. It wants to be dead, but medicine and magic prevent it from expiring. This requires constant checkups and regular fill-ups of implanted reservoirs. This upkeep is both expensive and time-consuming, and it inevitably results in death if not continued regularly.

Second, the constant nanite-driven DNA-resequencing that is part of cybermancy has not been perfected, and errors—mutations—inevitably develop. Mutating cells are not likely to spread far enough to cause actual physical deformities (they would be noticed and eliminated months or years before reaching such a stage), but they create a very real risk of cancer. The time frame for such a development has not been determined, but the risk increases steadily over time.

Third, the subject's overall physical integrity constantly becomes more unstable, due to the complexity of the biological, implant and cybermantic factors. If the subject's health is severely threatened, as might occur if the subject sustained severe trauma or wounds, the subject's system is more likely to collapse than the organic system of someone who still possessed their natural life force. Cybermantic subjects find it harder to recover from potentially fatal wounds and may die despite receiving immediate medical and magical assistance.

Fourth, cybermantic subjects suffer severe mental detachment, apathy and general malaise, known as chronic disassociation syndrome. If their minds are not regularly stimulated, their focus on remaining alive rapidly diminishes and they may fall into a catatonic state; from this point such subjects frequently lapse into comas and quickly die. To prevent this, all cybermantic subjects are fitted with an invoked memory stimulator implant (IMS, p. 21), which randomly triggers memories from the subject's brain. The effects of this device manifest as familiar background voices, lucid daydreams and random emotions.

Overstimulation can also be a problem, as the subject may become engrossed in minutiae without realizing it, again with the result that the spirit leaves the body and it dies.

Fifth, the subject's will to live dramatically decreases. Subjects of cybermancy seem to be barely aware that they are alive and fail to gain any fulfillment from still being so. While they don't consciously wish to die, they seem to lose many ingrained survival instincts, as well as the ability or desire to exert their mental strength.

The sixth drawback derives from the previous ones—cybermantic subjects are creepy, hard to relate to and generally shunned by others. Excessive implants tend to give them a monstrous and inhuman appearance, which is not at all offset by the subject's complete lack of presence, empathy or other emotions. This apparent lack of humanity has made it popular to refer to cybermantic subjects as cyberzombies.

The final and most interesting drawback is that the subject of cybermancy becomes permanently dual-natured. The impressive rituals involved in trapping the spirit in the body open up the subject to the astral plane, making them suddenly and constantly aware of a reality never before experienced. Subjects often have trouble comprehending things that they astrally perceive and frequently become entranced by particularly vibrant auras and astral forms.

In addition to leaving the subject vulnerable to astral dangers, this astral presence seems to have a polluting effect upon the mana around the cybermantic subject. In effect, such individuals create a wake of distorted mana wherever they go, effectively creating a movable background count.

Despite all these negatives, the techniques of cybermancy are constantly being improved and may eventually lead to greater survivability for cybermantic subjects.

WHERE TO FIND IT

The cutting-edge medical procedures necessary to practice cybermancy can only be obtained at a delta clinic, which are few and far between—and most delta clinics lack access to the necessary cybermancy rituals. The handful of elite magical groups who know the rituals generally refuse to teach cybermancy to others, because they find the ritual's effects counter to their philosophy of magic. A very few groups sell their expertise, but they require ritual samples from their "students" in order to control their use of the ritual.

While the number of delta clinics in the world has probably tripled in the past six years—from half a dozen to almost twenty—the number of these clinics capable of performing cybermancy without calling in outside resources remains low, at most five or six. Most of the rest possess the medical capability but must spend staggering sums of nuyen to hire the magical experts.

Each of the AAA megacorps, with the possible exception of Ares and Wuxing, have fully staffed delta clinics, as do several governments and AA corps, including Tír na nÓg and Universal Omnitech. Other delta clinics are rumored to exist, but details on these remain sketchy and confirmation is next to impossible.

THE MEGACORPS

More than once in recent years, sources within the UCAS government have leaked reports of a joint Ares–UCAS delta clinic project. The completion dates of this project are rapidly approaching, but it is almost certain that Ares still lacks the capability to perform the rituals of cybermancy.

For years, rumors have circulated of Aztechnology delta clinics, alternately in Tenochtitlan and hidden away in the Panamanian jungles. Reports of a run against the clinic have also circulated, prompting theories that its location has been moved—but to where, no one claims to know. In any event, given the Azzie taste for dark magics, it is almost certain that their experts have the ability to use cybermancy.

Employees of Cross Applied Technologies have exhibited delta-grade cyberware on several occasions, making it likely that the corp has its own clinic tucked away somewhere. Like Ares, there is no evidence that they have knowledge of cybermantic rituals.

Sources within Mitsuhama have established that the corp supports at least one delta clinic, but they have yet to make use of cybermantic operatives.

Novatech is assumed to have retained control of one of Fuchi's two delta clinics. Evidence points to this facility being located within the Pueblo Corporate Council, but other sites in NAN territory are also likely. The deaths during the corporate war of numerous cybernetic and magical researchers connected to this clinic diminish the possibility that Novatech possesses cybermantic capabilities.

Renraku inherited the second Fuchi delta clinic because it was controlled by the Nakatomi family. Reputedly located in the Nagano province of Japan, its security has recently been overhauled in light of the Seattle arcology situation.

No one doubts that Saeder-Krupp has a delta clinic or that it is cybermancy-capable. The real question is its location, though various clues point to the suburb of Ekrath, near

Dusseldorf, as the most likely site. One of the ultra-rich enclaves in that area is allegedly a cover for the clinic, a theory substantiated by several sightings of the premier Chinese cyberneticist Wei Xiong Chen in the area.

If Shiawase or Wuxing have operational delta clinics, they aren't advertising the fact. Some sources have pegged a Shiawase facility in the Philippines as a likely candidate, but its proximity to rebel Huk forces makes that theory implausible.

Yamatetsu's first delta clinic was relocated in its entirety from Japan to somewhere in Russia during the recent corporate war. They most likely have made their facilities available to the Russians and probably have the capability to perform cybermancy, but a standing order from Buttercup prohibits them from using it.

THE OTHERS

In addition to the Big Ten, a few of the second-tier corps have put together their own delta clinic facilities, including Universal Omnitech and Transys Neuronet.

As the designers of the first reliable move-by-wire system, Transys has always been in the forefront of the advanced cybernetics field, especially in neural systems research. Having acquired some extra brainpower during the corporate war, they now own enough experts to fully staff two delta clinics. Like Yamatetsu, they certainly have access to professionals capable of conducting cybermancy but seem to steer clear of it. Instead, they're focusing on neural connections for paranormal animals and advanced bioware packages.

Universal Omnitech most likely owes their cybermancy knowledge to Aztechnology, or at least Thomas Roxborough, and they haven't wasted any time researching and exploring its uses. The location of their clinic remains a secret, but holdings in Africa represent the primary possibility.

A few other large corps are well on their way to establishing delta clinics and may even have them up and running. Because their rivals are equally eager to see that they don't finish, delta-level cyberneticist extractions have become a corporate pastime. On the bench are Yakashima (through their subsidiary Biogene), Proteus AG and Phoenix Biotechnologies.

The only government that seems to have developed a clinic of their own accord, without megacorp backing, is Tír na nÓg. The elven nation supposedly has one stashed away in the province of Donegal, which they use to enhance the capabilities of their TRC special forces. If they practice cybermancy at this clinic, they have kept it well hidden—an ability this nation has thoroughly mastered.

At least five other active delta clinics are rumored, none of which have apparent megacorp backing. How these "independent" clinics keep afloat is a mystery, considering the significant overhead costs and competitive market for topnotch cyberneticists and implant technicians. While a few of them offer their services to the shadows (through carefully concealed channels), they are by no means cheap, and prospective clients can expect rigorous background checks and security precautions. The Istanbul and Vancouver clinics are reputed to be the best, though the quality of work at the Chiba and Swiss clinics is more than acceptable. The only one to have displayed expert thaumaturgical knowledge—and thus, possibly, knowledge of cybermancy—is the one rumored to be located in the heart of London.

CYBERMANCY RULES

Under normal circumstances, the Essence costs of cyberware limit the amount of cyberware *Shadowrun* characters can implant. Too much cyberware reduces the character's Essence to 0 or below and causes them to die. The cybermancy rules, however, enable characters and NPCs to remain "alive" even when their Essence Ratings drop below 0. This means that characters may implant a nearly unlimited amount of cyberware—provided they are willing to suffer the various side effects of a cybermantically sustained existence. This section provides rules for performing cybersurgery and cybermancy operations and for the resulting side effects.

ACCESS TO CYBERMANCY

Cybersurgery that lowers a character's Essence below 0 can only be performed at delta clinics (see *Finding Treatment,* p. 140) with the necessary magical resources. Unlike alpha and beta clinics, characters cannot simply find one of the world's few ultra-secret delta clinics in the local phone book or hear about one from friends. And even if some rare cosmic coincidence allows a character to stumble across such a clinic, he cannot simply walk in and get some work done. Every delta clinic operates under the tight control of a megacorp, nation-state or other powerful entity, and the staffs at these clinics only work on those whom their bosses okay.

These restrictions allow individual gamemasters to choose whether to allow cybermancy in their games. For those gamemasters who choose to incorporate cybermancy, note that characters cannot start the game with an Essence Rating of 0 or less. Because of this rule—and because of the potential impact of cybermancy on *Shadowrun* games—cybermancy should be connected to some plot element in a story. Gamemasters should ensure that becoming a cyberzombie is an extended, difficult endeavor full of extensive roleplaying rather than simply a matter of the appropriate dice rolls.

For example, a megacorp might provide a player character with access to a delta clinic in exchange for some extremely important work, or as a reward for some service yet to be performed. In the latter case, the character should perform one heck of a service and the megacorp should have an excellent reason for trusting that the runner will come through with the goods. Even if a runner does something amazing, like save the corp from destruction, and the corp hooks him up with a delta clinic for the repair work, his medical costs will mean that he owes the corp big-time. They'll consider him a personal guinea pig and expect him to gratefully follow their every "request."

GROUND RULES

Any character who undergoes cybersurgery that reduces his Essence to 0 or less will die unless the surgery is performed as part of a cybermancy procedure in a delta clinic. The attending cybersurgeons must have a minimum Biotech (Cybermancy) Skill of 8 and the magical group involved must know the cybermantic metamagical ritual.

The *Less than Zero* section provides rules for the cybersurgery/cybermancy procedure. The general characteristics of the actual cybermantic ritual are discussed in *Cybermantic Magic.*

LESS THAN ZERO

The cybersurgery/cybermancy operation is extremely risky. The actual surgery is a grueling task requiring multiple procedures. Unlike regular cybersurgery, which entails little risk of failure, a character undergoing a cybersurgery/cybermancy operation is likely to die on the table. The chance of dying increases the further the character's Essence drops below 0.

Cybermancy Procedure

Cybermancy surgery is conducted as a surgical procedure, in the same way as implant surgery (p. 146). The operation has a base planning time of 10 weeks (including deltaware modifiers and other modifiers). Because the cybermancy procedure determines whether the subject lives through the operation, that part of the procedure is performed before the numerous implants are installed.

The performing doctor makes a Biotech (Cybermancy) Test against a target number based on the desired Essence Rating (determined by calculating the total Essence Cost for the cyberware to be installed, including an invoked memory stimulator and an auto-injector) per the Cybersurgery/Cybermancy Survival Table.

To determine target numbers for desired Essence Ratings lower than those listed in the table, simply extrapolate from the progression shown. The lower limit is dictated only by the reduced possibility of surviving the procedure as the Essence drops below 0.

CYBERSURGERY/CYBERMANCY SURVIVAL TABLE

Essence Rating Desired	Target Number
0 to –.5	4
–.51 to –1	6
–1.01 to –1.5	8
–1.51 to –2	10
–2.01 to –2.5	12
–2.51 to –3	14
–3.01 and lower	16 (+2 for each .25)

Apply all appropriate modifiers listed on the Expanded Doctoring Table (p. 134), except that delta clinics are automatically considered intensive-care facilities (the –2 modifier for intensive care is already calculated into the target number). Because both the magical and surgical elements are part of the same operation, the Willpower-enhancing magic of the cybermantic ritual (*Changes to Willpower,* p. 58) does not apply in this test.

If the test fails, the character dies. The player cannot spend Karma on the doctor's skill test to improve his chances of success.

If the test succeeds, the character lives, and the implant procedures may be performed. All characters undergoing cybermantic operations automatically receive two pieces of cyberware: an invoked memory stimulator (IMS, p. 21) and an auto-injector (p. 25).

Auto-Injector: The auto-injector contains a cocktail of special drugs and nutrients that will keep the character's technically dead body alive. A 10-day supply of this mixture costs 3,000¥ x the absolute value of the character's Essence. If the system runs out of medicine, the character dies immediately. Depending on the arrangement the character has with the corp sponsoring his surgery, the gamemaster may allow the character to obtain refills of this cocktail at a discount of 1D6 x 5 percent, or even choose to have the corp supply the refills at no cost in nuyen—though the price might actually turn out to be quite high.

CYBERMANTIC MAGIC

Shadowrunners will never be able to use the spells, rituals and magical operations involved in cybermancy; even if by some wild stretch of the imagination a player character managed to learn cybermantic techniques, the knowledge would be worth nothing unless he also had access to a delta clinic and a dedicated medical staff at his beck and call for weeks on end. As a result, this section offers only general information about cybermantic magic.

In general, the magical ritual used for cybermancy requires a dedicated group, takes at least 24 hours to accomplish, involves the equivalent of an astral quest and includes powerful spirits in some way. In addition, some form of metamagic is used to enhance the magical "anchoring" of the subject's spirit to the body.

The Drain the ritual produces is, for all practical purposes, incomprehensible. Even the high-level initiates of a hermetic group who can use extra-effective Centering techniques against Drain do not undertake this ritual without powerful motivation and careful reflection.

Only a small number of hermetic organizations know the rituals necessary to perform cybermantic magic. Most of them are connected to the megacorps; they are not the corporate movers or shakers, but they willingly work for corporate interests. These magical organizations sell their cybermantic services to the corps for money, for the rush of power they get from performing the ritual and sometimes for even more sinister reasons. Part of their responsibility to the corp includes instructing select other corporate mages in those techniques required to perform cybermancy. However, all corporate employees taught these techniques must provide multiple ritual samples to ensure their commitment to complete secrecy and their unswerving loyalty. Further, the cybermancers keep certain levels of knowledge and specific rituals secret from even the corps, so that they will remain safe from their "students" and always be in demand.

If a player is thinking about trying to insert his character into a delta clinic to grab some of that sub-zero Essence action, remind him into whose hands he might be putting himself. Let

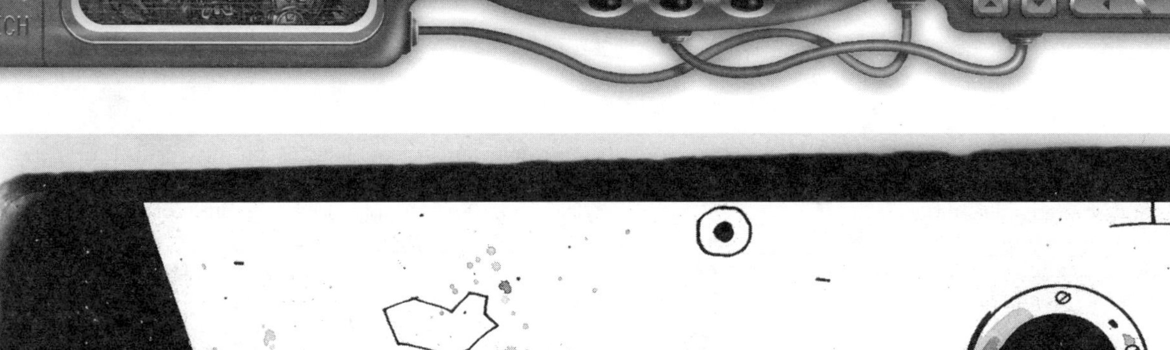

him worry about it a little before he makes his choice, because once he's gone through with the treatment, he will no longer know what worrying means.

SIDE EFFECTS

The actual cybersurgery/cybermancy operation is by far the riskiest part of using cybermancy. However, a successful operation does not mean the character is in the clear. When a character undergoes a cybermantic operation, he becomes the central participant in a magical ritual intended to fool his spirit into staying with his body. As a result, cybermantic techniques inflict several potentially lethal conditions and side effects on the character. One such condition, the need for an auto-injector medication system, is described in *Ground Rules.*

BETTER OFF DEAD

Ironically, cybermancy makes it easier for a character to die because it reduces the character's Physical Damage Overflow value (after calculating the bioware reduction) by half (round up). (See *Exceeding the Condition Monitor,* p. 125, *SR3.*)

Additionally, every time the character experiences Physical Damage Overflow and is healed or stabilized, the character must make a Willpower Test against a target number equal to twice the amount of overflow damage. If the test fails, the character dies, regardless of any magical or mundane healing measures applied. The character may spend Karma to prevent this (see p. 246, *SR3*), and cybermantic adjustments to Willpower apply to the test as well (see *Changes to Willpower,* p. 58).

MAGICAL RESISTANCE

Characters who undergo cybermantic treatment become more resistant to magic. To reflect this side effect, add the absolute value of the character's Essence Rating (for example, the absolute value of –2 is 2; round up) to the target number of any Spellcasting Test, critter power, metamagic or other magical tests made against him; this modifier does not apply to elemental manipulation spells. Unfortunately for the character, this modifier also applies to magical tests used for healing.

Their negative Essence and the cybermantic ritual make it impossible for cyberzombies to perform magic.

DUAL NATURE

A character who undergoes cybermancy becomes permanently dual-natured (see *Spirits and Dragons,* p. 260, *SR3*), existing on both the physical and astral planes simultaneously. This makes the character vulnerable to astral attack.

Even though cybermantic subjects are astrally active, their senses are not developed enough to perceive their astral environs with the same innate ability as an Awakened character. As a result, cybermancy subjects are often oblivious to the astral world, seeing only occasional ghostly forms and colors or otherwise sensing emotional imprints. Cybermantic subjects can, however, develop useful astral perception.

In game terms, cybermantic characters require the Aura Reading Active Skill in order to astrally perceive. Though it is usually available only to Awakened characters, those who have undergone cybermancy may purchase this skill. When used by cybermantic characters, it operates as a standard skill (use instead of Intelligence for astral perception), not a complementary skill. If they do not possess this skill, cybermantic characters must default to Intelligence for Astral Perception Tests.

If targeted by an astral attack, cybermantic characters can defend themselves using the standard astral combat rules (p. 174, *SR3).*

Cyberzombie Possession

A spirit or initiate possessing a cyberzombie faces some unusual and risky challenges. The magic that binds the cyberzombie's soul to his flesh also binds the astral form of any possessing entity to the body. The possessing entity immediately recognizes the trap and may attempt to break free.

Breaking free requires a Complex Action and a Willpower (or Force) Test. The target number is equal to the cyberzombie's absolute Essence (round up) x 3. Reduce the target number by the entity's Spirit Energy or the initiate's grade. If the entity succeeds, it breaks free. If not, it remains trapped. The entity may make a number of additional attempts to break free equal to the initiate's grade or the Spirit Energy (as appropriate), but modify the target number by an additional +2 for each attempt after the first.

If an initiate is trapped for too long, his physical body will die (see *While You Were Out …* , p. 173, *SR3*). When this occurs, the initiate's astral form survives, trapped in the cyberzombie as a permanent resident. Trapped entities will remain imprisoned indefinitely, until the cyberzombie dies or his handlers repeat the cybermantic ritual and purge the trapped astral form.

An entity that possesses a cyberzombie will also discover that it cannot control that body as easily as it can others. The possessor must defeat the cyberzombie in an Opposed Willpower Test; modify the possessor's target number by +2. If the possessor wins, it can control the cyberzombie; otherwise it fails and becomes trapped. If the cyberzombie is knocked unconscious, the possessing entity may control the body according to the standard rules.

KARMA HAZING

The term "Karma hazing" was coined by magicians who theorized that individuals with sub-zero Essence generate permanent astral pollution that may prove disastrous for the collective Karma of metahumanity.

Karma hazing makes the cybermantic character's astral presence increasingly noticeable to astrally active individuals and creatures, who can sense it from far beyond the standard ranges for assensing or astral awareness. The longer the character survives, the stronger the character's astral presence. It registers as a black shadow, a polluted zone, and he leaves a cloud of corrupted mana in his wake. To all who can sense this astral presence, it somehow feels *wrong.* Astrally active creatures and individuals either shun the affected character or take hostile action against him, and astral predators may be drawn to his vicinity.

In game terms, cybermantic characters produce background count wherever they go. This effect is not immediate but a gradual corruption of the mana around them. If a cybermantic character were to remain in the same location for an hour or more, that locale would develop a Background Count of 1. Over time, this background count may increase, up to half the character's absolute Essence value (round down). The gamemaster determines the rate at which this pollution intensifies. The staff of cybermantic delta clinics usually includes an initiate skilled in the metamagical technique of cleansing (p. 74, *MITS*), to keep the background count from interfering with cybermantic magic.

Cybermantic characters leave ugly-looking astral signatures wherever they go (see *Astral Signatures,* p. 172, *SR3*). Treat the astral signature as if it were created by a magical effect with a Force equal to the character's negative Essence value (round down). For example, a cyberzombie with Essence of –4.5 would leave an astral signature in his wake that would last for 4 hours.

Sooner or later, the Karma hazing will force *something* to take an active and hostile interest in the character. This something may be a critter wandering around the astra planel, or a much more dangerous entity with a much more specific purpose. This hostile attention could form the basis for an entire adventure in which the character must shake off the astral menace.

Fluorescing Astral Bacteria (FAB): FAB is attracted to the background count constantly generated by cyberzombies. Once it finds such a source of energy, a cloud of FAB will attach itself to the character. The cloud cannot drain magic or Essence from the character, but it does gain Force twice as quickly as indicated on the Strain-III Draining Table, p. 91 in *MITS.* For example, a Rating 5 cloud of FAB attached to a cyberzombie would gain an additional point of Force (become Rating 6) in only 9 hours.

CHANGES TO REACTION/PERCEPTION

Modify all Reaction Tests by +1 for each point or fraction thereof of the character's absolute Essence value in any situation in which the character is surprised (p. 109, *SR3*). For example, a character with an Essence Rating of –1.3 would suffer a +2 modifier.

Additionally, a cybermantic character receives a +1 modifier to all Perception Tests for every 2 points of negative Essence or part thereof.

LOST IN THE DETAILS

Sometimes a cybermantically sustained character can get lost in the details of what he is observing. Whenever a character takes a Simple Action to Observe in Detail (p. 106, *SR3*) and achieves no successes on all dice rolled for Perception Tests with modified target numbers of 5 or higher, he or she becomes completely absorbed by minutiae. To break free of this dangerous cycle, the character immediately makes a Willpower Test against the target number of the Perception Test. If the Willpower Test fails, the character remains lost in concentration.

The player may repeat the Willpower Test in each subsequent Combat Turn, or once per minute if not in combat. The target number increases by 1 each time the test is repeated. If the player fails five tests in a row, his invoked-memory stimulator kicks in and the target number is reduced by 1 per each Combat Turn or minute, whichever is more appropriate.

Other characters may also attempt to attract the cybermantic character's attention. Each such attempt reduces the Willpower Test target number by 1. During Combat Turns, characters must spend Simple Actions to make these attempts.

CHANGES TO WILLPOWER

For every half point of negative Essence or part thereof a character possesses, reduce his Willpower Rating by 1. A character with an Essence Rating of –.75, for example, would reduce his Willpower Rating by 2.

The cybermantic process, however, magically restores up to 4 points of Willpower lost as a result of negative Essence, up to the Willpower Rating the character possessed before undergoing cybermancy.

The character is also immune to any form of magic that can increase his Willpower Attribute, such as the Increase Attribute spell. Additionally, the cybermantic increase to Willpower cannot be dispelled or broken.

INVOKED MEMORY STIMULATOR

Whenever a cybermantically sustained character's invoked memory stimulator (IMS) kicks in, it brings up various pieces of the character's memories to reconnect the character to his body. For example, the character hears voices, sees faces, remembers people long dead or long forgotten and remembers good times and bad. The IMS and the memories it provokes have no specific game effects, but the gamemaster should use invoked memories as a roleplaying or storytelling tool.

On rare occasions, the character may confuse memory with reality, making the cyberzombie an inviting target for terrifying and/or humorous incidents.

SOCIAL AND KARMA PENALTIES

A sub-zero Essence rating causes characters to act strangely in social situations. Cybermantic characters suffer the penalties described under *Cyberware and Social Interaction*, p. 93, *SR3*, automatically giving a character with sub-zero Essence a +3 modifier. To reflect the additional social effects of walking around like a humanoid machine, add the absolute value of the character's Essence Rating as an additional Charisma and Charisma-linked skill modifier (round fractions up). For Essence Ratings below –2, double the penalty for the amount below –2.

These penalties apply even if a strong emotional bond once existed between the character and the individual with whom he is interacting. Gamemasters may even increase the penalties in such circumstances because people who once knew the character well may be especially disconcerted by his strange behavior.

Cybermantic characters cannot compensate for their loss of social skills by any magical means. The character has crossed an absolute threshold, and anyone who meets him knows this at a gut level.

These same scary social characteristics are a bonus if the cybermantic character is intimidating or interrogating someone. In such cases, use the modifiers described above as a bonus to the Open Test (see p. 93, *SR3*).

Sub-zero Essence also reduces a character's ability to accumulate Karma to one-half the usual rate (see p. 242, *SR3*).

Fred the cyberzombie has an Essence Rating of –3. He receives the following modifiers for Charisma and Charisma-linked skill tests:

+3 Every 2 points of Essence lost down to 0
+2 First 2 points of negative Essence
+2 Last point of negative Essence

Fred has a total of +7 in modifiers whenever he's negotiating, leading or otherwise smooth-talking. However, he's also pretty scary, so he gets the same +7 bonus to his Interrogation and Intimidation Open Tests.

LONG-TERM EFFECTS

Cybermantic treatments may also produce long-term side effects that may not be immediately apparent. These effects include chronic dissociation syndrome and cancer.

CHRONIC DISSOCIATION SYNDROME

Chronic dissociation syndrome (CDS) occurs when a character's response to his invoked memory stimulator (IMS) deteriorates. The IMS continues to provoke memories in the character's mind, but he ceases to respond to them in the same way. Instead, he experiences the memories as alien to himself. The memories produce the same disruptive effects described in *Invoked Memory Stimulator* (p. 58) and gradually lose their power to "anchor" the character to the real world. The images that occupy him are devoid of meaning, a jumble of disconnected events and appearances that serve only to confuse and the character and exist as a painful reminder of the life he once had. The character loses the will to live and seems to fade away, his last days spent in a catatonic state.

The gamemaster makes periodic Willpower Tests to determine whether a character develops CDS. The frequency and target number for the tests are determined by the character's Essence Rating, as shown on the Chronic Dissociation Syndrome Table. Willpower modifiers from cybermantic magic apply to this test, but similar modifiers from any other shorter-term magical source do not.

If a Willpower Test fails, CDS has set in and the character is lost to the world. He cannot initiate action, only react. For example, the character cannot initiate combat but can defend himself against attacks. CDS adds a +4 modifier to all Perception Tests the character makes and a +3 modifier for all other tests. Note that these modifiers are in addition to any other modifiers already applied to the character's tests.

A character with CDS quickly deteriorates in health, will not eat, develops untreatable insomnia and dies in a number of weeks equal to 3 + his Willpower Rating.

Chronic dissociation syndrome can be treated with magic, but only trained magicians—those capable of performing the cybermantic rituals—can perform the treatment, and this is part of the knowledge they keep secret. If the treatment is conducted in a delta clinic, the afflicted character makes a Spell Resistance (8) Test. If the test succeeds, the magic fails and the character dies. If the Spell Resistance Test fails, the syndrome is reversed and the character's IMS begins to function effectively, though it takes a few days for this to happen. The character makes a Willpower (6) Test to determine how quickly this recovery occurs. The base time for this recovery is 1 week; each success on the Willpower Test reduces the recovery time by 1 day.

CHRONIC DISSOCIATION SYNDROME TABLE

Essence Rating	Frequency of Tests	Target Number
0 to –0.50	1 every 6 months	3
–0.51 to –1.00	1 every 6 months	4
–1.01 to –1.50	1 every 6 months	5
–1.51 to –2.00	1 every 4 months	5
–2.01 to –2.50	1 every 4 months	6
–2.51 to –3.00	1 every 3 months	6
–3.01 to –3.50	1 every 2 months	6
–3.51 or lower	1 every 2 months	8; +1 to target number for every additional –0.5

CDS treatment becomes increasingly difficult each time the syndrome sets in, so reduce the target number for the Spell Resistance Test by 1 (to a minimum of 2) each time a character repeats the test.

CANCER

Cybermancy produces an artificial, forced alliance between a character's body and spirit. Magical and technological trickery is used to "fool" the spirit into staying, but this means that the body as well as the spirit develops problems.

Just as the insidious sickness of the spirit manifests as Karma hazing, the body's sickness manifests as cancer. At a very deep, cellular level, the body *knows* that the spirit is not truly present in it. As a result, the P46–gatekeeper/MIC gene systems present in every metahuman, which normally instruct body cells to die in a preprogrammed fashion, no longer send the right biochemical signals. Cells that should die remain alive and become cancerous. At the same time, cells that should stay alive die, and the body necrotizes. This is a ghastly end.

To determine whether the character will suffer this particular long-term effect, roll 2D6 during the initial cybermantic operation. If the result is less than double the absolute value of the character's desired Essence Rating, the character will eventually develop cancer (if he lives long enough). At the gamemaster's discretion, the die roll result may be increased by 1 if the character's unaugmented Body Rating is between 4 and 7, and by 2 if the Body Rating is 8 or better—high Body Ratings reduce the chances of cancer developing. If the individual has symbiotes (p. 69), the dice roll result can be modified by +1 at the gamemaster's discretion.

If the test fails, the character will develop cancer after 10D6 months. The cancer will be fast-growing, extremely nasty and incurable. It will kill the character within 5 to 10 weeks of its appearance (4 + 1D6). The gamemaster chooses when to inform the player of his character's condition.

The human body is complex and intricate—a machine made of organic materials and compounds. Naturally, corporations and scientists continually try to improve it through biotechnology, bionics and bioengineering.

The application of biotechnology—bioware—can allow an individual to perform far beyond his original parameters. While cyberware is machinery, artificial and invasive, bioware is subtle and of the flesh.

BIOWARE DEFINED

Bioware augments body functions and must be integrated into the body's own workings as if it were a natural feature. Essentially, doctors replace organs and tissue with other organic parts—a difficult process. While a cybertechnician can forcibly alter or replace whole elements of the body, a biotechnician cannot. Changing the fine balance of organic systems is a tricky business that can result in unforeseen complications and drastic side effects. The designer of bioware must study and understand each of the body's subsystems and organs before he can create successful and non-damaging biological equipment.

Bioware is undetectable, except by intensive medical examination. Casual searches, x-ray scans and the like cannot discern the difference between an augmented organ and the original. However, additional glands and organs can be detected by examining x-ray film. Apart from exploratory surgery, the only way to determine that an individual has undergone biological modification is through metabolic analysis—such as urinalysis or sophisticated blood tests.

Perhaps bioware's greatest advantage is its capacity for self-repair. Once implanted, bioware can call on the body's natural repair mechanisms.

IMPLANTING

Bioware does not require the neural changes that most cyberware does, nor is its impact upon the body's integrity as drastic. Bioware does not cause Essence loss.

Bio-implants can be installed in any metahuman with a matching blood type, and sometimes metatype or gender. Usually grown through advanced methods in a generic "organ donor," the implants are designed to be smoothly integrated into the body,

RNING!
D ACCESS

though they are not tailored for any body in particular. Installation usually requires a battery of immunosuppressive treatments, convincing the body that it should accept the implant as part of itself.

Cyberware and bioware can be integrated in the same body, though a few select implants are incompatible (see p. 78).

Implanting bioware, and the rules regarding surgery and its options, can be found in *Surgery* (p. 147).

BIOWARE GRADES

Like cyberware, bioware varies in quality and availability. The most common is basic bioware. Bioengineered by type, including blood classification and metahuman variants, it is considered off-the-shelf bioware.

Cultured bioware is tailor-made for the intended recipient, protein-matched and grown from a cellular matrix derived from the host. In medical terms, cultured bioware is actually a modified organ or set of biological material cloned from the person who will be receiving it. Vat grown from cells, this is the "friendliest" type of implant. Known collectively as neural bioware, these implants are usually attached to the brain or neural pathways. These pieces must be tailored to the customers to function.

Rules for bioware grades appear on p. 76.

Used Bioware

Called "secondhand" bioware, so as not to disgust the bargain hunters, this market is growing. While some parts are available from the original owners, bioware acquired from corpses or through other nefarious means is more common. Only basic bioware can be found secondhand. Cultured bioware is by definition protein-matched and cannot be implanted in another body. Basic bioware is genetically "indifferent" for the most part and homogenous in its cellular make-up, precluding the possibility of rejection.

Cosmetic Bioware

Bioware can offer a way to stay beautiful longer. Many of the more recent and more newsworthy innovations have come from this cosmetology area.

Cosmetic bioware appears on p. 76.

BIOWARE DRAWBACKS

Bioware users suffer from a number of drawbacks and side effects, as their natural systems have been thrown a little out of balance by modified organs and systems. Health problems can increase, ranging from minor annoyances to dangerous complications.

Bioware users also suffer from decreased immunity to pathogens, poisons and other compounds. Bioware tends to tie up immune system resources, as the body continuously attempts to adjust for the biotech changes. This can mean longer healing times, especially with more complicated biosystems.

BIOWARE AND THE AWAKENED

Bioware has an impact on the somatic and magical integrity of Awakened characters. Altering the body's make-up with bioware—even cultured bioware cloned from the Awakened character—alters the body's ability to channel mana. Metaphorically, if mana is viewed as electricity that is conducted through the Awakened body, then bioware is essentially a resistor, impeding the flow. This is not as detrimental as cyberware, however.

The drawbacks for magicians and adepts with bioware appear on p. 78.

BIOSYSTEM OVERSTRESS

Though bioware does not have an impact upon Essence, the body can take only so much augmentation before the delicately balanced human/metahuman metabolism begins to suffer. The maximum amount of bioware that a given individual can safely accept is represented by the amount of "meat" left in the body. Highly cybered users can accept less bioware, as so much of their body has already been modified.

This safety limit is termed "Essence Index." When the body is artificially pushed beyond this natural limit, dysfunction can result. If an individual exceeds his Essence Index for bioware, inherent drawbacks become exaggerated. Healing takes much longer, the person's immune systems are shredded, and he becomes plagued by a rash of minor health problems and complications.

THE POWER PLAYERS

Biotechnology tends to require more research and has higher front-end costs, so it doesn't rake in the nuyen like cybertechnology. Despite this, biotech is a hot and competitive field, with breakthroughs being made on a monthly basis.

THE IMPLANT KINGS

These two corps run the bio-implant world.

Shiawase

Shiawase has by far the largest amount of assets sunk into biotechnology research and is the primary provider of bioware implants throughout the world. Their Biotech Division is the foundation of the Shiawase empire, and it is well-diversified into all aspects of biotechnology—as well as the related fields of cybertechnology, nanotechnology, pharmaceuticals and health care. Subsequently, the corp is the biggest target for bioware research runs, and Shiawase-trained biotechnicians are a hot commodity in certain shadowmarkets.

Universal Omnitech

While Shiawase does it all, Universal Omnitech does it better. Though not a AAA megacorp, their strategic alliance with Aztechnology has allowed UniOmni to keep a foothold at the top of the biotechnology pyramid, despite every attempt from Shiawase to push them off. UniOmni is known for its biotech breakthroughs and has remained years ahead of the pack in new developments and research. Now that they rely on Aztechnology to market their discoveries and advances, they are an even larger threat to Shiawase and other biotech corps. Naturally, UniOmni facilities have spent a large percentage of their new earnings on security upgrades.

THE SECOND TIER

Aside from the two giants, four other corps wield significant power and influence in the field.

Cross Applied Technologies

Cross Biomedical has made some significant leaps into cultured neuralware in recent years and is continuing to pour funds into research. The primary focus has been modifications to the brain itself, rather than other aspects of the neurological system. The corp is considered to hold a stable of the world's top brain scientists, though rival corps such as Transys Neuronet have made subtle maneuvers to break Cross' lock in this area.

Proteus AG

Proteus AG has developed an array of biological modifiers to adapt metahumans to underwater conditions. The majority of these developments have yet to be released to the public. Rumors abound of more esoteric biotech research avenues, including efforts to adapt non-metahuman organs to metahuman biosystems.

Yakashima

Yakashima's subsidiary Biogene has gone through troubled times but has continued to be a world player in the biotech arena. The corp has been slow to release new developments, leading to a host of accusatory rumors about immoral and unconscionable research projects involving unwilling metahuman subjects. Yakashima has successfully to date fended off outside investigations.

Yamatetsu

Yamatetsu has the varied fields of biotechnology covered almost as well as it covers cybertech. The corp has also lived up to its usual standards, producing bioware that meets the needs of all metahumans. Their subsidiary—CrashCart—offers some of the cheapest prices for biotech procedures, giving Shiawase a run for its money.

OTHERS TO WATCH

Given the wide range of biotech options, several other corps also bear watching.

Aztechnology

The Big A is the world's leader in providing consumer-grade cosmetic bio-mods and has thousands of subsidiary bio-sculpting shops worldwide. It focuses on providing sterilization and birth control biotech, though its practice of providing it cheaper, or even free, in certain metahuman communities has been criticized as racist.

Saeder-Krupp

Naturally, Saeder-Krupp is involved in almost everything. The corp's most advanced bioware breakthroughs in recent months have involved bioware for critters, including some successful implants involving Awakened creatures.

Tan Tien

Though still a small outfit, Tan Tien is significant because it is almost as keen as Universal Omnitech when it comes to ideas and inventions. Rather than marketing its results, however, it usually sells the materials to the highest bidder—at a significant profit. Many other corps have made fortunes in biotechnology thanks to Tan Tien's breakthroughs.

Transys Neuronet

Most of Transys Neuronet's recent interests have involved bio-computers and cell-based memory storage systems. Much of its research has overlapped with Mitsuhama's wetware projects, leading to an exchange of runs between the corps.

THE HARVESTERS

One organization probably has more bioware filter through its grizzled white paws than most of the megas.

Tamanous

It was only a matter of time before implants became more valuable than flesh. One organization has taken the underworld by storm with its aggressive harvesting of organs and its human flesh farms. Tamanous officials—those whose identities are known—are on government Most Wanted listings. Still, the shady organization continues to spread into various major sprawls. Tamanous' origins are a mystery. There are rumors it is operated by ghouls, though this may not be true. Ghouls definitely aid the organization—and eat the scraps, but whoever is backing it remains deep in the shadows.

BIOWARE

What follows are descriptions of bioware products available to the general public. They are divided into three categories—basic, cultured and cosmetic.

BASIC BIOWARE

All basic bioware can also be purchased as cultured bioware (see *Bioware Grades*, p. 76). Each item lists the effects of various Stress levels (see p. 77).

ADRENAL PUMP

This is a small, muscular sac implanted in the lower abdominal cavity and connected to each of the two suprarenal, or adrenal, glands. When dormant, the pump serves as a reservoir for adrenaline and noradrenaline. When activated, the sac contracts, sending a surge of concentrates into the bloodstream. Stress and other emotional states such as anger, fear or lust will also activate the pump.

The actual combat effectiveness of the pump is variable, as the effects produced by hormones depend both on the amount secreted and the responsiveness of the tissue in question.

Game Effects

The adrenal pump comes in two levels. Once active, roll 1D6 for each level; the die result indicates the number of Combat Turns the hormones stay in the blood and, therefore, the number of turns the bonuses will apply.

The adrenal pump is normally triggered involuntarily, whenever the character suffers Physical or Stun damage. If the character has pain resistance bioware or magic that blocks pain, the pump will not activate until the character suffers wound modifiers. The gamemaster might also choose other conditions or emotions to trigger the pump. For example, the use of the Fear critter power would probably trigger the pump.

The adrenal pump can also be triggered on demand by inhaling a dose of the adrenocorticotropic hormone (see *ACTH,* p. 117). The drug MAO can suppress the effects of unwanted pump activation (see *MAO,* p. 120).

Each level of the pump adds 1 to Quickness, 2 to Strength, 1 to Willpower and 2 to Reaction for as long as the concentrates remain in the bloodstream. The Quickness bonus does not affect Reaction, nor does the Reaction bonus affect the Control Pool. However, the Quickness and Willpower bonuses affect the Combat Pool.

When the duration of the pump's effects ends, the character crashes from system shock and fatigue. He must roll Body to resist Deadly Stun damage with a Power equal to the number of turns the hormones remained in the blood.

Once the effects have worn off, the pump must regenerate its supply, a process that takes 9 + 1D6 minutes. If the pump activates again before the sac has been refilled, reduce the number of turns for its effect duration by half, rounding down.

Light Stress: Adrenal pump users are prone to twitchiness and sometimes suffer from uncontrollable shaking.

Moderate Stress: High levels of adrenaline and noradrenaline in the bloodstream contribute to high blood pressure. The character suffers –1 die on all Athletics Tests.

Serious Stress: Users are more prone to critical heart failure through sheer overexertion. Every time the pump is activated, roll 2D6. On a result of 2, the character suffers immediate cardiac arrest. This heart attack causes Deadly Physical damage, no resistance.

Deadly Stress: The adrenal pump ceases to function; it cannot be triggered accidentally or voluntarily. However, it does activate at random times, usually when the character least needs it.

CAT'S EYES

The recipient of cat's eyes receives a new set of replacement eyes, vat-grown and specially designed to incorporate a structure that amplifies light and enhances the user's night vision. The number of light-sensitive rods and detail-enhancing cones in the eye also increase. Like the eyes of a cat, this bioware incorporates a mirror-like organ in the cornea that reflects light toward the retina. Under low-light conditions, these eyes seem to be reflective and to glow in the dark. The pupils are also slitted like a cat's eyes, to increase the amount of light received. These eyes perceive color.

Game Effects

This bioware provides low-light vision. Like cybereyes, any racial benefits, such as thermographic vision, are lost. Unlike cybereyes, however, this vision counts as natural, not cybernetic, for purposes of visibility modifiers (p. 111, *SR3*). Cat's eyes are not compatible with cybereyes or retinal modification cyberware.

Light Stress: Users sometimes have difficulty distinguishing between colors and are sensitive to bright light.

Moderate Stress: Bright flashes have more effect against these eyes; apply an additional +1 Modifier to the effects of flash-paks and strobe lights.

Serious Stress: Users see the world only in shades of black and gray. Apply a +4 Perception Modifier to distinguishing between colors.

Deadly Stress: If the eyes fail, the user is essentially blinded (+8 to all visual Perception Tests and actions requiring sight).

CHEMICAL GLAND

A chemical gland is a sac lined with specialized and genetically tailored cells designed to produce a single naturally occurring compound. The compound is stored in the sac until used and can be deployed in one of four ways, described below. To prevent accidental injury from the internalized chemical, the character is also partially immunized against it.

Examples of these natural compounds include arsenic; venom; toxins from insects and spiders; ink, such as octopuses produce; royal jelly, a nutritious substance produced for queen bees; insulin; slime, as exuded by snails; and some mild acids.

Exhalation Spray: Implanted in the neck above the larynx, the gland is equipped with sphincters. When triggered via a "learned" reflex—such as a massive diaphragm contraction causing a deep inhalation, followed by a strong exhaling action—the sphincters open and the compound is exhaled much like an aerosol.

Spit: Also implanted in the neck, the gland collects the compound in a sphincter-equipped mucus reservoir sac. When contracted, the sac spits the compound, expelling it through the mouth.

Internal Release: The gland can be designed to regularly release measured doses of the compound into the user's bloodstream, thus serving as a biological auto-injector. This version can be implanted almost anywhere within the body.

Weapon Reservoir: Implanted next to a cyber-implant weapon, the gland secretes the compound into a reservoir, coating the weapon before use.

Game Effects

The sac can manufacture only one type of compound, which must be chosen prior to implantation. At the gamemas-

Bioware	Bio Index	Availability	Cost	Street Index	Legality
Adrenal Pump					
Level 1	1.25	10/16 days	60,000¥	3	5P–R
Level 2	2.50	10/16 days	100,000¥	3	5P–R
Cat's Eyes	.2	4/6 days	15,000¥	1	Legal

ter's discretion, some compounds might be unavailable. The gland requires 24 hours to manufacture one dose, and it can hold a maximum of five doses.

A character with a sac containing a compound, such as arsenic, receives double his unaugmented Body Rating to resist attacks against him made with that compound; in this case, arsenic.

The chemical gland costs 30,000 nuyen, plus 100 times the cost of one dose of the compound.

Exhalation Spray: To hit an intended target, the character must take a Complex Action and make a Ranged Attack Test, using Quickness as the attack skill—Combat Pool can be used. The maximum range equals one-half the unaugmented Body Attribute in meters, rounded down. The spray has a choke setting of two (use the shotgun spread rules, p. 117, *SR3*). The exhalation spray does not linger as a cloud.

Spit: To strike an intended target, use the same procedure as the exhalation spray, except the shotgun spread rules do not apply. The spit's range is equal to the character's unaugmented Body in meters and can only affect one target. Apply a +1 Target Number Modifier for every meter.

Internal Release: This gland constantly keeps the equivalent of one dose in the character's body.

Weapon Reservoir: When implanted next to a bladed cyberweapon, the gland coats the blade when it is retracted. Cyber dartguns and cybersquirts can also draw from this reservoir, though the dosage is limited.

Light Stress: The gland frequently becomes irritated and noticeably swollen, causing discomfort.

Moderate Stress: The gland only produces a new dose every 48 hours.

Serious Stress: The gland can only hold two doses at a time.

Deadly Stress: The gland fails and does not produce any more compounds until its host is healed.

DIGESTIVE EXPANSION

This involves a series of treatments that greatly expand the range of things a metahuman can safely digest. The stomach lining is toughened and modified to produce more enzymes and acids to break down matter, and the pancreas and liver are enhanced to produce improved bile and enzymes that aid in digesting food in the small intestine.

The result allows the user to safely consume a great variety of organic materials as food—including roots, grass, peat and a number of plants that are normally considered inedible. The improved digestive tract also provides protection against toxic materials, such as rhubarb leaves, smooth lepiota mushrooms and so on. This treatment also modifies the taste buds and olfactory senses, making it easier for the user to "stomach" unusual foods.

Game Effects

A character with digestive expansion can consume almost anything organic, from someone's cotton shirt to cactus to enriched soil. "Back to nature" types commonly acquire this bioware, as do others who may need to survive in harsh environments. Reduce Lifestyle costs by 20 percent for the character.

The hardened digestive process also provides immunity to things that would lead to food poisoning in normal metahumans. The Power of ingested toxins is reduced by half (round down). The negative effects can also be cut in half at the gamemaster's discretion.

Characters with this bioware have "dulled" taste buds and a poor sense of smell. Any taste- or smell-based Perception Tests are made at –1 die.

Light Stress: Heartburn, stomachaches and indigestion are common. Bulimia is a common psychological side effect.

Moderate Stress: The digestive system becomes less effective at breaking down toxins; the Power of ingested toxins is reduced by a quarter.

Serious Stress: Ulcers plague the character, causing him Light Physical and Stun wounds until treated.

Deadly Stress: The character's digestive system fails. The person cannot hold down food, and what little does stay down is painful to digest. The character is saddled with a Serious Physical wound, and he will die of starvation in a number of days equal to his Body x 10.

ENHANCED ARTICULATION

Enhanced articulation is a product of extensive procedures, including joint-surface coating, relubrication and tendon and ligament augmentation designed for fluid muscle and joint action. Studies show that individuals with enhanced articulation might be immune to many arthritic conditions.

Game Effects

Enhanced articulation allows a character to move faster and more precisely. Possessors roll an additional die when making any Success Test involving Combat, Physical, Technical and Build/Repair Skills. The bonus also applies to physical use of Vehicle Skills—driving a car via datajack or piloting a submarine does not qualify for the bonus.

Users gain a +1 Reaction bonus, which has no effect on rigging or decking and does not affect the Control Pool.

Light Stress: Muscle pains and cramps are common. Users usually must limber themselves up.

Moderate Stress: The user develops tendonitis; apply a +1 modifier to all actions involving the affected limb.

Serious Stress: Pulled muscles plague the user. Apply a +1 target number modifier to all physical activities.

Deadly Stress: A joint pops out of its socket. All tests using that limb are at +6. The character also suffers a Serious wound that cannot be healed until the joint is realigned, which takes a Biotech (6) Test. After realignment, the limb is still injured—incurring a +4 modifier to all tests involving it—until the Deadly Stress is healed. If a leg is affected, Movement Rate is cut in half and the individual cannot run.

EXTENDED VOLUME

An average adult's lungs contain approximately 2.5 liters of air. However, the actual tidal volume—the amount of air that enters and leaves the lungs with each breath—is only .5 liters. By augmenting the amount of flex in the diaphragm, it is possible to increase the tidal volume, thus increasing the efficiency of gas exchange and enhancing stamina.

Game Effects

Extended volume is available in three levels.

An average adult can hold his breath for approximately 45 seconds (see p. 47, *SRComp*). Each level of extended volume increases that amount of time by an additional 45 seconds. Each level also applies a –1 modifier to any tests involving stamina, such as fatigue (p. 47, *SRComp*).

Light Stress: Users have frequent bouts of hiccups and sleep apnea, inconsistent breathing that leads to poor sleep.

Moderate Stress: High anxiety or situations of high physical exertion can trigger hyperventilation if the character fails a Body (8) Test. Hyperventilating characters suffer –1 Willpower and Light Stun damage.

Serious Stress: The character's diaphragm tears, causing a hernia. He receives a +1 modifier when using Strength or Strength-linked skills. Any tests made with Strength or linked skills inflict 6L damage.

Deadly Stress: The character's lungs partially collapse, and he has difficulty breathing. A Serious Physical wound is inflicted until the Stress is lowered beneath Deadly.

METABOLIC ARRESTER

Similar to the suprathyroid, the metabolic arrester is a regulating gland grown on top of the thyroid. Under conditions where the body seems to be suffering from massive trauma, as measured by a severe drop in blood pressure and the presence of high levels of endorphins, the metabolic arrester supersedes the thyroid's metabolic functions, drastically decreasing the body's metabolic rate. As the heart and breathing rates slow to minimal levels and the body's temperature drops, the character takes on a death-like pallor. The lowered body functions help stave off the effects of trauma and lower nanite loss.

Bioware	Bio Index	Availability	Cost	Street Index	Legality
Chemical Gland	.6	10/4 days	Special	3	5–Q
Digestive Expansion	1	6/10 days	80,000¥	2	Legal
Enhanced Articulation	.6	5/6 days	40,000¥	1.5	Legal
Extended Volume					
Level 1	.2	4/4 days	8,000¥	1	Legal
Level 2	.3	4/4 days	15,000¥	1	Legal
Level 3	.4	4/4 days	25,000¥	1	Legal

Game Effects

When a character suffers at least 10 boxes of Physical damage, the metabolic arrester kicks in and places the body in near-metabolic stasis. The body's metabolic processes are slowed by a factor of five, similar to a Hibernate spell with 5 successes—see p. 194, *SR3*. If the character is not stabilized, he suffers an additional box of Overflow damage every (Body x 5) Combat Turn instead of every (Body) turn as normal.

When the metabolic arrester is active, it takes a Biotech (4) Test to determine that the character is still alive.

The metabolic arrester is not compatible with the suprathyroid (p. 69) or adrenal pump (p. 63).

Light Stress: The character tends to be tired and needs more sleep.

Moderate Stress: The arrester only slows the user's metabolism by a factor of two.

Serious Stress: The metabolic arrester becomes triggered when the user suffers Serious Physical damage. The individual falls unconscious and his metabolism slows.

Deadly Stress: The metabolic arrester doesn't function.

MUSCLE AUGMENTATION

Using a biological weaving treatment, special vat-grown muscle cables are braided into existing muscle fibers, enhancing the muscle's mass and performance.

Game Effects

Muscle augmentation is available in four levels. Each level adds 1 to the character's Strength, to a maximum bonus of +4.

Muscle augmentation is not compatible with muscle replacement cyberware. However, it is compatible with muscle toner bioware.

Light Stress: Muscle stiffness is common. Users must limber themselves up.

Moderate Stress: The user develops muscle tremors and spasms in a specific limb (gamemaster's choice); apply a +1 modifier to all actions involving that limb.

Serious Stress: Inflamed ligaments and tendons are common. Apply a +1 modifier to all tests involving physical activity.

Deadly Stress: The character's muscles tear, and his Strength is reduced to half of the unaugmented value. Apply a +2 modifier to all tests involving physical activity.

MUSCLE TONER

This treatment incorporates vat-grown elastic muscle fibers into existing muscle tissue, increasing muscle tension and flexibility. Users of this augmentation are quicker and more limber.

Game Effects

Muscle toner is available in four levels. Each level adds 1 to the character's Quickness, to a maximum bonus of +4. This Quickness bonus can increase the character's Reaction, except when rigging or decking. It can also increase the Combat Pool, but not the Control Pool.

Additionally, for every two full levels apply a –1 modifier to Athletics (Escape Artist) Tests (p. 46, *SRComp*).

Muscle toner is not compatible with muscle replacement cyberware. However, it is compatible with muscle augmentation bioware.

Light Stress: Muscle pains and cramps are common. Users must limber themselves up.

Moderate Stress: The user develops tendonitis in a limb (gamemaster's choice); apply a +1 modifier to all actions involving that limb.

Serious Stress: Inflamed ligaments and pulled muscles are common. Apply a +1 modifier to all tests involving physical activity.

Deadly Stress: The character's tendons and ligaments rip, reducing his Quickness to half of its unaugmented value. Apply a +2 modifier to all tests involving physical activity.

NEPHRITIC SCREEN

With the installation of a nephritic screen, the kidney is rebuilt to improve filtration and reclamation. Finer discrimination in the removal of waste products and the reclamation of useful materials causes a greater level of well-being.

Game Effects

Characters possessing a nephritic screen add 1 to their Body Attribute for tests to resist toxins and pathogenic agents. In addition, the screen acts to combat the effects of pathogens and blood-vectored toxins; reduce their Power by 1.

Light Stress: The nephritic screen begins to filter out needed nutrients as well as toxins. Users might need to take nutrition supplements.

Moderate Stress: The filter becomes overloaded, and the Power reduction bonus no longer applies.

Serious Stress: Occasionally, the nephritic screen accumulates a threatening mass of non-filtered toxic particles, which slowly leak into the user's system, poisoning him. In addition to numerous unpleasant side effects such as blisters, rashes and other ailments, the character is inflicted with a Light Physical wound until the screen is cleaned. Cleaning requires therapeutic surgery (p. 147).

Deadly Stress: The screen stops filtering, and the toxicity causes a urinary tract infection. The character suffers from a Serious Physical wound until the screen is repaired.

NICTITATING MEMBRANES

This process stimulates the growth of a clear protective

Bioware	Bio Index	Availability	Cost	Street Index	Legality
Metabolic Arrester	.6	6/8 days	20,000¥	1.5	Legal
Muscle Augmentation	.4/level	6/6 days	20,000¥/level	.9	4P–Q
Muscle Toner	.4/level	6/6 days	25,000¥/level	.9	4P–Q
Nephritic Screen	.4	4/4 days	20,000¥	1	Legal

membrane covering the eyes, similar to that possessed by many animals. This "inner eyelid" protects the eyes, keeping out sand, grit, smoke and other irritants. This eye protection eases underwater activities. The membranes are light sensitive and become tinted under bright light. Further, they are polarized to reduce glare.

Game Effects

Nictitating membranes reduce the effects of smoke and other eye irritants, such as CS/tear gas; reduce any modifiers applied by 1. They also act as flare compensation cyberware (p. 299, *SR3*) for defending against flashes and glare.

Nictitating membranes are not compatible with cybereyes or flare compensation retinal modification. They also prevent the recipient from wearing contact lenses.

Light Stress: Users develop watery eyes.

Moderate Stress: Nictitating membranes hinder the character's night vision; apply an additional +1 modifier under low light or worse conditions.

Serious Stress: The membranes become clouded and gummy, causing a +1 Perception Test modifier.

Deadly Stress: The membranes rip, providing no bonuses until healed.

ORTHOSKIN

Orthoskin weaves an energy-diffusing material just beneath the skin that provides the equivalent of personal armor. The individual's skin is peeled back section by section, and the body's dermal layer is fortified by grafts of sythagen (a strengthened and reinforced collagen-protein derivative), flextin (a synthetic and more resilient form of the elastin protein) and flakes of modified and laced cartilage. Once transplanted, orthoskin grows like normal skin and is virtually indistinguishable from unaugmented skin, as the underlying subdermis is altered at the same time. Orthoskin usually heals with little or no scarring. However, characters with orthoskin lose some degree of sensitivity of touch because of the increased density of the dermis.

ORTHOSKIN TABLE

Level	Armor	Concealability
1	+1 Impact	10
2	+1 Impact, +1 Ballistic	9
3	+2 Impact, +1 Ballistic	8

Game Effects

Much more durable and resistant to damage and environmental extremes, orthoskin gives a character extra levels of both impact and ballistic armor, which is cumulative with externally worn armor.

Orthoskin is available in three levels. The armor bonus provided at each level is detailed on the Orthoskin Table.

To reflect the loss of skin sensitivity, add the orthoskin level to the target number for tactile-based Perception Tests (e.g., orthoskin-2 adds +2 to such a Perception Test).

Orthoskin is not compatible with dermal plating or dermal sheathing.

Light Stress: Characters exhibit unsightly dry and flaky skin.

Moderate Stress: When damage is suffered, scars may develop (see *Scars,* p. 132). Apply a +2 modifier to the Body Test for scarring.

Serious Stress: The orthoskin becomes stiff and rigid, refusing to stretch easily. The character suffers a –1 Quickness penalty.

Deadly Stress: The orthoskin degenerates, and the character suffers from drastic eczema—uncomfortable rashes and blisters. Bits and flakes of cartilage also lodge themselves in joints and muscles. The character suffers a Light wound and the armor bonus is reduced by 1 until the Stress is healed.

PATHOGENIC DEFENSE

The pathogenic defense augmentation involves an enhancement of the spleen, spearheading the production of more effective and aggressive leukocytes, or white blood cells. These cells are then released into the bloodstream and lymphatic system to combat disease and infection.

Game Effects

Pathogenic defense is available in variable levels, up to a maximum of half the character's unaugmented Body (round down). When combating disease, allergens, microbiologicals, and other foreign particles—not including chemical compounds—reduce the Power Level of the biological attack by 1 for every level of pathogenic defense.

Light Stress: Users actually become more vulnerable to common colds and fevers.

Moderate Stress: Unhealthy pathogenic defense systems can lead to leukemia, as they produce large numbers of abnormal and defective leukocytes that overwhelm normal white blood cells. This leaves the character vulnerable to infection; reduce the Body dice for resisting disease by 1.

Serious Stress: The leukemia intensifies. Reduce the Body dice for resisting disease by 1 per level of pathogenic defense.

Deadly Stress: The character's leukemia becomes chronic, and the character loses all bonuses from the pathogenic defense.

PLATELET FACTORIES

Platelets are cell fragments in the blood that play a vital role in clotting. Platelet factories increase the body's ability to handle damage by selectively accelerating the production of platelets within bone marrow. More platelets in the bloodstream help to lessen the trauma from large wounds, as the bleeding quickly stops and clots.

Game Effects

Platelet factories remove one box from any Moderate or higher Physical wound. For example, a character implanted with platelet factories would mark off five boxes on the Physical Condition Monitor for a Serious wound, rather than the usual six.

A high concentration of platelets present the risk of thrombosis—the clotting/coagulation of blood. This can result in deadly embolisms—blocking of the arteries. To counter this risk, the character must take special anticoagulants daily. If the anticoagulant is not administered, make a Body Test every 12 hours against a Target Number 3, applying a +1 modifier for each day the character has not taken the anticoagulant. If the test generates no successes, the character has suffered a cardiac arrest or aneurysm stemming from an embolism; a Deadly Physical wound is inflicted immediately and no Damage Resistance Test is made.

The anticoagulant costs 20 nuyen a dose for an injected formula and 25 per dose for the orally administered pill.

Light Stress: Users suffer from poor circulation, leading to cold extremities and tingling sensations.

Moderate Stress: Platelet factories frequently produce temporary internal blood clots that can lead to painful vein inflammations. Each day the character does not succeed in a Body (6) Test, he suffers a Light wound.

Serious Stress: Platelet factories can overtax bone marrow, creating deficiencies in other bone marrow products, such as hemoglobin, making the character susceptible (–2 Body) to disease and infection.

Deadly Stress: A blood clot in the brain leads to a stroke. The character immediately suffers Deadly Physical damage and could suffer long-term impediments to certain brain or motor functions at the gamemaster's discretion.

SUPRATHYROID GLAND

The suprathyroid gland is a regulating gland that is grown and then implanted on top of an individual's existing thyroid gland. This suprathyroid gland supersedes the metabolic functions of the thyroid, optimizing catabolism (the breakdown of complex substances, such as starches into sugars) and anabolism (the chemical conversion of substances, such as the construction of complex sugars). The altered metabolism produces more energy and effectively supercharges the recipient. With the higher levels of energy available, characters with a suprathyroid have a tendency toward hyperactivity.

Individuals implanted with a suprathyroid gland must ingest twice as much food and drink as the normal person to fuel the higher metabolic rate.

Game Effects

A character with a suprathyroid gland receives +1 to all of his Physical Attributes and Reaction. Quickness raised in this fashion can also increase Reaction and the Combat Pool. The Control Pool is not affected by this bioware.

A character with a suprathyroid must increase their Lifestyle costs by 40 percent. This cost accounts for either extra food—eating twice as often—or the expense of a tailored diet.

If a character has both a suprathyroid gland and symbiotes, the increased food requirements are cumulative. A character who has a suprathyroid and Level 3 symbiotes, for example, would have to increase his Lifestyle costs by +100 percent (40 percent suprathyroid plus 60 percent Level 3 symbiotes). The lifestyle cost reduction (–20 percent) of digestive expansion (p. 65) can decrease the suprathyroid lifestyle costs.

As most reactions within the body are exothermic—they give out heat—a person with a suprathyroid gives off more heat, which permits observers with thermographic capability a –1 target modifier to notice him. The character's Signature is also reduced by 1 for sensor and sensor-enhanced Gunnery Tests.

The suprathyroid is not compatible with the metabolic arrester (p. 66).

Light Stress: Characters with a suprathyroid are usually hot and sweaty and tend to suffer from weight loss.

Moderate Stress: Users find it difficult to sleep, and they are often fatigued (+1 Perception Test modifier).

Serious Stress: Extreme fatigue plagues the user, as the body fails to relax. The character suffers –1 to all Mental Attributes.

Deadly Stress: The character suffers immediate cardiac arrest. This heart attack causes Deadly Physical damage, no resistance.

SYMBIOTES

Symbiotes consist of a number of tailored microorganisms that are introduced into the host's bloodstream. They dramatically enhance the body's regenerative functions, reducing the host's natural healing time. To fuel the symbiote activity, the character must increase his food and drink consumption. As this enhancement does not affect the stomach's capacity, the increased demand for food must be handled either by eating more often or by ingesting an expensive diet of tailored nutrients.

Game Effects

Symbiotes are available in three levels. The amount by which they reduce healing time are detailed on the Symbiotes Table, p. 70.

Bioware	Bio Index	Availability	Cost	Street Index	Legality
Nictitating Membranes	.1	4/6 days	8,000¥	1	Legal
Orthoskin					
Level 1	.5	8/8 days	25,000¥	.8	5P–N
Level 2	1	8/8 days	60,000¥	.8	5P–N
Level 3	1.5	8/8 days	100,000¥	.8	5P–N
Pathogenic Defense	.2/level	4/4 days	24,000¥	1.5	Legal
Platelet Factories	.4	5/8 days	30,000¥	1.5	Legal
Suprathyroid Gland	1.4	8/12 days	50,000¥	2.5	6P–Q

Characters with symbiotes must increase their Lifestyle costs by 20 percent per level to account for increased food intake. This percentage is cumulative with the cost increase of having a suprathyroid and is decreased by having expanded digestion (p. 65).

Lost blood volume due to physical trauma and bleeding does not greatly offset symbiote functioning. The symbiotes will regenerate and grow along with the replenishing blood supply.

Do not add in the Bio Index cost of symbiotes when calculating the effects of bioware on longer healing periods (see p. 78).

Light Stress: Characters with symbiotes suffer from weight loss.

Moderate Stress: The character's symbiote activities increase the body's exothermic reactions, meaning the character gives off more heat. This gives observers with thermographic capability a –1 target modifier to notice him. The character's Signature is also reduced by 1 for sensor and sensor-enhanced Gunnery Tests.

Serious Stress: The healing time percentage bonus provided by the symbiotes is reduced by half (95 percent Level 1, 85 percent Level 2, 75 percent Level 3).

Deadly Stress: The symbiotes do not provide a healing bonus.

SYMBIOTES TABLE

Level	% of Normal Healing Time
1	90
2	70
3	50

SYNTHACARDIUM

Synthacardium consists of artificially enhanced myocardium, the heart's muscle tissue. When added to the heart, it enables the organ to perform at higher levels.

Game Effects

Synthacardium is available in two levels. Each level adds 1 die to Athletics Tests and tasks. The character also becomes less prone to heart diseases and other cardiac-related problems. Characters receive an extra die for each level of synthacardium in their hearts for all tests to resist cardiac and circulatory-based conditions or ailments.

Light Stress: Recipients frequently suffer acute migraine headaches from high blood pressure.

Moderate Stress: Hypertension—abnormally high blood pressure—is common among synthacardium users, increasing the probability of a stroke. Whenever the character makes an Athletics Test, roll 2D6. On a result of 2, a stroke occurs. The exact effects are left up to the gamemaster, but they might include paralysis or loss of certain senses or mental functions, perhaps indicated by –1 Intelligence or Mental Flaw).

Serious Stress: The character suffers chest pains and is inflicted with Light Stun damage until the Stress is healed.

Deadly Stress: The bonuses provided by the synthacardium do not apply.

TAILORED PHEROMONES

Pheromones are chemical signals emitted by animals. These pheromones can subconsciously alter other animals' behavior. Pheromones are usually used as "presence scents," to establish a zone of dominance or attract members of the opposite sex.

By altering an individual's sweat glands, specially designed phero-mones may be released, dispersing into the area and subtly influencing others. These tailored pheromones are full-spectrum, boosting all pheromone scents, not just sex-oriented ones. Pheromone augmentation continues to function even if the person is in the presence of another person with tailored pheromones.

Pheromones are species-specific; though human and metahuman pheromones are similar, pheromones will have no effect on non-humanoid creatures. Tailored pheromones are designed to affect all metatypes equally.

Game Effects

Tailored pheromones are available in two levels. Each level adds 1 die to the recipient's Charisma and Social Skill Tests. Tailored pheromones have no effect on conjuring or astral abilities and skills.

Dispersion is largely dependent on atmospheric conditions. Under average conditions—for example, an open area with little or no wind—the effect extends from the source in a circle approximately 15 to 20 meters in diameter. Mild air currents can increase the area covered, but stronger winds will disperse the pheromones before they can take effect.

The effectiveness of pheromones depends on the olfactory system of the targets. Pheromones have no effect on individuals with impaired olfactory abilities or those unable to use their sense of smell, such as astral travelers. Tailored pheromones cannot be detected by standard metahuman senses.

Cultured pheromones are exceptionally powerful—double the normally acquired benefits, and extend ranges by an additional 50 percent.

Bioware	Bio Index	Availability	Cost	Street Index	Legality
Symbiotes					
Level 1	.4	5/10 days	15,000¥	1	Legal
Level 2	.7	5/10 days	35,000¥	1	Legal
Level 3	1	5/10 days	60,000¥	1	Legal
Synthacardium					
Level 1	.2	4/10 days	6,000¥	1.5	Legal
Level 2	.3	4/10 days	15,000¥	1.5	Legal

Light Stress: Characters leave a more lasting impression than usual on others.

Moderate Stress: The pheromones suffer a halved area of effect.

Serious Stress: For each person the character encounters, there is a 50 percent chance the pheromones have the opposite intended effect.

Deadly Stress: The pheromones fail to work properly; the character receives no bonuses.

TOXIN EXTRACTOR

The metahuman liver is the body's main organ for catabolism, or the breakdown of complex substances. As such, it is the first line of defense against potentially toxic compounds and drugs. The toxin extractor is a specially cultivated cluster of cells implanted in the liver to greatly improve the efficiency and to expand the spectrum of catabolic activity. Potential toxins that make their way into the bloodstream are filtered out in the liver, and with the aid of the extractor they are broken down into harmless fragments and then expelled.

Game Effects

Toxin extractors are available in multiple levels, with a maximum equal to half the character's unaugmented Body Attribute (round down). A subject with an extractor can reduce the Power of a blood-borne toxin attack by 1 per level. For example, in a 7D blood-toxin attack, a character with a Level 3 toxin extractor would resist against a 4D Damage Code.

Light Stress: The toxin extractor begins to filter out needed nutrients as well as toxins. Users may need to take nutritional supplements.

Moderate Stress: Strain on the liver causes weight loss and weakness. Reduce by one the number of Body dice rolled for Resistance Tests against any toxins or poisons.

Serious Stress: The extractor fails to break down accumulated toxins, leaking toxic particles into the user's system and in effect poisoning him. In addition to numerous unpleasant side effects such as blisters, rashes and other sicknesses, the character is inflicted with a Light Physical wound.

Deadly Stress: The extractor stops filtering, providing no bonuses.

TRACHEAL FILTER

When this is installed, traps and filters are implanted at the top of the trachea, just below the larynx. This cluster of specialized tissue absorbs airborne impurities and keeps them from reaching the lungs. Smoke, pollen and dust are easily blocked and expelled with an outgoing breath. Gaseous com-

Bioware	Bio Index	Availability	Cost	Street Index	Legality
Tailored Pheromones					
Level 1	.4	12/14 days	20,000¥	2	Legal
Level 2	.6	12/14 days	45,000¥	2	Legal
Toxin Extractor	.4/level	4/4 days	45,000¥/level	1	Legal

pounds are rendered inert or less effective through the various chemical reactions performed by the filters. Bacterial-sized impurities are not stopped by tracheal filters.

Game Effects

Tracheal filters are available in multiple levels, with a maximum equal to half the character's unaugmented Body, round down.

Each level of filter resists air-vectored compounds and other airborne nonmicrobiological attacks. Reduce the Power of such an attack by the filter's level. For example, an individual with a Level 3 tracheal filter facing an 8S gas attack would resist 5S.

Light Stress: Mucus constantly accumulates in the character's throat, causing coughing fits.

Moderate Stress: Swelling and tracheal irritation make breathing difficult; the character suffers a +2 modifier on Athletics Tests.

Serious Stress: The tracheal filter only works at half effectiveness (round down).

Deadly Stress: The filter shuts down (no bonuses), and swelling severely impedes the larynx. The character can barely talk and must take a Complex Action to spit out a short phrase.

CULTURED BIOWARE

CEREBRAL BOOSTER

Enhancing the brain via a cerebral booster requires that nerve tissue be added, along with convolutions and gyri (ridges and furrows), into the frontal lobes of the cerebrum. The extra cells and increased surface area improve brain functions.

Game Effects

The cerebral booster is available in two levels. Each level adds 1 to the recipient's Intelligence. This bonus affects both Reaction and Dice Pools.

A Level 2 booster also adds a Task Pool (see p. 48) of 1.

Light Stress: Recipients suffer acute headaches, at a frequency determined by the gamemaster.

Moderate Stress: Attention deficit disorder is common, making concentration on tasks difficult. Apply –1 die to all tasks requiring concentration, including magical activity.

Serious Stress: The character has trouble remaining aware of his surroundings and frequently "zones out." Apply a +2 modifier to all Perception Tests.

Deadly Stress: Once each day, the character has a 2-in-6 chance of suffering an epileptic seizure. The character suffers 8D Stun damage and convulses for 2D6 minutes. During this time he loses awareness of his surroundings.

DAMAGE COMPENSATORS

Compensators are implanted ribbons of transmissive nerve fiber that bypass the safety inhibitors. They allow their hosts to act while suffering from physical and mental trauma. Compensators do not block the actual damage, only the neurological and physiological effects of shock and fatigue on the body.

Game Effects

Damage compensators are available in nine levels. Subtract the user's level in damage boxes from his current damage before determining injury modifiers. Compensators work equally on Physical and Stun Condition Monitors.

Ace has Level 3 damage compensators. He has Moderate Physical and Stun damage (three boxes each), so his compensators allow him to ignore the effects of both wounds. If Ace had four boxes of Physical and three Stun, he would be suffering only the effects of a Light Physical wound (4 – 3 = 1 box, or Light damage).

The gamemaster might want to track the damage suffered by a player character, letting the player know that a hit has occurred, but not the severity of it. A Perception (6) or Biotech (4) Test could reveal the Damage Level of the hit.

Light Stress: Users feel phantom pain, perhaps from previously suffered wounds. The gamemaster decides when this occurs.

Moderate Stress: Users tend to overstress their bodies. Apply a +1 target number modifier to all Healing Tests.

Serious Stress: Only half the level (round down) of the damage compensators applies.

Deadly Stress: The damage compensators do not function and provide no bonuses until healed.

MNEMONIC ENHANCER

By attaching a highly concentrated growth of gray matter to the brain, the mnemonic enhancer can increase the capacity for both short- and long-term memory. A person with a mnemonic enhancer is less likely to forget events or information.

Game Effects

Mnemonic enhancers are available in three levels. Each level adds 1 die to memory-related Intelligence Tests, such as recalling a specific event or piece of information.

Bioware	Bio Index	Availability	Cost	Street Index	Legality
Tracheal Filter	.4/level	4/4 days	60,000¥/level	1	Legal
Cerebral Booster					
Level 1	.4	6/14 days	50,000¥	2	Legal
Level 2	.8	6/14 days	110,000¥	2	Legal
Damage Compensators					
Level 1–2	.2/level	6/6 days	25,000¥/level	2.5	6P–N
Level 3–5	.2/level	10/6 days	50,000¥/level	2.5	6P–N
Level 6–9	.2/level	12/6 days	100,000¥/level	2.5	6P–N

The increased retention of data facilitates the rapid comprehension of Knowledge and Language Skills. Level 1 adds 1 die on Language Skill Tests. Level 2 adds 2 and decreases the modifier for defaulting from a Knowledge Skill to Intelligence from +4 to +3. Level 3 adds 3, plus 1 die to all Knowledge Skill Tests.

Because memory retention is key to learning, the Karma cost for learning or improving skills is reduced by a number equal to the level of the mnemonic enhancer, to a minimum of 1.

Light Stress: Users suffer headaches and bouts of déjà vu.

Moderate Stress: Memories surface randomly, causing the user to talk in his sleep or mumble to himself in public. Such reflective tendencies inhibit concentration—reduce all tests requiring concentration by 1 die, including spellcasting and magical activity.

Serious Stress: A number of times a day equal to the mnemonic enhancer level (exactly when is up to the gamemaster), the character must succeed in a Willpower (6) Test or suffer a flashback. During the flashback, the character relives an old memory and is out of touch with the world for 1D6 minutes.

Deadly Stress: Whenever the character makes a Knowledge or Language Skill Test, he must also make a Willpower (6) Test or become distracted, suffering +2 to all actions (+4 for actions requiring concentration) for 2D6 minutes.

PAIN EDITOR

A pain editor is a cluster of specialized nervous tissue designed to filter sensory stimuli. Activation and deactivation of the editor is a learned reflex. When the editor is voluntarily triggered, the individual is no longer subject to pain sensations, including feedback pain. With the pain editor active, neither mental damage nor fatigue can render the character unconscious.

Game Effects

When a pain editor is activated, the character can no longer perceive pain. As a result, the player should not be told how much damage has been inflicted upon his character. The gamemaster should secretly keep track.

The character is even unaware of bullet wounds, knife stabs and so on, unless he can perceive them in other ways. He might see the weapon hit, note a big spreading spot of red on his shirt and so on. The character can make a Biotech (4) Test or consult biomonitor implants to analyze his condition.

Further, the character ignores all Initiative and target number penalties from Stun damage. Penalties from Physical damage are applied, but without the player's knowledge. The character will not be rendered unconscious from Stun damage, though he might fall unconscious if he reaches or surpasses Deadly Physical damage (see *Consciousness,* p. 131).

In addition to the pain-blocking feature, the subject gains +1 to Willpower when the editor is activated but suffers a –1 Intelligence loss for the duration. Because the editor works by filtering specific sensory stimuli, deterioration in the tactile sensitivity range also occurs. While the editor is engaged, the subject suffers a +4 to all target numbers for tactile-based Perception Tests.

When the pain editor is deactivated, the effects of any damage suffered are applied immediately—Initiative and target number penalties or even unconsciousness.

Light Stress: The character's sensitivity to pain and other stimuli randomly bounces up and down.

Moderate Stress: Pain editors occasionally dampen stimuli from other senses. The gamemaster should select a sense—sight, hearing, taste or smell—and apply a +1 Perception modifier.

Serious Stress: The character becomes particularly sensitive to pain. When calculating wound target modifiers, increase the character's Damage Level by one.

Deadly Stress: The pain editor fails to activate.

REFLEX RECORDER

With this enhancement, extra neural material is grown in small clusters around the thirty-one pairs of spinal nerves. These clusters allow memorization of certain "learned" motor reflexes.

Game Effects

Each recorder allows a character to retain reflexes related to a particular Combat or Physical Skill. Add 1 die to all uses of that skill.

Barring extreme circumstances, such as surgical reprogramming, the reflex skill, once learned, cannot be changed. Each reflex recorder modifies only a single, pre-chosen skill. The modifier is permanent and is applied whenever the skill is used.

Recorders can be constructed in two sizes, thus enabling two levels of "memorization." Large masses are used to augment entire base skills, while the smaller ones enhance skill specializations.

Reflex recorders are not cumulative and cannot be "stacked" to gain more than a single modifier to any single skill. However, multiple recorders can be implanted to gain benefits for multiple skills.

Light Stress: The character suffers from unwanted reflexive actions that match the skill given by the recorder.

Moderate Stress: When defaulting to the skill provided by the reflex recorder, the character suffers an additional +1 modifier.

Serious Stress: The reflexive actions interfere with natural improvisation. Any Combat Pool used to supplement the recorded skill is gained on a two-for-one. In other words, by spending two from the Pool, the character gains one die.

Deadly Stress: If the character uses the recorded skill, he gets caught in a reflexive loop, performing the same action again and again. The character must take a Complex Action and succeed in a Willpower (6) Test to break the activity.

SLEEP REGULATOR

This treatment modifies the hypothalamus region of the brain, which regulates body rhythms and numerous hormone-producing glands. These changes in body and brain chemistry allow for longer periods of wakefulness. The overall effect is that the recipient requires less sleep per day, and the sleep he gets tends to be deeper and more restful, with higher dream activity. This bioware is popular with professionals who have high-stress jobs and deadlines, as well as obsessive personalities who prefer tackling long-term tasks.

Game Effects

A character with this modification requires only three to four hours of sleep each night and can deprive himself of sleep for up to 48 hours without any modifiers.

The sleep regulator has no effect on healing periods; characters with this bioware must spend the standard amount of time resting and recuperating.

Light Stress: Users suffer from infrequent bouts of insomnia.

Moderate Stress: Despite the regulator, characters exhibit the responses of sleep deprivation—irascibility and irritability. Apply a +1 modifier to all Charisma and Social Skill Tests.

Serious Stress: The character suffers from chronic insomnia and nightmares. When awake, he suffers hallucinations and has a tendency to daydream. Apply a +2 Perception Test Modifier and reduce Reaction by 1.

Deadly Stress: Inability to rest plagues the character, who suffers a +1 modifier to all activities and cannot recover from any damage until the regulator is healed.

SYNAPTIC ACCELERATOR

With the implantation of a synaptic accelerator, the neural cells, which make up the spinal cord and other main nerve trunks, are encouraged to replicate and lengthen. This provides a wider "datapath" for the transmission of impulses and decreases the amount of time required for the signal to traverse the distance. Thus, more data can be sent from and received by the brain in a shorter period of time.

Game Effects

The synaptic accelerator is available in two levels. Each level adds a cumulative +1D6 to the recipient's Initiative. The synaptic acceleration process is incompatible with wired reflexes or move-by-wire systems. This Initiative bonus does not assist in rigging or decking, nor does it affect astral Initiative.

Light Stress: Characters with this tend to be jumpy.

Moderate Stress: The character suffers from unsteadiness and rapid uncontrolled eye movement; he receives a +1 modifier on Reaction Tests.

Serious Stress: Degeneration of the myelin sheath leads to a loss of muscle coordination. Apply a +1 modifier to all physical activities.

Deadly Stress: The dice provided by the accelerator are

Bioware	Bio Index	Availability	Cost	Street Index	Legality
Mnemonic Enhancer	.2/level	6/7 days	15,000¥/level	1	Legal
Pain Editor	.6	6/6 days	60,000¥	1.2	6P–N
Reflex Recorder					
Base Skill	.25	8/6 days	25,000¥	1.5	Legal
Specialization	.1	5/6 days	10,000¥	1.5	Legal
Sleep Regulator	.3	4/4 days	20,000¥	1	Legal

not rolled and are instead treated as if they each rolled a 1.

THERMOSENSE ORGANS

Derived from the heat-sensing organs found in pit vipers, the genengineered thermosense organs are grafted onto the sides of the head, just behind and below the ears. A cluster of specialized nervous tissue is also added to the sensory cortex of the brain, which interprets the signals of the thermosense organs. The recipient can detect the presence of other life forms near him by their heat signature.

HEAT-SENSING TABLE

Situation	Modifier
Target within 5 meters	–1
Target within 2 meters	–2
Warm environment (i.e., direct sunlight)	+1
Extremely hot environment	+2
Cool environment	–1
Extremely cold environment	–2
Every two additional heat-radiating persons/objects within 10 meters	+1
Thermal smoke	+6

Game Effects

Thermosense organs allow a character to make a heat-sense-based Perception Test against any life form or heat-producing object within 10 meters. The target number is based on the object's Signature Rating (p. 133, *SR3*), which is 6 for most human-sized biological forms; 5 for trolls. Apply any appropriate modifiers from the Heat-Sensing Table. If successful, the perceiving character knows that a heat-radiating person or object is nearby. Additional successes may provide information regarding the target's proximity, movement and heat-output but will give few other details.

Note that because this thermosense is not vision-based, a character cloaked with an Invisibility spell can be easily detected. Attacking an invisible character using only this sense would incur a +8 blind fire modifier.

Light Stress: Headaches and unplaced sensations are common.

Moderate Stress: The brain misinterprets signals from the organ, resulting in numerous "false positive" readings. In other words, the character constantly detects heat sources that aren't really there. When and how often this happens is up to the gamemaster.

Serious Stress: The organ's signals to the brain are befuddled with other sensory input, leading to confusing sensations. The character has a +2 modifier to all Perception Tests.

Deadly Stress: The thermosense organ fails to work properly; it cannot be used as a sense.

TRAUMA DAMPER

A trauma damper is a clump of specialized receptors, implanted at the base of the thalamus, near the midbrain. Upon receiving sensory information indicating fatigue, pain or physical trauma, the damper triggers the release of concentrated endorphins and enkephalins—naturally produced opiates and painkillers. These substances do not aid in repairing the trauma, but they may keep the user alive and conscious long enough for him to receive medical help.

Game Effects

Whenever Physical or Stun damage is inflicted upon a character with a trauma damper, the damper helps reduce the damage. If the damage, per wound, is Physical, shift one box from Physical to Stun; if the trauma stems from Stun damage, subtract one box. For example, a character who suffers a Serious Physical wound marks off five boxes of Physical damage and one box of Stun; if the Serious wound had been Stun damage, the character would only mark off five boxes of Stun.

A trauma damper subtracts 2 from the Open Test made by someone attempting to painfully interrogate the user. It also applies a –2 modifier to the target numbers for any tests made to resist the effects of pain—e.g., Body or Willpower Tests versus the symptoms of a painful disease.

Because of the feedback-driven nature of the trauma damper, it cannot function properly when used in conjunction with an activated pain editor. In characters implanted with damage compensators, the trauma damper will operate properly only when the compensators' ability to handle Physical and/or Stun damage has been exceeded.

Light Stress: The user tends to have mood swings, alternating between feeling good and feeling tired, and suffers from weight loss.

Moderate Stress: The trauma damper responds to pain stimuli more slowly. Damage affects a character normally at first, as if there were no trauma damper. At the end of the Combat Turn in which the damage is received, apply the effects of the trauma damper.

Serious Stress: The damper's response slows even more. Its effects are not applied until the end of the Combat Turn following the turn in which damage is taken.

Bioware	Bio Index	Availability	Cost	Street Index	Legality
Synaptic Accelerator					
Level 1	.4	6/12 days	75,000¥	2	5P–Q
Level 2	1.0	6/12 days	200,000¥	2	5P–Q
Thermosense Organs	.5	10/12 days	25,000¥	2	Legal

Deadly Stress: The trauma damper ceases to function and no bonuses apply.

COSMETIC BIOWARE

Cosmetic bioware usually involves less preparation than normal bioware.

Game Effects: Cosmetic bioware has little direct effect upon actual game mechanics; it is a vehicle for roleplaying. In some cases, the gamemaster might decide that cosmetic bioware has an impact on certain social situations.

Stress: Gamemasters are encouraged to create unusual side effects when cosmetic bioware becomes stressed.

CHLOROPLAST SKIN

This treatment introduces chloroplasts into the recipient's skin cells that turn the skin green. Chloroplasts engage in photosynthesis, a chemical reaction in which sunlight, water and carbon dioxide help create glucose and proteins. This process creates enough "food" for the recipient to sustain himself for short periods, though a supplemental diet with essential vitamins and nutrients is also necessary.

Chloroplast skin is incompatible with orthoskin.

CLEAN METABOLISM

With a series of alterations to the recipient's exocrine glands, liver and pancreas—and the addition of tailored bacteria to the intestines—this bioware more efficiently digests food and drink. The main effect, however, is that most of the more embarrassing and unpleasant effects of the digestive system are eliminated. Users rarely develop body odor, belch or pass gas. Even the person's sweat and bodily waste are sanitized. This treatment is popular among high-society players and trendy types who wish to avoid a social faux pas.

Clean metabolism is not compatible with digestive expansion (p. 65).

DIETWARE

This is for those image-conscious people who don't want to worry about gaining weight or losing their figure. It consists of a series of gastrointestinal tract modifications that limit the amount of food that is digested, in proportion to the user's metabolic rate. It ensures that no excess carbohydrates and proteins are created and converted into fat. In essence, the recipient won't pick up any extra pounds—no matter how much he eats.

Dietware is not compatible with digestive expansion (p. 65).

HAIR GROWTH

Hair and fur can be grown in excess or in unusual spots by treating the dermis skin layer to nurture hair follicles. The texture, color and thickness of the hair can be chosen in advance, allowing for a wide range of options—from a long green mane to a nice coat of leg fur so the user can wear shorts in the winter. Whiskers are a current favorite among the club scene.

Each treatment covers a region of skin approximately the size of the human head.

SCENT GLANDS

Simple changes to the exocrine sweat glands can be made, changing the scent that is exuded to almost anything imaginable. The recipient must choose the scent in advance, from a wide range offered on the market, including designer perfumes. This bioware can also change the way sweat tastes, making intimate occasions more interesting.

SENSITIVE SKIN

The number of nerve receptors in the skin's dermis layer can be increased with this process, slightly heightening the recipient's sensitivity to heat, cold, pressure and pain. The actual sensitivity change is minimal. It's not enough to cause increased damage, but it provides just the right tactile difference to satisfy pleasure-seeking hedonists.

Sensitive skin is incompatible with orthoskin.

SKIN PIGMENTATION AND BIO-TATTOOS

By altering the amount of melanin in the skin, and by introducing other natural pigments, metahuman skin can be altered to take on a wide range of colors—from pitch-black to bright red to bone white. The entire body can be colored, or just selected areas. The art of bio-tattooing is gaining popularity, especially with folks who want specific designs colored into their skin. Pigmentation applied in this way doesn't fade over time, though bio-tattoos can be designed so that they change slightly over long periods.

This bioware is incompatible with chloroplast skin.

The iris of the eye can also be altered in this manner, though this option is not compatible with cybereyes.

BIOWARE RULES

BIOWARE GRADES

Bioware comes in two grades: basic and cultured. Used bioware is available only at the basic grade. All can be installed

Bioware	Bio Index	Availability	Cost	Street Index	Legality
Trauma Damper	.4	6/8 days	40,000¥	2	6P–N
Chloroplast Skin	.2	6/8 days	10,000¥	2	Legal
Clean Metabolism	.2	4/4 days	10,000¥	1	Legal
Dietware	.2	4/4 days	10,000¥	1	Legal
Hair Growth	.1	4/4 days	2,000¥	1	Legal
Scent Glands	.1	4/4 days	5,000¥	1	Legal
Sensitive Skin	.2	6/6 days	10,000¥	2	Legal
Skin Pigmentation	.1	6/6 days	5,000¥	1	Legal

in any metahuman with a matching blood type—and sometimes metatype or gender. All are grown through advanced methods, and the process of installation usually requires a battery of immunosuppressive treatments that persuade the body to accept the implant as part of its organic self.

Basic bioware requires a generic "organ donor," as it is not tailored for any body in particular. Cultured bioware, on the other hand, is specifically created for an individual. It is cloned from the host's own cellular matrix. Use the Body Parts Table on p. 123, *SR3,* for basic growth times. Some items must be cultured bioware to even work; these are listed in the *Cultured Bioware* section (p. 72). Having bioware custom-grown takes much longer than merely finding someone with generic implants ready to go.

Basic bioware can also be obtained as cultured bioware, allowing it to be implanted with less impact on the user's body (25 percent less Bio Index; see below). The Availability and Street Index of this is also increased and does not include the cloning time (p. 128, *SR3*).

Implants available *only* as cultured bioware do not use these modifiers. They have already been calculated in the items' descriptions.

Cosmetic bioware can be purchased as cultured bioware as well, though there is rarely a reason to do so.

ACQUIRING BASIC BIOWARE AS CULTURED BIOWARE

Cost	Bio Index	Availability
x 4	x .75	+2/x 5

Used Bioware

Used bioware is available at 60 percent of its normal cost. Used bioware has 1 permanent Stress point that cannot be removed. Only basic bioware can be obtained used. Cultured bioware cannot be reused.

Because some bioware is actually more of a treatment or a medical process than an actual organ that can be easily transplanted, the gamemaster can rule that it is not available as used bioware. For example, enhanced articulation is a series of changes that cannot realistically be taken out of one person and placed in another.

EFFECTS OF INSTALLING BIOWARE

Bioware, being mostly organic in composition, does not have as much impact upon the body as cyberware. It costs no Essence to have bioware implanted. However, installing bioware does have an impact on the user—measured by an amount called the Bio Index—and has a number of side effects (see *Bioware Drawbacks*). After all, when a body's inherent composition is altered, some additional changes are bound to occur. It is also true that the metahuman body can only take so much augmentation before the system as a whole begins to suffer.

Note that a specific bioware implant can only be installed in a character once. A character cannot have, for example, two sets of damage compensators or two trauma dampers.

Bio Index

Each bioware implant has a cost called the Bio Index. This number serves as an indicator for how much of an impact the bioware has on the character's body. A character's total Bio Index value would equal the cumulative Bio Index costs of all his bioware implants.

Essence Index

The Essence Index indicates how much biological modification the body can take before it begins to suffer adverse effects. Because cyberware has a drastic impact on the character's wholeness and decreases the body's ability to sustain changes, cyberware implants affect this value as well.

A character's Essence Index is equal to his current Essence Rating +3. A character lacking cybernetic augmentation—naturally whole—has an Essence Index of 9. A chromed-to-the-max street samurai with only .05 Essence left would have an Essence Index of 3.05. Because the samurai has weakened his body's integrity, he is only capable of making a limited number of biological modifications before something becomes unbalanced.

When a character's total Bio Index value equals or exceeds his Essence Index, the character has overstressed his body's capacity for implants and suffers additional bad effects (see *Excessive Bioware Drawbacks,* p. 78).

Maximum Bioware

The absolute maximum amount of bioware a character can have is a total Bio Index of 9. No one can handle more changes. If a character has bioware implanted that exceeds 9 points of Bio Index, the character's body goes into shock and he dies.

Natural or Augmented

Because bioware is created to match the user's physiology, any Attribute bonuses conferred by bioware are treated as natural and unaugmented. In other words, they count as changes to the character's base Attributes.

BIOWARE DRAWBACKS

If bioware is installed, the character will suffer the following drawbacks, as appropriate.

Bioware Stress Levels

Any Stress damage that is applied to bioware lessens its performance. Bioware Stress damage is measured in levels, and each bioware item has a negative side effect listed that occurs when that level of Stress is achieved. For more details on bioware Stress, see p. 128.

Lesser Immunity

Because bioware tends to throw the body's physiology out of whack, users become more susceptible to diseases, compounds and toxins. For every 2 points of Bio Index, add 1 to the Power of any disease, drug, toxin or other compound the character is resisting.

Longer Healing Periods

The presence of bioware disrupts the body's capacity to repair itself, dragging out the healing process. Half of the character's Bio Index (round up) is applied as target number modifiers for any healing tests, including magical healing tests.

BIOWARE AND THE AWAKENED

Bioware has a definite impact on the somatic and magical integrity of Awakened characters. Altering the body's make-up with bioware—even cultured bioware cloned from the Awakened character—alters the body's ability to channel mana. Metaphorically, if mana is viewed as electricity that is conducted through the Awakened body to perform magic, then bioware is essentially a resistor, impeding the flow.

This is not as drastic as the effect cyberware has on Awakened characters, as the body's holistic make-up is not being chopped up or violated. However, the body has been changed and thus is not as conducive to magical activity as before.

In game terms, this effect is represented as a virtual reduction in Magic Rating (but not Essence). If an Awakened character has bioware, reduce the Magic Rating by the character's Bio Index and round down to the nearest whole number. This modified Magic Rating is used in place of the base Magic Rating for all effective game purposes. For example, it is used when calculating Drain (including determining whether the Drain causes Physical damage) and Spell Pool, determining the maximum levels allowed for an adept power (p. 168, *SR3*) and any other time Magic Rating is a factor, such as warding or astral combat. An adept whose Magic is reduced in this way cannot simultaneously use more Power Points worth of powers than his effective Magic Rating.

It is important to note that the Magic Rating is not actually reduced; it is only impeded. If a Magic Rating is modified to 0 (or less) by bioware, the character has not lost his ability to use magic—he just cannot use it as effectively because of what he has done to his body.

Geasa cannot be used to counteract a Magic Rating modified by bioware, as no Magic points are actually lost. A character can still initiate to raise his Magic Rating and decrease the effects of the bioware impediment.

EXCESSIVE BIOWARE DRAWBACKS

Whenever a character's Bio Index equals or exceeds his Essence Index, the body enters a state of imbalance, as its natural systems are constantly hampered by implants. The resulting state of flux has serious effects on the user's ability to sustain trauma. The character is also more likely to suffer breakdowns and other deleterious effects.

Easier to Die

A character with excessive implants must reduce his Physical Overflow by 1 for every point (or portion thereof) his Bio Index exceeds his Essence Index. For details on Physical Overflow, see *Exceeding the Condition Monitor,* p. 125, *SR3.*

Note that bioware bonuses to Body count as natural; apply them when determining Physical Overflow.

Rick has a Body of 6, Bio Index 5.4 and Essence Index 4. His Bio Index exceeds his Essence Index by 1.4 points (5.4 – 4 = 1.4). His Physical Overflow is normally six boxes (natural Body of 6), but because of his many implants, it is reduced to four boxes (1.4 is rounded to 2, 6 – 2 = 4).

Lesser Immunity

Excessive bioware has an even greater impact on the character's susceptibility to diseases, compounds and toxins. In addition to the increased Power, characters with excessive bioware lose 1 die on Resistance Tests for every 2 points (or part thereof) their Bio Index exceeds their Essence Index.

Longer Healing Period

Excessive bioware also leads to even longer healing times. These characters lose 1 die on Healing Tests for every 2 points (or part thereof) their Bio Index exceeds their Essence Index.

System Overstress

A character with a Bio Index greater than his Essence Index is in a constant state of overstress. Every bioware implant the character has is treated as if it were operating at a Light Stress Level. This condition cannot be repaired or reversed. It has no effect on the character's actual Stress Points for each implant; it is merely a measure of the body's overburdened condition.

BIOWARE COMPATIBILITY

In some instances, bioware and cyberware combinations can produce adverse reactions.

If an implant is described as "not compatible" with another implant, then the two should not be placed in the same body. If an implant is described as not compatible with a piece of external gear, then the gear cannot be used to assist or increase the effects of the implant and, at the gamemaster's discretion, could even hinder the implant's operation.

Adrenal Pump

Adrenal pumps are not compatible with move-by-wire systems, as the combination produces violent and uncontrollable responses that are out of proportion to stimuli and the body's natural reflexes. Such catastrophic overstimulation is unworkable.

Cat's Eyes

Cat's eyes are not compatible with cybereyes or retinal modifications.

Cosmetic Bioware

Chloroplast and sensitive skin are not compatible with dermal plating or dermal sheathing. Skin pigmentation and dermal sheathing are also incompatible.

Digestive Expansion

This bioware is not compatible with the ingested toxin filter system cyberware (p. 300, *SR3*).

Enhanced Articulation

This systemic implant cannot be integrated into a cyberlimb. The Reaction gain conferred by enhanced articulation is lost if the character gains a Reaction bonus from Quickness-enhanced cyberlimbs. All of the bonuses from enhanced articulation are lost if more than two of the character's limbs are partly or wholly replaced by cyberlimbs.

Extended Volume

This bioware is not compatible with internal air tank cyberware.

Mnemonic Enhancer

Bonuses from the mnemonic enhancer for Skill Tests do not apply toward skills obtained from skillsofts.

Muscle Enhancements

Muscle augmentation and muscle toner bioware are not compatible with muscle replacement cyberware, though they are compatible with each other. These bioware items cannot be installed within cyberlimbs; if a character has both, the effects of the bioware are reduced as described in *Cyberware Compatibility,* p. 32.

Nictitating Membranes

These implants are not compatible with cybereyes or flare compensation retinal modification.

Orthoskin

Orthoskin is not compatible with dermal plating or dermal sheathing. Orthoskin cannot be implanted on cyberlimbs, and the presence of cyberlimbs may reduce its effectiveness elsewhere on the body (see *Cyberware Compatibility,* p. 33).

Reflex Recorder

The reflex recorder is not compatible with skillwires. Skill bonuses from a reflex recorder do not apply toward skills obtained from skillsofts.

Suprathyroid Gland

Like the adrenal pump, suprathyroid glands are incompatible with the move-by-wire system.

Synaptic Accelerator

This bioware is not compatible with wired reflexes or move-by-wire systems.

Tracheal Filter

This bioware is not compatible with air filtration system cyberware (p. 300, *SR3*) or the OXSYS cybergill (p. 31).

BIOWARE AND MAGIC EFFECTS

Magic effects, such as adept powers and spells, are usually complementary to bioware effects. A few circumstances deserve special note.

Metabolic Suspension

If a metabolic arrester is activated at the same time a Hibernate spell or Suspended State adept power affects the character, only the strongest effect applies (i.e., the metabolic rate decrease is not cumulative).

Pain Resistance

Bioware such as damage compensators, pain editors and trauma dampers works against the effects of simulated-pain spells such as Agony and Mass Agony.

The adept power of Pain Resistance (p. 170, *SR3*) is incompatible with pain editors or damage compensators. A trauma damper will only affect any damage that the pain resistance power does not nullify.

Pain-resisting bioware is useless against the Nerve Strike adept power.

Reflex Boosters

If Reaction/Initiative-boosting bioware is used in conjunction with adept powers or spells that boost Reaction and Initiative, only the highest bonus applies.

Thermosense and Illusion Spells

Thermosense is not vision-based, so any illusion spells that target vision do not affect this sense. A character cloaked by Invisibility will be just as detectable as someone who is not.

The critter power of concealment hinders thermosense.

BIOWARE AND CRITTERS

Critters cope considerably better with bioware than they do cyberware, though corporations are rarely willing to conduct the research and design animal-equivalent bioware, given the cost. Critters are subject to the same bioware restrictions and drawbacks as characters.

Awakened critters also find their magical powers restricted by bioware, the same as Awakened characters (see p. 78).

Cyberware, at least the cyber/flesh interfaces, would not exist without nanites. Nanotechnology has been around in various guises since the inception of the cyberterminal and the end of the Euro-Wars. Still, these creations—invisible to the metahuman eye—were largely disregarded until the neo-AI Deus came along. Since then, nanotech has become one of the hottest research topics in the Awakened world.

NANOTECHNOLOGY 101

In simple terms, nanotechnology is the science of constructing machines on a near-molecular or cellular scale to be used in rearranging molecules. Nanotechnology relies on its parent sciences—chemistry, physics, biology, engineering and microelectronics. This gives rise to nanotechnology's "inferiority complex," since it is usually seen as a subsidiary to the broader primary sciences—including disciplines such as "nanoengineering" and "nanomedicine," which are viewed as specialties.

Nanotechnology includes the manufacture of optical chips, the installation of neural cyberware, and the building of precision machinery, each central to the corporate-dominated world.

INSIDE THE ARCOLOGY

Nanotechnology has recently entered a period of exponential growth, fueled at least in part by the incidents within the Renraku Arcology and the subsequent scramble to acquire the revolutionary technologies developed by Deus. Unlike the scientific community, Deus had no preconceptions of the world in which it found itself. Due to its constant access to the Matrix, its intimate understanding of its own construction and its ability to think in decidedly unmetahuman ways, Deus raised the bar on nanotech. The AI in effect became the archetypal "mad scientist," taking the limits of nanotechnology to wild and unpredictable heights. While metahuman scientists would have eventually duplicated what Deus was able to achieve so rapidly, many were constrained by residual ethics and morals—pressures not limiting an AI.

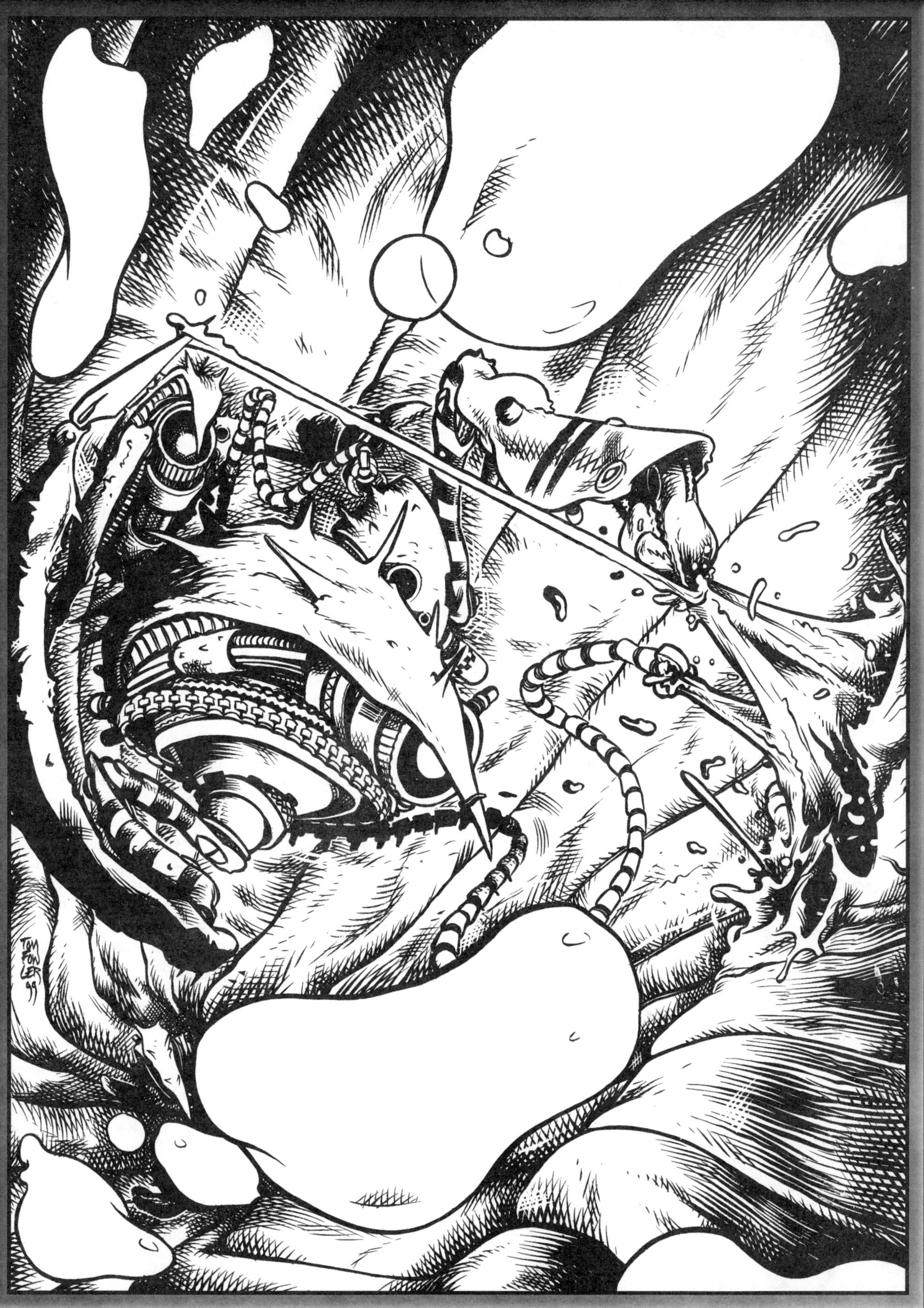
TOM
FOW
LER
'99

OUTSIDE THE ARCOLOGY

While shocked by Deus and what it has wrought, the megacorporations are working overtime to duplicate or surpass the AI's designs. Nanotechnology remains a very resource-intensive and competitive field. Design, testing and construction of nanites require nearly limitless resources (both financial and personnel) and a large corporate or governmental research system of laboratories, institutions, think tanks and state-of-the-art equipment. Successful nanite designs are always heavily patented, and intellectual property rights are jealously guarded. Not surprisingly, a thriving industry exists to steal and reverse-engineer proprietary nanite systems.

There are fortunes to be made through the mastery of nanotechnology, a fact of which the megacorporations are well aware. Each is scrambling to be the first, and hopefully only, corporation to dominate this industry. Society now relies on cyberimplants as a necessary part of everyday life, a revolution based on nanotechnology. The fact that nanotech affects both the molecular and the macroscopic structure allows metahumanity to effectively bridge the gap between what we can dream and what we can create.

This potential power, while pitched as a tool for the betterment of humanity, also has a dark side, which Deus eloquently demonstrated. The key to the progress of this technology, as always in the twenty-first century, will be whether nanotechnology's growth can be tied to commercial gain. The megacorporations are waiting eagerly to see their research pay off.

Despite the extraordinary potentials of nanotech, it isn't scientific magic, as it was billed in the early 2050s, and it isn't the cure to the Awakened world's ills. It has limits. Because the science is unrefined, underdeveloped and restricted, any progress will be slow in coming. After Deus' actions, it will take even Aztechnology's best spindoctors to sell the public on the most mundane uses of nanotechnology—in spite of its potential to refine the existing tools of medicine, chemistry, genetics and biotechnology.

THE NANOMACHINE EXPLAINED

Nanomachines, also called nanites or nanodrones, are tiny machines constructed on a micrometer scale. Theoretically, simple nanomachines can be constructed at the atomic scale, only a few dozen nanometers (one billionth of a meter) in size. However, most nanites in the world of *Shadowrun* are both functionally complex and relatively crude, and are larger by an order of magnitude. Nanites specific to the human body, nicknamed "nanoware" by street docs and cybertechnicians, are usually about the size of a human red blood cell—up to 10 micrometers (one millionth of a meter) in diameter—allowing uncomplicated transport throughout the human body. Nanodrones employed in other environments may vary from a fraction of this size to rare complex, roving automata at the threshold of visual perception. Even at their largest, nanites make the 10-centimeter Shiawase Beetle Crawler drone—the smallest on the market today—look gigantic.

CONSTRUCTION

At the most basic level, the structure of any object defines both its physical properties and its limitations; coal and diamonds, sand and silicon chips are all chemically comparable, yet structurally dissimilar. At all levels, variations in the arrangement of atoms in a structure define its worth, and nowhere is this more evident than in nanotechnology.

Nanites can be fabricated from a variety of materials, as fine control is more important than basic chemistry. Nanites are commonly constructed from silicon, carbon and the various metalloids, though almost any element has a potential application in nanotechnology. Carbon is unquestionably the material of choice for nanite construction. It is highly versatile and able to form radically different materials. Diamond, graphite and the more esoteric buckminsterfullerenes (so-called buckyballs and buckytubes) have ideal properties. Ordered carbon networks are extremely strong, stiff and light—a prime consideration for nanite construction. Additionally, these "diamondoids" have remarkable properties of thermal and electrical conduction and chemical stability, making them the dream material for microscopic construction. These carbon nanites are usually "grown" in a vacuum environment using Chemical Vapor Deposition and selective hydrogen abstraction, modifications on the same techniques used to make Dikote™ coatings.

Boron, silicon and the various metals are among the easier to work with, and the larger "species" of nanites can be wholly constructed from these materials by x-ray lithography and ultra-high precision machining ("nanolathing") techniques, which have been mainstays of industry since the early part of the twenty-first century. The ease of fabrication, and hence lower cost, of these materials is the primary motive for their use. This is counterbalanced by long-term drawbacks, such as corrosion, toxicity and decreased physical suitability, especially in a complex environment such as the human body. Despite this, many "one-shot" nanite treatments and the cheaper (and inferior) permanent systems rely on these materials—and even the best nanoware often includes sections composed of these elements.

The superiority of carbon as a manufacturing material raises the issue of using organic molecules, such as proteins and carbohydrates, as building blocks. The complexity of protein structures and their incredible flexibility would make them ideally suited for many nanotechnical roles. Natural proteins are used in current nanotechnology to protect the nanite from immune responses and to help the robot identify target cells or molecules. However, the core of every nanite is a manufactured robotic structure.

The very complexity of protein is the downfall of theorized wholly organic "bio-nanites"; no corporation has yet succeeded in establishing a general theory of biological structure that would allow them to fabricate a biological construct from scratch. Instead, they must adapt and coerce what nature has already built, using biochemistry and genetic manipulation. The line between metallic bacteria and fuzzy logic robots ("living nanites") is becoming increasingly vague. Protein nanotechnology is one of the "holy grails" of the industry and is consequently the focus of particularly vicious industrial espionage.

POWER SOURCES

Nanoware is virtually frictionless in operation, due to its miniaturization and the high precision of its manufacturing. Nanites can typically function for extended periods on internally stored chemical reserves or what they can procure from their environment. There are several means to provide nanites with the minimal energy they need to supplement their own reserves.

Internal power sources include miniature electrochemical cells that provide the tiny amounts of current required for the nanite's ambulatory systems. Also, nanites operate on such a small scale that they can derive a significant amount of power by using thermo-voltaic assemblies to draw on body heat. Other potential internal power sources include miniature fuel cells and atomic batteries, though the obvious problems with radioactivity preclude the use of the latter in biological applications, except perhaps by particularly unsympathetic organizations.

External sources of energy are often preferable, as the size and complexity of the unit is reduced by removing complicated onboard storage facilities and the nanite can cease functioning if the fuel is no longer supplied. In living systems, the nanites can be powered by the same molecules used by the body for energy—with the consequent problem of tweaking the supply to match. Nanites can also be fueled by added agents, such as various types of sugars. The choice of fuel is much wider in industrial systems, commonly including hydrocarbons and other gases.

SELF-REPLICATION

One of the most significant factors of nanotechnology is its ability to self-replicate. Given a sufficiently precise tool and adequate blueprints, any nanite can theoretically manufacture a copy of itself. In this respect, nanites seem to have many of the qualities of simple life forms.

However, replication is one area in which biological systems radically outperform nano-mechanical ones. Nanoware does not possess the same flexibility as bacteria and viruses; the machines are rigidly constrained by their design, and can only reproduce in a highly controlled environment.

An additional constraint upon *self*-replication is the scarcity of raw materials. The human body is three-quarters water, and most of the remainder is protein. Most nanites rely upon pure, highly reactive and unusual reagents for reproduction, which could damage their host. Nanite replication within the human body, therefore, will likely remain impossible for the foreseeable future.

Replication is possible in a controlled environment containing the appropriate raw materials. Currently, it takes 10 to 15 days for a nanite to be replicated, even in an ideal environment, due to the meticulous error correction necessary throughout the process. This "speed limit" is theoretically reducible.

The final barrier to replication is an entirely commercial one: it is not in a corporation's best interest to sell technology that can reproduce itself. Such "free goods" negatively affect the bottom line. All corporations retain tight control of their replication tools, and all of the nanite factories available on the open market rely on extremely specialized and proprietary raw materials or can build only "sterile" nanites incapable of further replication. Furthermore, corporations tend not to sell a nanite breed or the factory capable of producing it. Rather, they are leased on a periodic basis. These leases are monitored by the Corporate Court and are rumored to contain clauses that allow such options as the infamous Omega Order. Theft of proprietary nanotechnology is officially frowned upon, and those with ill-gotten research keep very quiet about it.

AUTONOMY

For a long time, the issue of control was one of the biggest challenges in making a useful nanite. Individual nanites are too small to control via remote computing, and external control wires are usually impractical or impossible. Each nanite must therefore incorporate its own computer capable of responding to external cues and must carry a "memory" of its task. This problem has been surmounted by the perfection and miniaturization of diamond circuitry and polymeric memory structures similar to DNA, combined with advances in knowbot command structures perfected in the Matrix.

Diamond nanocircuitry has greater thermal conductivity, higher temperature tolerance and more coherent signal transmission than silicon or other types of chips. This allows diamond-based components to be much smaller and faster, while avoiding the diffractive errors that affect equally fine optical circuits. Because of diamond nanocircuitry, the logic circuits of a nanite can occupy as much as half its volume. Even so, individual nanites are not much more complex than a pocket calculator.

The manufacture of very complex items is therefore beyond the capability of autonomous nanite systems. For these projects, an external control system is required, usually taking the form of a dedicated hardware and software package designed to send simple signals to the nanites. For extremely large projects requiring adaptability, an external semi-autonomous knowbot might be needed to direct the nanites. Rumors persist of research being conducted into designing true artificial intelligence dedicated to overseeing highly complex projects, and to perform other, far more advanced, functions, but naturally any parties concerned are keeping such knowledge close to their chests—especially in light of the recent Seattle arcology problem.

USES OF NANOTECH

Despite all the fears associated with nanotechnology, it is the most widely used "future tech" in *Shadowrun*—from Saeder-Krupp's and Ares' industrial applications and manufacturing in space to Yamatetsu's and Shiawase's augmentation of the human body. Few other technologies are as versatile or widely applicable as nanotech.

HUMANITY—CAUGHT IN THE GEARS

Nanotech is the key that allows flesh and machine to communicate. Without nanotechnology, all but the most basic cyberware would be so large and bulky that it would defeat its

purpose—and, in many cases, would cost more Essence than a being could spare. It is the nanites' task to continually maintain the body's neural system so that impulses of flesh and metal do not get rejected by each other. Nanites constantly maintain the neural highways to allow the electrical signals to pass between the body and its cyberware with no delay or impulse rejection, allowing street samurai to move in the blink of an eye, deckers to deck, riggers to rig and so on.

Nanites also control the microscopic circuits that form the retinal displays of cybereyes, weave and reweave the fibers of synthetic polymers used in dermal sheathing and are used in nearly every kind of modern surgery.

Outside the body, nanites act as SOTA sensors and controllers in high-temperature engines and as stress sensors and actuators in airframes—and in most, if not all, spacecraft and space stations. Modern bearings are polished by nanites to such a degree that if the bearing were earth-sized, the largest imperfection would be smaller than Mt. Everest.

Monofilament is also a product of nanotechnology. Originally intended to anchor ultra-heavy loads when woven into cables, it has instead become best known for the ultra-deadly monowhip.

Human Augmentation and Medicine

The primary value of nanotechnology—from a human perspective—lies in its applications in the medical and para-medical fields. Nanotechnology is the "silent wonder" of the cybernetics and bionics industries and has long been a staple of cyberware installation and implantation procedures. Without nanotechnology, invasive cyberware such as bone lacing, skillwires, dermal plating and even wired reflexes could never be attempted. And without the fine manipulations of the nanites, even installation of a simple datajack would be impossible. Because of this, the main focus of nanotechnology before Deus was in the medical field.

In the early stages of the cybernetics industry, genetically engineered bacteria, misleadingly nicknamed "nanites," laid the neural bridges during cybersystem implantation. This "old-world" nanite was responsible for the first implants, and its imprecision limited cyberware to a comparatively basic level and caused significant Essence loss even for very small implanted devices. The advent of true nanites rendered such clumsy tools unnecessary. True nanites are more precise and versatile, allowing larger devices, including limbs, to be implanted without such a loss of Essence that the body would shut down.

Cybernetics' reliance on nanotechnology is twofold; nanotech is used for implantation of stand-alone items of cyberware, and for producing the desired effects of other items. Nanotechnology is an absolute necessity for all cybernetic surgery, especially for the installation of bone lacing, balance augmentors, retinal duplication, orthoskin and dermal sheathing. Nanotech connects all cyberware to the neural pathways that go to the brain. In addition, nanites are directly integrated intomany cyberware devices, including cybereye accessories, filtration systems and chemical immunity and chemical analysis tools.

In the synthetic skin of a cyberarm, there are microscopic pressure, heat and cold sensors and monofilament-sized wires that detect cuts and abrasions and transmit "real" pain. In the ultra-high precision world of small mechanics, such as is found in cybernetic muscle replacements, nanomachines form a matrix of invisible motors that mimic natural muscle and provide machine-like strength.

Continuing progress in nanotechnology has created a medical renaissance. Nanotechnology has permitted revolutionary "bladeless surgery," made medical monitoring and reporting far simpler and expanded the range of monitorable medical data.

Targeted nanites permit rapid healing of wounds that seems near-miraculous. Nanite sutures, pain-suspension systems, coagulants, and other medical nanoware are transforming the face of controlled post-surgical and palliative operations and emergency/accident response treatments.

In some corporate jurisdictions, specialized nanites are injected into the most dangerous criminals, etching a unique metallic imprint onto the individual's skull as a sort of hardwired pass code. This wire can be read with a standard EM cyberware scanner and is used to track the prisoner within the institution. Several of the more paranoid megacorporations are rumored to use such bone etching as "un-forgeable" ID, and as a means of tracking or controlling the access of their employees within their securest facilities.

HEAVY INDUSTRY AND MANUFACTURING

Nanites are starting to occupy a less complex—but no less important role—in industry. The industrial sector began to implement basic nanotechnology during the late 2050s, which has accelerated dramatically into the 2060s toward a multibillion-nuyen market based around nanometer-scale refining, machining, etching and construction. This has produced such a leap in mechanical efficiency that the components of today behave in ways unthinkable even twenty-five years ago.

Perhaps the biggest impact of nanotechnology on industry is in the manufacturing of ultra-strong and ultra-light materials, as well as the fabrication of complex items as single parts. Structures without any flaws or stress points can be designed to far higher tolerances, and the unnecessary material that serves as insurance against failur, can be discarded. Building machinery in a single step is also economical, as large production lines are eliminated. For example, a jet turbine, which does not require further assembly and is "vat-grown" in one step, can perform well beyond normal limits and is comparatively cheap to produce.

Nanites can also perform security functions as taggants. Proprietary commodities are laced with simple nanites that carry a specific chemical code, allowing a company to detect counterfeits or copyright breaches. The use of nanites as taggants ensures that the taggants do not deteriorate and are not counterfeited.

Nanotechnology is also forging inroads into the environmental sector—nanites are used in personal-scale water purification filters to eliminate dissolved solids, bacteria and organic wastes (dioxins and so forth).

SPACE—THE DEEP BLACK

Outside of human-body augmentation, space is the arena in which nanotechnology has the single greatest potential for revolution. In the expensive and competitive theater of space exploration and exploitation, economic viability is a major consideration for those few corporations involved. Whether from earth to orbit or between the planets and the stars, payload weight defines cost and viability. Better engineering through nanotech allows a substantial reduction in the payload weight without sacrificing reliability or safety. The lower weight also dramatically increases the maximum attainable velocity, which in turn affects flight times and mission costs.

Nanotechnology advances slowly due to the high cost of research and implementation. In the space race, however, the cost of placing anything in orbit is so high that the cost of nanite technology is offset by the reduced cost of getting anything into space. AresSpace, for one, is gambling that nanotechnology will lead to a true renaissance in interplanetary travel, perhaps eventually allowing some of humanity to make the long dreamt-of pilgrimage to Mars.

In general, space exploration is no longer the province of human beings; in many cases, manned missions represent an unnecessary risk and expense. This is especially true when autonomous drones can perform the job equally well—and nanotechnology further extends this capability. Nanites can perform extremely complex tasks, and their ability to self-replicate enables a sufficiently patient corporation to send a tiny "seed" probe to perform an immense task, such as asteroid mining.

Nanotechnology's greatest achievements in space are the technological advances in space suits and solar sails. Current space suits are marvels of nano-engineering, weighing roughly half the mass of previous suits while being much safer. Ultrathin "lightsails" are currently in development by several corporations, particularly Yamatetsu, for use as cheap far-system and interstellar probes and as energy-collection devices to supplement the Earth's scarce reserves.

COMPUTERS

The first sector of industry to implement nanoscale manufacturing was the computer industry. Lithographic circuit etching techniques reached their absolute physical limits at about the same time as the Awakening. For a time, industry chose to develop massive parallel architecture while searching for an alternative to the established technology. Eventually, an alternative was found in the optical chip, which relies on a photoactive protein pigment to act as the binary logic circuit. The evolution of this circuit is continuing on an increasingly smaller scale. The first super-compact optical computer chips (OCCs) hit the market in the mid-2040s, products of basic nanotech. These same processes are now responsible for the production of the superconductor chips in cranial cyberdecks, which must be infinitely small and efficient to avoid brain-frying their owner.

WHAT IT CAN'T DO

Nanotech may seem amazing, and it holds great potential, but it is no miracle worker; nor is it magic. Nanotechnology must abide by the same rules of science as the rest of the world. And while it is uniquely suited to perform some feats previously beyond the reach of human engineering, it is a poor tool for many other tasks.

Nanoware cannot induce gross physical changes in a human body. Individual nanites operate on a cellular level, and even collectively they cannot directly alter the body significantly. That is not to say that they can't have major impact, but this will be an indirect consequence of the nanite population's actions.

Nanotechnology's greatest strength—its miniaturization—is also its greatest weakness. Nanites cannot store enough energy for anything other than powering their own functions. For example, they cannot alter overall body temperature enough to cook somebody from the inside. Their small size limits the control circuitry that can be built into them, restricting their adaptability and versatility. Their size also makes them vulnerable to the body's internal reactions to stress, shock and changing environments.

The limits their size places on internal control circuitry also means that external control of nanite systems must be very specific and absolute. In particular, large and adaptable projects performed by nanites require the rapid decision making, adaptability and heuristic learning of a semi-autonomous knowbot or even an AI. It is impossible for a human being to "rig" a nanite system, and no design system allows for metahuman/nanite interfacing, although a metahuman can change the programming on the knowbots or the program running the nanites.

Perhaps the greatest limitation of all is that nanites cannot replicate themselves within the human body. Nanite replication is a very precise activity that is impossible in such a chaotic and complex environment. Replication is also limited by the availability of raw materials and by the millions of operations required to construct a nanite. Even working at top speed, a nanite will take at least a week to replicate itself—if all other functions are suspended.

Finally, just as chemical, atomic and biological weapons raised the specter of terrorism and global destruction in previous decades, so do nano-weapons in the 2060s. Fortunately, though nanotechnology can perform incredible tasks, it does not make a particularly effective weapon. By virtue of their specificity, chemical, biological and physical weapons are better at causing whole-scale death than are nanites. That's not to say that nano-weapons do not exist or are not being developed, but the field needs much more refinement before nanowarfare can live up to its virulent potential.

WHO'S DOING WHAT TO WHOM

Much of the recent upsurge in nanotechnology in the corporate world is the result of the developments in Renraku's Seattle Arcology. The retaking of several Arcology floors by Renraku operatives stimulated new technological developments, as Renraku researchers strove to decipher Deus' creations and research data flowed from the embattled corporation via a steady barrage of corporate espionage.

The expertise and financial investment required for substantial nanotechnology research mean that most corporations currently specialize in one or two facets of nanotech—which has made for interesting intercorporate relations and marketplace synergy. Licensing deals, joint ventures, takeovers and shadow operations have been rife, particularly as the dust settles from the recent corporate shakeup.

THE BIG THREE

When it comes to nanoware, the market is clearly dominated by three major players contending for the best bio- and cybertechnology data and researchers.

Yamatetsu

Yamatetsu's involvement in the nanotechnology field is focused on cyberware installation and integration. The corp specializes in the production of such items as cyberware repair kits and cosmetic-modification nanosystems and is heavily involved in the cybernetic aspects of nanotech research. Such excellence has given Yamatetsu's cyberware products and their services built upon nanotech foundations have earned them a richly deserved reputation.

This corporation is the flamboyant leader of the nanotechnology market; its research is innovative and its engineering brilliant—and Yamatetsu staff publicists point this out at every opportunity. Yamatetsu nanoware is usually at the cutting edge, and the company's research tends to be the most creative and dynamic. This is a double-edged sword, of course—nanoware from Yamatetsu is often less reliable than that from other manufacturers, a natural consequence of "pushing the envelope" and consistently releasing the most advanced nanoware available.

Yamatetsu has a significant aerospace presence, greatly enhanced by its recent acquisition of the Baikonur orbital launch facilities in Russia. This affects the thrust of the company's nanotechnology research, but, unlike other prominent players in the aerospace industry, Yamatetsu has little interest in glory hunting or colonization in space. Its nanotechnology capabilities serve as a useful tool to help the company with other endeavors, such as orbital power generation, particularly through the construction of solar collectors analogous to stationary lightsails; biotechnological manufacturing facilities, where the products have high profit/yield ratios; and pure and applied biomedical research.

Unlike its competitors, Yamatetsu places comparatively little importance on industrial espionage, preferring instead to devote its resources to excellence in research and implementation, at which it has unquestionably succeeded. While other corporations struggle to play "catch-up," Yamatetsu is forging ahead. The corporation is leery of joint ventures, believing it has comparatively little to gain from an alliance that would dilute its premier position in the market.

Shiawase Corporation

Shiawase Corporation is responsible for much of the continuing progress in basic nanotechnology. Traditionally, Shiawase has concentrated less on dazzling leaps and more on steady technical improvement—in keeping with the corp's reputation as a builder rather than an innovator. Its ability to compete effectively is enhanced by its vaunted intelligence network in biotechnology. Shiawase almost always has the most recent data to build upon, although it exerts itself less often to obtain physical nanite samples. Very often, espionage targets don't even know their latest-greatest toy has been compromised until Shiawase comes out with its own version a month later—always just different enough to avoid infringing the patents, but clearly derived from its predecessor. Shiawase's ability to reverse-engineer the competitor's nanites, without reference to the underlying data, is rarely called upon and is less than impressive.

With its vast resources invested in medical facilities and biological research, Shiawase has produced many of the para-medical nanoware systems, including the Med-Alert System currently licensed to the Yamatetsu subsidiary CrashCart™. The company specializes in medical monitoring, wound mitigation and palliative-care nanotech systems. Public Shiawase medical facilities enjoy prestige as a result of their access to top-flight medical-grade nanotech systems.

Shiawase's strength in the manufacturing and service industries also means that many Shiawase nanotech products are targeted at institutional customers rather than individual end users. This means many of Shiawase's nanotechnology developments are licensed indirectly, which suits the publicity-shy corporation just fine. Many of these licensing arrangements are reciprocal, giving the corp some of the most widely stocked nanotechnology clinics in the business. To further its stake in this field, Shiawase is particularly targeting Universal Omnitech with some hefty intelligence-gathering. This is primarily to acquire cutting-edge nanotech research data but also serves to destabilize the smaller—but highly resilient—corporation in preparation for a future takeover.

Shiawase's major competitors in the burgeoning industrial nanotech field are Saeder-Krupp and Mitsuhama Computer Technologies. This presents some problems for Shiawase, as the dragon is more than protective of its perceived territories, and drawing MCT's disfavor is similarly a bloody proposition. Industrial espionage aside, Shiawase is currently experimenting with urban renewal nanotechnology, a system of solar-powered "digestive" nanites designed to tear down large urban structures, avoiding the risks inherent in conventional demolitions. However, controlling the tendency of these nanites to eat surrounding structures, including sewer systems and other public and private properties, is more problematic than anticipated, and commercial release of the system is unlikely in the near future.

Shiawase

RENRAKU COMPUTER SYSTEMS

Renraku Computer Systems

Renraku had a thriving nanotech division even before Deus seized the Seattle arcology. The Renraku arachnoid drone used much of the technology developed by the company's nanotechnology division. Renraku had several major "blue-sky" projects in development, which employed many of the top nanotech researchers in the world. Aside from the small number of projects directly lost within the Arcology, Deus' phenomenal advances rendered most of Renraku's precious research secrets worthless overnight. Since then, Renraku has been playing catch-up with all expected vigor.

Renraku's particular area of specialty lies in nanite control systems. Renraku's nanites act "smarter" and adapt better than its competitors. Its cybernetic and biological implementation are not as flashy as either Yamatetsu or Shiawase, and they aren't as innovative, but the products are usually dependable. There is, however, a certain consumer wariness, as many people are concerned that a Renraku nanotech system could stage an arcology-style takeover of their body, turning them into puppets of the AI.

Renraku currently has a major advantage in that it has primary access to the Seattle Arcology and all the treasures it contains. This has given the company a significant jump in understanding and reproducing Deus' toys, but the other megacorporations are slowly acquiring similar artifacts. Aside from its knowbot control systems, Renraku has produced little that is extraordinarily innovative or commercially successful. Once it runs out of buried treasure in the Arcology—or Deus turns it into a fusion slag pile—the company may lose its status as serious competition to Yamatetsu and Shiawase in the nanoware market.

Renraku also has a significant stake in other areas of nanotechnology. The corporation traditionally has been a market leader in computer-control systems and artificial intelligence research, and these strengths have given it a significant advantage in the wider nanotechnology market. In particular, Renraku excels in large-scale nanotechnology projects with sophisticated external controls, such as complex construction and maintenance in inimical environments.

LEAN AND MEAN

While Yamatetsu, Shiawase and Renraku are the most ubiquitous entities in the field of nanotechnology, there are many other corporations eager to make their mark on such a fundamental industrial enterprise. Most are either up-and-comers in the field, lacking the long years of dominance or major market share to truly threaten the "Big Three," or specialize in particular fields of nanotechnology at the expense of a comprehensive mastery of the market.

Aztechnology/Universal Omnitech

Aztechnology prefers to maintain its aura of mystery, so on the surface it appears to be doing little in the field of nanotech. However, the corporation dabbles in many facets of nanotechnology. Aztechnology's few specialized areas of nanotech investment are in high-end consumer goods and combat-oriented nanoware. They also compete well with Saeder-Krupp for industrial nanotech systems designed to control chemical processes.

One of the biggest movers in the nanotech industry is Genetique—the wholly owned biotech subsidiary of the Big A. One of Aztech's board members, Thomas Roxborough, believes that nanotech can alleviate his degenerating condition. He is using his influence to secure huge amounts of funding for Genetique, enabling it to buy up large chunks of Algonkian-Manitou real estate and topnotch talent from around the world.

Also through Roxborough's dealings, Universal Omnitech's research facilities have been sharing knowledge and resources with Genetique—and thus Aztechnology. This level of connection has many insiders worried; as a member of the Pacific Prosperity Group, Universal Omnitech is in a prime position to make a successful attempt to gain access to Yamatetsu's secret vaults.

Cross Applied Technologies

Market analysts consider Cross Biomedical the contender to watch in the nanoware field; it draws from a range of productive subsidiaries and has a stable of aggressive and innovative researchers supplying cutting-edge data to its production facilities. If Yamatetsu nanoware is considered state-of-the-art, that coming out of Cross Biomedical in Boston is only a step behind. Aiming to replace Yamatetsu as the media darling and market leader, CATCo has taken a leaf out of Shiawase's book and applied the formidable intelligence-gathering resources of the Seraphim against any and all competitors.

Cross Applied Technologies has traditionally focused on pure research, licensing its results to other corps for production. This is changing rapidly now that CATCo is playing with the big boys, but a significant portion of Cross research breakthroughs are still farmed out to other megacorporations in very lucrative licensing deals. Cross tends to select AA-rated megacorps, such as Universal Omnitech, for these deals, though it still keeps a wary eye on its bedfellows.

Its market share is growing rapidly, at the expense of the Big Three.

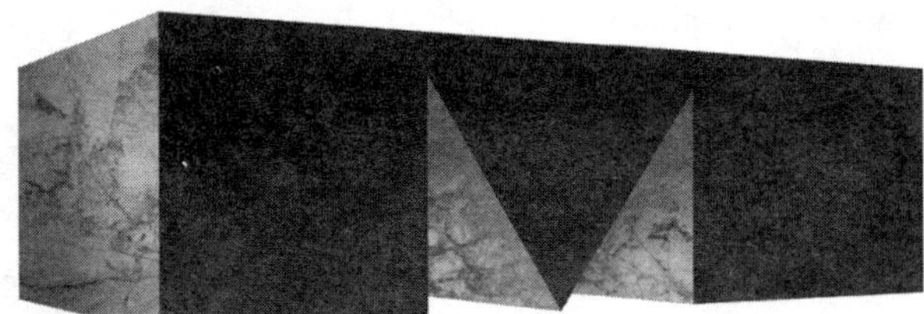

Mitsuhama Computer Technologies

Mitsuhama's emphasis with nanotech is on robotics and drone industries. The company was quick to acquire samples of Deus' drone tech and has been successful in reverse-engineering and implementing these technologies. As a consequence, Mitsuhama remains the undisputed world leader in remote-piloted vehicle technologies, building the smallest and best-designed vehicles on the market.

As an extension of the drone industry, and as one of its few space ventures, Mitsuhama specializes in sophisticated autonomous space vehicles. To give it a more substantial presence, the corporation is seeking to form a limited partnership with Ares Macrotech to develop a nanotech lunar mining facility.

MCT is also giving Renraku some competition in the field of semi-autonomous knowbot systems. The corporation is continuing its research into "biocomputing," accelerated by nanotech.

Saeder-Krupp

Breaking the mold of the other corps, Saeder-Krupp does not specialize in any one type of nanotechnology. Rather, its interests are as diverse and pervasive as the corporation itself, spanning the range from industrial manufacturing to agriculture to military technology. As a consequence, truly revolutionary breakthroughs are rare, but the corporation can maintain its second-rank position with ease.

Saeder-Krupp's focus on nanotechnology is toward direct exploitation of nanotechnology in heavy machinery and industry rather than the biomedical and metahuman augmentation fields. The majority of its proprietary nanite systems are profitable, whether in "smart corrosive" agents or as aids to high-precision orbital manufacturing. Despite its dominance of the heavy-industrial and mining fields, its lunar mining colony uses barely any nanotechnology—which leaves it vulnerable to competition from Ares.

The Draco Foundation

Rumors abound that the group controlling Dunkelzahn's legacy has been active in the high-priced nanotech market. The Foundation has been aggressively gathering nanotech scientists, implant specialists and cutting-edge researchers. Their

big coup was grabbing the nano-savant Dr. Chandra Patel out of the CFS.

It seems the Draco Foundation's pro-Dunkelzahn, pro-metahumanity, pro-"new world order" ideal appeals to many of the disillusioned scientists who slave in obscurity for the corps. The fact that many corps have made seemingly miraculous breakthroughs in nanotech—without the help of the AAA boys club—means that the Draco Foundation might be harder at work than most players will admit.

SITTING IN THE NANO-DUST

Currently, these corporations are far behind the movers and shakers on the nanotechnology bandwagon. Some have avoided the market entirely; others rely on nanotechnology leased from other corporations. As with any major corporation, any of them could become players in the next few years—given the requisite investment, and a few key extractions.

Ares Macrotechnology

The American Giant has surprisingly little interest in nanotechnology and associated basic research. Ares has traditionally focused on military, industrial and populist markets, leaving biotechnology, medicine and cybernetics to other corporations. As a result, Ares has been slow to develop an interest in nanotech, and what little it does have is restricted to a few fields. Ares' minor interests in nanotechnology arise from its dominance of the aerospace and armaments industries and its complementary interests in heavy industry. Aside from a comprehensive range of increasingly smaller and more complex smart weapons, the former NASA assets incorporated into AresSpace is the only other area from which Ares draws its nanotech interests.

As far back as the 1980s, before nanotechnology was anything but a theory, NASA proposed building a complex, self-sustaining, unmanned nanotech lunar mining facility. These plans had little substance and were shelved when NASA became AresSpace and its energies were directed toward immediate profit. However, the mining facility project has recently been reactivated and given top priority by Damien Knight himself. Saeder-Krupp represents direct competition to Ares in space, and the fact that S-K beat Knight to

establishing a profitable lunar mining colony is a blow to his considerable ego. Rapidly establishing a nanotech mine in the moon's Aitken Basin would neatly turn the tables on the dragon and reassert Ares' dominance of the field. It would also give Ares a head start in exploiting and colonizing the near-Earth asteroids.

Ares cannot fully develop its own niche in nanotechnology, as the company has little interest in either cyber- or biotechnology. Rather, Ares acquires whatever nanotech it needs via license arrangements and espionage, and by reverse-engineering what it cannot otherwise acquire. This has left the company behind the tech curve, as the market leaders are obviously unwilling to license out their cutting-edge wares.

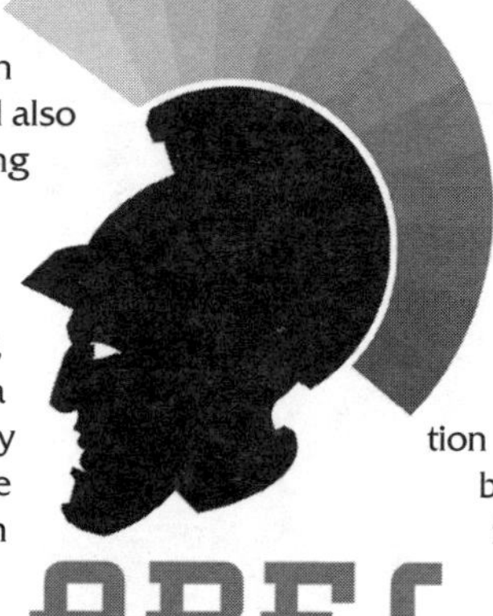

To finance the huge Aitken Basin project, Ares is considering a limited partnership, through a subsidiary, with a corporation with complementary interests. MCT is currently the foremost contender to provide the expertise Ares lacks. Many smaller A-level corps in the Pueblo Corporate Council have recently become close to Ares. While unable to provide the resources and commitment that MCT could, Ares would have a 100 percent open-door policy on its research, and that may sway the votes of Knight, Vogel and Daviar.

This is obviously preferable to shifting Ares away from its single-minded goal of dominating the arms and space industries, but it has the UCAS government more than a little concerned. Fears in the UCAS of losing their last all-American mega to Japanese investment or the PCC are real and growing. Phrases such as "protection of vital industries" and "anti-trust" are the current buzz words of the Senate.

NOVATECH

Ares is slowly developing a few highly specialized nanotechnology research facilities under the aegis of AresSpace, to enhance their already awesome aerospace capability. There is much speculation over the location of these facilities; current rumor lists their mysterious habitat *I Helios* or Tranquillity Base, their lunar research facility near the site of the Apollo 11 landing, as top contenders.

Novatech Incorporated

Though Novatech is embarking upon an aggressive plan of corporate acquisition, it has so far ignored the promising nanotech industry. Novatech needs to secure its future as an AAA megacorp and can ill afford to take expensive risks on unproven technologies such as nanotech. Rather, the corp is working on consolidating its stranglehold on high-end matrixware and on expanding its orbital presence in preparation for the space race looming on the horizon.

WUXING

Richard Villiers is a superlative corporate predator, and once he has secured the future of his corporation, he will undoubtedly seek to develop a strong presence in the nanotech industry—preferably at the direct expense of his competitors. In the meantime, Walker Aerodesign, a former subsidiary of Fuchi Orbital, is one of the few Novatech subsidiaries with a credible nanotech focus, specializing in the manufacture of SOTA propulsion systems and orbital vehicle components.

Wuxing, Incorporated

Wuxing is conspicuous among its megacorporate brethren because of its almost complete lack of domestic nanotech capability. The corporation is wholly preoccupied with expanding its primary business interests in consumer goods, agriculture, finance and mystical research. Wuxing is content to let the rest of the pack conduct all of the research and exploration, selectively investing in and acquiring only those technologies that have proven track records. Wuxing uses its significant financial muscle as leverage against the smaller fellow Pacific Prosperity Group members to bargain for whatever nanotech it needs. Wuxing also has gained access to many of the best technologies of Yamatetsu, Gaeatronics and Universal Omnitech in return for magical research data and other concessions.

As Wu Lung-Wei has stated many times, "Technology is good, and we all owe it a great debt. But he who controls the magical forces that surround us all, controls the world."

NANOTECH GEAR

The gear described in this section functions according to the rules that begin on p. 96. Because these descriptions use terms specific to nanotechnology, players should review the rules for this section before using this gear.

Nanotech gear falls into three categories. *Nano-implants* are cyberware that interacts with nanites or nanoware systems. *Nanoware* (p. 91) includes transient and free-floating nanite systems implanted in a metahuman body. *Nanogear* (p. 95) covers miscellaneous tools and gear that involve the use of nanites.

NANO-IMPLANTS

Some nano-implants, such as the nanite facilitator and the hive, are necessary for free-floating nanites to exist within a metahuman body. Others, such as the nano-biomonitors, facilitate the operation of nanites within the body.

All nano-implants are considered cyberware (see p. 8) and follow the basic cyberware rules, including Essence cost. Some nano-implants can be installed within cyberlimbs; these have the ECU and other costs listed in their descriptions.

NANITE FACILITATOR

This cyberware system is essential for all characters desiring permanent or long-term free-floating nanite systems (see p. 98). The facilitator system comprises a range of minor modifications to the liver, kidneys and spleen. In effect, nanite facilitators ensure that nanoware systems are not filtered out along with bodily waste and by-products.

Game Effects

Nanite facilitators allow a character to possess nanoware without suffering from degradation (see *Nanite Loss,* p. 99).

The Essence cost for this item is reduced for characters possessing blood filtration system cyberware (p. 300, *SR3*), as the systems are complementary. Each level of blood filtration cyberware reduces the Essence cost of the nanite facilitator by .05.

NANITE HIVE

This invaluable piece of cyberware is particularly useful for shadowrunners. Designed for use in the long-term administration of free-floating nanoware, it contains the hardware and software necessary for replicating a particular species of nanite. It is capable of producing enough new nanites to maintain a normal level, replacing those naturally excreted by the body and replenishing depleted levels after injury.

In addition to the actual construction machinery, the nanite hive incorporates a system for monitoring nanite levels in the blood, as well as reservoirs of raw materials in gel form. The hive is a sealed unit that is hardwired to produce only what it was programmed for at creation.

Game Effects

If a free-floating nanoware system is supported by a hive, nanite function is restored by 5 percent each day (see *Nanite Loss,* p. 99). For example, it would take 10 days to recover full nanite function after a Deadly wound.

Nanite hives must be replenished approximately every six months, costing 10 percent of the price of the nanite breed they produce (see *Maintenance,* p. 100).

Each hive is a sealed black, gray or blue box, individually numbered and often incorporating a tracer device. Most will contain several hundred or thousand nanite replication units, as well as the controllers and ancillary machinery. Nanite hives generate significant amounts of heat, making their integration into the metahuman body problematic, so they include a layer of insulation to prevent the body's defenses from attacking it.

If it is placed in a cyberlimb it takes up 1 ECU (see p. 36), reduces Concealability by –1 and costs .1 Essence.

NANO-BIOMONITOR SYSTEMS

Several corporations took the basic biomonitor cyberware system (p. 26) and integrated free-floating nanite systems. Two such implants are on the market: CrashCart's Med-Alert and Cross Biotech's Guardian Angel.

These are generally more effective than the basic model, as they also analyze body chemistry and hormone levels and generally operate on a finer scale. Like basic biomonitors, they are programmed with the range of normal values for the user, considering age, gender and race. If the medical results exceed the preprogrammed tolerances, the unit automatically triggers a warning display—if it is integrated with a display unit or other neural interface—and can be programmed to send an emergency call.

CrashCart Med-Alert: Originally designed by Shiawase, the product was licensed to Yamatetsu, which has aggressively marketed it through its CrashCart subsidiary.

Guardian Angel: This military-grade nanotech system includes an advanced processor and nanites that are programmed with specific trauma control functions.

Game Effects

Nano-biomonitor systems are advanced versions of the basic biomonitor systems. Each combines the biomonitor—actually a free-floating nanoware system—and the diagnosis processor. The subdermal display (p. 27) must be purchased separately. Both systems include a nanite hive to sustain the nanoware component.

CrashCart Med-Alert: This implant functions as a Rating 6 medkit. If implanted in a cyberlimb, it costs .2 Essence and has no effect on Concealability, though it takes up 2 ECU.

Guardian Angel: This implant also functions as a Rating 6 medkit, and it provides a –2 target number modifier to Biotech (First Aid) Tests. If the character falls unconscious, the Guardian Angel will attempt to revive him. If the character receives a Deadly wound, it will attempt to stabilize him. Failing that, it will double the amount of time in which Overflow damage is incurred (to 1 box every Body x 2 Combat Turns).

This implant is not compatible with metabolic arrester bioware (p. 66).

If implanted in a cyberlimb, it costs .3 Essence and has no effect on Concealability, though it takes up 2 ECU.

NANOWARE

BIOWARE REGENERATOR

This fixed transient system is implanted as a cluster of tiny capsules situated around an item of bioware. Each capsule contains a concentrated nanite and nutrient suspension and is situated so the nanites within can analyze the bioware implant's status. If the nanites detect problems or damage, or determine that the bioware is operating outside normal parameters, they are expelled from the capsules. Programmed to repair the implant, the nanites attempt to stabilize chemical levels; repair tissue; clean and remove dead tissue, waste and toxins; and stabilize the bioware implant's environment.

Nanogear	Essence	Cost	Availability	Street Index	Legality
Nanite Facilitator	.3	9,000¥	10/1 mo	2	Legal
Nanite Hive	.7	80,000¥	18/2 mo	4	4P–R
CrashCart Med-Alert	1	100,000¥	8/2 wks	1.5	Legal
Guardian Angel	1.2	130,000¥	12/1 mo	4	4P–R

Game Effects

The regenerator nanites are triggered when the bioware implant they are attached to accumulates Moderate Stress or higher. They automatically reduce the implant's Stress by 1D6 ÷ 2 points per day. Regenerator nanites cannot heal permanent bioware Stress or repair failed bioware.

Replenishing regenerator nanites requires implant surgery (repair cyberware procedure; see p. 147).

Reduced Effect: The bioware regenerators only remove 1 Stress per day.

CARCERAND-PLUS

This upgraded version of carcerands (see p. 111) occupies the boundary between chemistry and nanotechnology. Normal carcerands are passive, designed to break down within a narrow period. This version can be programmed to respond to external stimuli such as the presence of a certain molecule or an electrical charge. Once triggered, the carcerand-plus nanites release their chemical into the bloodstream.

Game Effects

Carcerand-plus nanites contain the equivalent of one dose of a compound. Once injected, they circulate through the body until the trigger condition is met or they are purged. The trigger condition must be specified before the nanites are installed.

Carcerand-plus nanites are available as free-floating or transient systems.

CUTTERS

Gruesomely known as "juicers" on the streets, this rare example of effective nano-weaponry was copied from a weapon carried by "bumblebee" drones inside the Renraku Arcology. Designed by Aztechnology's Genetique subsidiary, cutters are gaining notoriety as an assassination tool.

CUTTERS

Vector	Speed	Damage
Injection	2 minutes	9M

Once injected, cutters distribute themselves throughout the victim's body. They then enter a supercharged power mode and begin to indiscriminately cut their way through blood cells, blood vessels and organ tissues. The nanites remain active for at most 30 seconds using internal energy reserves. However, this is sufficient time to produce tremendous internal bleeding and damage and a shock response in the victim. Victims usually die painfully and convulsively.

Game Effects

Cutters will continue to cause damage (9M Physical) to the character for 1D6 + 3 consecutive Combat Turns. After that point, the nanites have burnt themselves out. Stage this damage per the *Additional Dosage* rules, p. 107.

CYBERWARE REPAIR UNIT

Similar to bioware regenerators, this fixed transient system is implanted as a cluster of tiny capsules situated around an item of cyberware. Each capsule contains a concentrated nanite and nutrient suspension and is connected to the implant's fault-checking circuitry (if any). If the nanites detect a major malfunction or damage, or determine that the cyberware is operating outside normal parameters, they are expelled from the capsules. Programmed to repair the implant, the nanites rejoin neural connections, seal fractures, repair circuitry and fix other minor damage.

The repairs they make are somewhat haphazard, as the nanites cannot discriminate between individual wires and neurons. Repair nanites cannot restore function in cases where severe trauma has occurred, such as lost limbs.

Game Effects

The repair nanites are triggered whenever the cyberware implant they are attached to accumulates Moderate Stress or higher. The nanites automatically reduce the implant's Stress by 1D6 ÷ 2 points per day that they are active. Repair nanites cannot heal permanent Stress, nor can they repair failed cyberware.

Replenishing repair nanites requires implant surgery (repair cyberware procedure; see p. 147).

Reduced Effect: The repair nanites reduce 1 Stress per day.

FINGERPRINT MAPPERS

This treatment involves programming a nanoware system with a scanned fingerprint or palm print. Once injected, the nanites rebuild the subject's skin layers, changing the ridges on the pads of the fingers or the palm to match the print.

Game Effects

This nanoware system has a rating between 1 and 10 that is used in an Opposed Test with the print scanner (see p. 235, *SR3*). The re-mapping of the skin takes (Rating) hours, during which the character's hands tingle and itch. This process also renders the finger tips very tender for the duration of the re-

Nanoware	Nanite Type	Cost	Availability	Street Index	Legality
Bioware Regenerator	Fixed Transient	10% of implant cost	10/2 wks	2	Legal
Carcerand-plus					
	Free-floating	30,000¥	12/2 wks	2	Legal
	Transient	7,000¥	10/1wk	2	Legal
Cutters (per dose)	Transient	20,000¥	20/1 mo	5	2–Y
Cyberware Repair Unit	Fixed Transient	10% of implant cost	8/2 wks	1.5	Legal
Fingerprint Mappers	Transient	Rating x 5,000¥	12/1 mo	2	5P–Y

GEMINI						
Vector	**Speed**	**Damage**	**Addict.**	**Tolerance**	**Edge**	**Fix Factor**
Injection	1 minute	—	6M	—	2/20	3 days

mapping procedure, imposing a +2 target number modifier to all tactile-based Perception Tests. Once re-mapped, the character's natural prints will grow back and replace the fake print after 30 days. This treatment affects one hand only.

Reduced Effect: If the re-mapping of the fingerprint is still in progress, the fingerprint's rating is reduced by half (round down).

GEMINI

Gemini is a nanotech-based drug recently developed by Mitsuhama as a side effect of their attempts to render cybered animals more tractable. Once injected, Gemini nanites traverse the body until receiving a preprogrammed trigger signal, which can be anything from hormonal levels to a chemical presence to an ultrasound signal. When triggered, the nanites stimulate neural responses in the same fashion as chemical narcotics. By targeting a wide variety of cellular drug receptors, the nanites can produce a specific preprogrammed emotional response in the host. This emotion can range from towering rage to deep sadness to sublime contentment. Unlike BTLs, Gemini produces its effects, and causes addiction, through emotional manipulation rather than full sensory immersion.

Game Effects

A character dosed with Gemini is susceptible to the preprogrammed emotional state when the nanites are triggered. The character must play out the emotion for the duration of the nanites' existence. If the character wishes to display another emotion, he must take a Complex Action and succeed in a Charisma (8) Test. If successful, he can emote what he wishes for the next Combat Turn. After that, the Gemini-controlled emotional state returns.

While under the influence, characters receive a +1 bonus to Willpower.

Reduced Effect: The character needs to make a Charisma (6) Test to successfully display another emotion.

GREMLINS

Gremlins are nanites programmed to seek out cyberware within the host's body and sabotage it. Specifically, gremlins target neural connections, fiber optics, superconductive pathways, microelectronics and implant casings. By cutting connections, power sources and processing ability, gremlins can severely damage an implant in a short time.

Game Effects

Once injected, gremlins rapidly scour the body, looking for cyberware implants and doing their best to damage them. Each full day that the gremlins are active, roll 1D6. The result is the number of cyberware wound effects (see p. 126) that the character suffers.

Reduced Effect: The gremlins inflict 1D6 ÷ 2 wound effects each day.

NANITE HUNTERS

These nanites are designed to hunt and destroy another specified nanoware system.

Game Effects

Nanite hunters must be programmed to target a specific nanoware system (nano-symbiotes, for example). Once injected, nanite hunters reduce the targeted nanite system by 1D6 percent every hour.

Reduced Effect: The hunters reduce the nanoware system by 1D6 ÷ 2 percent every hour.

NANOSYMBIOTES

Similar to organic symbiotes (p. 69), nanosymbiotes are free-floating nanites that aid the body's regenerative capabilities. Nanosymbiotes remove or repair damaged cells, stimulate cell growth, help fight infection and engage in numerous other activities to spur healing. Unlike the bioware, these nanites do not require increased food intake, and they are susceptible to degeneration through blood loss, as other nanites are.

Game Effects

Nanosymbiotes reduce the base time for healing by one Damage Level (see the *Healing Table*, p. 127, *SR3*). For example, a character healing a Moderate Physical wound would use a base time of 24 hours—the base time for Light—instead of 10 days.

If using the optional *Healing Physical Damage* rules (p. 134), calculate the base time as if the wound modifier were one level lower. For example, a character without bioware would heal one box of Moderate in a base time of 24 (24 x 1) hours instead of 48 (24 x 2) hours.

Note that damage decreases the percentage of nanosymbiotes in the system by 5 percent per box, as normal. Nanosymbiotes are incompatible with symbiotes.

Reduced Effect: Determine the revised base healing time as above, but then increase that period by 50 percent (x 1.5).

Nanoware	Nanite Type	Cost	Availability	Street Index	Legality
Gemini (per dose)	Transient	20,500¥	14/48 hrs	3	2–Y
Gremlins	Transient	20,000¥	14/2 wks	3	2–Y
Nanite Hunters	Transient	20,000¥	16/3 wks	3	4–Y
Nanosymbiotes	Free-floating	70,000¥	12/1 wk	2	Legal

NANOTATTOOS

Nanotattoos are prized because they can change shape, size, color and even texture over time—according to their programming. The field has drawn a number of artists who create unique designs for those willing to pay for the privilege of wearing them.

Game Effects

The potential variations of nanotattoos are staggering, and it is up to the gamemaster to limit exactly what can and can't be accomplished artistically. Price may also vary, depending on the artists, uniqueness of the design, size and other factors.

Reduced Effect: The tattoo's quality and rate of change are diminished.

NANTIDOTES

Similar to the carcerand-plus nanoware, nantidotes are designed to carry antidotes and neutralize toxins. Ideal for dispensing exact quantities of drugs at specific sites and minimizing side effects, nantidotes are also useful against neurotoxins and other compounds that have rapid effects.

Nantidotes are tailored to combat one type of toxin and circulate in the bloodstream in a dormant state. When they detect the toxin, they activate and release their antidote at the site of poisoning.

Game Effects

Nantidotes can be purchased as transient or free-floating systems. Each nantidote system is only effective against a particular toxin. At the gamemaster's discretion, closely related compounds can also be affected (Green Ring 3 and Green Ring 8, for example).

If nantidotes are present in the system when the toxin is introduced, or injected before the toxin's Speed duration expires, the toxin has no effect.

If nantidotes are injected after the toxin's Speed period, the nantidotes prevent further damage. They also reduce the target number on tests to heal the toxin's damage by 2.

Reduced Effect: If present before the toxin's Speed duration expires, the toxin's Power is cut in half (round down), and its Damage Level is reduced by one—for example, from Serious to Moderate. If applied after the toxin has caused damage, any further damage is reduced as stated, and the character receives a –1 modifier on tests to heal the toxin's damage.

OXY-RUSH

These nanites are essentially diamondoid oxygen bottles, carrying a cargo of highly compressed oxygen. In effect, they can provide enough oxygen and remove enough carbon dioxide that the host can exist without breathing for at least several hours. The nanite-distributed oxygen also helps the body achieve greater levels of performance and helps to counter the effects of low blood pressure from damage and shock.

Game Effects

A character with oxy-rush nanites can hold his breath for hours—until the nanites wear out. These nanites also provide +2 bonus dice to Athletics Tests and provide the equivalent of 1 level of Pain Resistance (see p. 170, *SR3*).

Oxy-rush is incompatible with oxygenated fluorocarbons (p. 113); if both are applied, use only the strongest effect.

Reduced Effect: The character can still hold his breath, but he receives only +1 die for Athletics.

RETINAL TAILORS

Retinal tailors are nanites that rework the retinal pattern of the user's eyes to match a retinal print they have been programmed with.

Game Effects

This nanoware system has a rating between 1 and 10 that is used in an Opposed Test with the print scanner (see p. 235, *SR3*). The re-mapping of the retina takes (Rating) hours, during which the character's eyes itch. This change is permanent; if the character wants to retun to a previous retinal print or any other, retinal tailors must be applied again.

These nanites are not compatible with cybereyes or retinal duplication cyberware.

Reduced Effect: If the re-mapping of the retina is not complete, reduce the print's rating by half (round down).

TAGGANTS

Taggants are nanite systems designed to mark the user in some way for security purposes. Presently, two types are used: etchers and markers.

Etchers: This transient system inlays a magnetic metallic pattern onto a section of bone. Usually used to permanently mark convicts or employees, the imprint left by etchers is detectable by magnetic anomaly detectors (MADs) and cyberware scanners. The latter can actually read the imprint, which usually contains information such as the convict's SIN or employee ID code.

Nanoware	Nanite Type	Cost	Availability	Street Index	Legality
Nanotattoos	Free-floating	5,000¥	8/2 wks	3	Legal
Nantidotes	Free-floating	500¥ x toxin's cost	10/2 wks	2	Legal
	Transient	200¥ x toxin's cost	8/1 wk	2	Legal
Oxy-rush	Transient	10,000¥	8/2 wks	2	Legal
Retinal Tailors	Transient	Rating x 6,000¥	12/1 mo	2	5P–Y
Taggants					
Etchers	Transient	5,000¥	6/1 wk	1.5	Legal
Markers	Free-floating	10,000¥	8/2 wks	2	Legal

Markers: This free-floating system is nothing more than a blood-borne information capsule. The marker nanites are usually encoded with identifying information, which can be analyzed and read by a nano scanner. Some security systems attempt to "tag" runners by injecting them with marker nanites so that they can be identified later. Markers are also used as a discreet message delivery system, sometimes via unknowing accomplices.

Game Effects

Taggants have no reduced effect; they operate as normal until gone.

Etchers: The target number for a MAD system or cyberware scanner to detect an etching is 3. Etchings are usually permanent. Specially programmed etcher nanites can remove them, as can surgery to open up the bone and scrape it.

Markers: Marker nanites can hold 5 Mp of data.

NANOGEAR

MONOWIRE

Superfine monofilament wire, constructed via nanotech "buckytubes," can be used for a wide range of security purposes. Nearly invisible, monowire can be stretched atop fences or in a maze pattern across doorways and hallways. Many other clever uses have been devised, such as coiling the monowire in a special wrist-worn container with a pull tab at one end, to be used as a lethal garrote.

Game Effects

Rules for using monowire as a physical security measure appear on p. 234, *SR3*. When extended and taut, monowire has a Concealability Rating of 8.

NANOSCANNER

Nanoscanners are hand-held devices that test blood, saliva, tissue or other materials for nanoware—especially taggant nanites. Located nanites can be analyzed for any data they carry (such as that carried by marker nanites), as well as for their general construction and purpose.

Game Effects

Nanoscanners have a rating from 1 to 10; this determines the number of dice rolled to detect nanites in the sample. See *Nanoware Detection,* p. 100.

SAVIOR™ ADVANCED MEDKIT

Designed by Shiawase Biotech and marketed as a personal backpack or satchel unit, the Savior™ advanced medkit combines cutting-edge nanotech with a system capable of diagnoses far superior to those of generic models. When activated, the medkit injects a mixture of diagnostic and repair nanites into the bloodstream, as well as the standard stimulants, coagulants and painkillers. Under direction from the expert system, the nanites rejoin damaged tissue, stop blood loss and minimize the onset of shock.

Game Effects

The Savior is a Rating 6 medkit and follows all the normal rules for medkits (see p. 136). It also provides a –1 target number modifier for Biotech (First Aid) and Body Tests to stabilize.

The system has a limited supply of nanites and will be exhausted on 1D6 die roll result of 1–2 following a treatment.

SMART CORROSIVES

This system consists of a swarm of nanites suspended in a clear chemical solution. Each nanite carries a payload of a corrosive compound. The nanites are programmed to seek out a certain substance, bind to it and use the corrosive to melt it. Because the nanites can tell the difference between the target substance and anything else, the corrosive is applied in a manner that affects only the target, while everything around it remains untouched.

Game Effects

Smart corrosive solutions can be applied via squirtguns, spray canisters, splash grenades and a variety of other methods (see *Chemtech Application Gear,* p. 115). Each solution is programmed to corrode only a specific substance, from skin to metal to plasteel. The corrosive carried by the nanites will affect only that substance.

The costs below do not include the cost of the corrosive carried. Corrosives are detailed on p. 111.

NANOTECH RULES

Nanotechnology is among the newest scientific toys to hit the streets. From cyberware to monowire, the effects of nanotechnology have been evident for some time. However, its earlier effectiveness to the average shadowrunner were minimal.

That all changed when an AI took over the Renraku Arcology. Deus' constructs became public knowledge and nanotechnology became a buzz word for science out of control. Soon items began to appear in the shadows—items that could only be created or maintained with nanoware.

This shift opened up a Pandora's box that will rival cybertechnology in scope.

NANOTECH AND ITS USES

Nanites come in two basic forms; *nanoware,* which is implanted or injected into a metahuman's body, and *nanodrones* (also called *nanorobots*), which can function outside the body and work on anything from mining and manufacturing applications to molecular and even atomic reconstruction.

In *Shadowrun* terms, nanites are microscopic semi-autonomous drones (see p. 67, *Rigger 2*). The technical level of *Shadowrun* does not allow for "freethinking" nanites able to adjust their programming code. Therefore, nanites are not considered to be fully robotic.

Unlike normal drones, nanites do not need a constant radio signal. They have a Pilot Rating equal to the number of functions they can perform, which means that the vast majority of nanite systems have a Pilot Rating of 1. More adaptable nanites with higher Pilot Ratings are correspondingly more expensive and rarer. Since they are not robots, nanites do not have Learning Pools.

Nanites act like compounds or chemicals within a host system and therefore do not need an Initiative rating.

NANODRONES

Used throughout high-tech and heavy industry, nanodrones excel in precision work and single-step manufacturing. They are particularly valuable in inhospitable environments such as space and seafloor facilities. A simple nanotechnological "production line" for a single manufacturing process costs about 10 million nuyen. For more complex processes, the costs become stratospheric. Use the base costs below for nanotech facilities to determine a base cost. There are no nanotech shops.

This is a new and highly technical field, which means that street index and availability are irrelevant. These are not available on the street level. The gamemaster can determine how practical nanotech facilities are in his game.

Industrial nanorobotics is a complex discipline, represented in *Shadowrun* by the Nanorobotics specialization of the Engineering Knowledge Skill.

Programming Nanites

Reprogrammable nanites are a rarity in *Shadowrun,* though their popularity is increasing as research obstacles are overcome. Such advanced types of nanites are used in industrial processes where adaptability is a prime consideration.

All nanites are produced with their programming already coded into them, but in some cases their instructions can be modified. Any nanite system with a Pilot Rating of 1 is a spe-

Nanogear	Conceal	Weight	Availability	Cost	Street Index	Legality
Monowire (per meter)	8	—	24/14 days	2,000¥	3	1–K
Nano-scanner	6	1	Rating/1 wk	5,000¥ x Rating	2	8P–U
Savior Advanced Medkit	—	4	6/1 wk	1,500¥	2	Legal
Savior Supplies	8	—	6/1 wk	300¥	2	Legal

	Availability	Cost	Street Index	Legality
Smart Corrosives (per dose)	12/1 mo	7,000¥	3	3P–Y

NANOTECH FACILITY COSTS

Nanotech Research Facility	(Max. Pilot Rating of nanite +10)^2 x 100,000¥
Reprogrammable Nanite Facility	(Max. Pilot Rating of nanite +10)^2 x 250,000¥
Single-use Nanotech Production Line	Calculate as if it were a nanotech research facility and add that cost to that of the facility without nanotech—as per the rules on p. 288 of *SR3*.
Multi-use Nanotech Production Line	Calculate as if it were a reprogrammable nanite facility and add that cost to that of the facility without nanotech—as per the rules on p. 288 of *SR3*.

cialized single-purpose "breed" with hardwired instructions. It cannot be reprogrammed.

Any nanite with a Pilot Rating of 2 or greater can be reprogrammed, as long as one of those hardwired instructions is the ability to be reprogrammed. A semi-autonomous knowbot or a computer host—of at least Orange-10 security level, or any Red system—must be used to reprogram nanites to perform new functions.

The knowbot or computer host must be able to analyze and reprogram the nanite system in its own "language," and must be able to communicate with the nanites. Directed ultrasound, microwave or UV transmission—as defined by the design of the original nanite—can carry the reprogramming signal. The transmission has a maximum effective range of 1 meter, and the transmitter's Rating must be equal to the nanites' Pilot Rating. Nanites cannot receive any other radio transmissions.

Reprogramming and re-deploying a nanite population to perform a new task takes a significant amount of time, as described in the table below. During the reprogramming, the nanites suspend whatever operation they were performing. The time can be reduced by a successful Engineering (Nanorobotics) roll against a Target Number 6. Knowbots can use their Utility Pool in place of the Engineering Skill for this test.

TIME TO REPROGRAM NANITES

Controller	Base Time
Orange Host	Nanite Pilot Rating x 36 hrs
Red Host	Nanite Pilot Rating x 24 hrs
Knowbot	Nanite Pilot Rating x 12 hrs

Whitelight is browsing the MCT Chiba host looking for their nanotech-manufacturing controller, because she needs a new engine for her Fed-Boeing Eagle. Assuming she can successfully subjugate the host to her will (it's a Red host controlling a Pilot Rating 3 nanorobot system), she can tell it to make jet engines instead of Rotodrones, and the host will reprogram the nanites accordingly.

If she successfully performs a Control Slave operation to take command of the process, the host will begin modifying the nanite programs. Because it's a Red host, it will take three days to complete the reprogramming, reduced by any successes on an Engineering (6) Test. And because Control Slave is a monitored operation (see p. 215, SR3), Whitelight has to watch over the process until reprogramming is complete. At that point, construction of her engine will commence unmonitored. Better hope she has an IV drip or a top-rated Engineering skillsoft.

Direct Control

Though nanites are considered to be drones, they cannot be rigged. They are built specifically with a hardwired function. The only way a rigger or decker would be able to reprogram them is via the methods listed above.

Shutting Down Nanites

A nanite unable to perform its function is considered "shut down." Nanites can be shut down in multiple ways. They may be coded to shut down automatically when a particular condition is fulfilled, such as a chemical or physical trigger, or receiving a particular transmission. Or their energy source could be cut off, if supplied externally. Programmable nanites can be shut down at the completion of a particular task.

Nanites by nature perform simple, repetitive tasks until told to stop. It is this very tenacity that makes controlling Shiawase's experimental solar-powered urban renewal nanites so difficult. Their energy source cannot be permanently depleted, and individual nanites are very difficult to control in an open-air environment.

Use of a chemical trigger is common in nanoware systems, employing the introduction of a particular compound designed to block some or all of the nanite's abilities. This chemical is specific to the receptors of a particular "breed" of nanite and can be in a gas, liquid or molecular form—sometimes even borne by a different type of nanite.

Shut-down nanites can be restarted later given appropriate cues. But in most cases they will begin to decay when they no longer function. Certain breeds of nanites are capable of, or even designed to, scavenge "dead" nanites for raw materials.

NANOWARE

While nanotech has many applications, nanoware is the tech that is specific to characters. Nanoware does not interfere with magic or the use of magic.

There are two main categories of nanotechnology in the physiological context—free-floating and transient nanites. Either category can be a fixed system. The nanites that monitor the flesh/cyber interface are considered part of the cyberware implant and do not fall under the nanoware classification.

Fixed systems are segregated from the rest of the body, usually isolated in a protected capsule or sac until required. These systems include damage-repair nanites, cyberware "repair kits" and other systems in which nanite function is triggered by a specific event or localized to one region of the body. Once released, they are considered either transient or free-floating until their job is finished.

Free-floating nanites are carried in the blood and extracellular fluids. Such systems are ideal for general monitoring of bodily conditions and rapid response to a range of physiological damage. Characters can have two free-floating nanite systems at the same time. They cannot have more because of physiological limits on blood volume, coupled with the problems of heat and waste produced by active nanites.

If a third nanite system is introduced into the host, it fails to function, and the other nanoware in the host's system suffers diminished effectiveness. See *Nanite Loss,* p. 99.

Transient nanite treatments are used for procedures such as cyberware implantation, "bladeless surgery," cosmetic modification, antidote treatments and the like. Such nanites have a short-term presence in the body, as they are cleaned from the blood by the body's filtration and immune systems.

ACQUIRING NANOWARE

Nanotech is the newest technology to hit the streets and is still comparatively rare among the gutter trash. It is not a simple matter of wandering down to your corner street doc and getting a shot in the arm. Most street docs won't be able to acquire any nanoware, except what they need to implant cyberware.

Having nanoware legally installed is more involved than acquiring cyberware or bioware. Nanite systems require considerable resources to design, develop, test and manufacture. Nanotechnology research and production is a significant economic enterprise, and the resulting nanotech systems are usually patented and imprinted with some code that only their mother corporation knows about.

A large percentage of the cost of registered nanotech stems from the licensing fee that the big players charge the little ones. Any required surgery or hospitalization costs are extra, of course. If the customer chooses to have a nanite hive (see p. 91) installed, he must pay a further, and rather hefty, fee to have the unit programmed with the specifications of the proprietary nanite system chosen. Each nanite hive is specialized for a given type of nanite, and separate hives must be installed for every nanite system the customer wishes to have maintained.

Finding a Shadowclinic

Most shadowrunners do not acquire their "edge" legally. Acquiring illegal nanoware is a difficult process. The same shadow-clinics that first gave runners access to beta- and deltaware are the same ones now allowing nanotech to trickle into the shadows. Finding a nanoware clinic follows the rules for finding a clinic, p. 140. Only beta- or delta-level clinics can provide nanoware treatments.

Most nanoware is bleeding-edge. In the interest of game balance, and as with beta- or deltaware, gamemasters should not permit starting characters access to it.

Legality

The majority of current nanotechnology systems are heavily patented, and possession without the appropriate licenses is a significant infringement of intellectual property laws. Perhaps more significant than this, however, is a lingering perception of nanotech as a highly dangerous technology in the wake of the Renraku Arcology debacle.

Most personal-augmentation nanoware systems are legal if the possessor carries an appropriate permit. Other implementations of nanotechnology often meet with less approval from local authorities. Nanite systems can range in legality from fully legal to Class B Controlled Substances (Legality Rating Y), depending on the local government and the capabilities of the system in question. In particular, authorities tend to frown upon nanotechnology capable of self-replication.

On a corporate level, unlicensed possession of proprietary nanotechnology is a more serious offense, and few corporations will openly supply pirated nanotech to any but their most trusted agents.

INSTALLATION

Each type of nanoware has different requirements for installation.

Fixed systems require surgery to implant, using the same rules as cyberware implantation (see p. 146) or transimplation, depending on whether they are being fixed to cyberware or an organ.

Free-floating nanoware requires no surgery to install—a considerable advantage over other methods of physical augmentation. Introducing free-floating nanite systems into the body merely involves an injection followed by a brief hospital stay—one day in intensive care followed by two days in regular care (see p. 240, *SR3*). The period in regular care can be reduced to one day by making a Body (6) Test. This period of hospitalization is for monitoring and adjusting the body and nanites.

Characters who do not spend this time in medical care must make a Body (12) Test. If this test succeeds, the nanites are fine, as is the new host body. If the test fails, the character suffers extreme pain (S Stun) as his body rejects the nanites.

Transient systems are usually a simple liquid suspension delivered by injection and thus require no surgery.

NANITE EFFECTIVENESS

Percent Loss	Effect
100% to 50%	Nanite system works properly
49% to 25%	Nanite effectiveness noticeably reduced (see specific nanite system description for game application)
24% to 0%	Nanite system no longer works

Modified Filtration System

Installing nanites into humans is a delicate procedure. Though nanotechnology in *Shadowrun* is relatively reliable, introducing foreign entities into the human body risks disturbing the sensitive balances between physiological systems. Modifications must be made to the body's waste filtration systems, and care must be taken to match the nanites with the body's immune system.

If a free-floating system is intended, a host of minor cybernetic modifications can be made to pre-existing organs. These alterations keep the body from filtering out nanites like other waste and cellular "detritus." Without this cyberware, called nanite facilitators (p. 90), the long-term effectiveness of free-floating nanoware systems is limited.

Immune System Tailoring

This process tailors the nanites to the host's immune system to avoid raising an immune response—which would otherwise quickly render the nanites useless. Therefore, all nanites interacting directly with the body are specifically tailored to mimic the immune markers the body uses as its "identification tags."

All free-floating nanotech systems are customized to match the immune markers of their host. In many respects this matching is like blood-typing, and since people have more than seventeen different molecular factors determining cellular identity, it is not a simple matter of taking a nanite package off the shelf and injecting it. The need for nanite personalization is responsible for the high cost of free-floating nanoware and makes an illicit nanotechnology clinic a risky proposition for the customer. Any mismatches in immunotyping would be detected during the period of hospitalization following implantation. The pathogenic defense bioware implant and nanites can work together just fine as long as the match is made and adjusted in the post-injection stage.

Transient systems don't need this kind of camouflage because the immune response when these nanites are activated is a comparatively minor price to pay for the useful function they serve. Also, for some systems it is desirable that the nanites eventually lose their effectiveness.

Manx wants to maintain his edge, and cyberware's just not enough anymore. So he makes a few discreet inquiries after reading about nanoware in Street Sam's E-Monthly. *A few discreetly placed bits to his contacts, and he's lucky enough to find a semi-reliable lab. The usual deal of how Manx will scratch their back if they "upgrade" his flesh is made, and Manx is ready for the injection.*

Because these are the first pieces of nanoware being installed in Manx, he needs to have a little cyberware as well—the nanite facilitators (see p. 90) are essential if he wants his nanoware to last more than a couple of days. Manx already has a topflight blood filtration system (see p. 300, SR3*), so it doesn't cost him any extra Essence, just money. And now he can get whatever nanoware he chooses.*

For now, all Manx wants is nantidotes to combat Neurostun VIII. His nantidotes are a free-floating system, so he doesn't require any surgery. The doc injects the serum and dispatches Manx to the clinic's recovery wards for monitoring. Manx rolls two sixes on his Body Test, so he spends a day in intensive care and one day in regular care. Then he's back on the street and no longer has to fear the riot police for the next month or so.

NANITE LOSS

Nanites are not permanent like bioware or cyberware, although they are longer-lasting and do not have the addiction penalties of chemicals and compounds. Nanites are transitory and will degrade, get flushed out or get crushed in the microscopic mixmaster of a metahuman's circulatory system.

The type of nanite in the system, the length of time it's there and bleeding are all factors that can reduce the effectiveness of the nanite's performance. Since there are millions of microscopic entities in one implantation, nanites can function even when some loss has occurred.

Nanite effectiveness is measured as a percentage of lost nanites. Implanted nanoware loses a percentage of nanites due to time and bleeding. Each loss is cumulative until the nanites no longer work.

Nanite loss is noticeable when their numbers are reduced below 50 percent. This reduced effectiveness has game applications, and each nanite "breed" has its own signs of degrad-

NANITE LOSS

	Transient	Free-Floating without Facilitator	Free-Floating with Facilitator
Per Box of Physical Damage	–5%	–5%	–5%
Time	–10% per day	–3% per day	—

ing. Any nanite breed that has losses of 75 percent or greater is ineffective, and all benefits are lost.

Time

Time is the biggest factor in loss of nanites. Systems cannot self-replicate in the human body without impeding their intended function or causing parasitic damage to the host body. Therefore, all nanites will eventually be cycled out of the body, regardless of preventative measures. Each nanite type has a length of time that it remains working in the body. This is measured by the percentage of nanites lost per time period. That percentage can be found in the Nanite Loss Table.

If the character has a free-floating system supported by a nanite facilitator, he does not suffer a percentage loss over time.

Bleeding

Nanites are carried by the blood system, but shadowrunners have a distressing tendency to leak blood all over the landscape, thus causing a corresponding loss of nanites. For each box of physical damage a character suffers there is a 5 percent loss of nanites.

While some physical wounds may not cause actual blood loss, nanites are also lost in clots, hemorrhaging, and through bruising.

Healing has no effect on nanite loss. While it removes the physical damage, it does not restore lost nanites.

Excessive Nanoware

If more than two free-floating nanoware systems are introduced into a body at the same time, every system after the second fails to operate. Additionally, each system already in place suffers a 25 percent loss for each additional nanoware system introduced beyond the limit of two.

Spock-O made a deal with the devil—or, to be more precise, with a megacorp. They hook him up for a free-floating nanite treatment called nanosymbiotes that help to heal him. They will stay in his system long enough so he can go on a little run for his new bosses. The run takes place three days later, so Spock-O has already lost 9 percent (3 percent per day) of his nanites. No problem, because the nanosymbiotes are still working. Spock-O gets into a firefight in the lab and suffers a Moderate Physical wound. That's 15 percent more nanites lost (5 percent per box of damage). That means Spock-O has lost 26 percent of his nanite treatment.

After stealing what his bosses wanted, he is shot again and suffers a Serious Physical wound. That's a loss of 30 percent of his remaining nanites (6 boxes of damage). He has now lost more than half of his nanites, and the nanosymbiotes will begin to show reduced effectiveness.

Maintenance

There are two primary ways to maintain nanite levels: periodic replenishment treatments from weekly to twice-yearly, depending on the nanites installed, or installation of a nanite hive (see p. 91).

A character does not have to wait to heal before injecting new nanites; he can get them replaced immediately if he so desires.

THERMOGRAPHIC DETECTION

Like every other machine, nanites require energy to function, and many nanoware systems have a comparatively high-energy output. Operational nanoware (particularly fixed-point and transient nanites) can also produce symptoms similar to a mild fever—sweating, accelerated heart rate and elevated body temperature. Gamemasters should apply a –1 target number modifier to any thermographic detection or Sensor Tests against a character with active nanites. This includes all transient and free-floating nanoware, and fixed nanites when activated.

NANOWARE DETECTION

Nanoware is very difficult to detect. A nano scanner must be used. This is standard gear in hospitals and clinics. The target number for detecting nanoware can be found on the Nanoware Detection Table. A test must be made for each nanite system.

NANOWARE DETECTION TABLE

Type of Nanoware	Target Number
Fixed (inactive)	10
Free-floating	6
Transient	8
If the system is working below 50%	+1
If the system is not working (below 25%)	+3

An individual with a sound understanding of this science—which deals with the composition, structure, reactions and properties of matter—is like an accomplished sculptor with a mound of clay. He has the material he needs to create.

THE BASICS

In 2061, chemistry has a direct impact on daily life. It is a field widely researched by the corporations that drive the world's economy, especially the megacorps. Advances have improved medicine, fuel, energy and construction materials. Chemists are called upon to produce numerous compounds used to build, heal, protect and destroy.

In the world of *Shadowrun,* the applications of chemistry are divided into three main areas: pharmaceutical, industrial and alchemical. Pharmaceutical science involves medicines and compounds that affect body chemistry, including poisons. Industrial chemistry deals with just about every other mundane use of the science, from manufacturing cleaning products and plastics to creating new corrosives and superconductors. Alchemy became important following the Awakening in addressing compounds and magical effects.

Shadowrunners know that chemical technology is useful, perhaps even lifesaving. In the course of their adventures they will discover that the chemical sciences can be exploited by anyone with the right skills. Tools are inexpensive and readily available, and most chemicals are easy to obtain or manufacture. Some compounds can be found under the kitchen sink in the guise of traditional household products. And despite corporate and government attempts to restrict various materials, a skilled chemist can produce explosives and toxins from over-the-counter cleaning agents.

APPLIED INDUSTRIAL CHEMISTRY

Chemical products abound in modern industry—from the lubricant that greases machine gears to the plastic used to wrap the final product. Scientific breakthroughs continue to have a significant impact on industry and society. For example, plasteel and similar polymer-based alloys enjoy widespread use because they are lightweight and impenetrable, making them an integral component in vehicles, buildings and armor. Piezoelectric compounds, which twist and bend when voltage runs through them, have

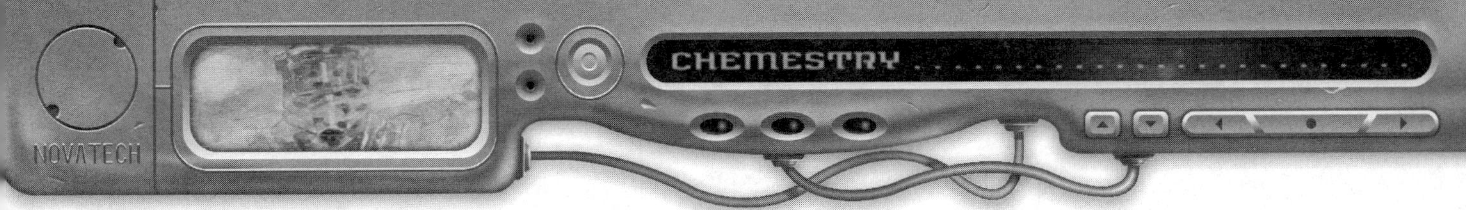

made the use of "smart" materials in vehicles and other devices more commonplace. Optical chips, which are a cornerstone of modern electronics, rely on the chemical reactions of bacteriorhodopsin, a photosynthetic organic pigment. Many security guards are equipped with chemical weapons and crowd-control gases and foams. The pollution and other toxic wastes that result from industrial chemical applications are discreetly hidden when possible or subjected to chem-based "environmental cleanings" when brought to the public eye.

The corporations responsible for these and similar products exploit them to their fullest. Megacorp equipment and gear are often built using state-of-the-art compounds, which are slowly and purposefully leaked to smaller corporations and eventually wind up in household goods.

Like other research, applied chemistry is rife with corporate espionage. Any company with a "chemical edge" has a lead on the rest of the pack. Competition is keen in discovering and manufacturing rare elements, as the conflict over molybdenum mining rights has proved. Orbital chemistry is also a growing field, as its remoteness promises security while the advantages of microgravity suggest interesting possibilities.

IN THE SHADOWS

Shadowrunners and underworld figures have found many uses for chemical technology. Though expensive, chemical weapons can be handy for a team wishing to take the opposition by surprise. A chemistry shop can provide a skilled runner with the means to break into a facility (corrosives), maneuver a drone past the guards (smart materials) and even blow the place apart (explosives). Like the corps, the shadows are constantly experimenting with chemtech, improvising new uses and finding unexpected applications.

PHARMACEUTICALS

A moral and ethical gap has developed between "medicine" and "drugs." *Medicine* largely refers to chemicals of a beneficial nature, while the term *drug* is often assigned to compounds that lead to self-indulgence and self-destruction. Most drugs have some medicinal properties, but they are often used excessively, and they are addictive. The difference between toxins and medicine is mostly a matter of dosage. For example, when used in low concentrations, many poisons are useful in treating certain ailments. Any medicine can become toxic when administered in excess.

CATEGORIES

Pharmaceutical chemicals can be broken down into several broad categories:

Stimulants quicken physical or mental activity and vary from broad-spectrum (adrenaline) to narrow-focused (digitalis, which stimulates heart muscles, or diuretics, which stimulate the kidneys). A stimulant requires a certain amount of "reserve energy" in the organ to be effective. Using a stimulant in the absence of such a reserve is akin to whipping a fatigued horse. Overuse of stimulants leads to massive exhaustion, as the body taxes itself until all its energy is drained. Repeated overuse invites death.

Tranquilizers suppress mental and physical activity and are known for their addictive calming effect. Tranquilizing drugs include narcotics, sedatives and hypnotics. A sedative reduces the activity of the nervous system (diminishing excitement and irritability); hypnotics aim to produce sleep; and general tranquilizers, such as sedatives, squelch mental stress. Narcotics are on the borderline between sedatives and hypnotics, relieving pain while inducing sleep. The results of substance-abuse research show that tranquilizing drugs are the most commonly misused chemicals—even more than hallucinogens.

Hallucinogens alter mental and emotional processes. They have been used throughout history as mind and sensory enhancers, and they are potentially the most dangerous of all drugs. Many hallucinogenic drugs carry additional side effects—psychotomimetic action being among the most distressing. Psychotomimetic drugs stimulate mental illness, eventually causing permanent mental trauma, brain dysfunction and neurosis. Hallucinogens and psychedelics are commonly referred to as "escapist" drugs, allowing the user to flee into a world of sensory splendor. In actuality, they are letting their advocates "escape" only into neurological oblivion.

Other pharmaceuticals are placed under the catchall category of *utility compounds.*

USE OF PHARMACEUTICALS

In *Shadowrun,* pharmaceuticals are primarily used to treat injuries and can be found in hospitals and in portable medkits. They are also used by security agencies and shadowrunners and are part of the street drug culture.

Street Drug Use

Though still widespread, the use and abuse of illegal street drugs have declined following the introduction of simsense and Better-Than-Life chips. BTLs provide a more intense "high" than all but the most potent of street drugs, and they are less detrimental to the addict's health.

Some drug syndicates work hard to compete with simsense and BTLs. As a result, many of the latest street drugs are more potent and addictive, so that the users are more easily hooked. The price of street drugs is kept low, making them more attractive to individuals strapped for cred—and there's no need for a chipjack or simdeck. Just to keep things interesting, the cartels have made a significant effort to market drugs synthesized from Awakened plants, which frequently have strange and unusual side effects.

A high percentage of street drug users come from the corporate ranks, as the suits seek a way to escape from the stress of their careers. Designer drugs and so-called "smart drugs" are especially popular, as are stimulants that help the users cope with their fast-paced lifestyles. While many corps frown on drug activity, perhaps even conducting regular drug testing, others encourage it—either turning a blind eye or even providing corp-sponsored substances at a discount so their execs can stay on the edge. Rumors also abound that certain corps covertly dose their employees through tainted food, water and air, though most such claims are merely malicious rumormongering (or so the corp news tells us).

DUCT FIVE
5
GOBI
SATAN'S BREATH

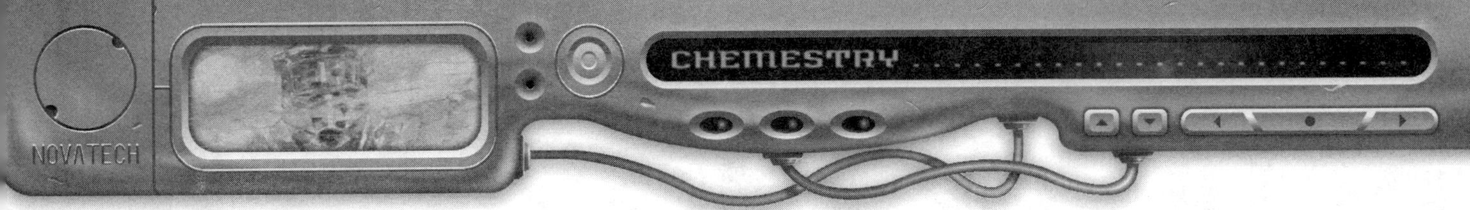

Hallucinogenics are popular among some of the Awakened, particularly shamans and those from tribal backgrounds who use them for meditation, rituals and vision quests. Natural organic hallucinogenics are preferred over synthetic substances, and most such users practice restraint in their drug use.

Security Uses

Never ones to let a good chemical go to waste, the corps rely on pharmaceuticals as part of their security measures. Many companies do not have the resources or won't spend the money to equip and train a sizable security force. As an alternative, they turn to tailored amphetamines to give their men that extra edge and keep them competitive with their cybernetically enhanced and biologically augmented opponents. It is more economical to use "pumped-up" men than to arm security guards with bioware and cyberware, which cost thousands of nuyen. Few guards dosed in this fashion live long enough to apply for the medical severance their employers offer.

Corp security forces are frequently armed with tranquilizers. Individuals who manage to penetrate a complex's perimeter defenses can be neutralized by these chemicals—which are more cost-effective and efficient than mobilizing security teams and risking employee injury and property damage. If prisoners are taken, pharmaceuticals that function like truth serums are employed to get to the bottom of the break-in.

CHEMISTRY AND ALCHEMY

Following the Awakening, chemistry and magic were combined, bringing about a renewed interest in the ancient discipline of alchemy.

RADICALS AND ORICHALCUM

Magical "radicals"—arcane compounds used in the creation of enchanted items—are formed through a complex process that combines magic and chemistry and that astounds traditional scientists. Researchers try to explain the process, and corporations attempt to exploit it. However, all attempts to employ alchemy in mass production have failed—the art requires weeks of personal attention and direct involvement from an Awakened alchemist. Nevertheless, many megacorps continue to pursue methods of replicating alchemical processes in the hopes of someday mass-producing compounds with esoteric and useful properties.

Even more intriguing is the substance known as orichalcum, which seems to defy scientific laws by its very elemental composition. Its method of production has been intensely scrutinized, but all attempts to replicate it through mundane methods have failed. Added to this mystery are persistent but unlikely rumors of orichalcum appearing naturally in secluded and well-guarded areas. Most scientists, including many alchemists, regard this as an impossibility.

Alchemy is discussed in detail under *Enchanting*, p. 39, *Magic in the Shadows*.

MAGICAL COMPOUNDS

In remote areas rich with magical power, tribal shamans have discovered how to use Awakened plants to bestow magical effects that are similar to those enjoyed by Awakened creatures. The cultivation methods vary among the tribes, though it is most likely accomplished via tightly guarded metamagical techniques.

The plants play an important role in the tribe's spiritual beliefs and rituals. For example, the Anasazi bands living deep within the Mojave Desert consider these plants their "spiritual helpers," bestowed to aid them as caretakers and protectors of the land. The Anasazi view the use of these plants as part of their birthright and fiercely protect the secrets of where they grow and how they are cultivated. In fact, any tribal member who reveals this information to outsiders risks being put to death.

Because of their controlled nature, these magical plant compounds are in high demand by researchers, many of whom hope to synthesize the plants' active chemicals. As of yet, few formal studies have been made.

THE POWER PLAYERS

At some point, every multinational turns to chemistry, if only to reduce manufacturing costs. No large corporation can avoid employing the science.

NECK AND NECK: S-K AND Z-IC

The two chemical giants in 2061 are Saeder-Krupp (S-K) and Zeta-ImpChem (Z-IC). A decade ago, Z-IC was the largest chemical manufacturer in Europe, if not the world. Its only real competition was from AG Chemie Europa—of which Z-IC owned a significant chunk. Z-IC made the mistake, however, of trying to expand its focus and muscle Transys Neuronet out of its cyberware research niche—an effort that failed. While they were pre-occupied, S-K quietly capitalized on every opportunity that Z-IC missed. Before Z-IC realized the threat, S-K had become the world's largest producer of chemical goods.

Z-IC has a reputation for ruthlessness. It is known for illicit medical testing, dumping toxic chemicals and pushing out products that either haven't been properly tested or that are suspected of being harmful—such as they did in the Polydopa scandal of '42.

S-K is diversified, covering almost every branch of chemical research. Its connections with the remnants of the old petroleum industry hierarchy and its orbital factories and lunar mining operation give it distinct advantages.

SECOND TIER

AG Chemie Europa

A conglomerate of large chemcorps, AG Chemie claims an impressive array of specialized subsidiaries. Its primary strength lies in pharmaceutical production and plastic engineering, and it has built an impressive empire within Greater Frankfurt—which for all practical purposes it owns. As a competitor, AG Chemie's edge is dulled, as its primary opposition (S-K and Z-IC) both own controlling shares in several of AG Chemie's core companies.

Mitsuhama Computer Technologies

MCT focuses on the application of industrial chemicals, specifically in robotics and other heavy industry. They are the foremost developers of piezoelectric smart materials used in drone and vehicle construction. Their magical research divisions have an interest in synthesizing magical compounds, but with little success to date.

Shiawase

Shiawase is known for its rare-metal mining projects and is a major supplier of raw materials for industries. Almost as diversified as S-K, Shiawase has developed many useful agricultural chemicals and has delved deeply into narcotics research—which has generated a number of interesting products and rumors.

Yakashima

Yet another mining and pharmaceuticals giant, Yakashima has made a fortune by developing chemicals for the military, from fuel-air explosives to war gases to lightweight armor polymers.

SPECIALISTS

Aztechnology

No one churns out optical chips like the Azzies do, and the chips have been a core of their business empire for years. They are also breaking ground with research and distribution of combat drugs, allegedly tested extensively in their Yucatan conflict.

Debeers-Universal Omitech

Boasting the development of Dikotė and related materials, Debeers-UO is the leader in carbon coating and diamond industrial tools.

United Oil Industries

One of the longest-lived petrochemical corps, UniOil is responsible for many of the refinement techniques and tools widely used today. The company has recently expanded into researching other chemical fuel methods, with limited success.

DRUG RULES

Drugs, including medicines and toxins, affect characters as described under *Diseases and Toxins*, p. 249, *SR3*. The following rules expand upon that, clarifying how drugs work and detailing several additional attributes and ratings gamemasters can use to determine their effects upon characters.

DOSAGE

In *Shadowrun*, drugs and other compounds are measured in units called *doses*. A dose is a generic quantity of the substance necessary to produce an effect. In real life, the actual amount of any given dose can vary. For game purposes, it is simpler to keep the amount abstract. A single dose can be considered an amount equivalent to the liquid in a needle, a shot from a squirtgun or the gas inhaled during a single Combat Turn.

DRUG ATTRIBUTES

Each drug has four Attributes that determine how it affects a character: Vector, Damage Code, Speed and Effects.

Vector

The exposure vector is the method by which the drug is administered. Only four vectors are possible: contact, ingestion, inhalation and injection.

Contact: This drug works by touch. In effect, it is absorbed through the skin and works its way into the character's bloodstream. Liquid chemicals can soak through clothes and armor, seeping into the skin.

Ingestion: This drug is swallowed and absorbed through the character's stomach lining into the bloodstream.

Inhalation: This is inhaled and absorbed into the character's bloodstream through the lungs.

Injection: This drug must be physically injected into the bloodstream to affect the character.

Damage Code

A drug's Damage Code is broken down into Power and Damage Level, just like other Damage Codes (p. 114, *SR3*). However, there are differences, and these are noted.

Power: A drug's Power is used as the target number for any Damage Resistance Tests against the chemical's effects. Depending on how a target is exposed to the drug, the drug's Power can be altered (see *Drug Effects*).

Damage Level: This indicates the severity of the damage inflicted by a single dose of the chemical. It cannot be staged up, though it can be staged down. Increased dosage can increase the Damage Level (see *Additional Dosage*, p. 106).

Speed

This refers to the period of time between when exposure occurs and the target begins suffering damage and other effects from the chemical.

Effects

Many drugs have side effects in addition to physical damage. Unless otherwise stated, these are applied to any character exposed to the drug—even if the character resists any physical damage the compound inflicts. The effects can be mitigated by the extent of the character's exposure.

DRUG EFFECTS

To determine how a drug affects a character, use the following rules, which expand upon the details given in *SR3*.

Determine Exposure

To determine if a character is exposed to a drug, consult the drug's Vector and judge whether it is applicable.

Depending upon the extent of the exposure, the gamemaster might choose to raise or lower the drug's Power. For example, if a character places a wet rag over his mouth and nose to avoid breathing in a drug with an inhalation vector, the drug's Power could be reduced. If a character falls into a vat filled with a drug with a contact vector, the drug's Power could be altered by as much as +4.

The Exposure Modifiers table provides for various situations.

Chemsuits: As described on p. 293, *SR3*, each chemsuit has a rating. This rating reduces the Power of any drug or toxin deployed against the chemsuit's coating and air filter.

Envirosealed Armor: Security armor fitted with environmental controls (p. 284, *SR3*) protects the wearer from contact-vector compounds. The installed respirator protects as described below.

Hazmat Gear: As described on p. 116, hazmat and X-E suits protect the wearer from contact and inhalation vector compounds. Gas masks protect the wearer from inhalation vector attacks.

Respirators: Though equipped with their own air supply, respirators are not completely sealed against gases. Reduce the Power of any inhalation-vectored compounds by 2 and the Damage Level by one.

EXPOSURE MODIFIERS

Vector and Situation	Power Modifier
Contact	
Full body exposure	+4
Fireman's coat/semi-protective gear	–2
Chemsuit	–Rating
Ingestion	
Character vomits before Speed	–4
Stomach pumped before Speed	–8
Inhalation	
Wet rag over nose and mouth	–1
Chemsuit air filter	–Rating
Respirator	–2 (also –1 Damage Level)

Exposure Via Weapons

Some weapons—from dartguns to squirtguns—are designed to expose characters to drugs. Only drugs with a contact vector (squirtguns, coated blades) or injection vector (dartguns, needles) can be used in this way. If the attacker strikes the target and the target does not completely dodge the attack, he is considered exposed to the drug and must resist its effects.

Good attacks—those with many successes—will more fully expose the target, such as contacting more skin or piercing a good vein. Conversely, poor attacks—those with few successes—will limit exposure, such as only splashing the target or missing primary veins.

Successes from the attack can raise the drug's Power by 1 for every 2 successes. If the attack method also causes damage (a blade coated with a drug, for example), any successes cannot be used to stage up the weapon's Damage Level.

Impact armor worn by the target will reduce a drug's Power by half the armor rating, rounded down.

Coated Blades: Blades can only be coated with a single dose; once a target is struck, the dose is used.

Called Shots: A character can intentionally target a non-armored body part. A successful called shot nullifies any Impact armor worn. If the weapon used also causes damage, the called shot modifier can either negate armor *or* stage the weapon's Damage Level.

Body Resistance Test

A character exposed to a drug makes a Damage Resistance Test using Body to resist the drug's effects once the Speed period has passed. If the drug's Speed is instantaneous, the character resists it at the end of that Combat Turn.

If the drug is delivered via a damage-causing weapon, the character makes two Damage Resistance Tests—one immediately for the weapon and one for the drug after the Speed period has passed. Combat Pool can be used for both tests; any spent applies toward both. Combat Pool must be spent when the attack is made, even if the drug doesn't take effect until later.

Gordie accidentally startles a woman who mistakes him for a mugger. She whips out a can of pepper punch (contact and inhalation vectors) and sprays him, getting 3 successes. Gordie uses half his Combat Pool to dodge but manages only 2 successes. He's been pepper-sprayed!

The pepper punch has a Speed of 1 Combat Turn, meaning it won't actually affect Gordie until the end of the following Combat Turn. If the Speed was Immediate, he would be resisting it at the end of this Combat Turn. Just in case, Gordie allocates his three remaining Combat Pool dice right now to help resist its effects later. Lucky for him, he has no need of them for the rest of this turn.

The aerosol spray inflicts no physical trauma, so Gordie is okay for now. If he had been attacked with a damaging weapon, he would have had to resist that too.

At the end of the next Combat Turn, the pepper punch kicks in. The damage is 12L Stun, but Gordie is wearing 5 points of Impact armor, so that's reduced to 10L (5 ÷ 2 = 2.5, rounded to 2; 12 – 2 = 10). He has a Body of 3, plus the three Combat Pool dice he allocated when sprayed. So he rolls six dice to resist. He cannot use any of his Combat Pool from the current turn. He rolls: 1, 1, 3, 3, 4 and 11—only 1 success. That's not enough to stage it down, so he takes Light Stun.

On top of that, Gordie must also resist the side effects of the pepper punch (described on p. 121). He makes a Body (5) Test, getting only 1 success. That means he will be suffering an additional +4 to all actions for the next eight minutes—ouch!

Applying an Antidote

If an antidote is used before the Speed period has passed, the drug is nullified and the character will not suffer any damage or effects.

If an antidote is applied after the Speed period, the character suffers no further damage from the drug, though other effects still apply at half-potency. Additionally, the character receives a –2 target number modifier bonus for tests made to heal the drug's damage.

Additional Dosage

If a character is exposed to an additional dose before the Speed period has elapsed, stage up the Damage Level of the drug by one. Further doses beyond that will not raise the

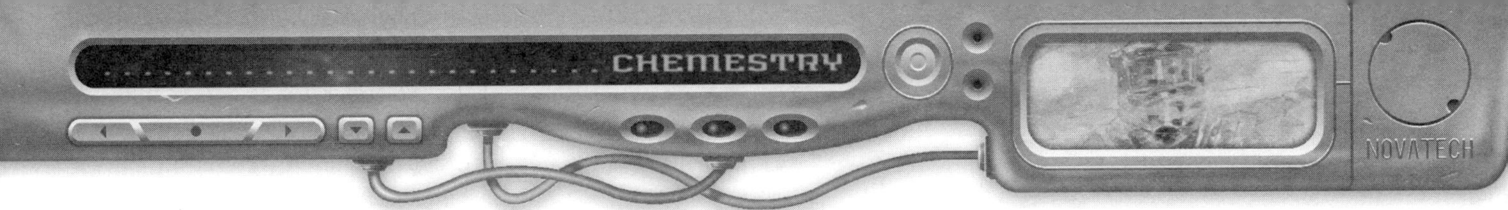

Damage Level but will raise the drug's Power by 1 per additional dose.

If a character is exposed to additional doses after the Speed period has elapsed, the character must make another Body Resistance Test. As long as the character is continuously exposed, he must resist every time the Speed period goes by. However, a character will never suffer more total damage from doses higher than the drug's base Damage Level +1. Once the character has suffered this maximum damage, increased dosages will have no further effects—except for possible overdosing (see below).

Unless otherwise stated, any other effects of the drug will not be modified by additional doses.

Despite his attempts to calm her, the frightened woman sprays Gordie twice more with the pepper punch before the first dose has even kicked in. The second dose raises the Damage Code by one (from L to M), and the third raises the Power by 1 (from 12 to 13). That means Gordie is actually rolling six dice against 13M Stun.

If the woman had instead waited for the first dose to affect Gordie and then sprayed him again, the outcome would be slightly different. Another Combat Turn (the punch's Speed) after suffering the Light Stun, Gordie would again be facing another 12L Stun. As long as the woman keeps spraying him, Gordie will continue to face 12L Stun every Combat Turn. However, Gordie will never suffer more than Moderate Stun damage (the base Damage Level plus 1) total from the pepper punch. Too many doses, however, and he might suffer from a pepper punch overdose!

Overdosing

Extreme amounts of anything can kill a metahuman. The exact point at which "a lot" becomes "too much" and causes toxicity varies, depending on the substance in question. It is the gamemaster's call to decide when this point is reached and when to start applying additional damage to the character. As a general guideline, inflict an extra box of damage every (Body) dose.

WORKING WITH CHEMICALS

A character with the Chemistry Skill and the right tools can be a useful asset, manufacturing a number of essential compounds.

CHEMICAL TOOLS

Like other tools (p. 288, *SR3*), chemistry equipment can be found in kits, shops, and facilities. They have a Cost multiplier of x 3.

Chemistry Kits

In addition to a number of basic chemicals and handling tools (gloves, goggles, beakers, tubes, Bunsen burners and so on) and a reference library, kits feature built-in chemical analyzers and gas spectrometers (which function like the cyberware, p. 13) with a Rating 3 reference program.

Chemistry Shops and Facilities

Chemistry shops and facilities can perform the same function as a chemkit, and they feature a wider array of equipment. They can synthesize and create compounds, assuming the base elements are present and the shop's software knows the formula.

To control the production of compounds that are highly dangerous, explosive or toxic (basically, any compound with a Legality Rating), chemical shops and facilities have a Legality Rating of 2P–X and are required by law to incorporate security features to prevent unauthorized users from handling the equipment.

Shops and facilities also have built-in safety features that act as a Rating 3 chem sniffer (p. 292, *SR3*), constantly scanning for noxious or toxic chemicals in the air.

HOME COOKING TABLE

Compound	Target Number	Base Time
Street drugs	4	24 hours
Designer drugs	6	48 hours
Toxin	4	6 hours
Improvised grenade	6	12 hours
Plastic explosives	8	48 hours
Fuel-air explosive	8	72 hours

MAKING CONTROLLED SUBSTANCES

Chemistry tools are used to synthesize controlled substances, from explosives to pharmaceuticals to corrosives. Enterprising shadowrunning teams with the right skills and gear are likely to take advantage of this fact, so gamemasters should be prepared to improvise costs, target numbers and base times—based on the difficulty of the work.

In most cases, the Knowledge Skill of Chemistry would be used for such tasks, as the character's knowledge of the chemicals and procedures involved is what counts. However, any task involving the manufacture of explosives requires the Demolitions Skill, though Chemistry can be used as a Complementary Skill for such tests. A chemistry shop or facility may also be necessary.

The first step, of course, would be obtaining any necessary ingredients. Depending on the substances, this could be an adventure in itself. Some key chemicals might be heavily restricted, or just plain rare. Some that can be used to create explosives are mixed with trace elements, nanites or even radioactive isotope markers, which can be traced back to the source by investigators.

The next step is obtaining a formula. If the correct ratios and mixtures are not available, the experiment could go awry. While most explosive and illegal drug recipes are restricted, they are readily available from Shadowland and other Matrix sources.

When assigning target numbers for such tasks, the gamemaster can use the Difficulty Number Table (p. 92, *SR3*) or base it off the examples on the Home Cooking Table, below. Appropriate modifiers, such as those given on the Build/Repair Table (p. 95, *SR3*), should be applied.

SUBSTANCE ABUSE

All drugs, whether a chemical, BTL, or other addictive substance, have several ratings.

Addiction Rating: This number denotes the potency of the substance's addictive qualities. It is used as a target number for tests to resist addiction. The higher the number, the more easily it can hook characters.

Addiction Code: Addiction can be physical (P), mental (M), or both. The Addiction Code indicates how the drug is addictive, appearing after the Addiction Rating. A drug can have separate ratings and codes. Mental addictions are resisted with Willpower, and physical addictions are resisted with Body. Mental dependence usually stems from the emotional gratification derived from use of a drug. Physical addiction is a much "harder" addiction and results from the body becoming dependent on the substance for its continued "survival."

Tolerance: This measures how easy it is to become "immune" to the effects of the substance. The higher the number, the easier it is to develop a tolerance.

Edge: This rating indicates the ease with which dependency (addiction) and immunity (tolerance) are acquired in long-term use of the drug. The number to the left of the slash indicates pre-addiction Edge, and the number to the right measures post-addiction. Every time the number of applications taken equals a multiple of the compound's (pre- or post-) Edge Rating, add 1 to both the Addiction and Tolerance Ratings. The higher the number, the slower the build-up.

Fix Factor: The Fix Factor is the maximum period that can go by before an addict must get another "fix" of the drug.

BECOMING ADDICTED

The first time a character uses an addictive substance, he must make a test to determine if he becomes addicted. The character uses unaugmented Willpower (if mentally addictive) or Body (if physically addictive) against a target number equal to the substance's base Addiction Rating. It takes only one success to remain unaddicted (if the substance is both physically and mentally addictive, make a separate test for each one). If the test fails, the character becomes addicted to the substance. A dwarf receives +2 Body dice for resisting physical, but not mental, addiction.

If a character continues to take the substance, the odds for addiction increase. When a number of doses equal to the pre-addiction Edge Rating have been taken, the drug's Addiction and Tolerance Ratings each rise by 1. For example, if the drug's pre-addiction Edge Rating is 5, every fifth dose adds 1 to both ratings. These modifiers are cumulative, so the more the substance is sampled, the more likely it is that the character will get addicted or develop a tolerance.

When the Addiction Rating is raised, the character must make another Body or Willpower Test against the modified Addiction Rating. If the test fails, the character becomes addicted. Once addicted, the Addiction Rating reverts to the base rating +1.

Twitch has been taking lots of Cram (Addiction 4M, Edge 5/50) to boost his combat abilities. The first hit didn't hook him, as he easily made the TN 4 with his Willpower of 5. On his fifth use, the Addiction Rating is raised +1 to 5, and he must make another Willpower (5) Test. Again, he makes it.

Skipping ahead another 10 doses, the modified Addiction Rating has been raised to 7. Twitch rolls 1, 2, 2, 2, and 5. He fails and is now mentally hooked on Cram! Now that he is addicted, the Addiction Rating reverts to the base rating (4) +1, or 5.

GETTING A FIX

Once addicted, the character must use the substance regularly to fulfill his craving. The substance's Fix Factor determines the maximum time period a character can go between doses. This period can be extended once by making a successful Body/Willpower Test—both, if necessary—against the current Addiction Rating. If successful, the character can skip a Fix Factor period before craving another dose.

If a character fails to get a dose in time, he goes into immediate withdrawal (see *Forced Withdrawal*, p. 110).

For each (post-addiction Edge) number of uses, a substance's Addiction and Tolerance Ratings increase by 1. Further use by the character will continue to increase these ratings.

The Fix Factor for Cram is two days. Every two days, Twitch needs another dose. If necessary, he can extend that period to four days with a successful Willpower (6) Test (6 being the Cram's modified Addiction Rating for him).

ACQUIRING A TOLERANCE

Starting with the first time a character uses a drug—and every time the Tolerance Rating of the drug is raised for that character (every Edge number of uses)—the character must make a Body (Tolerance) Test to determine if he has developed a tolerance. If the character fails to roll any successes, he has become immune to the substance. Once immune, the substance will no longer appease the character's craving. A stronger version (higher base Addiction Rating) becomes necessary for the character to get his fix. This can be a new variant of the drug, or it can be a more addictive drug of the same general type (amphetamine, barbiturate, BTL and so on). Doubling the dosage of the current drug will also work, though overdosing is a danger (see *Overdosing*, p. 107).

The modified Addiction Rating for the new drug or increased dosage is equal to the Addiction Rating of the old drug or dosage.

If the character fails to get a stronger drug or dosage, he goes into forced withdrawal (see p. 110).

The tests to determine tolerance are made after the drug has been administered and its effects have worn off.

Note that tolerance to a substance does not necessarily mean the character does not suffer any game effects from using it; it merely means the substance does not satisfy the character's addiction any longer. At the gamemaster's discretion, such drugs might have half their normal effect. For example, if the substance added two dice, a character with tolerance to it would get one die.

After a year of being a Cram junkie, Twitch's Tolerance for Cram has risen to 8. Twitch makes his Body (8) Test, gets a 1, 2, 2, 5 and 7, and fails! This means he has developed a tolerance to Cram. He needs to either switch to something stronger (a base Addiction Rating higher than Cram) or increase his dosage. Twitch decides he'll just increase his dosage for now, meaning that he has to take two doses to get the same effect.

ADDICTION EFFECTS

In addition to cravings, an addicted character must make a Body and/or Willpower (Addiction Rating) Test once a month. If it fails, the character loses one point from Body; this is a permanent loss.

When a character's Body reaches 1, the character will not lose any further points (unless the Attribute is raised). However, the character's Racial Modified Limit and Attribute Maximum (p. 245, *SR3*) for Body are permanently reduced by 1. Additionally, each week after that, the character will either lose one box from either the Physical or Mental Condition Monitor or permanently lose a quarter point of Essence (.25)—the player's choice.

Awakened characters losing Essence this way must check for Magic Loss (see p. 160, *SR3*). If a character's Essence reaches 0, he dies. Boxes taken from the Condition Monitors are taken from the Light end; treat them as boxes filled in by damage. The first box taken from the Condition Monitor affects the character as an omnipresent Light wound and inflicts a +1 modifier to all target numbers. A character filling up 10 boxes of Physical dies; a character filling up 10 boxes of Stun goes into a coma.

At the end of his first month of addiction, Twitch's modified Addiction Rating for Cram is 7. He makes a Willpower (7) Test and easily makes it.

A year later, Twitch's Addiction Rating has risen to 10. He makes his Willpower (10) Test and fails it miserably. He loses a point of Body—ouch!

A few months later, Twitch has hit bottom. His Body has been reduced to 1, and after another week he must choose to lose either Essence or Condition Monitor boxes. Being a samurai, he doesn't have much Essence to lose, so he opts to take a box of physical damage. In gameplay, Twitch has been reduced to a sickly wretch, still eager for his next fix. If he doesn't kick the habit soon, he'll be dead within a few months.

KICKING THE HABIT

At some point, an addicted character might want to "kick the habit." Quitting an addiction is difficult. To begin the process, the character must make a successful Willpower Test against the substance's current Addiction Rating + 1 (if mental), Addiction Rating + 3 (if physical) or Addiction Rating + 4 (if both mentally and physically dependent). This roll can be modified by mitigating external circumstances, such as strong peer support, a long stay at the Mercurial Clinic and so on. Addiction recovery attempts can only be made if the gamemaster believes they are warranted—a player cannot decide that his character is cured without cause.

If the character succeeds, he forces himself to avoid the substance and goes into immediate withdrawal. If the character fails, he caves in and does whatever he can to get his next fix. If other characters physically prevent him from getting his fix, he goes into forced withdrawal.

Twitch has a momentary sanity relapse and realizes he has to get off Cram before it kills him. He makes a Willpower Test to try and kick the drug. His target number for his mental addiction is his current Addiction Rating (13) + 1. He throws some Karma into it and gets a 2, 4, 7, 9 and 17! That day he locks himself in his squat with loads of soykaf and munchies and prepares to ride it out.

Withdrawal

When undergoing withdrawal, the drug's Addiction Rating drops 1 point every two days, assuming the character has the strength and courage to weather the recovery process. Once the rating drops to its base rating (it may never drop below its starting rating), the character is no longer addicted.

During the withdrawal process, all losses from substance abuse are temporarily halted but not removed. In addition, the individual suffers a +2 penalty to all his target numbers (+4 for concentration tasks, including spellcasting). This is due to the ordeal of withdrawal pains and mental/physical shock.

The penalties of withdrawal vanish immediately if a dose of the "required" drug is administered. In that case, however, the recovering character is automatically considered addicted once again, and the drug's current Addiction Rating increases by 1.

With an Addiction Rating of 13, it's going to take Twitch a good 26 days (2 x 13) to kick his habit. That's almost a month with a +2 TN modifier (+4 if concentration is required).

Forced Withdrawal

In other circumstances—perhaps the character cannot obtain the addictive drug in time—he might suffer forced withdrawal. This is not a recovery process, but a failure to satisfy artificially induced substance cravings.

Losses due to addiction accrue throughout a forced withdrawal period. The character could feel physically and emotionally drained and wish he were dead. All his target numbers suffer a +3 performance penalty (+6 to tasks requiring concentration, including spellcasting). Also, the individual is in a state of constant pain and will behave as if suffering from the effects of a persistent Moderate mental wound (cumulative with addiction-caused Stun damage).

The effects and penalties associated with the withdrawal process are immediately removed once a dose of the "required" drug is administered. However, this only reinforces the addiction; the drug's current Addiction Rating immediately increases by 1. Characters undergoing forced withdrawal will do just about anything to get a hit of their desired substance.

For each 24-hour period a character manages to get through without a dose, the drug's current Addiction Rating drops by 1 point. The individual is still considered addicted, however, and will experience forced withdrawal until he is administered a dose. Once the Addiction Rating has dropped to the substance's base rating, the character is no longer addicted.

Magic cannot directly aid in recovering from substance addiction, as such dependency is not—technically—a toxin, a disease or a wound. A spell such as Resist Pain can alleviate the agony associated with forced withdrawal, however.

Before his 26 days are over, Twitch's Cram dealer visits the squat to see why his buddy has been out of touch. The dealer passes Twitch a few free doses of Cram. The gamemaster tells Twitch to make a Willpower Test, which he fails miserably. Twitch can't help himself and takes the dose. Bam—he's back to being addicted, at an Addiction Rating of 14 (13 + 1).

Twitch's friends have had enough of his junkie habits. They stash him inside a safehouse, where they can watch him closely as he goes cold turkey. For 10 days (current Addiction Rating of 14 – base rating of 4), Twitch screams and rants and suffers. He attempts various activities, but his TN mods make everything difficult. Finally, the period ends—and Twitch has gotten over his addiction!

Recovery

Once the character has beaten the addiction, he must rest a length of time equal to the drug's Addiction Rating to restore his physical and mental health. During this time, his shock penalties drop to +1 for his target numbers (+2 for concentration-based activities). The character recovers the damage (lost boxes) on his Condition Monitors at a rate of one physical and one mental box for every three days of rest. Once the rest cycle has elapsed, all performance penalties are removed. Essence and Racial Maximum losses from substance abuse can never be recovered. All other Attribute losses can be improved using standard rules.

Staying Clean

Even after withdrawal and recovery, cravings for the substance may linger. If the character is offered a substance he was recently addicted to, the gamemaster might require him to make a Willpower (Addiction Rating) Test to refuse it. Modifiers for passed time, exceptional therapy, counseling and so forth can be applied. If a character takes a dose, he is immediately addicted again, with +1 to the Addiction Rating.

Given enough time, a Tolerance Rating will also decline, but never below its base rating. Every 30 days minus the pre-addiction Edge of not using that particular drug, decrease the Tolerance Rating by 1. If the character uses the drug again, check again to see if he is "tolerant" to it.

Drug addiction is a very debilitating experience. The best solution is prevention—not to become dependent in the first place.

APPLIED CHEMTECH COMPOUNDS

ACIDS AND CORROSIVES

Most acids are relatively mild; they are used as solvents and generate heat when mixed with water. Typically, it is dangerous to add water to acids, as it causes a reaction in which the acid might froth and splash the area. Mild acids may have some caustic effects on skin; they are particularly dangerous to eyes, and poisonous if taken internally.

Stronger concentrated acids are more dangerous and can cause severe burns. They are highly corrosive, capable of dissolving metals and alloys. Acids must be kept in containers that will not corrode.

If handled properly, acids can be used for creative endeavors such as melting through locks and doors, etching walls or windows, and even as a weapon. Acid burns generate nasty scars and can be used to blind individuals.

Game Effects

For game purposes, each strong acid has a rating that indicates its strength and corrosive power.

When applied as a corrosive to a barrier, compare the acid's rating to the Barrier Rating, as described under *Barriers* (p. 124, *SR3*). The effect occurs at the end of that Combat Turn. A corrosive will continue to eat through a barrier for a number of Turns equal to its rating. This continued corrosion stops when the acid is washed off or a base is applied.

Noxious fumes and smoke can be generated as an acid corrodes something; apply a +4 modifier to anyone in the area who could be affected.

If used as a weapon, a dose of acid inflicts (Rating)M Physical damage. Acid will severely damage worn gear, including armor. Reduce by 1 both the Ballistic and Impact values of any acid-stricken armor.

CARCERANDS

Carcerands are molecular bodies whose structures resemble empty spheres. When created, small amounts of a compound may be trapped within them. The carcerand can then be injected, where it circulates through the organism's system, carrying the chemical. Carcerands are degraded by acids and enzymes within the target organism, and the trapped compound is slowly released into the organism's body. Depending on its composition, a carcerand can degrade as quickly as one hour or as slowly as one year after introduction.

Carcerands are used by those who need regular medication. Rather than taking a periodic shot or pill, they have carcerands injected every few months. Carcerands are also useful as persuasion devices—the target is injected with a toxin-carrying carcerand and forced to do something to receive the antidote in time.

Game Effects

Each carcerand has a delay period. This is the amount of time between when the carcerand is injected and when the compound it contains is released.

Carcerands are not affected by blood filters.

Prices for carcerands are based on their delay periods. They do not include the cost for the compounds the carcerands contain.

DIKOTE™

Dikote is a process that deposits a thin diamond film on any solid surface. The diamond film imparts more structural strength and resilience. Dikoted surfaces are smooth and relatively frictionless, conduct heat well and can be modified to conduct electricity.

Not everything can be glazed with Dikote. The item treated must be able to withstand the heat generated by the plasma used in the glazing process. Cloth and plastic cannot be coated, though ceramics and most metals can.

Game Effects

Dikoting a surface adds 2 to the Barrier Rating and 1 to any ballistic and impact armor. If used to coat a vehicle or drone, Dikote adds 1 to the vehicle's Body and Armor Ratings; it takes up no CF.

When Dikote is used to coat a melee, throwing or projectile weapon, add 1 to the Power of any attack made with the treated weapon. If applied to an edged instrument such as a sword, the weapon's Damage Level is also increased by one. For example, a sword that is normally (STR + 2)M would have a Damage Code of (STR + 3)S if Dikoted.

Barriers use their normal ratings against Dikoted melee weapons (as opposed to the standard double ratings against melee attacks).

Dikoting costs 1,000 nuyen per 100 square centimeters (minimum 1,000 nuyen cost).

DMSO

Dimethyl sulfoxide (DMSO) is a utility chemical with a number of applications, though its most common use is as a carrier that forces the skin to absorb delivered chemicals. DMSO is soluble in acetone, alcohol, ether and water; it is liquid at room temperature and is nonreactive with most other compounds. Upon contact with skin, DMSO, and whatever other compound is dissolved in solution with it, is instantly absorbed into the body.

Game Effects

Any chemical mixed with DMSO is deployable via the contact vector.

Compound	Availability	Cost	Street Index	Legality
Acid (per dose)	(Rating)/6 days	500¥ x Rating	2	6P–X
Carcerands (per dose)	4/10 days	100¥ per day	2	Legal
Dikote	6/14 days	See text	2	Legal

Porous armor (such as armor clothing and Kevlar™ weaves) offers little protection against DMSO, as it soaks right through. Only individuals in fully sealed rigid armor or in protective suits specifically designed to protect against chemical/biological agents are immune to the penetrating effect of DMSO.

DMSO is a necessary ingredient for weapons such as the cybersquirt, SuperSquirt and Cascade (see pp. 41 and 115).

FREEZE FOAM

This coats the target area with a sticky, thick, white foam that begins to harden almost immediately to a solid, dense consistency. Once hardened, the concretized foam restricts movement, though it does remain porous to reduce the risk of suffocation. The solid foam quickly breaks down over a period of hours and can be easily dissolved with a simple solvent.

Freeze foam is used in trauma situations to immobilize broken limbs in protective casts. Riot police use it to incapacitate rioters and to construct foam barricades. Police versions of the foam typically include chemical stain markers that show up under ultraviolet light, so rioters can be identified later.

Game Effects

Medical-purpose freeze foam is dispensed through a handheld spray tank (p. 116). Improvising characters can use the foam to create temporary restraining devices.

Riot freeze foam is dispensed through a high-pressure water cannon (p. 307, *SR3*). Conduct the water cannon attacks as normal. At the end of each Combat Turn, any character struck by the foam must make a Quickness Test against a Target Number of 4 plus the successes made on the attack. Characters who fail become immobilized.

Solidified foam has a Barrier Rating of 12. This is reduced by 1D6 points an hour as the foam breaks down. Applying the solvent dissolves the foam immediately.

The semi-permanent UV dye in riot freeze foam wears off after 1D6 days; scrubbing will not help.

Water cannon freeze foam tanks contain 100 liters (1 liter per "shot").

FUEL-AIR EXPLOSIVES

A fuel-air explosive (FAE) is a devastating weapon. A standard FAE bomb contains a mixture of highly volatile gases under pressure, with an ignition device. When triggered, the gas fuel is released, dispersing over a wide area in a fraction of a second. This cloud is then ignited, creating a powerful area-effect explosion.

Game Effects

FAEs are large bombs, requiring large amounts of fuel to cause extensive damage. Unlike other explosives, FAEs have a blast radius in which the Damage Code is a constant. The blast radius is equal to Rating x (kilograms ÷ 50) in meters and the Damage Code is (Rating x 2)D throughout. Beyond this radius, the Power is reduced by –1 per meter. The *Blast in a Confined Space* rule (p. 119, *SR3*) does not apply to FAEs, but they use twice their Rating against barriers.

The Power of FAEs is reduced by impact armor. The detonator used to trigger a FAE bomb requires a bigger bang, and so costs twice as much as listed in *SR3*.

INSECTICIDES

Popular among agricorps and sprawl residents, insecticides took on a new dimension when the Universal Brotherhood was exposed as a front for insect spirits and the subsequent bug explosion and quarantine in Chicago was reported. Though Chicago allegedly has been "cleaned out," almost every household has a decent stash of insecticide—just in case. Bug hunters have also developed a number of nasty insecticide-based weapons to aid in their extermination projects, including splash grenades and sprayguns.

Game Effects

Though insecticides are irritating to insect spirits and other creatures with Vulnerability (Insecticides), they are more of a nuisance than a danger. Large amounts, such as released from an insecticide spray tank or splash grenade (p. 117), can have minor caustic effects (4L Physical damage). A creature so attacked is likely to either become enraged and go berserk (like a Bear shaman, p. 163, *SR3*) or flee in pain and terror—both options are left to the gamemaster's discretion.

A weapon coated with insecticide that is used against a creature with Vulnerability (Insecticides) increases its Damage Level by one (from Moderate to Serious, for example). This effect also applies to insecticide-laden ELD-AR pellets (p. 115).

High concentrations of insecticide can be toxic to metahumans, and characters might be overcome by strong insecticide fumes. The exact effect is left up to the gamemaster.

OXYGENATED FLUOROCARBONS (P4MO)

The oxygenated fluorocarbon compound known as perfluoro-4-methyl-octahydroquinalidine (P4MO) is widely used as a blood substitute. Its use in emergency situations helps to prevent the mismatching of blood types.

Fluorocarbons like P4MO also exceed the capabilities of the blood's natural hemoglobin as a vehicle for gaseous exchange. In other words, P4MO dissolves a higher percentage of oxygen from the lungs into the blood. When introduced into healthy subjects, P4MO allows them to achieve higher levels of physical performance.

P4MO is purged through perspiration without being metabolized. P4MO has a half-life of about one week, so treatments are not usually effective beyond that period. Replacing the P4MO lost due to half-life deterioration is not recommended until fluorocarbon levels in the blood drop below 25 percent, which occurs about three weeks after initial application. If replaced too early, P4MO dramatically increases the chance of death by "bubble embolism."

Game Effects

P4MO is added to the bloodstream in 5-liter treatments. This treatment adds two dice to all Athletics Tests and effectively doubles the amount of time a person can hold his breath (i.e., 90 seconds instead of 45). This effect lasts one week; after the initial week, all benefits are lost until P4MO levels are replaced.

If P4MO treatments are taken in rapid succession (before the fluorocarbon level decreases—three weeks or less), the character can suffer an embolism and die. Roll 2D6—on a 2, the character dies. Repeated doses increase the chance of embolism by 1. The next roll, the character would die on 2 or 3, and so on.

PLASTISTEEL–7 CATALYST

Many dependable plasteel alloys are on the market, but the alloy known as Plastisteel–7 merits special notice. Developed by a small industrial corp called Plasnetics, Plastisteel–7 was released at competitive prices, and large stockpiles were quickly bought. Shortly after Plasnetics mysteriously went out of business, data hit the shadows that Plastisteel–7 could be destabilized with a special catalyst spray. When the catalyst is applied to Plastisteel–7, the affected area grows warm, bubbles for several minutes and turns into a gooey substance with the consistency of chewing gum. Several hours later it returns to normal.

Naturally, most users of Plastisteel–7 recalled their products. A number of facilities still feature Plastisteel–7 in walls and other structural components, simply because they couldn't afford to replace it.

Game Effects

Plastisteel–7 looks much like other plasteel alloys, so a successful Chemistry or Engineering (8) Test would be necessary to visually identify it.

Any Plastisteel–7 that is sprayed with the catalyst bubbles for 5 minutes; anyone who touches the area during this time suffers 6L damage from heat burns. After this period, the Plastisteel–7 has the consistency of gelatin and can be pushed through. The altered Plastisteel–7 will not stick to anything and will retain its form unless relentlessly mangled out of shape. After 1D6 hours, it returns to its normal state.

The catalyst comes in a spray can containing enough solvent to affect a troll-sized section of wall. Though the formula is hard to come by, a character can easily synthesize it with a chemistry shop, a Chemistry (6) Test and a base time of 8 hours.

Compound	Availability	Cost	Street Index	Legality
DMSO (per dose)	2/12 hrs	10¥ + chemical cost	1.5	Legal
Freeze Foam (per liter)	2/12 hrs	20¥	1	Legal
Solvent (per liter)	2/12 hrs	5¥	1	Legal
FAE Bomb (per kilo)	12/72 hrs	Rating^2 x 5¥	5	2–J
Insecticide (per liter)	Always	10¥	1	Legal
P4MO Treatment (5 liters)	4/48 hrs	4,000¥	1	Legal
Plastisteel–7 Catalyst	10/48 hrs	500¥	1	Legal

RUTHENIUM POLYMERS

Ruthenium polymers undergo a color change with the application of a small voltaic charge. The charge alters the polymer's chemical composition, allowing it to shift between a wide spectrum of hues. Since these polymers are also very durable and can be applied in layers of less than about .1 micron thick, they can be put on virtually any surface without any appreciable loss of flexibility or function. This makes ruthenium polymers useful for chameleon cloaking technology.

A chameleon effect can be achieved by combining ruthenium polymers and imaging scanners. The scanners view the surrounding environment and send the data through an imaging processor. The processed data is then fed to the ruthenium polymer surface so that the surface mimics the color and image of whatever is around it. At least four imaging scanners, strategically placed to receive full surround information, are required for the effect. More scanners give cleaner and more "correct" images.

The imaging processors are quick enough to cloak a walking person, but they are unable to shift fast enough to cloak running people or moving vehicles.

Game Effects

To achieve a cloaking effect, the entire object must be covered with ruthenium. A metahuman can manage this by wearing a ruthenium-covered cloak or body suit.

When activated, the target numbers needed to perceive such a cloaked object are increased by 4. For each extra scanner beyond four, add 1 to the final target number for detection. The maximum modifier attainable is +12.

Ruthenium systems are powered by gel packs with 10 hours' duration; new packs cost 50 nuyen. Ruthenium that covers a vehicle can be powered by the vehicle's power supply.

Radar, thermographic and ultrasonic systems are not affected by the ruthenium's cloaking effect. This means that dwarfs and trolls, ultrasound-using characters and vehicle sensors reduce the target number modifiers of the ruthenium by half, rounding down.

Ruthenium is only effective on stationary or slow-moving targets (6 meters or less a Combat Turn). If a character or vehicle is moving faster, reduce the Perception modifier by 1 for each extra 2 meters/Turn. Exceptionally fast characters or vehicles will likely be more obvious (–2 Perception modifier), as the ruthenium rapidly switches colors in an attempt to keep up with the landscape.

SLIP SPRAY

Developed as a crowd-control device, slip spray is a slick, frictionless gel dispensed by a spray tank, water cannon or splash grenade. Slip spray is a top-quality lubricant that makes any movement extremely difficult. Holding an object coated in slip spray is also challenging.

Slip spray breaks down over a short period and easily washes off.

Game Effects

Any area covered with slip spray is considered difficult ground. A character attempting to move across such a surface must succeed in a Quickness (8) Test or fall prone; vehicles must make a Crash Test (p. 147, *SR3*). Attempting to hold on to a coated item if either the character or item moves requires a Quickness (8) Test as well. This test applies to firing guns that have recoil; apply recoil modifiers to the test.

Slip spray breaks down in 1D3 hours.

SPLAT GLUE

Also known as "tangler," "loogey" and "goober," splat glue is a gooey and sticky adhesive gel designed for nonlethal restraint. Usually launched from specialized splat guns (p. 116), splat glue can be applied on the ground and other surfaces to catch anyone or anything that touches it.

Splat glue is biodegradable and can be dissolved with a special solvent.

Game Effects

Anything that comes into contact with splat glue sticks to it. Removing an object or person from the glue requires a Strength (6) Test. Objects might require several successes to remove.

SPRAY FOAM EXPLOSIVE

This stable explosive is a sticky foam distributed from a simple canister—much like shaving cream. It is similar to plastic explosives in that it is detonated by electric current.

Game Effects

Spray foam explosives are available in cans that hold approximately 4 kilos. The explosives come in three ratings (3, 6 and 12), each equivalent to the commercial and plastic explosives described on p. 283, *SR3*.

THERMITE

Thermite is an incendiary material sometimes used in welding operations. When ignited, thermite burns at extreme-

Compound	Availability	Cost	Street Index	Legality
Ruthenium Polymer	5/14 days	10,000¥/m^2	2	Legal
Imaging Scanner	5/14 days	5,000¥	2	Legal
Slip Spray (per liter)	4/48 hrs	100¥	1	Legal
Splat Glue (per liter)	6/72 hrs	100¥	1	Legal
Solvent (per liter)	2/12 hrs	5¥	1	Legal
Spray Foam Explosive Can	10/48 hrs	Rating x 30¥	2	4–J
Thermite (per kg)	12/14 days	500¥	2	4P–U
Burning Bars	14/21 days	1,000¥	2	3P–U

ly high temperatures and is capable of eating through iron, steel and plasteel.

Sometimes packaged as a "burning bar," it consists of a rod of thermite and compressed oxygen mounted on a "handle" and in a frame. Though difficult to find, burning bars are favored by safecrackers, as they can be used to easily melt holes through thick metal.

Game Effects

Ignited thermite can melt through 5 centimeters of a Rating 12 barrier each Combat Turn. If the Barrier Rating is higher or lower, decrease or increase this amount by the appropriate percentage (for example, it would cut through 2.5 cm of a Rating 24 barrier each Combat Turn).

Thermite burning bars melt a hole 5 centimeters in diameter; thermite formed in other shapes will burn holes sized to those shapes.

Thermite normally burns for 30 seconds (10 Combat Turns). Flammable materials, including clothing and gear, will ignite and catch fire. Any character touching burning thermite suffers 10D damage and will likely catch fire. Fire causes 6M damage at the end of each Combat Turn; increase the Power by +2 per Combat Turn. Burning thermite is both incredibly loud and bright; anyway facing it will suffer a +6 modifier from glare, –1 per 5 meters of distance, and reduced by –1 per turn. Flare compensation will reduce this modifier by half.

CHEMTECH APPLICATION GEAR

ARES SUPERSQUIRT II

Produced by Ares Arms, the SuperSquirt is a popular nonlethal weapon. It features two removable clips, the first being a reservoir of DMSO gel and the second being chemical capsules. Each clip is designed with a different shape, color and grooves, so it cannot be confused and wrongly inserted.

The SuperSquirt uses compressed air technology, making it silent and recoilless. The DMSO and chemical are dissolved together and launched at the target. A solid hit is all that's needed, as the DMSO penetrates most armor and soaks into the skin.

Game Effects

The SuperSquirt counts as a light pistol; a character firing it uses the Pistol Skill. It may be drone-mounted, but it cannot accept any top-, barrel- or under-barrel-mounted accessories.

This weapon uses DMSO (see p. 111) in a reservoir clip, good for 20 shots. The chemical clips contain 20 capsules, or "shots," with each capsule considered one dose. Extra clips of either cost 10 nuyen.

The grip of the SuperSquirt contains a canister of compressed CO_2 that is good for 50 shots. It can be recharged for 50 nuyen.

ARES CASCADE RIFLE

Expanding upon the popular Ares SuperSquirt, the Cascade offers increased range and an expanded reservoir. The Cascade also features a selectable nozzle so the user can choose between a long-range stream and a wide-angle spray.

Game Effects

The Cascade is a rifle version of the SuperSquirt; a character firing it uses the Rifle Skill. The DMSO gel reservoir clips are good for 100 shots; each extra clip costs 20 nuyen. It uses the same chemical clips as the SuperSquirt.

This weapon has two modes: stream and spray. In stream mode, the Cascade has the range characteristics of an SMG. In spray mode, treat the Cascade as a shotgun with an effective choke of 2 (cannot be changed).

The Cascade can be drone-mounted. This weapon accepts all standard top- and under-barrel-mounted accessories, but no barrel-mounted accessories.

ARES ELD-AR ASSAULT RIFLE

Used by the UCAS military and various corporate security forces, the ELD-AR (Encapsulated Liquid Delivery—Assault Rifle) has been a standard in training missions for years. The ELD-AR fires a gel-coated round filled with biodegradable paint or other marking or chemical agents. Its compressed gas canister provides a silent and recoil-free shot, even under burst-fire conditions.

Game Effects

A character firing the ELD-AR uses the Assault Rifle Skill.

The standard ammunition for the ELD-AR is paint rounds, which cost 5 nuyen per 10 rounds. Dye that is normally invisible but shows up under ultraviolet or thermographic vision is also commonly used. Gelcoat rounds can also be fashioned with materials costing 300 nuyen. Self-made rounds can carry any chemical desired, though some chemicals can eat through the pellets or cause some other undesirable reaction.

The ELD-AR creates negligible recoil, which is absorbed by the shoulder stock. Treat the weapon as having a sound suppressor.

The ELD-AR may be drone-mounted. The weapon accepts all standard top- and under-barrel-mounted accessories, but no barrel-mounted accessories.

Refillable compressed air canisters in the stock, each good for 50 shots, power the weapon. Refilling a canister costs 50 nuyen.

Gear	Conceal	Ammo	Mode	Damage	Weight	Cost	Avail.	St. Index	Legality
SuperSquirt II	7	20/20(c)	SA	Special	2	800¥	9/14 days	1.5	6P–E
Cascade	4	100/20(c)	SA	Special	5.5	1,800¥	12/14 days	2	6P–F
ELD-AR	4	50(c)	SA/BF	4L Stun	4.5	950¥	9/7 days	2	Legal
Paint Rounds (per 10)	8	—	—	See rules	.15	5¥	2/24 hrs	1	Legal

DART GUNS

These pistols and rifles deliver chemical-coated darts, most commonly narcoject (p. 250, *SR3*). The darts can effectively pierce most armors.

Game Effects

For range purposes, treat the dart pistol as a light pistol and the dart rifle as a shotgun. A character firing them would use the Pistol or Rifle Skill, respectively.

The dart rounds below do not include the cost of the chemical.

HAZMAT GEAR

In some cases, a standard chemsuit or respirator doesn't provide quite enough protection against hazardous materials (hazmat) and environments. Commercial hazmat suits and military-grade X-E chemsuits are designed to keep the wearer safe from military gases capable of penetrating lesser gear.

Hazmat and X-E suits cover the entire body in thick, specially treated plastics and polymers. The hood features a clear faceplate and several emergency rip patches. Gas masks and air tanks (available separately) provide an hour's worth of breathable air.

Game Effects

A character wearing a hazmat or X-E suit is safe from contact or inhalation vectors, unless the suit is breached. A character wearing a gas mask and air tank is immune to inhalation vectors.

The gloves on hazmat and X-E suits are bulky; apply a +1 to the target number of any action involving finger or hand use, including handling weapons.

If a character suffers damage from projectiles or sharp melee weapons, his suit gets a hole in it. A Complex Action is required to apply a patch, and in the meantime the character may be exposed to outside toxins.

Gas masks and air tanks are not concealable, and they weigh 10 kg.

Hazmat suits provide 1 point of both Ballistic and Impact protection. X-E suits have an Armor Rating of 3/2.

SLAP PATCHES

These are adhesive-backed disks that are applied to the skin and that are coated with a chemical mixed with DMSO (p. 111) to dispense a drug into the user's bloodstream.

Game Effects

Any drug can be mixed onto a slap patch, giving it a contact vector. As described on p. 305, *SR3,* dermal armor and blood filters impede the drug's exposure.

SPLAT GUN

This compressed air gun is used to launch one-liter "rounds" of splat glue (p. 114) at targets. The rounds are packaged in a safety wrap that is ejected upon launch.

Game Effects

A character firing a splat gun uses the Launch Weapons Skill; the weapon uses shotgun ranges. Two characters standing within 1 meter of each other may be targeted simultaneously. Struck targets must make a Body (8) Test to avoid knockdown; they will also be covered in glue and stuck to everything in the immediate vicinity (walls, the floor, gear and so on). The character will be immobilized, requiring a successful Strength (6) Test with a number of successes equal to the net successes generated on the Attack Test to take any physical action.

Refillable compressed air canisters in the stock, good for 50 shots, power the guns. Refilling a canister costs 50 nuyen.

SPRAY TANK

Similar to a fire extinguisher, this is a chemical-filled tank with an attached hose. Designed to be strapped to the back or slung over a shoulder, the tank is triggered by depressing a lever, which admits carbon dioxide into the main tank, forcing whatever chemical is inside out through the hose.

Almost any compound can be stored inside a spray tank, from slip foam to insecticide, for dispersal over a wide area.

Game Effects

The Active Skill Spray Weapons is used to spray the contents of a tank at a target. Spray Weapons Skill is linked to Strength and grouped with Heavy Weapons. Specializations include Firehose, Flamethrower and Spray Tank.

Spray tanks use taser ranges, but their hose nozzles can be adjusted like a shotgun's choke, using shotgun spread rules. Any target that does not completely dodge the attack is hosed; see *Drug Effects,* p. 105.

The carbon dioxide used to power the tank is good for 50 uses; recharging it costs 50 nuyen. Spray tanks hold up to 2 liters of any chemical.

Compound	Availability	Cost	Street Index	Legality
Gas Mask and Air Tank	4/12 hrs	1,000¥	1	Legal
Hazmat Suit	6/1 wk	5,000¥	1.5	Legal
X–E Suit	8/2 wks	15,000¥	2	Legal
Slap Patch	6/72 hrs	50¥ + chemical cost	2	Legal

Gear	Conceal	Ammo	Mode	Damage	Weight	Cost	Avail.	St. Index	Legality
Dart Pistol	7	5(c)	SA	Special	1.5	600¥	6/2 days	2	Legal
Dart Rifle	4	10(c)	SA	Special	3.25	1,700¥	8/2 days	2	Legal
Dart Rounds (per 10)	8	—	—	See rules	.15	200¥	4/48 hrs	2	Legal
Splat Gun	4	2(m)	SS	Special	3	600¥	9/7 days	2	Legal

Z-IC SPLASH GRENADES

Developed by Zeta-ImpChem, these grenades disperse a chemical spray over a wide area. The chemical is often mixed with DMSO (p. 111). A wide range of compounds is available, from gamma-scopolamine to insecticide.

Game Effects

Splash grenades soak everything within a 5-meter radius with their chemical spray. See *Drug Effects,* p. 105 for details on chemical effects. Each grenade holds roughly 1 liter (10 doses) of a compound.

The cost below does not include the chemical's cost.

PHARMACEUTICAL COMPOUNDS

ACTH

Adrenocorticotrophic hormone (ACTH) is a naturally occurring hormone used primarily as a trigger for voluntary activation of the adrenal pump. Packaged in inhalers with six doses, once administered it instantly activates the adrenal pump. Though ACTH is not addictive, a tolerance builds up over time, rendering it ineffective as an external trigger.

Game Effects

When inhaled, ACTH triggers the adrenal pump (p. 63). The cost includes an inhaler with 6 doses.

ANABOLIC STEROIDS

Mimicking the effects of testosterone, steroids are used to promote the growth of muscle tissue. Popular with athletes, body builders and samurai wannabes, steroids have a number of unpleasant side effects associated with long-term use.

Game Effects

When taken regularly in large doses and combined with muscle-building exercises, steroids can help to increase strength. Such a character can reduce the Karma cost for raising the Strength Attribute by half (round up) or the Body Attribute by a quarter (also round up). To obtain this bonus, the number of weeks of steroid use and exercise should equal the desired Attribute score.

Gear	Conceal	Ammo	Mode	Damage	Weight	Cost	Avail.	St. Index	Legality
Spray Tank	4	20	SS	Special	5	100¥	3/12 hrs	1	Legal

Gear	Conceal	Damage	Blast	Weight	Cost	Avail.	St. Index	Legality
Splash Grenade	5	Special	—	.25	50¥	8/4 days	2	3–J

Continued steroid use may result in adverse effects such as acne, hallucinations, aggressive behavior, hair loss, sterility, impotence, muscle spasms and hypertension—among others. Gamemasters can simulate these effects with appropriate Flaws or modifiers, or perhaps even with occasional Stress damage.

ARSENIC

Though widely found in small quantities throughout nature (in soil, water and metahumans), arsenic is poisonous in large quantities. It is a cumulative poison, meaning that it can be administered slowly, over time, until it has reached a level toxic to the body.

Game Effects

Arsenic can be delivered in a single lethal dose. It can also be delivered in minute quantities over time, by tainting the target's food and drink. Each mini-dose delivered has an escalating Damage Code; the Power equals the number of mini-doses ingested, and the Damage Level is equal to the number of mini-doses in damage boxes. For example, the first dose does 1L (effectively 2L), the second 2L, the third 3M, the fourth 4M, then 5M, 6S, 7S, 8S, 9S and 10D.

Upon taking the sixth mini-dose, the side effects of arsenic poisoning become apparent. They include numbness (–2 dice for tactile Perception Tests), tingling sensations, vomiting and diarrhea.

ATROPINE

Atropine is a distilled alkaloid and the active component of the medicinal agent belladonna, which is derived from the deadly nightshade plant. Extreme in its action, powerful and poisonous, it is a tranquilizer that relaxes the involuntary muscle system. Atropine acts on the vagus nerve, inhibiting the actions of the organs.

Game Effects

Initial application results in a +1 modifier to all Active Skill Target Numbers.

Victims of atropine poisoning experience the following symptoms: increased pulse rate, dryness of mouth, inability to focus on near objects (raising target numbers by an additional +1 for melee and Short Range ranged attacks), mental confusion (+2 to all Knowledge, Technical, Build/Repair, Language and Magic Skill use), hallucinations, hot and dry skin and hyperpyrexia (high fever because of the inability to sweat). Some subjects might also develop a rash.

The subject continues to suffer damage every 15 minutes until the atropine has either been neutralized or filtered out of the system.

CS/TEAR GAS

Commonly referred to as tear gas, CS gas is an irritant that affects the skin, eyes and mucous membranes, causing them to burn and water. It also stimulates a physiological panic response—increased heart rate, shortness of breath and so forth.

Game Effects

Characters dosed with CS gas must make a Body (5) Test; they receive a +3 modifier to all actions, –1 per success. The effects of CS gas last for 5 minutes, –1 minute per success.

Victims of CS gas also suffer a –2 reduction to Willpower for any tests to resist fear or intimidation.

CYANIDE

Cyanide is one of the most rapidly acting of all poisons. Its presence is noted by a momentary burning sensation in the mouth (if the cyanide is swallowed or inhaled), the smell of bitter almonds and an almost instant lapse into spasmodic breathing.

Cyanide works by inhibiting and blocking the enzyme that controls the oxygen release from red blood cells. The result is death by cellular asphyxiation. Oxidizing agents, such as hydrogen permanganate or potassium permanganate, can transform cyanide into a harmless oxamine, but they must be applied immediately.

Game Effects

If inhaled or injected, the effects are instantaneous; if ingested by other means, cyanide's effect occurs 1 minute after exposure.

GREEN RING 3

Green Ring 3 is a colorless and odorless nerve gas developed from research done in the 1970s.

Compound	Availability	Cost	Street Index	Legality
ACTH	5/12 hrs	100¥	1	Legal
Anabolic Steroids (per dose)	4/12 hrs	40¥	1	Legal
Arsenic (per dose)	4/12 hrs	40¥	1	Legal
Atropine (per dose)	5/12 hrs	600¥	1	Legal
CS Gas (per dose)	4/36 hrs	10¥	1	Legal

Compound	Vector	Speed	Damage	Addict.	Tolerance	Edge	Fix Factor
ACTH	Inhalation	Instant	—	—	3	10/—	—
Anabolic steroids	Ingestion, injection	—	—	3P	—	10/10	1 wk
Arsenic	Ingestion	1D6 hrs	10D	—	1	20/—	—
Atropine	Injection	Immediate/15 min	7D	—	—	—	—
CS/Tear Gas	Contact or inhalation	1 Combat Turn	Special	—	—	—	—

Game Effects

Victims suffer cramping, nausea, double vision and crippling pain. For every two boxes of damage taken due to gas exposure, add a +1 modifier to all target numbers. These effects continue for 10 cumulative minutes per +1 modifier. Green Ring 3 persists for 1 hour, after which the gas has oxidized and become inert.

GREEN RING 8

An improved version of Green Ring 3 developed by MCT, this is designed to penetrate standard chemsuits. It is colorless and odorless.

Game Effects

A standard chemsuit does not reduce the Power, but it adds 2 Combat Turns to the gas' speed. Only hazmat or X-E suits (p. 116) will keep the gas out.

Green Ring 8 causes cramping, nausea and double vision. For every two boxes of damage taken due to exposure, add a +1 modifier to all target numbers. These effects persist for 10 minutes per +1 modifier; the gas oxidizes and becomes inert after 10 minutes of exposure to air.

HYPER

Hyper is a direct neural stimulator, acting on the nerves connected to the lobes of the brain that interpret most nervous sensations, including taste, smell, sound and sight. Hyper artificially produces the effects of hyperaesthesia, a condition of excessive acuteness to sensory stimuli, resulting in pain from even the most minor sensations. A tap, for example, feels like a sharp blow, a whisper becomes a shout and so on.

Game Effects

Upon initial exposure, the victim suffers mild vertigo (apply a +1 to all target numbers). The effects of hyper last for 10 minutes per box of damage suffered. During this time, the individual is bombarded with intensely magnified sensations. All concentration tasks attempted suffer a +4 target number modifier (including spellcasting).

Due to sensory overload, any damage suffered while under the effects of hyper will result in additional damage boxes. This is Stun damage, equal to half the damage boxes suffered, rounded up. For example, a Serious Physical wound (6 boxes) would also cause 3 boxes of Stun damage.

JAZZ

Developed by Lone Star's R&D Division, jazz was designed to better the odds for run-of-the-mill law-enforcement officers who run up against wired and chromed street samurai. Designated as an "energizer," jazz significantly boosts the user's reflexes and reactions for a short period. Jazz users frequently suffer a crash period, and long-term users suffer brutal side effects.

Game Effects

Usually taken from a single-dose inhaler (or "popper"), jazz increases the user's Quickness by 2 (which can increase Reaction) and Initiative by +1D6. Jazz has a duration of 10 x 1D6 minutes.

When jazz wears off, the user crashes and is flooded with despondent and miserable emotions. The user must resist 8L Stun damage with Body. Also apply a +1 modifier to all tests involving concentration and a –1 penalty to Quickness for 10 x 1D6 minutes.

KAMIKAZE

Kamikaze is a tailored amphetamine combat drug. In moderate doses, kamikaze can give users an edge, somewhat equalizing the odds when unaugmented (either biologically or cybernetically) individuals face augmented opponents in combat. As use continues and addiction grows, the individual requires larger doses, and adverse side effects begin to manifest. Large doses can cause excitement, tremors, momentary euphoria and dilated pupils. Excess doses (bordering on overdose level) cause anxiety, hallucinations and uncontrolled muscular movements. Even higher dosages lead to death.

Game Effects

Used as a battle stimulant, kamikaze adds +1 Body, +1 Quickness, +2 Strength, +1 Willpower and +1D6 to calculated Initiative (these bonuses may also increase calculated reaction and Dice Pools). It also provides pain resistance equivalent to four levels of the adept power (p. 170, *SR3*). The effects of kamikaze last 10 x 1D6 minutes.

Compound	Availability	Cost	Street Index	Legality
Cyanide (per dose)	3/48 hrs	360¥	1	4P–X
Green Ring 3 (per dose)	14/2 wks	500¥	5	2–K
Green Ring 8 (per dose)	16/2 wks	800¥	5	2–K
Hyper (per dose)	4/24 hrs	180¥	.9	4P–X
Jazz (per dose)	8/4 days	40¥	3	4P–X

Compound	Vector	Speed	Damage	Addict.	Tolerance	Edge	Fix Factor
Cyanide	Ingestion, inhalation, injection	Immediate or 1 min	7D	—	—	—	—
Green Ring 3	Contact or inhalation	Immediate	8S	—	—	—	—
Green Ring 8	Contact or inhalation	Immediate	10S	—	—	—	—
Hyper	Inhalation or injection	Immediate	6S Stun	—	—	—	—
Jazz	Inhalation	Immediate	—	4M/5P	2	2/8	3 days

When kamikaze wears off, the user crashes and suffers –1 Quickness and –1 Willpower for 10 x 1D6 minutes. They must also resist 6M Stun with Body.

The repeated use of kamikaze has a destructive effect on the user's metabolism. On top of the likelihood of addiction, every four applications of the drug inflict an automatic wound effect (see p. 126), causing damage to the character's cyberware or bioware.

LAÉS

Developed by the government of Tir Tairngire, laés erases short-term memories in a retrograde fashion, beginning the moment the drug is injected and flowing backward. Subjects also fall unconscious. Laés is used by the Tir to memory-wipe border infiltrators, who are dumped outside the nation.

Game Effects

When laés is injected, the subject must make a Body (6) Test. The drug erases 12 hours of memory, minus 1 hour for each success. Unless the subject manages to resist the entire effect (12 successes), he also falls unconscious for 120 minutes, minus 10 minutes per success.

Memories erased by laés may not be recoverable by any means (including magic), as the drug changes the chemical structure of the memory neurons.

LONG HAUL

A combination of synthesized hormones and other brain-regulating chemicals, long haul stimulates the brain and keeps the user awake, obviating the need for sleep. A long haul user can go without sleep for approximately four days but suffers a tough "crash" period afterward.

Game Effects

A character dosed on long haul can remain awake for four days—without incurring any modifiers from fatigue or weariness. After this time, however, the user immediately passes out and sleeps soundly for 8D6 hours. If the character is kept awake during this period, he suffers +6 to all target numbers and is inflicted with hallucinations and disorientation, as well as an inability to concentrate.

If a second dose of long haul is taken after the first has worn off, the character can stay awake an additional 1D6 ÷ 2 days. However, after that period, he suffers 10D Stun damage and must crash as detailed above. Long haul cannot keep a character awake past this point, no matter how many additional doses are administered.

MAO

Monoamine oxidase (MAO) is an enzyme that promotes rapid oxidation of adrenaline, thus removing the effects of adrenaline. It can be used to counter the effects of the adrenal pump (p. 63).

Game Effects

Upon its injection, MAO lowers a target's Reaction Attribute by 1 and reduces the individual's Initiative by 1D6.

On targets with an active adrenal pump, MAO inhibits some of the pump's benefits to the character's physical Attributes. An individual with a Level 1 adrenal pump receives only the Reaction bonus (his total Reaction is then modified as above). A character with a Level 2 adrenal pump receives his normal Reaction bonus (+6, but with the total Reaction modified as above)—but all other attributes are modified as if he had only a Level 1 pump (i.e., only +1 Quickness, +1 Strength and +1 Willpower).

MAO's duration is 10 Combat Turns, minus 1 Turn per success on a Body (4) Test.

Any further applications of MAO have no effect until the current dose has been flushed out of the subject's system.

NAUSEA GAS

Designed to incapacitate riotous crowds and break their willingness to cause a disturbance, nausea gas is a potent and loathed weapon.

Game Effects

A victim who breathes nausea gas will feel the need to vomit. Further, the character suffers a +5 modifier to all target numbers, –1 per Body (5) Test success. For example, a character with 2 successes would suffer a +3 modifier.

Characters who suffer a higher target number modifier than their Willpower must make another Body (5) Test or vomit. Vomiting characters are incapacitated for 3 Combat Turns.

Nausea gas lasts for 5 minutes per +1 modifier. Thus, a character with a +3 modifier is sick for 15 minutes.

NEURO-STUN GASES

In addition to the commonly used neuro-stun VIII (described on p. 250, *SR3*), two other varieties are available.

Compound	Availability	Cost	Street Index	Legality
Kamikaze (per dose)	5/4 days	50¥	5	3P–X
Laés (per dose)	21/21 days	1,000¥	2	Legal
Long Haul (per dose)	6/6 days	500¥	2	Legal
MAO (per dose)	5/36 hrs	280¥	2	4P–X

Compound	Vector	Speed	Damage	Addict.	Tolerance	Edge	Fix Factor
Kamikaze	Inhalation	Immediate	—	5P	2	2/10	2 days
Laés	Injection	Immediate	Special	—	—	—	—
Long Haul	Injection	10 min	—	2M	2	10/10	2 wks
MAO	Injection	Immediate	12L Stun	—	—	—	—

Neuro-stun IX becomes inert more quickly than neuro-stun VIII, and so is more useful in situations when timing and clearing the air are important. Neuro-stun X delivers a more powerful punch, with the same duration as neuro-stun IX.

Game Effects

Whereas neuro-stun VIII is inert after 10 minutes, neuro-stun IX and X become inert after only 1 minute. Wind and other environmental conditions may disperse the gas more quickly. All neuro-stun varieties are colorless and odorless.

PEPPER PUNCH

Pepper punch uses oreocapsicum, derived from hot peppers, as an active ingredient. It is mixed with other irritants, such as CS gas, and deployed as a gas, liquid or foam spray. Liquids and foams frequently incorporate ultraviolet dye so that the target may be identified later.

Game Effects

A victim dosed with pepper punch feels an intense burning on any affected skin, and his eyes and nose will water. Eyes that are sprayed will burn fiercely, and the victim will have difficulty seeing. The throat and nasal passage will be irritated, making breathing difficult.

Victims must make a Body (5) Test or receive an additional +5 modifier to all actions, –1 per success. The effects of pepper punch last for 2 minutes per +1 modifier.

PSYCHE

This designer smart drug, allegedly produced by MCT, is especially prized by magicians.

Game Effects

Psyche users gain +1 Intelligence for 12 – Body hours (minimum 1 hour), as the drug stimulates their brain into hyperactivity. Awakened users also gain the Focused Concentration Edge (p. 28, *SRComp*), allowing them to suffer only a +1 modifier for each spell they have sustained.

SEVEN–7

Like Green Ring 8, Seven–7 is a cutting-edge war gas developed by Mitsuhama and capable of permeating normal chemsuits. It is colorless and odorless.

Game Effects

Except for the onset time and damage, Seven–7 has the same effect as Green Ring 8 (p. 119).

STREET DRUGS

Despite the popularity of BTLs, a number of old-fashioned brainbenders still circulate. The variety of street drugs has grown immensely, as dealers seek to expand their market with enticing new chemicals. The drugs listed below are but a few examples.

Bliss: A tranquilizing narcotic, bliss is an opiate synthesized from poppy plants.

Burn: In the never-ending quest to avoid sobriety, burn is the latest synthahol intoxicant beverage, named for its simultaneous effect on the throat and brain.

Cram: The most recent amphetamine to make the rounds, cram is an energizer drug designed to give the user an energy boost.

Nitro: A combination of potent drugs, including novacoke and several other narcotics and stimulants, nitro's effects can easily kill a user. It is favored by troll gangers.

Novacoke: A stimulant derived from coca plants, novacoke is a highly addictive social drug.

Zen: A psychedelic hallucinogen, zen is popular among those looking to escape reality or seeking trance-like states.

Game Effects

If a character gets high on street drugs, roleplaying should be encouraged. Most people on drugs change dramatically. They may become less inhibited, euphorically happy, sexually aroused, paranoid, hyper-aware, mellow and incoherent, or enter a berserk psychotic rage. Gamemaster characters often have Professional Ratings of 4 when on drugs because they're too high to realize they could get hurt.

Compound	Availability	Cost	Street Index	Legality
Nausea Gas (per dose)	4/48 hrs	10¥	2	8P–X
Neuro-stun IX (per dose)	6/36 hrs	20¥	2	6P–X
Neuro-stun X (per dose)	8/48 hrs	30¥	2	6P–X
Pepper Punch (per dose)	2/4 hrs	5¥	1	Legal
Psyche (per dose)	8/72 hrs	500¥	2	Legal
Seven–7 (per dose)	20/2 wks	1,000¥	5	2–K

Compound	Vector	Speed	Damage	Addict.	Tolerance	Edge	Fix Factor
Nausea Gas	Inhalation	5 Combat Turns	Special	—	—	—	—
Neuro-stun IX	Contact or inhalation	1 Combat Turn	6S Stun	—	—	—	—
Neuro-stun X	Contact or inhalation	1 Combat Turn	8S Stun	—	—	—	—
Pepper Punch	Contact or inhalation	1 Combat Turn	12L Stun	—	—	—	—
Psyche	Ingestion	10 min	—	4M	2	10/20	1 wk
Seven–7	Contact or inhalation	1 Combat Turn	10D	—	—	—	—

Bliss: Using bliss reduces Reaction by 1, adds 1 to all target numbers and provides pain resistance equal to three levels of the adept power. Duration is 6 – Body hours, minimum 1 hour.

Burn: The effects of this synthahol are simulated by the Stun damage taken.

Cram: Users add 1 to Reaction and 1D6 to Initiative for the duration (12 hours – Body, minimum 1 hour). When this effect wears off, users crash and suffer Moderate Stun damage for an equivalent duration.

Nitro: The heavy hitters who take nitro receive +2 Strength and Willpower and pain resistance equal to six levels of the adept power. They also receive +2 to all Perception Tests. The drug's duration is 10 x 1D6 minutes, after which the subject suffers 8D Stun damage.

Novacoke: Users gain +1 Reaction, +1 Charisma and a +1 Perception Test modifier. They also gain pain resistance equivalent to one level of the adept power (p. 170, *SR3*). The drug's duration is 10 – Body hours, minimum of 1 hour. After it wears off, the user's Charisma is reduced to 1 and his Willpower is reduced by half (round down) for an equivalent duration.

Zen: Zen users suffer a –2 Reaction and a +1 to all physical-related target numbers, but they also receive +1 Willpower. Duration is 10 x 1D6 minutes.

MAGICAL COMPOUNDS

The following magical compounds are derived from Awakened flora and are traditionally prepared via secret metamagical techniques by a tribal "medicine man," such as a brujo and bruja of the Anasazi tribes. The compounds appear in many forms—from potions and salves to cooked plant matter or matter dried for smoking.

All of these concoctions are rare and difficult to acquire, as the tribes staunchly defend their secrets. Even if an Awakened plant is obtained, without knowledge of the preparation, it is useless. In fact, many such plants have active ingredients that are toxic.

Each of the magical balms and liquids described here bestows powers on their users. Their use also incurs some disadvantages specific to each compound. Any character can use these potions, whether Awakened or mundane. However, because many of these mixtures impact the user's life force, heavily cybered individuals will not get the same boost from them.

The preparations tend to go stale after a few weeks. Each compound has a shelf life of 1D6 weeks. After that, while it no longer provides the advantages described, its disadvantages and drawbacks remain potent.

The compounds are listed by their Anasazi names; other tribes may use different terms.

Speed: Each of these magical compounds has a Speed of immediate.

Duration: The duration of the powers conferred by spiritual helpers is the Essence of the character using them + 1D6 hours, up to a maximum of 12 hours.

ANIMAL TONGUE

This paste is prepared primarily from the pulp of the manzana cactus and gifts the user with abilities similar to the ani-

Compound	Availability	Cost	Street Index	Legality
Street Drugs (per dose)				
Bliss	5/48 hrs	15¥	2	5–X
Burn	2/30 min	5¥	1	Legal
Cram	4/12 hrs	20¥	1	6P–X
Nitro	6/48 hrs	100¥	1	4–X
Novacoke	3/12 hrs	20¥	1	6–X
Zen	3/6 hrs	5¥	1	8–X

Compound	Vector	Speed	Damage	Addict.	Tolerance	Edge	Fix Factor
Bliss	Inhalation, injection	1 Turn	—	5M/5P	2	2/30	2 days
Burn	Ingestion	10 min	3D Stun	2M	2	20/100	1 day
Cram	Ingestion, inhalation	10 min	—	4M	2	5/50	2 days
Nitro	Inhalation	1 Turn	4D	5M/8P	3	2/5	3 days
Novacoke	Inhalation, injection	1 Turn	—	6M/5P	2	3/50	2 days
Zen	Inhalation	5 x D6 min	—	3M	2	5/50	2 days
Deepweed	—	—	—	7P	2	5/20	1 wk

mal control power observed in Awakened beings. Anasazi warriors typically use it for protection against animal attacks and to reconnoiter large areas through the eyes of desert birds. It is also used to induce mystical visions.

Vector: Ingestion.

Advantages: This mixture grants the critter power of Animal Control (see p. 262, *SR3*).

Disadvantages: When animal tongue wears off, the user has an unnatural fear of animals for a period of time equal to the mixture's duration. Treat this as if animals—mundane or paranormal—that come near the character exude the fear power (p. 263, *SR3*). Spirits do not count as animals.

DEEPWEED

Also known as "bad karma," this substance is derived by Caribbean houngans from an Awakened form of kelp. Naturally laden with nicotine and THC, deepweed is especially enticing to the Awakened and is sometimes used to dose targets for possession.

Vector: Ingestion or inhalation.

Advantages: Deepweed increases Willpower by 1 and forces any magically active smoker to astrally perceive, even if the user is an adept without astral access.

Disadvantages: Besides being addictive, once its effects have worn off, deepweed users suffer a +2 penalty to all target numbers for an equal duration.

IMMORTAL FLOWER

This compound is prepared from the petals of a small Mojave flower of the same name.

Vector: Ingestion.

Advantages: This mixture grants the critter power of regeneration (p. 13, *Critters*).

Disadvantages: For every 20 boxes of damage sustained while under the influence, the character must permanently remove one box from his Physical Overflow. These boxes can never be regained. If the character's Overflow is reduced to 0, every box of damage suffered past that point (while under the compound's influence) reduces the character's Essence by .1.

A character with cyberware or bioware who takes this drug also suffers 2D6 wound effects when the drug wears off, as the regeneration ability attempts to "repair" the implants.

LITTLE SMOKE

When smoked, this blend of mosses and green leafy substances gifts the user with abilities similar to the concealment and confusion powers associated with Awakened beings.

Vector: Inhalation.

Advantages: Concealment and confusion powers (pp. 262–63, *SR3*).

Disadvantages: Perception and Willpower are reduced to 1 when the mixture wears off, for as long as the mixture's effect lasted.

ROCK LIZARD BLOOD

This bluish-green paste is made from the mashed pulp of the desert's weeping tree.

Vector: Ingestion.

Advantages: It grants the power of immunity (pathogens, poisons). See p. 264, *SR3*.

Disadvantages: When the immunity wears off, the character suffers a Light Physical wound. If the character already has Physical damage, increase the Damage Level by one for the duration instead.

SPIRIT STRENGTH

Prepared from small black mushrooms, this pasty mixture is often distributed to tribal warriors before an expected combat and before hunting expeditions.

Vector: Ingestion.

Advantages: This compound grants the critter powers of enhanced physical Attributes (p. 9, *Critters*), movement (self only, p. 265, *SR3*), enhanced reactions (p. 9, *Critters*) and one enhanced sense (p. 263, *SR3*) of the gamemaster's choice.

Disadvantages: When the advantages wear off, the user crashes for an equal duration. During this time, the character's natural Body, Quickness and Strength Attributes are reduced to 1 and the character's natural Reaction becomes 1 + 1D6.

WITCH'S MOSS

Made of unknown ingredients, this mixture looks like green porridge.

Vector: Ingestion.

Advantages: Grants the critter power paralyzing touch (p. 13, *Critters*).

Disadvantages: The character's arms become crippled and useless once the power wears off, for an equal duration. Apply a +6 modifier to any test involving the use of the arms.

The following rules describe how to resolve what happens to a character who takes damage during game play. These rules include a simple system for determining the effect of wounds on cyberware, bioware and Attributes. The maintenance required to keep cyberware and bioware in good working order is also described, along with rules for reducing and eliminating Stress. This section includes rules for remaining conscious after receiving Deadly damage and for acquiring scars.

A number of optional rules also appear here, covering first aid, doctoring tables and a system for healing Physical damage box by box.

STRESS POINTS

Damage to implants or the organic body is represented by Stress Points. Stress Points measure wear and tear on the implant or Attribute and are used to determine implant or Attribute failure. An implant or Attribute suffering from Stress is on its way to breaking down.

For all implants and Attributes, Stress Points mark the progression of damage; each time an implant or Attribute takes Stress, the player must make a Stress Test to determine if the part fails. In addition, bioware function degrades from the presence of Stress; as the number of Stress Points reaches certain thresholds, bioware malfunctions in increasingly more critical ways.

All new implants and Attributes begin with 0 Stress Points; used cyberware begins with 1D6 ÷ 2 permanent Stress Points and bioware begins with 1 permanent Stress Point.

For rules on removing Stress, see *Stress Maintenance,* p. 130.

Stress from Wound Effects

When an implant or Attribute is damaged by a wound effect, (see p. 126) it suffers 1D6 ÷ 2 Stress Points (the Rule of Six does not apply to this roll) and the player must make a Stress Test. These points are cumulative with any existing Stress Points.

Other Sources of Stress

While most accumulation of Stress Points is a result of damage, gamemasters may also choose to require regularly scheduled implant maintenance. Implants that are not

SEEING 135
TOM FOWLER '99

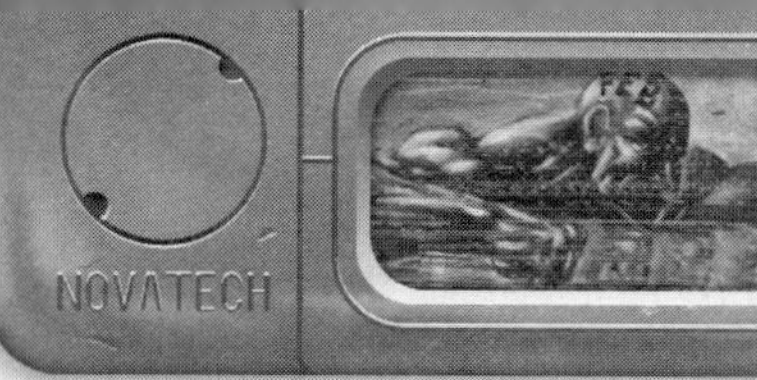

regularly serviced will suffer Stress at a rate determined by the gamemaster.

STRESS LEVEL

The Stress Level, as shown on the Stress Level Table, indicates the amount of Stress an implant or Attribute currently suffers. This indicator is used for determining bioware malfunctions and the requirements for repairing Stress damage to cyberware and healing Stress damage to bioware and Attributes. The ratio between Stress Points and Stress Level is roughly equivalent to the ratio between damage boxes and Damage Levels.

If an implant or Attribute's Stress Points reach Deadly Stress Level, the implant or Attribute automatically fails.

STRESS LEVEL TABLE

Stress Points	Stress Level
1–2	Light
3–5	Moderate
6–9	Serious
10+	Deadly

STRESS TEST

Whenever an implant or Attribute takes Stress, the player must make a Stress Test.

The number of dice rolled for a Stress Test depends on the implant's grade, as shown on the Stress Dice Table. Use half the unaugmented Attribute Value for Attribute Stress Tests. The Fragile and Rugged implant surgery options affect this number of dice (see *Surgical Options,* p.148). For used cyberware and bioware, roll a number of dice equal to the equivalent grade.

The target number for the Stress Test is the current Stress Point total. Only one success is needed to avoid a system failure. For cyberlimbs with integrity enhancement (p. 39), reduce the target number by the Integrity Rating. For an Attribute boosted by bioware, add the value of the Attribute boost to the target number. If the test results in no successes, the Stress causes an implant system or Attribute to fail.

Gamemasters may also require Stress Tests in situations in which the implant or Attribute is subject to extreme conditions. For example, if your cyberware is not well-maintained and you get very sick while marching through a jungle, your cyberware may develop problems even if nothing happens to the cyberware to incur Stress.

STRESS TEST TABLE

Base Target Number: Current Stress Point Total

Situation	Modifiers
Cyberlimb Integrity Enhancement	– Integrity Rating
Attribute boosted by bioware	+ boost value

STRESS DICE TABLE

Wound Effect Affects:	Number of Dice to Roll
Cyberware	
Basic	1
Alphaware	2
Betaware	3
Deltaware	5
Bioware	
Cosmetic	1
Basic	2
Cultured	4
Attribute	unaugmented Attribute ÷ 2

Leggy's reaction enhancer, nephritic screen and Reaction are all suffering wound effects from a powerbolt he took. He rolls 1D6 ÷ 2 for the cyberware and gets a 3; the enhancer gains 3 Stress Points. Now he must make a Stress Test to see if the inflicted Stress actually breaks the implant. The enhancer is a basic cyberware item, so he rolls 1D6 against a Target Number of 3 with a result of 2. Looks like the powerbolt shorted out the enhancer.

Rolling 1D6 ÷ 2 for the bioware, Leggy gets a 1—it takes only 1 Stress Point. Unfortunately, the nephritic screen had 3 Stress Points from a previous incident, so his Stress Test Target Number is 4. He rolls 2D6 (because it's basic bioware), resulting in 3 and 5. He achieves 1 success, so the screen is still functional.

Leggy also rolls 1D6 ÷ 2 for his Reaction and determines that it has taken 3 Stress Points. He makes a test using half his unaugmented reaction against a Target Number of 3 and easily achieves the needed success, so he doesn't have to worry about Attribute failure.

WOUND EFFECTS

Shadowrun's damage system allows players to apply the effects of damage to characters in an abstract fashion that does not allow the gamemaster to easily determine additional complications that a wound might cause. For example, a wound may have caused damage to a cybernetic or biotech system, or it may require medical attention and inhibit a character's physical performance.

Whenever a character takes damage, whether Physical or Stun, there is a chance that the wound may cause other effects in addition to general trauma. These wound effects may inflict damage in the form of Stress Points on a character's cyberware, bioware or Attributes.

Injuries that result in damaged implants or altered Attributes will always require a doctor's care to heal.

DETERMINING WOUND EFFECTS

When a character makes a Damage Resistance Test, compare the highest die result rolled to the number of boxes of damage inflicted by the attack. In other words, use the results of the Damage Resistance Test as if it were a Success Test, with a target number equal to the number of damage boxes inflicted. If the character fails (does not roll any numbers equal to the target number), the character suffers a number of wound effects equal to the margin of failure (the difference between the highest roll and the number of damage boxes suffered).

Leggy's in trouble. An enemy shaman has just zapped him with a Serious damage powerbolt (6 boxes). On his Spell Resistance Test, Leggy rolls a 1, 1, 2, 2 and 3. Comparing the highest number rolled (3) to the number of boxes of damage taken (6) means Leggy suffers (6 – 3) 3 wound effects.

Each wound effect a character suffers may cause lasting damage to an implant system or the character's body. Roll 1D6 for each wound effect and compare the result to the Wound Effect Table. Consult the appropriate section to determine the damage caused.

If a character with no cyberware rolls a cybersystem damage result, or a character with no bioware rolls a bioware damage result, ignore that wound effect.

WOUND EFFECT TABLE

D6 Result	Wound Effect Type
1–2	Cybersystem damage (below)
3–4	Bioware damage (p. 128)
5–6	Organic physical injury (p. 129)

Leggy rolls a die for each wound effect, getting a 1, a 3 and a 6. One wound effect has a chance of damaging Leggy's cyberware, another his bioware and the third gives him an organic physical injury.

CYBERSYSTEM DAMAGE

If the character rolls a wound effect of 1 or 2, the wound may have inflicted damage to a cyberware system. The more cyberware a character has, the more likely it is that something will be damaged in an attack.

Electrical Damage: Attacks that cause electrical damage automatically affect cyberware and may even damage more than one system simultaneously. This includes damage from tasers, stun batons, electrified fences, electrical critter powers, lightning elemental manipulation spells and so on.

For each wound effect from an electrical attack suffered by a character with cyberware, apply the wound effect as described in Determine System Affected, and roll an additional 1D6; on a result of 1 or 2, the attack damages another piece of cyberware. For example, if in the previous example Leggy had been hit by a lightning bolt rather than a powerbolt, he would have had to roll 1D6 for each wound effect to determine which cybersystem was damaged, then roll 1D6 three more times, once for each wound effect, to determine whether the attack damaged additional pieces of cyberware.

Assign Essence Slots

In order to determine the cyberware that takes damage, all cyberware systems must be assigned to one of six Essence slots (one slot for each point of Essence). Each slot holds 1 Essence point of cyberware. Implants with an Essence Cost of more than 1 will take up more than one slot. Begin filling Essence slots with slot 1, and fill each slot completely before assigning cyberware to the next slot, in ascending order.

Treat any system installed in a cybereye, cyberear or cyberlimb system as part of that system, unless the character paid Essence for the item. For example, any cybereye accessories that take up the .5 "free Essence" in a cybereye are counted as part of the basic cybereye system. If, however, the character has an additional eye modification that cost Essence to install, it would take up part or all of an Essence slot.

Cyberzombies: Characters who have undergone cybermancy (p. 50) will have more cyberware than Essence slots. In this case, the player must "double up" on his slots, making it possible for two systems to be damaged at the same time. Cyberzombies always take damage from cybersystem wound effects.

Determine System Affected

To determine which cyberware system is damaged by a wound effect, roll 1D6 and compare the result to the character's Essence slots. If the die roll result indicates a slot that contains no cyberware, ignore that wound effect. If the die roll result indicates a slot that contains cyberware, one of the implants listed for that slot is damaged. The gamemaster can simply choose an appropriate cybersystem from that slot, choose randomly, or roll a ten sided die if available, to choose the system damaged (subdivide the Essence slot by the Essence Cost for items assigned to that slot and roll 1D10 to determine the system damaged).

If a cyberlimb, cybereye or cyberear is damaged, the gamemaster may decide that the whole system (including all internal accessories) is damaged, or he may decide that only a randomly determined subsystem suffers damage.

Damage to a cybersystem inflicts 1D6 ÷ 2 Stress Points, and the player must make a Stress Test (p. 126).

Leggy has a lot of cyberware, so there's a good chance some implant is going to take damage. His implants include: VCR 2 (alphaware, Essence Cost 2.4), two reaction enhancers (Essence Cost .6), wired reflexes 1 (alphaware, 1.6), cybereyes with mods (.2), datajack (.2) and a smartlink (.5). Assigning all his cyberware to Essence slots produces the following results:

Slot 1	*VCR 2*
Slot 2	*VCR 2*
Slot 3	*VCR 2, 2 reaction enhancers*
Slot 4	*wired reflexes 1*
Slot 5	*wired reflexes 1, cybereyes, datajack*
Slot 6	*smartlink*

The first five of his Essence slots are full, but the last one (slot 6) is only half full, because the smartlink only costs .5 Essence.

Leggy rolls 1D6 for his potential cyberware wound effect, getting a 3. The gamemaster has a choice between the VCR or a reaction enhancer being damaged; he rolls randomly and gets one of the reaction enhancers.

If Leggy had rolled a 6, he might not have taken any damage at all because that slot is only half full. In that case, the gamemaster would have declared a 50–50 chance between the smartlink getting hit and no damage being done.

CYBERWARE FAILURE

When a cyberware implant fails, the gamemaster chooses exactly how the device malfunctions. The implant may merely cease to function, or it may go on the fritz in spectacular, unusual or even amusing ways. For example, a broken set of wired reflexes may simply cease to function, turn on and off at random intervals and cause the character to tremble visibly or cause the character to suffer from frequent, violent twitching and spasms.

Cyberware that represents primarily a structural or physiological change (for example, dermal plating, boosted reflexes, bone lacing and muscle replacement) does not actually degrade in performance when damaged but instead breaks in such a way that a doctor must repair and maintain it. For example, having bits of loose dermal plating poking into your guts tends to make everything a little more difficult.

Gamemasters may instead choose to use the Cyberware Failure Table to generate a specific effect for an item's failure. Roll 1D6, consult the table and use whatever modifiers are applicable to the damaged implant.

For repairing cyberware Stress, see p. 130. For repairing cyberware that has failed, see *Implant Surgery*, p. 146.

Because a reaction enhancer simply adds +1 to Reaction, Leggy's gamemaster decides that he loses that bonus when the implant fails. Before he chooses any other drawbacks, the gamemaster reviews the description of the equipment and finds that a reaction enhancer is superconductive material wrapped around the spine. At best, the enhancer's failure means that some of the superconducting material was dislodged; at worst, it may be creating neural feedback. The gamemaster decides that Leggy has had enough bad luck and imposes the least hampering option. Leggy will be at –1 Reaction until the enhancer is fixed.

CYBERWARE FAILURE TABLE

1D6 Roll	Cyberware Failure Effect
1	Cyberware's bonus/rating at 50 percent, +1 target number modifier to use
2	Cyberware's bonus/rating at 50 percent, +1 target number modifier to use, +1 modifier to all target numbers from feedback/discomfort
3	Cyberware's bonus/rating at 50 percent, +2 target number modifier to use, +1 modifier to all target numbers from feedback/discomfort
4	No bonuses from cyberware, rating reduced to 0, +2 target number modifier to use, +1 modifier to all target numbers from feedback/discomfort
5	No bonuses from cyberware, rating reduced to 0, +2 target number modifier to use, +2 modifier to all target numbers from feedback/discomfort
6	No bonuses from cyberware, rating reduced to 0, +3 target number modifier to use, +3 modifier to all target numbers from feedback/discomfort

BIOWARE DAMAGE

On a wound effect roll of 3 or 4, a bioware implant may be damaged. To determine which bioware system suffers damage (if any), use the same rules as for damaged cyberware, but substitute Bio Index slots for Essence slots. Because some characters may have more bioware than slots, they may have to double up on Bio Index slots, as do cyberzombies for Essence slots.

Leggy also rolled a bioware wound effect, so he must check to see if any of his bioware implants are damaged. Leggy only has two bioware items, a nephritic screen (Bio Index .4) and tailored pheromones (level 2, Bio Index .6), so he has a 1 in 6 chance of taking bioware damage. His Bio Index slots fall into place as follows:

Slot 1	*nephritic screen, tailored pheromones*
Slot 2	—
Slot 3	—
Slot 4	—
Slot 5	—
Slot 6	—

Leggy rolls 1D6 and gets a 1—it's not his day. His gamemaster now gets to choose which of the two implants takes the hit. Rolling randomly, he determines it's the nephritic screen.

BIOWARE FAILURE

All Stress damage applied to bioware affects its functioning. Listed in the description of each bioware item is a negative side effect that manifests at a specific level of Stress (see p. 126). These Stress Level effects are cumulative; for example, a character suffering the Moderate Stress Level effects of a damaged bioware item also suffers the Light Stress effects of that item.

Bioware that fails a Stress Test is considered to be at a Deadly Stress Level, which means the equipment has failed and the character suffers the effects described for Deadly Stress.

For more information on bioware Stress repair, see p. 130. For repairing failed bioware, see *Therapeutic Surgery*, p. 147.

Leggy's nephritic screen has 4 Stress Points, which puts it at a Moderate Stress Level. Consulting the nephritic screen description (p. 67), Leggy will be suffering the effects of both the Light Stress Level (screen filters out nutrients) and the Moderate Stress Level (filter becomes overloaded and the Power reduction bonus no longer applies).

ATTRIBUTE DAMAGE

In *Shadowrun,* the Condition Monitor penalizes tests and Initiative to simulate the effect of trauma, but a character's basic Attribute-determined abilities often remain unchanged. Organic damage simulates damage to natural body parts such as organs and limbs. While the specifics of this damage are left up to the gamemaster's creativity (bruised ribs, hamstrung legs, broken bones and so on), the effects are represented by Stress Points applied toward character Attributes.

When a character receives an organic damage wound effect, roll 1D6 and consult the Organic Damage Table (p. 130) to determine the Attribute affected. Damage to an Attribute inflicts 1D6 ÷ 2 Stress Points, and the player must make a Stress Test (p. 126).

Injuries that result in damaged Attributes always require a doctor's help to heal.

Leggy rolls 1D6 to determine which Attribute was affected by the third wound effect. He rolls a 6, and so the powerbolt impedes his Reaction.

ATTRIBUTE FAILURE

An Attribute failure means that the character's physical capabilities have been impaired in some way by the wound(s) he has received. In game terms, this means the character's Attribute value may be temporarily reduced or that use of the Attribute and linked skills will be impeded. Gamemasters are encouraged to develop a fictional explanation for these modifiers; for example, reduced Quickness could result from severed tendons or a smashed bone.

The gamemaster may also choose to use the Attribute Failure Table (p. 130) to randomly generate game effects for a failed Attribute. Roll 1D6 and consult the table. If the suggested modifiers reduce an Attribute to 0, the character has become an invalid and must remain bedridden until the Attribute is healed. Such characters cannot use the failed Attribute or any linked skills.

For details on repairing Attribute Stress, see p. 131. For repairing a failed Attribute, see *Therapeutic Surgery,* p. 147.

Deadly Wounds and Permanent Damage

The wound effect rules do not replace the rules for *Deadly Wounds and Permanent Damage* described on p. 127, *SR3.*

The wound effect rules do modify those rules as follows: whenever a character suffers a Deadly wound and makes a Body Test to determine if they suffer any permanent damage, add the character's highest Attribute Stress Points to the target number.

Later on in Leggy's illustrious career, he runs afoul of an enemy mage and takes a Deadly damage manabolt. Checking for possible permanent damage, Leggy makes a Body Test. Normally the target number is 4, but Leggy has 3 existing points of Reaction Stress, so the target number is 7 (4 + 3). If Leggy also had 5 points of Quickness Stress, he would use the higher Stress value for a Target Number 9.

ORGANIC DAMAGE TABLE

1D6 Roll	Damaged Attribute
1	Body
2	Strength
3	Quickness
4	Intelligence
5	Willpower
6	Reaction

STRESS MAINTENANCE

Implants and Attributes can be repaired and/or healed to remove the effects of Stress. Cyberware implants that have existing Stress may undergo maintenance to remove the Stress Points. Bioware implants and Attributes with Stress can heal naturally over time.

Stress repair or healing will not restore functionality to implants or Attributes that have failed because of Stress; to correct such failures, the character must undergo either implant surgery (p. 146 for cyberware) or therapeutic surgery (p. 147 for bioware and Attributes).

CYBERWARE STRESS REPAIR

Cyberware Stress Points may be removed through standard maintenance work. This work requires a cyberware tool shop and should be performed in a medical facility (work not performed in a medical facility suffers penalties per the Expanded Doctoring Table, p. 134).

Cyberware suffering a Serious or Deadly Stress Level always requires surgery to repair, and the gamemaster may also make surgery a requirement for maintaining certain types of cyberware. For example, to repair a punctured internal air tank, the technician needs to be able to access the tank, which requires cutting the patient open. This implant surgery would be considered a Repair Cyberware procedure (see *Implant Surgery*, p. 146).

Repair Test

The technician performing the overhaul must make a Repair Test using one of the following appropriate skills: Biotech (Cybertechnology Implantation), Computer (Cybernetics) B/R or Electronics (Cybertechnology) B/R. The gamemaster determines what constitutes an appropriate skill based on the cyberware in question and the extent and type of the damage. For example, Computer (Cybernetics) B/R is useless for repairing bone lacing because bone lacing doesn't incorporate any computers.

The target number for the technician's test is equal to the implant's Stress Points; apply modifiers from the Expanded Doctoring Table (p. 133). Every 2 successes reduce the Stress Points by 1; Stress that remains may be repaired later with another overhaul. If the test fails, 1 of the Stress Points becomes permanent and can only be removed by a cybertechnician with better tools and a higher skill level. Eventually, a piece of cyberware may prove too difficult to maintain; the character may attempt an overhaul, but it may be more effective to simply remove and replace the cyberware.

The grade of the cyberware may also make the repair more difficult. For each grade above basic, modify the target number for the Repair Test by +2.

An implant's Stress Points can never be reduced below 1; once an implant has been pushed beyond its limits, it never performs perfectly again.

A cyberware maintenance overhaul costs 100 nuyen in replacement parts per Stress Point removed, plus labor costs (see *Paying the Price,* p. 151). The procedure requires a number of hours equal to the item's Essence Cost x 5 (any successes beyond the first can be used to decrease this time, per p. 95, *SR3*).

BIOWARE STRESS REPAIR

Because of the organic nature of bioware, such systems can potentially heal Stress Points on their own, in much the same way that the metahuman body can heal itself. Bioware that has failed, however, must be repaired using therapeutic surgery (p. 147) to remove Stress.

Healing bioware follows roughly the same procedure as *Healing Physical Damage* (pp. 126–127, *SR3*). The character first makes an unaugmented Body Test against a target number from the Healing Table (p. 127, *SR3*), replacing Damage Level

ATTRIBUTE FAILURE TABLE

1D6 Roll	Result
1	+1 TN modifier to Attribute Success Tests and use of linked skills
2	–1 to Attribute value, +1 TN modifier to Attribute Success Tests and use of linked skills
3	–1 to Attribute value, +2 TN modifier to Attribute Success Tests and use of linked skills
4	–2 to Attribute value, +2 TN modifier to Attribute Success Tests and use of linked skills
5	Attribute value halved (round down), +2 TN modifier to Attribute Success Tests and use of linked skills
6	Attribute value halved (round down), +3 TN modifier to Attribute Success Tests and use of linked skills

with the bioware's Stress Level. If this test succeeds, the bioware can heal the Stress without medical attention. If it fails, the character must undergo a doctor's care in a clinic (medical shop) in order to heal.

Once a bioware item has taken damage, its Stress Points can never be reduced below 1.

Self-Healing Bioware Stress

Without help, bioware heals in the same manner as Physical damage, as described in *Stages of Healing* (p. 127, *SR3*). Replace the phrase "Damage Level" with "Stress Level" in the appropriate paragraphs and follow the same procedure. The optional *Healing Physical Damage* rules (p. 134) may also be used.

Medical Care of Bioware Stress

If medical attention is required to heal bioware Stress, the character must undergo therapeutic surgery (p. 147).

Magical Healing and Bioware Stress

Because it is an organic component of the body, damage to bioware can be reduced through healing magic. Spells such as Heal and Treat must use the highest Damage or Stress Level present in the body. For example, when using a Heal spell on a character with a Light Physical wound, Moderate Stress to his cerebral booster and Serious Stress to his adrenal pump, the spell would be cast against Serious damage (adjust the Drain accordingly). Each success from the spell can be used to either remove a box of Physical damage or remove a Stress Point (to a maximum equal to the spell's Force). Like other damage, Stress can only be healed magically once. Any remaining Stress must be healed normally, though any new Stress incurred can be healed magically.

ATTRIBUTE STRESS REPAIR

Attribute Stress may also heal on its own, though complications may require medical attention. Attribute Stress uses the same rules for healing (and magical healing) as bioware Stress.

An Attribute that has failed cannot be healed until it is repaired. Attribute Stress can always be reduced to 0. If an Attribute acquires permanent Stress Points, the character must undergo therapeutic surgery (p. 147) to restore the Attribute's function.

USING STRESS

Gamemasters are encouraged to use Stress Points creatively, inflicting them on characters to represent the result of strenuous activities or harsh circumstances. Additional Stress Points can be incurred by pushing an implant beyond its performance capabilities, straining physical capabilities, incompetent surgery or even other circumstances such as chemical poisoning. Likewise, the gamemaster can also call for Stress Tests when an implant or Attribute is tested to the extent of its capabilities. These mechanics should be used primarily to present the players with challenges and to provide some comic relief. They should not be used simply to make a character's life difficult.

The following rules suggest expanded uses for Stress.

Cyberware Upkeep

Implants are not designed to last forever, and eventually even the best designed systems develop flaws from wear and tear. Most cyberware is designed to function at top efficiency only when given maintenance overhauls on a regular basis. Depending on the implant, this overhaul could consist of a simple diagnostics check, or it could require cleaning, recharging power sources, lubrication, refilling reserves, reprogramming, tightening a few bolts and so on. Most cyberware is on a yearly maintenance schedule, but some require more frequent checkups (such as cybereyes and wired reflexes) or perhaps even fewer (bone lacing and cyberskulls). Higher-grade cyberware tends to require more frequent upkeep, to keep the more sophisticated systems running smoothly.

At the gamemaster's discretion, a character who has not maintained his cyberware on a regular basis may incur Stress Points as the implants slowly get dirty, run out of necessary chemicals, fall out of alignment and so on. Stress Points accumulated in this way should be inflicted gradually and infrequently—for example, 1 point every three months. The effects of this wearing-down process should be manifestly evident to the player. Implants may start to make an irritating noise, need to be whacked to work properly or even get stuck in odd positions.

Stress for Attribute Dice

Under certain circumstances, the gamemaster may allow characters who are stretching their abilities to willingly take an Attribute wound effect (1D6 ÷ 2 Stress Points) in exchange for an extra die for an Attribute Test (the wound effect and extra die must both apply to the same Attribute). This option should be allowed only when the character is pushing the Attribute to the limit. Only one die may be obtained in this manner per test. This rule applies only to Attribute Tests or when defaulting to an Attribute. A Skill Test cannot receive an extra die this way.

CONSCIOUSNESS

In *Shadowrun,* when a character receives Deadly Physical or Stun damage, they are knocked unconscious. In the real world, however, a person who suffers a massive or even life-threatening injury may remain conscious right up until they die. The following rules establish guidelines for characters who may remain conscious after receiving Deadly damage.

Whenever a character fills 10 boxes of either Stun or Physical damage, the player makes a Willpower Test against a Target Number 6 plus injury modifiers and Bio Index (round down). One success means the character remains conscious and can act normally; failure means the character is unconscious.

These consciousness rules allow a character with the Pain Resistance adept power or damage compensator bioware to remain conscious until they have reached 10 + level/rating boxes of damage. A character with a pain editor makes the Willpower Test as normal but ignores the injury target number modifier.

REVIVING UNCONSCIOUS CHARACTERS

A character with Biotech Skill can help (or force) a person with Deadly (or more) damage to regain consciousness. The character uses a Complex Action and makes a Biotech (First

Aid) (8) Test, adding any appropriate modifiers from the Expanded First Aid Table. The patient is revived for a number of minutes equal to the number of successes, or until the character takes more damage and passes out again.

EFFECTS OF RETAINING CONSCIOUSNESS

Characters who remain conscious after suffering Deadly damage frequently exhibit reduced respiration, blood pressure and stimulus response—they're in bad shape. These effects are represented by the following Deadly damage modifiers applied to such characters: +4 to all target numbers; –4 to Initiative; reduce their Quickness by half (round up) for determining Movement Rate; such characters cannot run.

Any damage taken by the character, whether Stun or Physical, after exceeding the Deadly Damage Level requires another Willpower Test, with an additional +1 target number modifier for each additional test.

Disablement

A character who remains conscious after receiving Deadly Physical damage will become incapacitated when his Physical Damage Overflow exceeds half his Body (round down). Incapacitated characters may still be conscious but generally can't move or act. They may speak, look around and perform non-strenuous gestures, but they must make Perception and Communication Tests for even easy things, using applicable injury modifiers.

As with all characters who take Deadly Physical damage, the character continues to take an additional box of damage every (Body) Combat Turns, until they receive medical care or die. Each box of damage requires another Willpower Test to determine if the character remains conscious.

Generally, incapacitated characters are disoriented and only partly aware of their surroundings. The gamemaster may require the character to make Willpower Tests to refrain from babbling secrets or attacking friends (though in their weakened condition, these attacks will be quite ineffective). The character's best option is to lie down somewhere safe before he passes out.

SCARRING MODIFIERS

Healing Conditions	Modifier
Healed in hospital or clinic	–4
Healed under bad conditions (Barrens, slums, etc.)	+2
Healed under terrible conditions (cesspool, sewers, swamp, etc.)	+4
Magically healed of half damage or more	–4
Magically healed of less than half damage	–2
Character has dermal plating	+3
Character has dermal sheath	+2
Damage caused by fire or acid	+4

SCARRING TABLE

Number of Successes	Scar
0	Grotesque
1–2	Conspicuous
3–4	Romantic
5+	No visible scar

Characters with pain-resisting bioware or magic are still subject to disablement. Even a character with a pain editor will find that his body isn't working right and that he's having trouble concentrating, even though he feels no pain.

SCARS

Whenever a character takes a nasty wound, there is a chance that they may develop a scar.

After a character heals the damage from a Serious or Deadly Physical wound, the player makes a Body Test to determine if the wound left a scar. Make the test against a target number equal to the number of boxes of damage taken; apply the appropriate modifiers from the Scarring Modifiers table. Compare the number of successes to the Scarring Table to determine the type of scar created, if any.

Conspicuous and Romantic scars can be removed through simple cosmetic surgery (p. 146); Grotesque scars require moderate cosmetic surgery. At the gamemaster's discretion, the scar's location and visibility may affect the character's social interactions (for example, by imposing a +1 penalty to such interactions, a bonus to Intimidation Tests or even a bonus to negotiations—the target may consider people who have scars to be particularly attractive).

EXPANDED FIRST AID TABLE

	Modifier
Patient	
Is Awakened	+2
Has bioware	+(Bio Index ÷ 2, round up)
Is cyberzombie	+(absolute Essence value)
Is suffering Attribute failure	+1 per Attribute affected
Has Guardian Angel nano-implant	–2
Has Savior™ advanced medkit	–1
Patient's Body Attribute	
1–3	+0
4–6	–1
7–9	–2
10+	–3
Conditions	
Bad	+1
Terrible	+3
No medkit available	+4
Paramedic does not know cause of injury	+2

Nanosurgery: Wounds healed through nanosurgery (see p. 150) leave no scars.

DERMAL ARMOR DAMAGE

Whenever a character with dermal armor (plating or sheath) takes a Serious or Deadly wound, the dermal fiber weave's innate self-repairing properties may not function correctly. Roll 1D6; on a result of 1 for dermal sheaths or 1–2 for dermal plating, the armor has suffered damage that it cannot self-repair.

A spray bonder treatment is available for such circumstances, containing specially designed nanites that re-weave the armor fibers. This spray bonder costs 500 nuyen for 10 applications, and it must be used within 24 hours of taking the damage.

If the spray bonder is not applied in time, the dermal armor takes 1 Stress Point and the character must make a Stress Test.

OPTIONAL RULES

The following rules offer options that may not fit the gaming style of every group. All members of the group should review these rules before adding any of them to their game.

EXPANDED FIRST AID MODIFIERS

In addition to the modifiers given in the First Aid Table (p. 129, *SR3*), several other conditions may affect attempts at using Biotech (First Aid). These additional modifiers are listed on the Expanded First Aid Table.

Expanded First Aid Table Notes

Patient has bioware: Bioware upsets the body's natural balance, making healing more difficult and medical complications more common. See *Bioware Drawbacks,* p. 77.

Patient is cyberzombie: See *Cybermancy,* p. 50.

Patient is suffering Attribute failure: See *Wound Effects,* p. 126.

Patient has Guardian Angel nano-implant: See p. 91.

Patient has Savior advanced medkit: See p. 95.

Paramedic does not know cause of injury: In many cases, the cause of injury is apparent (bullet holes, knife in the back and so on). If it is not, the injuries are more difficult to treat and may even be misdiagnosed and treated incorrectly. The gamemaster may make a Medicine Test to determine if the medic correctly identifies the cause of injury.

EXPANDED DOCTORING

If a character fails their attempt to heal damage on their own (pp. 126–127, *SR3*), the character requires medical attention. The Expanded Doctoring Table offers additional modifiers for the test to determine how long it takes for the damage to heal.

Expanded Doctoring Table Notes

Doctor's Biotech (Extended Care) Skill: A skilled doctor can improve a character's chance of healing more quickly.

EXPANDED DOCTORING TABLE

Situation	Modifier
Care conditions (only one applies)	
Intensive care (hospital only)	–2
Not in hospital or clinic	+2
Bad conditions	+3
Terrible conditions	+4
Long-term magical care	–2
Patient is Awakened	+2
Patient's natural Body/Willpower Attribute is (apply for both)	
1–3	+0
4–6	–1
7–9	–2
10+	–3
Doctor's Biotech (Extended Care) Skill	
0	+4
1	+0
2	–2
3–4	–3
5–6	–4
7+	–5
Patient has undocumented bioware	+Bio Index
Patient has documented bioware	+(Bio Index ÷ 2, round up)
Patient has undocumented cyberware	
Essence 5.01–6	+0
Essence 3.01–5	+1
Essence 1.01–3	+2
Essence .01–1	+3
Cyberzombie	+(3 + absolute value of Essence)
Patient has documented cyberware	
Essence 3.01–6	+0
Essence 1.01–3	+1
Essence .01–1	+2
Cyberzombie	+(2 + absolute value of Essence)
Patient/doctor communication severely impeded	+2

OPTIONAL HEALING TABLE

Condition	Modifier
Not maintaining minimum lifestyle (see *Healing Table,* p. 127, *SR3*)	+2 per level below minimum
Better than minimum lifestyle	–1 per level above minimum
Bad conditions	+1
Terrible conditions	+3
Consistent recovery assistance provided (min. Biotech (Extended Care) Skill of 3)	–(Biotech ÷ 2, round down)
Patient has bioware	+(Bio Index ÷ 2, round up)
Rest required to heal previous box interrupted by activity	+1

Undocumented/Documented Bioware or Cyberware: Implants are considered documented if the character has told the doctor about all of them, or the doctor has scanned them all (see *Diagnosis and Profiling,* p. 144).

Patient/Doctor Communication Severely Impeded: If the doctor cannot communicate at all with the patient because of language barriers or refusal to cooperate, or because the patient is unconscious, apply this modifier.

HEALING PHYSICAL DAMAGE

The rules on pp. 126–127 of *SR3* describe the stages of healing Physical damage. The following optional rules replace those rules and allow characters to heal Physical damage box by box instead. These rules are more complex, but they allow players to more closely manage their characters' recovery—in effect, letting their characters feel better sooner.

These rules are also appropriate for healing bioware and Attribute Stress (see *Stress Maintenance,* p. 130).

Healing without Medical Care

Each box of damage is healed separately. To determine how much time it takes to heal one box, make an unaugmented Body Test against a target number equal to the total number of boxes of Physical damage, plus wound modifiers and appropriate modifiers from the Optional Healing Table. The base time to heal the box is equal to 24 x the total wound modifiers in hours, divided by the number of successes. If the test results in 0 successes, the base time is doubled.

Only time spent resting counts toward this healing time, though the resting period may be interrupted. Any type of physical activity or any type of strenuous mental activity (such as rigging or decking) does not count as resting.

At the end of the healing period, the Physical damage is reduced by 1 box, and the player determines the time required to heal the next box of damage. If during any healing period a character takes new Physical damage, the healing process is aborted and the character must begin again.

Healing with Medical Care

If the character requires medical care, use the rules provided in Healing without Medical Care, with the following exceptions: the base healing period per box is double the period described; apply modifiers from the Expanded Doctoring Table (p. 134); and the rest period cannot be interrupted.

A doctor's care for a patient consumes a base number of hours per day equal to the patient's boxes of Physical damage. Divide this time by the doctor's Biotech Skill plus the rating of his tools to determine the actual hours required. The cost of this care appears on p. 128, *SR3.*

Whenever the character's damage is reduced to a new Damage Level, the character may make a new Body Test against the target number listed on the Wound Table, p. 126, *SR3.* If the character achieves 2 successes, he no longer requires medical care and may be discharged. A character whose damage is reduced to a Light wound is automatically discharged.

CALLED SHOTS AND WOUND EFFECTS

An attacker who makes a successful called shot (see p. 114, *SR3*) against a target may choose to have the shot cause a wound effect rather than increasing the Damage Level of the attack. The called shot may cause additional wound effects, but at least one is guaranteed. For that wound effect, the gamemaster may use the Wound Effect Table or choose a specific wound effect type appropriate to the attack.

DEADLIER OVER-DAMAGE AND WOUND EFFECTS

When used in conjunction with wound effects, deadlier over-damage has the following results. For every 2 successes remaining after an attack has been staged to Deadly damage, the character suffers a wound effect. These wound effects are in addition to any caused by the damage from the attack itself. Use the Wound Effect Table to determine the wound effect type.

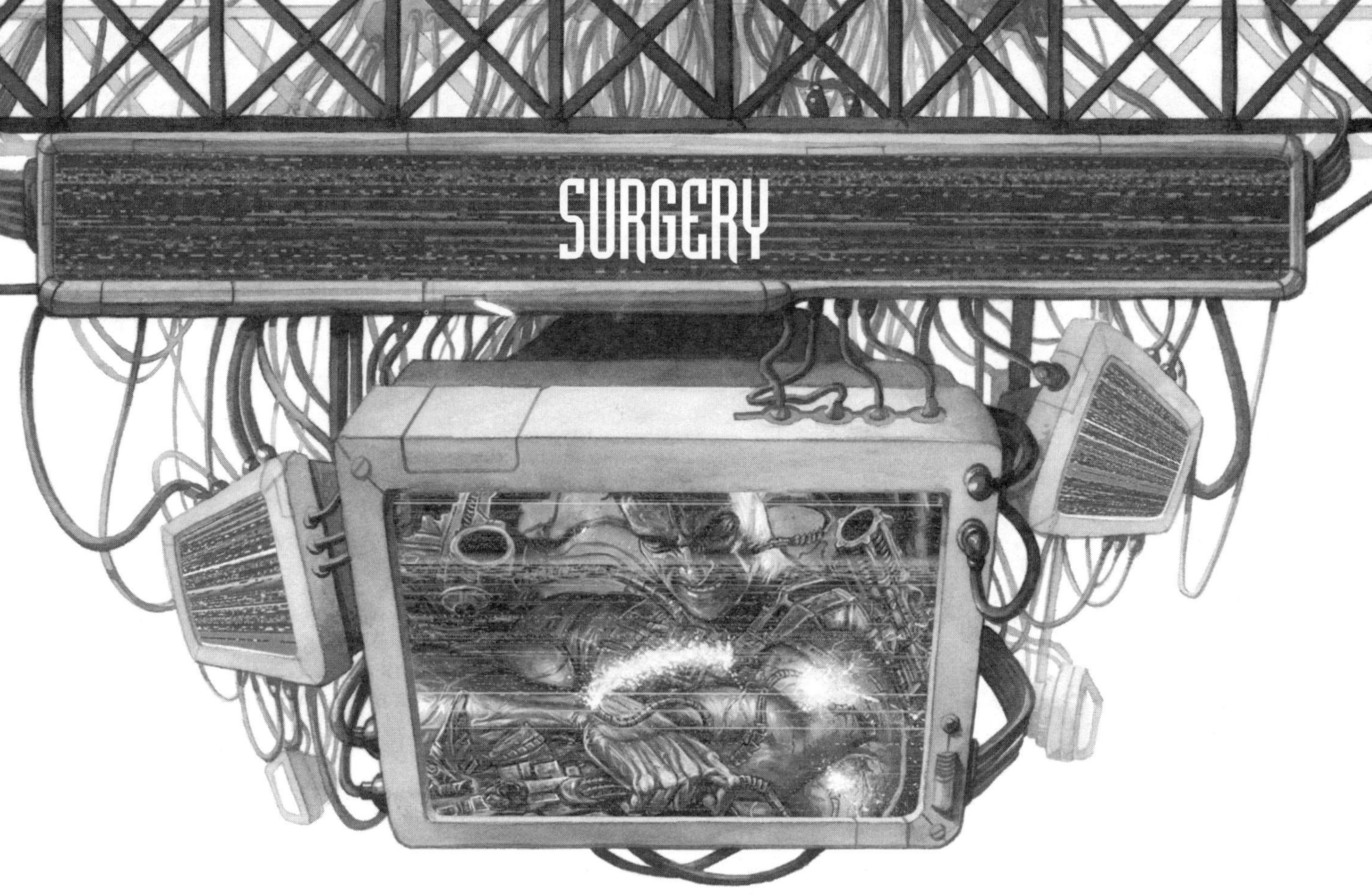

Sometime during a shadowrunner's career, he is bound to go under a surgeon's laser. Whether the runner is having the latest state-of-the-art implant installed; getting a face-lift to hide from old enemies; or having a few wounds tended to from a brawl with a troll, surgery will be necessary. The quality of the work can vary. Did the runner seek the hottest black clinic in town? Did he opt for the budget job in the nearest bar's back room, swigging down a pint of Jack for anesthetic? Maybe he had no say in the matter, and his life is in the hands of an emergency room doctor he's never met.

In 2060, surgery is no longer a hands-on, cut-'em open, grisly and direct procedure. Many techniques are programmed into automated surgical machines. Nanites, micro-drones and cellular-level manipulation allow precise medical monitoring and "bladeless" surgery. Medical care and even surgery are now possible from remote locations. Despite the technology, however, nothing beats a skilled doctor prepared to get his gloves bloody to save someone's life.

Detailed in this section are surgery rules for players and gamemasters, including the skills and gear needed, the challenge of finding medical care, an overview of the surgical process, pre-surgery diagnosis, planning, types of surgeries and procedures, surgical options and the costs.

SURGICAL SKILLS

No matter what tools and procedures are used, most surgeries require the same basic skill: Biotech. Several other Active and Knowledge Skills can also play a part.

ACTIVE SKILLS

Biotech

In *Shadowrun* all medical procedures use the base Active Skill of Biotech. The following Biotech specializations, as listed on p. 88, *SR3*, give an overview of what can be accomplished with this skill. Standard skill use and defaulting work the same for this skill and specializations.

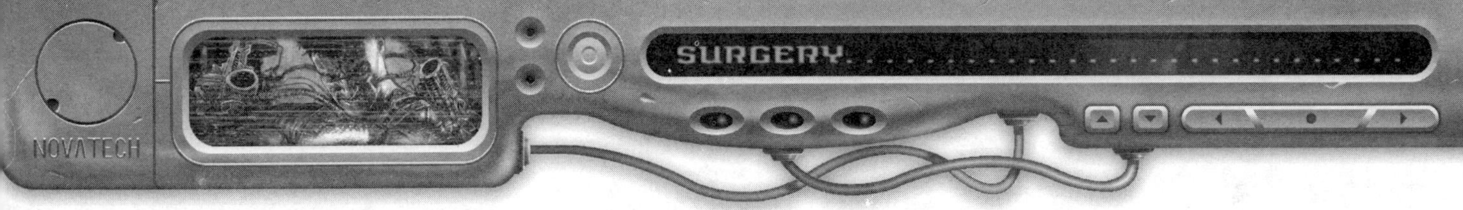

Cybermancy: This specialization is used for cybermantic surgery, as described on p. 55.

Cybertechnology Implantation: This specialization is used for implant surgery (p. 146) involving cyberware.

Extended care: This specialization focuses on post-op and recovery and long-term medical procedures. Many nurses have this specialization. It is used by medical personnel helping a character heal Physical damage (see *Stages of Healing,* p. 127, *SR3*).

First Aid: All the basic lifesaving techniques are covered by this specialization, including the Heimlich maneuver, treating bleeding, applying tourniquets, splinting broken bones, resuscitation, coping with shock and immediate wound care.

Magical Health: This new specialization of Biotech is used for extended care of Awakened patients. It includes knowledge of holistic healing methods, using astral perception to assess the subject's injuries and to identify possible healing complications, and using health spells (Prophylaxis, Resist Pain, Heal, and so on).

Organ Culture and Growth: This specialization handles the care and growth of organic body parts, including cloned replacements and biotechnology-enhanced implants. It also focuses on maintaining healthy transplant parts taken from donors.

Surgery: Used for cosmetic, therapeutic and trauma surgery, this specialization deals with all surgical procedures except those covered by Cybertechnology Implantation and Transimplant Surgery.

Transimplant Surgery: This is the specialization used for transimplant surgery (p. 147) involving bioware or replacement body parts.

Computer (Cybernetics)

The Cybernetics Specialization of Computer Skill includes knowledge of any cybertechnology that incorporates computerized systems, whether hardware or software. It focuses on the neural interface between such devices and the brain and nervous system, as well as datalinks to other devices.

Computer Cybernetics B/R: This Build/Repair Skill is called upon by implant surgeons repairing headware, skillwires, matrixware, riggerware and other computerized systems.

Electronics (Cybertechnology)

The Cybertechnology Specialization of Electronics deals with cyberware that incorporates electronics, especially senseware, cyberlimbs, smartlinks and other powered devices. Power and control systems, diagnostics, flux and communication, motorization and micro-engines are covered.

Electronics (Cybertechnology) B/R: This Build/Repair Skill handles the construction, maintenance and repair of electronic cyberware.

KNOWLEDGE SKILLS

Knowledge Skills represent the schooling and the specific medical background of a doctor and often separate a doctor from a mere medical technician who has only the Biotech Skill. The Knowledge Skill Medicine is a must for anyone wanting to be a doctor.

In addition, several other Knowledge Skills are particularly useful: Biotechnology, Cybertechnology, Genotechnology and Nanotechnology.

Other Knowledge Skills might also come in handy, such as Biology, (Para-)Zoology, (Para-)Botany, Chemistry and other physical science skills. Many doctors also have Psychology or Sociology Skills.

Medicine

This skill is used for diagnosis of medical problems (p. 144) as well as planning surgical procedures (p. 145). A doctor with no specialization in Medicine is considered a general practitioner or "family doctor."

Specializations: By specific biological system (cardiovascular, neurological, pulmonary and so on); also Traumatology (trauma surgery and care), Pathology (the study of diseases) and Toxicology (the study of toxins and poisons).

MEDICAL GEAR

Most shadowrunners are familiar with the standard (Rating 3) medkit (p. 304, *SR3*), but that only scratches the surface of what is available. Unlike other tools, medical kits are available in different ratings, as are med-shops (known as clinics) and med-facilities (known as hospitals).

The rules that define kits, shops and facilities on p. 288 of *SR3* give an abstract definition of what each unit contains; these apply toward medical tools as well. Each unit contains a basic assortment of necessary gear. Thanks to advances in genetics and nanotechnology, many medical tools are universal. For example, instead of storing a broad range of specialized drugs, most clinics produce drugs using their laboratory equipment.

Low-rated tool units are either outdated, might lack gear or might have broken components. If a medical kit, shop or facility is rated less than 3, the gamemaster should feel free to impose penalties upon its use, including target number modifiers and other minor effects.

Max Rating: The maximum rating of medical gear available to players is 6. Though certain facilities in the world of *Shadowrun* may have higher ratings, they are beyond the reach of shadowrunners.

Implant Grade and Surgery Tools: Shops and facilities that conduct implant or transimplant surgery and repair have the same price multipliers and availability adjustment as the implants themselves. For example, a clinic that can repair alphaware charges double the usual price.

Renting Access Time: Characters can access some clinics and hospitals simply by renting them. The character must have the appropriate permits. If the character is renting access time from an illegal black clinic, then he must pay the Street Index.

MEDKITS

Medkits perform the functions described on p. 304, *SR3.* They consist of basic medical sensors, reference programs and general-use legal drugs. A medkit allows a user to treat a single patient at a time. Medkits are legal.

If used by a character without Biotech Skill, medkits provide Biotech Skill equal to their rating. If used by a character

OOT
TOM FOWLER 99

MEDICAL TOOLS TABLE

Gear	Availability*	Cost*	Weight	Street Index
Medkits	(Rating – 1)/24 hrs	(Rating + 2) x 40¥	Rating	1.5
Medical Shops	Rating + 2/1 wk	$(Rating + 4)^3$ x 200¥	NA	2
Medical Facilities	Rating x 2/1 mo	$(Rating + 6)^4$ x 4,000¥	NA	3
Access to tools for personal use:				
Medical Shop (Clinic)	—	Rating x 100¥/day	—	3
Medical Facility (Hospital)	—	Rating x 300¥/day	—	3

* If the tools are used for graded implants, modifiers for grade also apply.

with Biotech Skill, they provide Complementary dice for Biotech Tests equal to their rating. In either case, medkits do not function independently; they require a living user to follow instructions and undertake tasks (applying bandages, injecting drugs and so forth).

MEDICAL SHOPS (CLINICS)

In the world of *Shadowrun,* many small clinics and doctors' offices operate with only a single medical shop. Clinics can accommodate one doctor per rating point and up to three nurses or biotechnicians per rating point. They are designed to allow a doctor, nurse or biotechnician to keep tabs on a number of patients at any given time equal to its rating number.

Most such operations are legal, though illegal black clinics also do a thriving business, as do quasi-legal clinics. A rating of 3 is the minimum a clinic must have to get a medical permit from the UCAS or Seattle government. Other territories can have higher (Tir Tairngire) or lower (Tsimshian) standards. Many illegal street docs operate in low-rated clinics.

Medical clinics do not usually have long-term care options.

A permit is required to purchase equipment for a medical clinic. Use the rules for obtaining a permit (pp. 273–274, *SR3*). Also required is proof of medical staff; at least one doctor and one nurse per rating point must be under contract. This staff must be registered as medical providers, though the staff's presence is not required to be awarded the permit. Permits cost 15 percent of the total cost of the shop.

Clinic Components

Clinics suffice for most medical purposes—as well as for many surgical operations. They act as a medkit equal to their ratings and as a stabilization unit (p. 305, *SR3*).

A standard clinic includes a computer with $Rating^2$ x 100 free Mp, powerful medical scanners, ASIST-based diagnostics, advanced reference programs equivalent to a medical library, subminiature "laproscopic" surgical drones, an assortment of controlled substances and prepared genetic and nanite treatments. It also has the capability to synthesize most drugs.

Clinics also possess the capability for remotely operated medical operations (see *Medical Telepresence Gear,* p. 139).

MEDICAL FACILITIES (HOSPITALS)

In *Shadowrun,* a hospital is designed for use by as many doctors as its rating x 5, and up to 10 x rating nurses and biotechnicians. It allows each doctor, nurse, and biotechnician to monitor a number of patients equal to the hospital's rating.

Most hospitals are owned by corporations. Individuals can purchase the equipment for a hospital but must first pass a DNA screening and obtain a permit. Getting a permit (pp. 273–274, *SR3*) requires proof of medical staff and at least 5 doctors and 10 nurses per rating point must be under contract. A separate head doctor and head nurse also must be contracted. All of these individuals must be registered as medical providers with the governing body. At the time a permit is awarded, the head doctor and nurse must be present and undergo DNA identity-check scans. Permits cost 25 percent of the total cost of the facility.

Hospital Components

Hospitals represent the most advanced medical technology available: from quantum resonance imaging to "knifeless" surgical methods. They can perform all the tasks of a clinic, and then some.

Each hospital includes a mainframe host with a Security Value equal to half its rating (round up); this is generally a user-friendly Green host. This limited-function dedicated host cannot be used for nonmedical purposes without temporarily reducing the rest of the facility to the effectiveness of a medical shop. The mainframe host provides the majority of current medical reference texts and a medical VR environment. This host is a part of the facility and is not usually hooked up to the Matrix. However, most hospitals expand their computer resources and link this base host to a more developed Matrix presence—usually behind a choke point.

Hospitals also have the capabilities for remotely operated medical operations (see *Medical Telepresence Gear,* p. 139), including everything a Valkyrie module is capable of.

MOBILE MEDICAL SHOPS

Hospitals—and sometimes clinics—employ ambulances and emergency medical technician (EMT) vehicles to respond to emergencies, pick up patients and so forth. In effect, these vehicles contain a medical shop specifically designed for in-vehicle use. Due to limited space, mobile clinics can only be simultaneously used by a number of doctors, nurses, or biotechnicians equal to their rating ÷ 3 (round down), though they can keep tabs on a number of patients equal to the shop's rating. The number of patients generally depends on the size of the vehicle.

In general, mobile clinics have a rating 2 less than the clinic or hospital they are associated with.

Mobile clinics possess the capability for limited remote medical operations, but not for tele-operated surgery (see *Medical Telepresence Gear).*

Vehicle Modification

The Vehicle Medical Clinic Table gives the statistics necessary to design or customize a vehicle with a medical shop, following the rules given on p. 108, *Rigger 2*. Note that any vehicle designed to carry a medical shop has a +1 Mark-Up Factor (see p. 114, *Rigger 2*). This does not include space for patients.

MEDICAL TELEPRESENCE GEAR

When combined with simsense technology, medical gear can be used to perform many medical procedures via telepresence. A biotechnician who is connected to a medical shop or facility via the Matrix or simsense broadcast can diagnose a patient's condition, plan procedures, issue instructions to a medkit and so forth. In effect, he can use the medical tools remotely.

At the gamemaster's discretion, certain procedures might not lend themselves to remote performance. Surgery, for example, is out of the question, unless a Valkyrie module is used.

VEHICLE MEDICAL CLINIC TABLE

Design Specifications
- **Design Cost:** (Rating + 4)^3 x 3 Points
- **Maximum Rating:** NA
- **CF Consumed:** Rating x 2
- **Load Reduction:** Rating x 75 kg

Customization Specifications
- **Part Cost:** (Rating + 4)^3 x 800¥
- **Parts Availability:** (Rating + 3)/(Rating x 2) days
- **Street Index:** 3
- **Maximum Rating:** NA
- **Base Time:** (Rating) days
- **Skill:** Appropriate Vehicle B/R Skill, Electronics B/R
- **Target Number:** Rating
- **Equipment Needed:** Vehicle Shop, Electronics Shop
- **CF Consumed:** Rating x 3
- **Load Reduction:** Rating x 100 kg

Valkyrie Module

A Valkyrie module is essentially a one-patient medical shop robotic drone designed for tele-surgery. The Valkyrie is fitted inside a vehicle (see the Valkyrie Module Modification Table, p. 140, for statistics); it has no self-mobility. The Valkyrie operates like a self-contained, expert-system-driven medical shop and can function as a mobile medical shop, though for only one patient at a time. Patients are placed inside, and the remote operator instructs and manipulates the Valkyrie in medical procedures, including surgery. The Valkyrie's numerous sensors, mechanical limbs and automated treatment systems take care of the rest.

The Valkyrie is specifically designed to handle a number of interface protocols. The remote operator can access the Valkyrie via a cyberdeck or remote control deck. It has satellite-uplink capability, as well as Matrix interfaces and rigger control adaptation.

In most cases, the tele-operator will be commanding the Valkyrie through "captain's chair" mode (see p. 154, *SR3*). The Valkyrie will be using its Pilot Rating (5) for all medical skill tests. The gamemaster may decide that certain esoteric surgical procedures require a Comprehension Test on the Valkyrie's part, to determine if its programming can understand the tele-operator's intentions (see *Issuing Commands,* pp. 66–67, *Rigger 2*).

If the tele-operator is communicating with the Valkyrie through a rigger remote control deck and has a VCR, he can "jump into" the Valkyrie and perform the surgery using his own Biotech Skill. Unlike normal rigging, this surgeon can use only 25 percent of his Control Pool (round down) on medical tests.

Valkyries are robots and have a minimum Learning Pool of 1 that can be applied toward medical tests (see *Robots,* p. 67, *Rigger 2*). At the gamemaster's discretion, the Learning Pool can be increased to 2 or 3 if the clinic or hospital the unit is affiliated with is of a particularly high rating.

Valkyrie modules are popular among shadowrunners and underworld biotechnicians because the virtual interaction allows for privacy and security. The biotechnician retains anonymity, while the patient retains control of his physical environment—no worrying about those pesky biological samples. Of course, some people do not trust Valkyrie modules, and reasonably so. Matrix intrusion or electronic signal interference is a potential problem. And without careful inspection, one can never be quite sure who built the unit and what "extras" they might have installed. As with the shadow clinics, the cutting edge of medicine always carries an element of risk.

DocWagon and other private medical providers rarely use Valkyrie modules, as their system of response teams and clinical care is less expensive in the developed areas they cover.

BODY PARTS

When a character loses a body part, he might opt to replace it with a transplant rather than cyberware or bioware. Such organic parts may have originated from a donor, or they might have been vat-grown from cloned tissue.

Organic parts are contingent upon availability and compatibility. While cloned organs are less likely to be rejected by the patient, they take time to grow. Donated organs are sometimes immediately available, but the user runs the risk of rejection and failure.

Transplanted body parts are subject to Stress (p. 124), similar to cyberware and bioware implants. They do not acquire Stress through damage; instead, the gamemaster determines when and how such transplants accumulate Stress, and when Stress Tests are necessary. If the transplant fails, the body has rejected it and the character must find a replacement. Such failures can have drastic effects upon the character's health.

Awakened characters who have non-cloned parts transplanted will lose Magic, as described under *Magical Characters and Damage,* p. 129, *SR3.*

Donated Parts

Donated parts are transplanted from another metahuman. "Donated" may be a misnomer, as many parts in fact come from the thriving organlegging trade and could have been stolen. Many parts are also taken from recently deceased people. Most governments and extraterritorial corps automatically require the dead to be "harvested" for useful organs, though this varies from jurisdiction to jurisdiction. This, of course, has led to competition over corpse retrieval in some areas—sometimes leading to an even higher body count.

In most cases, an effort is made to find a donor who is physiologically compatible with the intended recipient, to minimize the chance of rejection. This requires a medical profile (p. 144) of both the recipient and donor, which is usually not available in the cases of organlegged parts. Donated parts that are compatible with the patient are called "Type O" parts, as opposed to generic transplants.

Most hospitals have an ample supply of generic parts in storage and available for emergencies. Finding a Type O part takes time searching Matrix medical databases. This period is up to the gamemaster, depending on the common or uncommon nature of the patient's physiology. In rare cases, a well-stocked hospital may have a Type O part on hand. Both medical shops and facilities are capable of storing body parts; the longer they are stored, the less viable they become.

Use the costs on p. 128, *SR3,* for Type O donated parts; reduce the price by 60 percent (x .4) for generic parts.

Cloned Parts

As DocWagon and other medical services proudly advertise, body parts can be cloned from a patient's DNA. Cloned parts are a near-precise match and are rarely rejected. Of course, this process requires the patient to surrender some of his own cells for growth, which many shadowrunners are reluctant to do. Cloning parts generally takes a long time, despite accelerated growth methods. An often-used forced-growth process speeds up the timing significantly, though it still takes weeks at the minimum.

Parts cannot be grown individually—an entire clone body must be grown, which can then be harvested. Clones of this sort are barely considered metahumans and are usually little more than animals or slabs of living flesh. Forced-growth clones mature even faster, developing as full adults in less than two months, and are considered nothing more than meat.

Awakened characters usually reject forced-growth cloned parts. Only standard cloned parts will work. Note that the clones of Awakened people cannot be considered Awakened themselves.

In preparation for emergency situations, DocWagon and other emergency medical providers automatically grow and "care for" a cloned counterpart for purchasers of super-platinum or higher contracts. These can be used as sources for parts as soon as three months after the contract is signed.

Only special single-purpose medical facilities have the capability to grow cloned tissue, especially forced-growth clones. The base growth time for cloned parts appears on p. 128, *SR3.* For basic cloned parts, double the cost; quadruple it for forced-growth parts.

VALKYRIE MODULE MODIFICATION TABLE

Design Specifications
Design Cost: 3,000 Points
Maximum Rating: NA
CF Consumed: 10
Load Reduction: 400 kg
Customization Specifications
Part Cost: 1,000,000¥
Parts Availability: 10/2 wks
Street Index: 3
Maximum Rating: NA
Base Time: 5 days
Skill: Appropriate Vehicle B/R Skill, Electronics B/R
Target Number: 5
Equipment Needed: Vehicle Shop, Electronics Shop
CF Consumed: 15
Load Reduction: 500 kg

Notes: Includes rigger adaptation, satellite uplink, datajack port, Pilot 5, Learning Pool 1 and space for one patient.

FINDING TREATMENT

Finding a doctor to give you a checkup, treat a minor injury or administer long-term care is easy—just look in an online city reference or visit a local clinic. However, finding a doctor who isn't busy, who will accept payment after treatment or who will keep your injuries and illegal implants a secret is a little more difficult and more expensive.

Good medical skills and facilities are unquestionably important to shadowrunners, but the characters won't always have a choice. Knowing the ratings of a doctor's skills and tools is important for the gamemaster, who will be making the tests to determine how medical procedures go. The following rules offer two methods of determining those ratings, depending on whether the medical care is an emergency—the bullet-ridden character was picked off the street by DocWagon—or non-emergency, such as the character seeking a nice black clinic for some implant surgery.

MEDICAL PROVIDERS

In the medical profession, expert doctors, nurses and technicians are worth their weight in orichalcum. Medical-care providers fit into four categories—corporate, private, public and illegal. Each operates differently, and this can have an impact on a character's options and choices.

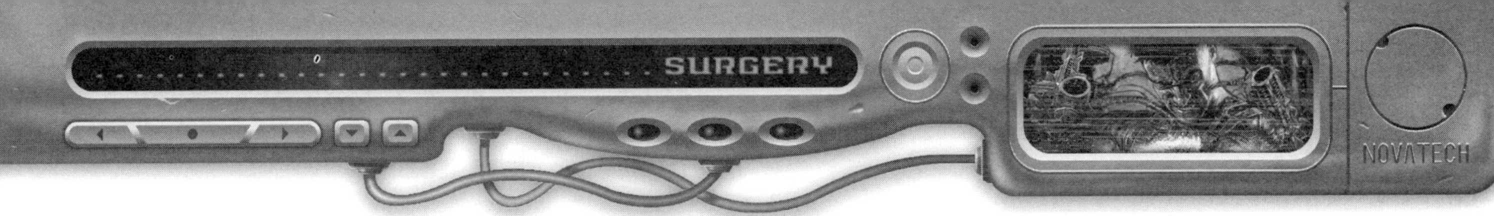

Corporate

Many corporations, from non-rated nationals to AAA megacorps, operate health-care centers usually only available to employees or corporate citizens. To receive medical services from these centers, the character is required to have a corporate ID and SIN, or at least good forgeries. Many will also only accept payment in corporate scrip. Company men and women are usually given access to such sites for trauma and implant care. It is also possible for shadowrunners to work out a deal with a corporate Johnson to gain access to such services.

Corporate medical providers are often the only source for certain procedures or implants. Corporate sites are also more likely to have alpha-grade or better gear, and their doctors are usually more skilled. Some even offer emergency medical services similar to DocWagon, though usually at much steeper rates and with slower service.

The primary bonus for many AA and AAA corp medical centers is their extraterritoriality. A piece of cyberware that cannot be legally installed within a Seattle public hospital might be obtainable from the Yamatetsu clinic two blocks over, as they operate under Yamatetsu laws. Many extraterritorial corporate med-centers pay lip service to local laws regarding implants to maintain good relations and a community-service façade. But the right cred can inspire them to conveniently ignore such trivialities behind their sovereign closed doors.

There are several drawbacks to using corp-sponsored medical centers. The corp will know what implants a character is packing and what procedures he has undergone—information many privacy-loving shadowrunners aren't willing to give. The corp controls the medical environment, so there is also the possibility that it might retain biological samples (for forensics and ritual sorcery); include some unwanted implants ("Did we mention the cortex bomb we installed?") or use the character to test some experimental procedures or devices.

DocWagon: DocWagon and equivalent services are popular with shadowrunners because their clinics maintain extraterritorial status; a patient's location and records are generally confidential. DocWagon generally acknowledges extradition requests from Lone Star and other corporate security institutions.

Private

Private clinics and hospitals are owned, funded and operated by a private interest and are only available to selected clientele. This includes private-practice medical professionals, military health services, university clinics and those maintained by special interest groups. Even tribal shamans and medical personnel fall into this category.

Unlike public med-centers, private practices can select to whom they sell their services. They tend to focus on specific sectors and criteria. Characters may be able to obtain services by meeting those criteria, doing them a favor or just paying them off.

Private health care staff is a notch above public, though such personnel may be dedicated to a particular purpose that is at odds with the character's goals.

Public

Theoretically, anyone can walk into one of these centers and get care. Realistically, if an individual doesn't have cred or a SIN, he's pushed to the end of the line and may even be legally denied service despite the Hippocratic oath. Public health centers are usually overwhelmed by masses of the poor and downtrodden, who have no other access to medical care. Getting medical attention usually requires a wait of at least several hours, unless the character's situation is dire. Certain procedures require payment up-front.

Public health care is usually government-run, though many sites are also privately owned, usually held by corporations looking for a public relations boost, or by some "charitable" entity such as the Catholic Church. Privately owned centers tend to be more professional and less disease-ridden than government sites.

Public hospitals usually offer emergency medical services to the surrounding community. Unlike DocWagon or other armed medical providers, no high-threat service is available. If the ambulance or EMT encounters a combat situation, they will immediately withdraw and contact the police.

EMERGENCY CARE TABLE

Situation	Modifier
Medical Provider	
DocWagon	+2
CrashCart/other corp service	+1
Private	+0
Public/Illegal	–1
*EMT Response Team**	
High-threat	–1
Standard/crisis	+0
*Medical Contract**	
Super-platinum	+3
Platinum	+2
Gold	+1
Basic	+0
None	–1
Neighborhood Rating	
AAA or AA	+1
A or B	+0
C or D	–1
E or Z	–2
Character is SINless	–1
Patient is a prisoner/under arrest	–2

*These refer to DocWagon-specific services. Services from other providers should be approximated.

EMERGENCY RATING TABLE

Modified 2D6 Roll	Skill Rating	Gear Rating
0 or less	None	None
1	2	1
2	3	1
3	3	2
4	4	2
5	4	2
6	5	3
7	5	3
8	5	3
9	6	4
10	6	4
11	7	4
12	7	5
13	8	5
14	9	6
15 or more	10	6

The quality of service in public hospitals is average at best. Most doctors find better-paying corporate jobs. Racism and class bias are prevalent; a human suit can expect to see a doctor faster than an ork squatter.

Public med-centers must follow local laws. Many public-service medical professionals supplement their meager incomes by undertaking illegal operations on the side. In some cases, entire hospital wings might be engaged in illegal services. It is not uncommon for public-hospital staffers to have seedy sidelines. They may be buying or selling corpses or used implants with organleggers, engaging in illegal testing or worse.

Black Clinics

Any illegal med-center falls under the black clinic category. These can range from street docs who remove bullets in the corner bar's back room to clinics for hire that engage in illegal procedures. The high-end black clinics are usually sponsored by some powerful interest group, including dragons, policlubs and even corps. The majority are corp- or underworld syndicate-connected, allowing them the resources for high-tech procedures.

Black clinics specialize in illegal goods. In fact, many don't even bother offering legal wares and procedures. They never require ID or SINs, though they do require payment in advance.

Black clinics usually have connections for obtaining used implants and replacement organs.

FINDING EMERGENCY MEDICAL CARE

When a character receives medical care from a random source (passerby, emergency response ambulance or nearest clinic), roll 2D6 to determine the ratings of the attending biotechnician's skills and tools. Make a separate check for each. Apply appropriate modifiers from the Emergency Care Table and consult the Emergency Rating Table for the result.

A modified roll that results in "none" can mean several things. Perhaps the "doctor" doesn't have the necessary skill and must default. He might not have the proper gear. Or he may just refuse to aid the character for some reason, such as the character being SINless.

Twitch has been shot up pretty good on a run gone bad in Renton. His team left him behind, and when Lone Star arrives, they cuff him and call the nearest hospital—which happens to be a small public place called Maple Valley General Hospital. The gamemaster rolls 2D6 a few times to determine the service Twitch gets. He rolls a 9 for the hospital's rating and an 11 for the emergency-room doctor's Biotech Skill. The modifiers to these rolls are –1 (public hospital), –1 (Twitch has no medical contract), –1 (neighborhood is rated C) and –2 (Twitch is a Lone Star prisoner), for a total of –5. With the modifiers, the gamemaster checks the table and notes that the hospital is Rating 2 (9 – 5 = 4, which equals a 2) and the doctor's Biotech is 5 (11 – 5 = 6, which equals a 5). Twitch could have gotten much worse.

NON-EMERGENCY MEDICAL CARE

Whenever a character spends the time to work his contacts and seek out medical care in a non-emergency situation, his success will depend on several factors: who he knows, what kind of clinic and surgery he's looking for, the grade of any implants he desires, illegality and so on. The gamemaster should consult the following to determine how well the search proceeds.

The character should first decide what he's looking for and then consult the Medical Search Table for modifiers to this test. For example, if the character wants an illegal black clinic to install some security-grade alphaware, he's facing modifiers of –1 (illegal clinic), +1 (implant surgery), +2 (alphaware) and +1 (security grade), for a total of +3.

The character then makes an Etiquette (4) Test, plus modifiers, to see if he is able to track down what he's looking for. One success is all that's needed. The base rating and search time are given on the Medical Ratings Table (p. 144). Extra successes may be used to reduce this time (divide the time by successes) or to increase the rating of the medical gear (+1 per success, maximum 6).

To determine the skill ratings of the attending biotechnicians, roll 2D6 and apply the skill modifier listed on the Medical Ratings Table. Take the modified result and consult the Emergency Rating Table (p. 142) to determine the skill rating. Roll separately for each skill.

MEDICAL SEARCH TABLE

Situation	Modifiers
Appropriate Contact	
Fixer, government official, organlegger, etc.	–1
Street doc, DocWagon medtech, etc.	–2
Provider Sought	
Corporate	+2
Private	+1
Illegal	–1
Public	–2
Clinic	+0
Hospital	+2
Type of Surgery	
Cosmetic	–1
Implant	+1
Therapeutic	+0
Transimplant	+1
Trauma	+0
Nanosurgery	+2
Implant Grade	
Basic cyberware	+0
Alphaware/basic and cosmetic bioware	+2
Betaware/cultured bioware	+4
Deltaware	+8
Nanoware	+4
Legality	
Legal	–1
Paralegal/Class A	+0
Security grade/Class B	+1
Military grade/Class C	+2
Each extra skill required	+1

Medical Search Table Key

Appropriate Contact: Depending on what the character is looking for, some contacts might give him a few pointers. For example, a city official will likely know of public medical centers but will not be useful if searching for a black clinic. Medical professionals of any type are always helpful and provide a –2.

Provider Sought: See p. 140 for details on different provider types.

Type of Surgery: See pp. 146-148 for descriptions of the surgery types. Nanosurgery is any surgery incorporating the nanosurgery option (p. 150).

Implant Grade: See the sections on *Cyberware Grades* (p. 45) and *Bioware Grades* (p. 76) for info on implant grades.

Legality: Legality Codes are explained on p. 273 of *SR3*.

Each Extra Skill Required: Medical providers are assumed to have Biotech (p. 135) and Medicine (p. 136) Skills. Certain procedures may require other skills, however, as noted in their descriptions. Any additional such skills required incur a +1 modifier.

GETTING IN THE DOOR

Once a character has found a medical provider, he must negotiate for the service he wants. Certain factors can pose difficulties, depending on the provider (see the descriptions on p. 140). The character may lack a SIN, be unable to pay up-front, might be asking them to break the law, may not have corp ID or corpscrip and so on. The provider could demand to keep records on the patient, file paperwork with higher authorities and keep tissue samples.

Shadowrunners asking for certain regulations to be "overlooked" or "special considerations" to be made must make an Etiquette Test

MEDICAL RATINGS TABLE

Provider	Base Rating	Skill Modifier	Search Time
Standard illegal	2	–2	1 day
Standard private/public	3	–1	2 days
DocWagon/corp-owned	4	+0	1 week
Alpha/bioware-equipped	5	+1	2 weeks
Beta/cultured bioware-equipped	6	+2	1 month
Nanoware-equipped	6	+2	2 months
Delta-equipped	8	+4	6 months

equal to the med-center's rating. Apply any appropriate modifiers from the Medical Search Table (p. 143) and Social Modifiers Table (p. 94, *SR3*), plus any others the gamemaster feels are appropriate.

The character can attempt to bribe his way in, using nuyen to grease the wheels. Most doctors have no problem with extra compensation, and the threat of losing a medical license is lessened due to the realities of extraterritoriality. The going rate for such bribes is 10 percent of the service's total cost. Offering this amount or more generally makes breaking the rules advantageous to the provider (apply a –2 modifier to the Etiquette Test).

If the Etiquette Test fails, the doctor refuses. Intimidation or other attempts at coercion could help, but this could also persuade the provider to turn the character over to the authorities. Of course, many doctors have been known to perform surgery with an AK-97 pointed at them.

SURGERY OVERVIEW

The several different types of surgery (p. 146-148) all follow roughly the same formula. First, the patient is scanned and diagnosed. Using this medical data, the doctor then plans the surgery (p. 145).

Surgery is a complex process. Within each type of surgery are a variable number of *procedures* (p. 145) that can be undertaken. For example, under implant surgery, there are several possible procedures, including implant cyberware, remove cyberware, repair cyberware and so on.

When planning a procedure, the results of the surgery are tabulated in a *Procedural List,* with each Surgical Test success having a listed result, as shown on the Procedural List Example. Each of the entries is called a *surgical option* (p. 148). Each procedure must list two negative options and a number of positive options. The exact options used are chosen by the patient and doctor and are listed during the planning stage.

When the surgery is undertaken, a test is made against a target number determined by the procedure. The number of successes is compared to the Procedural List to determine the surgery's outcome. At 0 successes it fails. At 1 success, it succeeds but both negative options apply. At 2 successes, it succeeds, but only the second negative option applies. Break-even is 3 successes, and each success past that means that a positive option was achieved.

Additionally, each Surgery Test made is treated as an open-ended Success Test. The target number for this is called the Surgical Threshold. The base Threshold is the test's base target number. Count down the Procedural List, marking off options achieved by the successes. Surgical options can modify the Threshold as options are reached on the Procedural List. Apply any Threshold modifiers; all such modifiers are cumulative. If the high result of the Surgical Test does not meet the modified Threshold, that option is not achieved, nor are any others further down the list, even if there are successes remaining.

More than one procedure may be conducted during a surgical session, though additional procedures become more difficult.

DIAGNOSIS AND PROFILING

Before surgery, the patient undergoes medical checks and scans to build a *medical profile* to assess general health and magical activity. This helps to avoid complications, such as allergies, location of implants, diseases, blood filters, nanoware and the like. These tests also help to diagnose any problems or conditions the character could unknowingly have.

Medical profiles are also useful for determining matches for Type O transplants (see p. 140)—of course, this entails taking blood and tissue samples. Medical profiling, including implant detection (p. 145), is mandatory for anyone wishing to sign a platinum or super-platinum contract with DocWagon or a similar medical-care provider.

Some shadowrunners avoid medical profiles, as they don't want to put themselves at risk for having illegal implants or risk letting their medical data fall into the wrong hands.

Creating a medical profile requires a medical shop or facility and a base time of 48 hours. The profiling character must succeed in a Medicine (4) Test; extra successes can be used to reduce the base time. The patient being profiled must be present for a quarter of the total time.

PROCEDURAL LIST EXAMPLE

Successes	Result
0	Failure
1	Succeeds, with 2 Negative Options
2	Succeeds, with 1 Negative Option
3	Succeeds, with 0 Negative Options
4	Succeeds, with 1 Positive Option
5+	Succeeds, with 2 Positive Options (+1 more Positive Option per extra success to limit)

At the gamemaster's discretion, certain procedures and options might require a specialized medical profile, one that delves deeply into areas a general profile doesn't cover. Medical profiles are also time-sensitive, as a person's physiology changes, especially as new implants and wounds are introduced.

DETECTING IMPLANTS

Undocumented implants can cause problems during surgery and can interfere with first aid and other medical care. If a character has chosen not to tell—or is incapable of telling—a doctor about certain implants, use the following to determine whether they are found.

First, make a Perception Test for the doctor against the Concealability Rating (if any) of implants that are potentially noticeable through a visual scan.

Next, every clinic and hospital features equipment for detecting implants. These devices can scan for both cyberware and bioware, but each requires a separate test. The rating of the detection gear equals the clinic or hospital's rating. The target numbers for these tests and the results of successes are listed on the Implant Detection Table. Each scan, for cyberware and bioware, takes a base time of 60 minutes; extra successes can be used to decrease this time. No successes means the test only reveals the basic Essence Rating or Bio Index of the character.

IMPLANT DETECTION TABLE

Implant Type	Target Number Clinic/Hospital
Cyberware	
Basic	4/3
Alphaware	6/5
Betaware	8/7
Deltaware	10/9
Bioware	
Basic	6/5
Cultured	10/9
Nanoware	8/7

Successes	Details
1	Type of implant or nanite
2	Implant manufacturer, any ratings
3	Grade
4	Amount of Stress or degradation
5	Options used on it, nanite manufacturer

SURGERY PLANNING TIME

Type and Procedure	Base Time
Cosmetic	24 hrs
Implant	
Install/Remove/Upgrade	72 hrs
Repair	36 hrs
Therapeutic	48 hrs
Transimplant	60 hrs

Surgery Involves	Base Time Modifier
Alphaware	x 2
Betaware	x 4
Deltaware	x 8
Cultured Bioware	x 6
Nanoware	x 4
Each Positive Option	x (Threshold Modifier)

SURGICAL PLANNING AND PREPARATION

Given the high-tech and automated nature of most surgical techniques in 2060, it is necessary to plan everything step by step. The exception is trauma surgery, which is usually fast and improvised. Surgery that is not planned out suffers modifiers as noted on the Surgery Table (p. 146).

To plan the procedure, a doctor must have the Knowledge Skill Medicine and the other skills needed to perform the surgery—at the minimum, Biotech.

OPTIONS

Though the patient usually indicates which options he would prefer, and in what order, the final choice is up to the surgeon. Unscrupulous doctors, or those with hidden agendas, can choose and order the options. Unless the actual surgical plan is analyzed, or the surgeon is monitored by someone with knowledge in Biotech—a Biotech (6) Test—the different procedure will not be noticed until it is too late. While this gives the gamemaster some leeway for plot development and twists, it should not be abused merely to make the character's life more difficult.

Two negative options must be listed on each Procedural List. These represent the basic difficulties of surgery. The negative options can be chosen by the gamemaster. Unless it is noted, the same option can be used twice.

The doctor planning the surgery can list as many positive options in the procedure equal to his Medicine Knowledge Skill. The number of positive options cannot exceed the rating of the medical equipment being used—no gear, no positive options! In 2060, most surgical options are common knowledge in the medical field, and the details of each are accessible via numerous Matrix archives and libraries. At the gamemaster's discretion, certain procedures can be limited—these would be state-of-the-art and known only to a select few.

CREATING A PROCEDURE

To thoroughly plan the surgery, the doctor must have access to the patient's medical profile (see *Diagnosis and Profiling,* p. 144) and a computer with enough memory to hold the surgical prep data.

Each type of surgery, with the exception of trauma surgery, has a base planning time (listed on the Surgery Planning Time table). Each positive option that is included in the Procedural List requires an additional amount of medical data preparation.

The biotechnician must make a successful Medicine Test against a Target Number

4, +1 for each positive option. Successes may be used to reduce the base time.

Surgical data has an Mp size equal to the Base Time (with modifiers) x 2.

SURGICAL TESTS

There are five types of surgery in *Shadowrun:* cosmetic, implant, therapeutic, transimplant and trauma. Each follows roughly the same rules, with some variations.

Surgery is normally performed in a medical facility, but it can be performed in a medical shop or even on the street—with appropriate modifiers, of course. Surgery involving implants of grades higher than basic must be done with tools of that grade (see *Medical Gear,* p. 136).

Most surgical procedures are assumed to require anesthesia; the patient is brought to D Stun damage and cannot recover until the surgeon finishes.

The base target number for each type of surgery below depends on the exact procedure, as listed on the appropriate table. Available negative and positive options are also listed; these are detailed under *Surgical Options* (p. 148).

The Surgery Test uses Biotech Skill or an appropriate Biotech Specialization. Apply any fitting modifiers from the Surgery Table. The medical gear rating may be used as Complementary dice.

Surgery takes a number of hours equal to the Surgery Test target number. Any extra successes not used for options may be used to decrease this time.

SURGERY TABLE

Situation	Modifier
Surgery Location	
Medical facility/hospital	–2
Medical shop/clinic	–1
Mobile shop/clinic	+0
Elsewhere	+3
Elsewhere without a medkit	+5
Surgery Conditions	
Bad conditions	+3
Terrible conditions	+4
Medical gear of better grade than necessary	–2
Lacking medical profile	+1 (or more)
Lacking surgical data	+1
Via telepresence	+1
Additional doctor(s) (Biotech and Medicine of 4+)	–1
Magical care provided during surgery	–1
Each prior procedure done this surgical session	+1
Prior procedure attempt failed	+2
Patient Condition	
Essence 2 or less	+1
Cyberzombie	+(Absolute Essence Value)
Patient has bioware	+(Bio Index ÷ 2, round up)
Patient is Awakened	+1
Implant Surgery	
Alphaware	+1
Betaware	+3
Deltaware	+6
Therapeutic Surgery	
Cultured bioware	+1
Attribute enhanced by cyberware or bioware	+1
Transimplant Surgery	
Cultured bioware	+1
Generic non-matched transplant	+1
Type O transplant	+0
Cloned transplant	–1
Trauma Surgery	
Trauma patch used on patient	+1

COSMETIC SURGERY

Cosmetic surgery is designed to change the appearance of the patient—from minor modifications, such as nose jobs and crafting pointed ears for elf-posers, to tummy tucks, liposuction and full facial reconstruction. More esoteric options, such as adding scales, fur and other minor biotechnology changes, are also possible. Cosmetic surgery is relatively non-invasive.

To notice cosmetic surgery requires a successful Perception Test at a Target Number 8. The Natural Looks option can be used to increase this target number.

There are three variations of cosmetic surgery: simple, moderate and serious.

SIMPLE COSMETIC CHANGE

These procedures involve changes such as snubbing ears or removing scars. Minor cosmetic surgery causes the character a Light Physical wound.

MODERATE COSMETIC CHANGE

This involves mildly invasive changes: elongating ears, skin grafts, nose jobs, liposuction and so on. Moderate surgery causes a Moderate Physical wound.

SERIOUS COSMETIC CHANGE

Serious surgery involves facial reconstruction or the addition of cosmetic bioware (see p. 76). This causes a Serious Physical wound.

IMPLANT SURGERY

Implant surgery includes the installation, removal, upgrading and repair of cyberware.

CYBERMANCY

Surgery that involves cybermancy requires this procedure. See *Less than Zero* (p. 55) for details on this surgery.

INSTALL CYBERWARE

This is used to install cyberware of all grades. Characters who begin the game with cyber-implants are assumed to have gone under the laser for implant surgery prior to game play. The rules included here are advanced rules intended for subsequent cyber-enhancements and they should not be used for starting characters.

Implant surgery sometimes follows immediately after trauma surgery, as damaged body parts or limbs are replaced with metal and chrome. Unless contingency plans have been made and filed in advance, such post-trauma implant surgery can only install basic or alpha-grade cyberware. If the post-trauma character is under the care of a street doc or illegal med-center—or if he is in legal care but has no SIN or no nuyen—there is a 50 percent chance that used cyberware will be installed.

If the procedure fails, the implant is installed, but the body rejects it. The character cannot heal and suffers an additional point of Physical damage per day until the cyberware is removed.

This procedure also covers the installation of fixed nanoware (p. 98) and nanoware implants such as the nanite facilitators (p. 90), which require the nanosurgery option.

COSMETIC SURGERY TEST TARGET NUMBERS

Procedure	Target Number
Simple	3
Moderate	5
Serious	6

Negative Options: Essence Loss, Marred Appearance, Scarring
Positive Options: Human Looking, Improved Looks, Nanosurgery, Natural Looks

REMOVE CYBERWARE

Cyberware that is removed does not restore the character's lost Essence. Removing cyberware incurs permanent damage to the implant (1D6 ÷ 2 Stress).

If this procedure fails, the cyberware is not removed, it suffers 1D6 ÷ 2 Stress, and it must make a Stress Test.

REPAIR CYBERWARE STRESS

Repairing Stress damage to cyberware implants requires surgery. If successful (3 successes are achieved), 1 Stress Point is removed from the implant. The rest of the implant's Stress remains. If the test fails, 1 Stress Point becomes permanent and can never be repaired. Removing the remaining Stress requires a doctor with a higher-level Biotech Skill.

Cyberware repair is never conducted in post-trauma surgery.

REPAIR CYBERWARE FAILURE

A cyberware implant that has failed due to Stress can be repaired with this procedure. If successful (3 successes are achieved), the implant is fixed and the Stress Points are reduced to 6 (Serious Level). If the test fails, 1 Stress Point becomes permanent and can never be repaired.

Cyberware repair is never conducted in post-trauma surgery.

UPGRADE CYBERWARE

Cyberware can be upgraded without its removal; the cost and Essence Cost of the new part equal the total costs of the upgrade implant minus the old implant costs.

Failure means that the cyberware is not upgraded, and it suffers 1 Stress Point. Upgrading is never conducted in post-trauma surgery.

IMPLANT SURGERY

Procedure	Target Number
Cybermancy	Special (see *Less than Zero*, p. 55)
Install cyberware	4
Remove cyberware	3
Repair cyberware Stress	3
Repair cyberware failure	4
Upgrade cyberware	4

Negative Options: Essence Cost, Fragility, Obvious, Sensitive
Positive Options: Concealed, Essence Reduction, Essence Slot, Nanosurgery, Redundancy, Remove Stress Point, Rugged

THERAPEUTIC SURGERY

Therapeutic surgery is needed to repair damaged bioware. Lasting injuries represented by Attribute Stress and failure can also be repaired through therapeutic surgery. Separate Surgery Tests are required for each bioware item and Attribute.

Therapeutic surgery requires at least 3 successes.

CORRECT STRESS

This procedure is designed to remove Stress from a particular bioware item or damaged Attribute. If successful (3 successes are achieved), the targeted bioware or Attribute is reduced in Stress by 1. If the test fails, 1 Stress Point becomes permanent and never can be repaired. Only a doctor with a higher Biotech Skill can remove the remaining Stress.

CORRECT FAILURE

This procedure is designed to repair a particular bioware implant or Attribute that has failed due to Stress. If successful (3 successes are achieved), the targeted bioware or Attribute becomes functional again, and the Stress Points are reduced to 6 (Serious Stress Level).

TRANSIMPLANT SURGERY

This is called for to replace damaged organs and limbs and to install and remove bioware. Separate Surgery Tests are required for each bioware item and replacement part.

Transimplant surgery often follows trauma surgery, as body parts that are excessively damaged need to be replaced. Removing bioware usually means that a replacement organ must be installed.

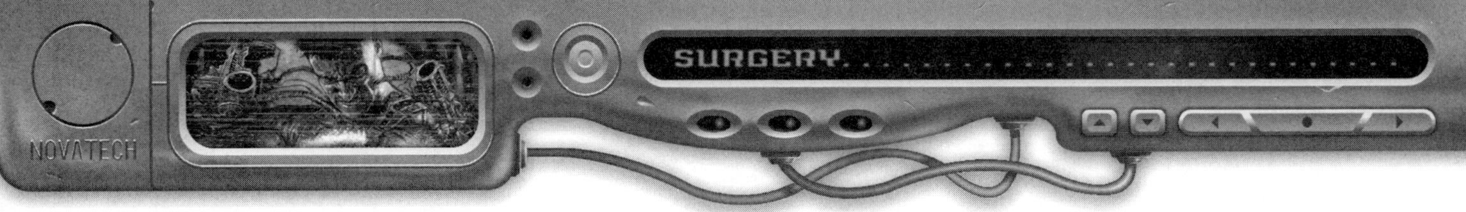

INSTALL BIOWARE

Whenever bioware is implanted, this procedure is used. The bioware implant itself must be available (see *Bioware Grades,* p. 76).

If this procedure fails, the bioware is implanted, but the body rejects it. The character cannot heal and suffers an additional point of Physical damage each day until the item is removed.

REMOVE BIOWARE

If bioware is removed, the character does not regain the implant's Bio Index. Removing bioware incurs permanent damage to the implant (1 Stress point).

Removing bioware usually requires that a replacement part be found and transimplanted.

If this procedure fails, the bioware implant is not removed; it suffers 1 Stress point, and it must make a Stress Test.

TRANSPLANT ORGAN/LIMB

Replacement body parts, whether transplanted from another person or a cloned "spare" (see *Body Parts,* p. 139), are implanted using this procedure.

If this procedure fails, the part is transplanted, but the body rejects it. The character cannot heal and suffers an additional point of Physical damage each day until the part is removed.

TRAUMA SURGERY

DocWagon and street docs specialize in this—emergency life or death surgery. This involves everything from removing mangled limbs to removing bullets. Trauma surgery is designed to correct life-threatening bodily malfunction or damage in emergencies.

In game terms, trauma surgery is necessary when a character has suffered a Deadly wound (10 boxes or more of Physical damage), even if the character has been stabilized. If the character has been magically healed below Deadly, surgery is not necessary. Trauma surgery is also necessary when a character has suffered 16 boxes of combined Physical and Stun damage.

Trauma surgery is often immediately followed by additional surgery—such as transimplant or implant. This additional surgery is usually necessary to replace irreparably damaged limbs and organs (see *Deadly Wounds and Permanent Damage,* p. 127, *SR3*).

The base target number for trauma surgery is equal to the character's Physical damage modifiers, plus half Stun damage modifiers, plus half Overflow damage (round fractions down). For example, a character with Serious Stun and 3 boxes of Physical Overflow would have a TN of 4 (Physical damage modifier) + 1 (Serious) +1 (Overflow), or 6.

TREAT DEADLY WOUNDS

Every character requiring trauma surgery needs this. A character must first be stabilized (see *Deadly Wounds and First Aid,* p. 129, *SR3*). Remember that any medical shop or facility incorporates a stabilization unit (p. 305, *SR3*). An unstabilized character will die before the surgery is completed.

If the procedure succeeds, the character is reduced to Serious Physical damage; characters who had taken half their Overflow damage or more are only reduced to Deadly damage. The character heals normally.

If this procedure fails, a second attempt may be made at +2. If this procedure also fails, the patient dies.

TREAT PERMANENT DAMAGE

Any character who has sustained permanent damage (see *Deadly Wounds and Permanent Damage,* p. 127, *SR3*) must undergo this procedure to remove a mutilated organ or limb. Body parts can be replaced with cyberware (see *Implant Surgery,* p. 146), bioware or transplants (see *Transimplant Surgery,* p. 147).

If this procedure fails, a second attempt can be made at +2. If this also fails, the patient's organ or limb cannot be replaced with cyberware, bioware or a transplant. In some cases, the character could die.

SURGICAL OPTIONS

As described in *Surgery Overview* (p. 144), each surgery requires two negative options and could have positive options. Positive options also list a Threshold Modifier, which increases the target number for the Surgery Test (see *Surgical Tests,* p. 146).

As an optional rule, gamemasters might want to allow surgical options for starting characters as Edges or Flaws (see p. 15, *SRComp*). Each negative option can be taken as a 1 point

THERAPEUTIC SURGERY

Procedure	Target Number
Correct bioware Stress	4
Correct bioware failure	5
Correct Attribute Stress	5
Correct Attribute failure	6

Negative Options: Bio Index Gain, Scar Tissue, Surgical Stress
Positive Options: Nanosurgery, Remove Stress Point, Rugged

TRANSIMPLANT SURGERY

Procedure	Target Number
Install bioware	5
Remove bioware	4
Transplant organ/limb	5

Negative Options: Bio Index Gain, Fragility (bioware only), Sensitive (bioware only), Surgical Stress
Positive Options: Bio Index Reduction, Bio Index Slot, Nanosurgery, Rugged

TRAUMA SURGERY

Target Number: Physical damage modifier + (Stun damage modifier ÷ 2) + (Physical Overflow ÷ 2)

Negative Options: Essence Loss, Mangled Part, Marred Appearance, Wound Effect
Positive Options: Improved Healing, Nanosurgery, Trauma Control

Flaw; positive options would be worth a number of points as an Edge equal to their Threshold Modifier.

NEGATIVE OPTIONS

Bio Index Gain (Therapeutic/Transimplant)
The surgery goes badly, and the character gains 1D6 x .1 permanent Bio Index from the procedure. If the character is Awakened, he must also immediately check for magic loss.

Essence Cost (Implant)
Add 5 percent to the Essence Cost of the implanted cyberware. Apply the total of all similar adjustments as one multiple, not separately.

Essence Loss (Cosmetic/Trauma)
The character loses 1D6 x .05 permanent Essence from the procedure. If the character is Awakened, he must immediately check for Magic Loss.

Fragility (Implant, Transimplant)
Add 1 to the target number of Stress Resistance Tests for the cyberware or bioware. Additionally, whenever the implant takes Stress, add 1 to the total Stress it takes.

Mangled Part (Trauma)
This option can only be used for the treat permanent damage procedure. The organ or limb is mangled so badly, either through damage or botched surgery, that it cannot be replaced with bioware or transplants. Cyberware replacement is still available.

Marred Appearance (Cosmetic, Trauma)
The character's appearance is marred by cosmetic surgery. He receives +1 to all Charisma and Charisma-linked Skill Tests when face to face with others. This has no effect on Conjuring or on astral abilities or skills.

Obvious (Implant)
This option is only available to cyberware with a Concealability Rating. Reduce its Concealability by –1.

Scarring (Cosmetic)
The surgery leaves a large and visible *conspicuous* scar (see p. 132) that can be used to identify the character.

Scar Tissue (Therapeutic)
The affected area develops a mass of scar tissue that can never be healed; 1 Stress Point becomes permanent and cannot be healed.

Sensitive (Implant, Transimplant)
This piece of bioware or cyberware is easily stressed. When making an Essence/Bio Index Slot list (p. 127) to determine implant damage, this device takes up space equal to twice its Essence Cost or Bio Index. This option can only be taken once per item.

Surgical Stress (Therapeutic, Transimplant)

The surgery causes a wound effect (1D6 ÷ 2 Stress) in another body system (either a bioware implant or Attribute).

Wound Effect (Trauma)

The character incurs a randomly determined automatic wound effect, either implant or Attribute Stress (see p. 126).

POSITIVE OPTIONS

Bio Index Reduction (Transimplant, +1 Threshold)

This option can only be used when installing or removing bioware. For installed bioware, the Bio Index of the implant is reduced by 5 percent. For removed bioware, the leftover Bio Index "slot" is reduced by 10 percent of the implant's total Bio Index.

Bio Index Slot (Transimplant, +2 Threshold)

If the character previously had bioware removed, a new implant with this option can be installed within the "Bio Index hole" left by the earlier implant. In other words, the old implant's leftover Bio Index can be subtracted from the new implant's Bio Index.

Concealed (Implant, +1 Threshold)

This option is exclusive to cyberware with a Concealability Rating. Increase its Concealability by +1.

Essence Reduction (Implant, +2 Threshold)

This option is exclusive to the Installing or Upgrading Cyberware procedures. Reduce the Essence Cost of implanted cyberware by 5 percent. Apply the total of all similar adjustments as one multiple, not separately.

Essence Slot (Implant, +2 Threshold)

If the character previously had cyberware removed, a new implant with this option can be installed within the "Essence hole" left behind by the earlier implant. In other words, the old implant's Essence Cost can be subtracted from the new implant's Essence Cost.

Human Looking (Cosmetic, +2 Threshold)

A dwarf, elf or ork character undergoing serious cosmetic surgery can choose this option. It provides the same effect as the Human Looking Edge (p. 41, *SRComp*).

Improved Healing (Trauma, +1 Threshold)

Each improved healing option gains an additional die for healing tests. (This only counts for current damage, not any damage accumulated in the future.)

Improved Looks (Cosmetic, +2 Threshold)

The character's looks have been remarkably improved, adding 1 to Charisma. This option can be taken once per character. This has no effect on conjuring or astral abilities and skills.

SURGERY DAMAGE TABLE

Type of Surgery	Wound Level
Cosmetic	
Minor	L
Moderate	M
Serious	S
Implant	
Implant/Remove/Upgrade Cyberware	See *Surgery Damage*, p. 151
Repair Cyberware Stress/Failure	L
Therapeutic	
Repair Stress	M
Repair Failure	S
Transimplant	
Implant/Remove Bioware	See *Surgery Damage*, p. 151
Transplant Limb/Organ	S

Nanosurgery (Cosmetic, Implant, Therapeutic, Transimplant, Trauma, +2 Threshold)

Only clinics and facilities capable of performing nanosurgery can offer this option. Damage resulting from the surgery is reduced by one level—or 2 boxes in the case of implant/transimplant surgery. The healing time is cut in half. This option can be taken once per procedure.

Natural Look (Cosmetic, +1 Threshold)

This option makes it more difficult for the changes made by cosmetic surgery to be noticed; add 2 to the target number for Perception Tests to notice the surgery (see *Cosmetic Surgery*, p. 146).

Remove Stress Point (Implant/Therapeutic, +1 Threshold)

Each of these options removes 1 additional Stress Point from the cyberware, bioware or Attribute.

Redundancy (Implant, +2 Threshold)

When an implant with this option suffers Stress, reduce the amount it takes by one. Using this option adds 50 percent to the cost of the implant.

Rugged (Implant, Therapeutic/Transimplant, +1 Threshold)

The bioware or Attribute in question receives one extra die for future Stress Tests (p. 126). Each implant or Attribute can gain this option once.

This option can be applied once to any transplanted organ or limb for use against a specified Attribute Stress Test. The chosen Attribute should be appropriately related to the body part.

Trauma Control (Trauma, +2 Threshold)

Each trauma control option gains an additional die for any transimplant or implant Surgery Tests that immediately follow this one.

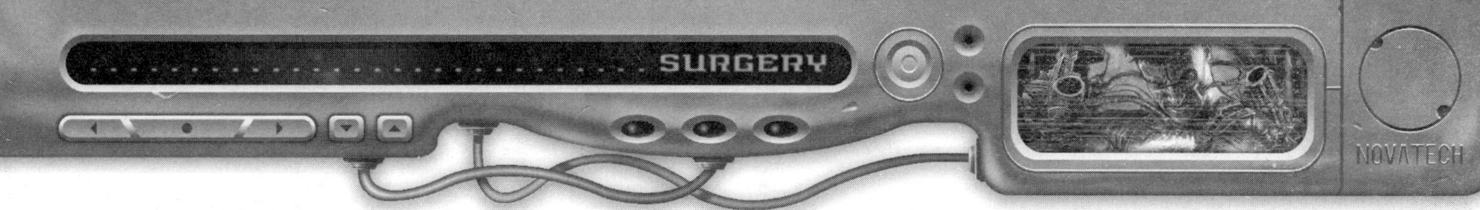

IMPLANT SURGERY DAMAGE

Implant Essence Cost/Bio Index	Boxes of Physical damage
Less than .2	1
.2—.29	2
.3—.49	3
.5—.79	4
.8—1.29	5
1.3—2.09	6
2.1—3.39	7
3.4—5.49	8
5.5—8.89	9
8.9+	10

SURGICAL COSTS TABLE

Service	Cost
Paramedic first aid for:	
Deadly wound	400¥
Serious wound	200¥
Moderate wound	100¥
Light wound	50¥
Doctor's services:	
Preparing a medical profile	20¥ x Medicine Skill
Planning a surgical procedure	100¥ per Mp
Implant surgery	40¥ x Biotech Skill
Therapeutic surgery	30¥ x Biotech Skill
Transimplant surgery	40¥ x Biotech Skill
Trauma surgery	50¥ x Biotech Skill
Medical provider charges:	
Hospitalization lifestyle	500¥ per day
Intensive care (Deadly wounds only)	1,000¥ per day
Stabilization	100¥
Emergency pickup	500¥
Mobile clinic use	500¥
Valkyrie module use	1,000¥
Magical care provided	500¥ per day
Doctor/provider charge modifiers:	
Alpha-equipped gear use	x 2
Beta-equipped gear use	x 4
Delta-equipped gear use	x 6
Cultured-equipped gear use	x 5
Nanosurgery-equipped*	x 4
Doctor's outpatient services:	
Deadly wound	400¥ per day
Serious wound	200¥ per day
Moderate wound	100¥ per day
Light wound	50¥ per day
Body parts (time to grow):	
Eye or small organ (3 weeks)	7,500¥
Large organ (5 weeks)	15,000¥
Hand/foot (6 weeks)	15,000¥
Limb (8 weeks)	25,000¥
Stress repair:	
Cyberware parts	100¥ per Stress Point
Outpatient Stress therapy (bioware/Attribute)	100¥ per day

* This multiplier is in addition to any multipliers from other gear grades available.

SURGERY DAMAGE

Most surgery involves cutting open the body, so it is natural that characters who undergo surgery suffer some damage. The damage inflicted is always Physical and is dependent upon the type of surgery. Consult the Surgery Damage Table (p. 150) to determine the type of wound. A character who suffers Deadly damage through surgery does not need to check for stabilization or permanent damage. Awakened characters must check for Magic Loss (p. 160, *SR3*).

Trauma surgery does not inflict any extra damage upon the character.

Implant surgery causes a number of boxes of damage dependent upon the item's Essence Cost or Bio Index (see the Implant Surgery Damage table). Use the base Cost/Index, before any modification from grade or surgical options. Double the Cost/Index if the implant is mostly neural-related or is based on numerous neural connections (wired reflexes, datajack, encephalon and so on).

Characters can also suffer other side effects from the surgery, depending on the operation. For example, eyes that were operated on will be blind until the surgical damage is fully healed.

PAYING THE PRICE

Surgery is expensive, from preparation to post-surgical care. The Surgical Costs Table expands upon the costs listed on the Medical Costs Table (p. 128, *SR3*).

EQUIPMENT TABLE

HEADWARE

BRAINWARE

	Essence	Cost	Availability	Street Index	Legality
BattleTac Cyberlink	.2	30,000¥	12/30 days	4	2P–R
Chipjack	.2	1,000¥	3/72 hrs	.9	Legal
Chipjack Expert Driver	Rating x .1	Rating x 5,000¥	4/48 hrs	1	Legal
Cranial Bombs					
Kink Bomb	—	28,000¥	12/14 days	1.5	2–R
Microbomb	—	65,500¥	18/48 hrs	1.25	2–R
Area Bomb	—	500,000¥	20/14 days	1	2–R
Data Compactor					
Rating 1	.1	9,500¥	6/60 hrs	1	Legal
Rating 2	.15	19,000¥	6/60 hrs	1	Legal
Rating 3	.2	28,500¥	6/60 hrs	1	Legal
Rating 4	.25	38,000¥	6/60 hrs	1	Legal
Data Filter	.3	5,000¥	6/36 hrs	1.5	Legal
Datajack	.2	1,000¥	Always	.9	Legal
Data Lock	.2	1,000¥ + Encryption Cost	6/36 hrs	1.5	As Encryption
Encephalon					
Rating 1	.75	40,000¥	6/12 days	2	Legal
Rating 2	1.5	115,000¥	6/12 days	2	Legal
Induction Datajack	.3	3,000¥	5/4 days	2	Legal
Induction Adaptor	—	100¥	4/48 hrs	1.5	Legal
Invoked-Memory Stimulator	.25	100,000¥	10/2 mo	4	3P–Q
Knowsoft Link	.1	1,000¥	3/24 hrs	1	Legal
Math SPU					
Rating 1	.1	2,000¥	6/60 hrs	1	Legal
Rating 2	.15	5,000¥	6/60 hrs	1	Legal
Rating 3	.2	11,000¥	6/60 hrs	1	Legal
Memory	Mp ÷ 300	Mp x 150¥	3/24 hrs	.8	Legal
Multi-slot Chipjacks					
2 Slots	.25	2,000¥	3/72 hrs	.9	Legal
3 Slots	.3	3,000¥	3/72 hrs	.9	Legal
4 Slots	.35	4,000¥	3/72 hrs	.9	Legal
RAS Override	.05	1,000¥	4/48 hrs	1	Legal
Router	.1	1,000¥	Always	1	Legal
Each Port	.01	200¥ or 500¥ (see text)	Always	1	Legal
Tactical Computer	1.5	400,000¥	12/60 days	4	2P–R
Each Dedicated Port	.1	10,000¥	12/60 days	4	2P–R
Each Generic Port	.1	5,000¥	12/60 days	4	2P–R
Tactical Sense Program	—	5,000¥	8/1 mo	4	6P–R
BattleTac Modification	—	+10,000¥	+6/—	4	2P–R

COMMUNICATIONS

	Essence	Cost	Availability	Street Index	Legality
Commlink	.3	Rating x 5,000¥	3/48 hrs	1	Legal
Internal Voice Mask	.1	Rating x 4,000¥	6/48 hrs	1	6P–Q
High-frequency Modulator	—	8,000¥	6/48 hrs	1.25	6P–Q
Low-frequency Modulator	—	8,000¥	6/48 hrs	1.25	6P–Q
Radio	.75	Rating x 2,000¥	2/24 hrs	.8	Legal
Radio Receiver	.4	Rating x 1,000¥	2/24 hrs	.8	Legal
Subdermal Speakers	.1	650¥	4/72 hrs	2	Legal
Subvocal Microphones	.1	850¥	4/72 hrs	2	Legal
Telephone	.5	3,700¥	3/24 hrs	.9	Legal
Transducer	.1	2,000¥	4/1 wk	1.5	Legal
External Transducer	—	1,000¥	3/72 hrs	1	Legal

MATRIXWARE

	Essence	Cost	Availability	Street Index	Legality
ASIST Converter					
External Plug-in	—	50¥	4/24 hrs	1	Legal
Datajack Accessory	—	1,000¥	6/36 hrs	1.5	Legal
Cranial Cyberdecks					
Allegiance Sigma	1.9	14,000¥	4/1 wk	.8	4P–S
Sony CT–360–D	2.5	75,000¥	6/2 wks	1	4P–S
Novatech Hyperdeck-6	2.7	150,000¥	6/2 wks	1	4P–S
CMT Avatar	2.8	300,000¥	8/2 wks	1	4P–S
Renraku Kraftwerk-8	2.9	450,000¥	10/1 mo	1	4P–S
Transys Highlander	3.0	700,000¥	14/1 mo	1	4P–S
Novatech Slimcase-10	3.2	1,500,000¥	18/1 mo	1	4P–S
Fairlight Excalibur	3.5	2,000,000¥	24/2 mo	1	4P–S

RIGGERWARE

	Essence	Cost	Availability	Street Index	Legality
BattleTac FDDM	.15	200,000¥	10/21 days	3	5P–R
BattleTac IVIS	.15	150,000¥	8/14 days	3	5P–R
Protocol Emulation Module	.2	Rating x 5,000¥	(Rating + 2)/(Rating) days	2	Legal
Remote Control Deck	.3	Rating x 25,000¥	4/72 hrs	2	Legal
RC Encryption Module	.2	Rating x 10,000¥	(Rating)/(Rating) days	3	8P–W

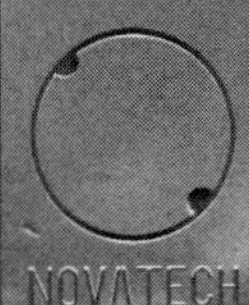

	Essence	Cost	Availability	Street Index	Legality
Remote Control ECCM					
Ratings 1–3	.2	Rating x 15,000¥	4/7 days	2	Legal
Ratings 4–6	.3	Rating x 35,000¥	6/14 days	3	6P–Q
Ratings 7–9	.4	Rating x 75,000¥	12/28 days	4	5P–R
Rating 10	.45	900,000¥	18/45 days	5	4P–R
Rigger Decryption Module	.2	Rating x 17,500¥	(Rating + 2)/(Rating) days	3	8P–W
SENSEWARE					
Chemical Analyzer and Gas Spectrometer	.2	2,500¥	4/6 days	1	Legal
Built-in Program	—	Mp x 200¥	4/6 days	1	Legal
External Program	—	Mp x 150¥	5/4 days	1.25	Legal
Internal GPS	.1	2,000¥	5/6 days	1.5	Legal
Olfactory Booster	.2	Level x 1,000¥	6/8 days	1	Legal
Oral Dart	.25	3,600¥	6/1 wks	2	6P–Q
Oral Gun	.4	5,600¥	6/72 hrs	3	6P–Q
Oral Slasher	.25	10,500¥	8/1 wk	2.5	6P–Q
Orientation System	.25	15,000¥	5/6 days	1.5	Legal
Tooth Compartment					
Breakable	—	700¥	3/48 hrs	1.5	10P–Q
Storage	—	1,500¥	2/48 hrs	1.25	Legal
Ears					
Balance Augmenter	.4	14,000¥	8/2 wks	2	Legal
Cosmetic Modification	—	1,000¥	2/24 hrs	.8	Legal
Cyber Replacement	.3	4,000¥	2/24 hrs	.75	Legal
Dampener	.1	3,500¥	4/48 hrs	1.25	Legal
Hearing Amplification	.2	3,500¥	4/48 hrs	1.25	Legal
High Frequency	.2	3,000¥	4/48 hrs	1.25	Legal
Low Frequency	.2	3,000¥	4/48 hrs	1.25	Legal
Recorder	.3	7,000¥	8/48 hrs	2	12P–N
Select Sound Filter (Levels 1–5)	.2	Level x 10,000¥	6/48 hrs	1.25	Legal
Spatial Recognizer	.2	1,200¥	4/48 hrs	2	Legal
Eyes					
Camera	.4	5,000¥	6/24 hrs	2	Legal
Cosmetic Modification	—	1,000¥	2/24 hrs	.75	Legal
Cyber Replacement	.2	5,000¥	2/24 hrs	.75	Legal
Display Link	.1	1,000¥	4/36 hrs	1	Legal
Eye Dart	.25	4,200¥	8/2 wks	2	7P–Q
Eye Datajack	.25	2,200¥	6/48 hrs	2	4P–N
Eye Gun	.4	6,400¥	6/1 wk	3	6P–Q
Eye Laser System					
Low Power	.2	3,000¥	8/72 hrs	2	5P–N
Medium Power	.3	5,000¥	8/1 wk	2	5P–N
High Power	.5	8,000¥	8/2 wks	2	5P–N
Laser Designator	.1	6,000¥	12/1 mo	3	5P–R
Laser Microphone	.1	Rating x 2,000¥	(Rating)/72 hrs	2	5P–N
Optiscan Link	.15	2,500¥	8/72 hrs	3	3P–N
Optiscan Remote Adaptor	—	2,000¥	8/2 wks	2	3P–N
Tool Laser	.15	3,000¥	8/1 wk	2	5P–N
Eye Light Systems	.2	1,200¥	4/72 hrs	1.5	Legal
Brightlight Feature	.2	2,200¥	8/2 wks	3	7P–Q
Superflash	—	+500¥	8/2 wks	3	7P–Q
Flare Compensation	.1	2,000¥	5/48 hrs	1.25	Legal
Image Link	.2	1,600¥	4/48 hrs	2	Legal
Independent Cybereyes					
Pair	.5	15,000¥	6/72 hrs	2	Legal
Single	.3	10,000¥	6/72 hrs	2	Legal
Low-Light	.2	3,000¥	4/36 hrs	1.25	Legal
Microscopic Vision	.1	5,000¥	5/48 hrs	1	Legal
Opticam	.5	20,000¥	5/72 hrs	2	Legal
Protective Covers	—	500¥	4/48 hrs	1.5	Legal
Retinal Clock	.1	450¥	3/24 hrs	1	Legal
Retinal Duplication (illegal)	.1	Rating x 25,000¥	8/7 days	2	3–Q
Thermographic	.2	3,000¥	4/36 hrs	1.25	Legal
Ultrasound Vision	.5	10,000¥	6/48 hrs	2	Legal
Vision Magnification					
Optical 1	.2	2,500¥	4/48 hrs	1	Legal
Optical 2	.2	4,000¥	4/48 hrs	1	Legal
Optical 3	.2	6,000¥	5/48 hrs	1	Legal
Electronic 1	.1	3,500¥	5/48 hrs	1	Legal
Electronic 2	.1	7,500¥	5/48 hrs	1	Legal
Electronic 3	.1	11,000¥	8/48 hrs	1	Legal
BODYWARE					
Auto-injector					
Reusable	.1	1,000¥ + contents	4/72 hrs	1.5	6P–N
One-shot	.05	1,500¥ + contents	4/72 hrs	1.5	4P–Q
Extra Dose Capacity	—	+500¥ per dose	4/72 hrs	1.5	As above
Balance Tail	.5	10,000¥	8/1 wk	2	Legal
Biomonitor	.3	5,000¥	6/72 hrs	2	Legal
Diagnosis Processor	.2	2,500¥	6/72 hrs	2	Legal
Subdermal Display	.1	500¥	4/48 hrs	1	Legal

EQUIPMENT TABLE

	Essence	Cost	Availability	Street Index	Legality
Body Compartment	.2	5,000¥	4/48 hrs	1	Legal
Injector	—	500¥ + contents	4/72 hrs	1.5	6P–N
Lockpicks	—	500¥	8/2 wks	3	6P–Q
Lockpick Gun	—	Rating x 250¥	8/2 wks	3	6P–Q
Synthetic Fingerprint	—	Rating x 2,000¥	(Rating x 2)/1 wk	3	4P–Q
Scanner Accessory	—	Rating x 500¥	(Rating)/72 hrs	3	6P–V
Bone Lacing					
Plastic	.5	7,500¥	5/14 days	1.5	6P–N
Kevlar	1	20,000¥	6/21 days	2	6P–N
Aluminum	1.15	25,000¥	5/14 days	1.5	6P–Q
Ceramic	1.5	40,000¥	6/21 days	2	6P–Q
Titanium	2.25	75,000¥	5/14 days	1.5	6–R
Boosted Reflexes					
Level 1	.5	15,000¥	3/24 hrs	1	8P–Q
Level 2	1.25	40,000¥	3/24 hrs	1.25	6P–Q
Level 3	2.8	90,000¥	3/24 hrs	1.5	5P–Q
Cyberfins	0.3	10,500¥	5/48 hrs	1.25	3P–N
Dermal Plating					
Level 1	.5	6,000¥	4/12 days	1	6P–N
Level 2	1	15,000¥	4/12 days	1	6P–N
Level 3	1.5	45,000¥	4/12 days	1	5P–N
Dermal Sheath					
Rating 1	.7	24,000¥	6/14 days	1.5	6P–N
Rating 2	1.4	60,000¥	6/14 days	1.5	6P–N
Rating 3	2.1	120,000¥	8/14 days	1.5	5P–N
Ruthenium	+.2	+150,000¥	+2/+4 days	+.25	4P–N
Image Scanner (each)	+.05	+8,000¥	—	—	—
Filtration Systems					
Air	Rating ÷ 10	Rating x 15,000¥	6/4 days	1	Legal
Blood	Rating ÷ 5	Rating x 10,000¥	6/4 days	1	Legal
Ingested Toxin	Rating ÷ 5	Rating x 10,000¥	6/4 days	1	Legal
Fingertip Compartment	.1	3,000¥	3/24 hrs	1	Legal
Flex Hands	.4	8,000¥	6/72 hrs	2	7P–N
Foot Anchor	.4	14,000¥	6/7 days	2	Legal
Hand Blade	.1	7,500¥	6/5 days	1.5	4P–R
Retractable	.25	10,000¥	6/5 days	1.5	3P–R
Hand Razors	.1	4,500¥	3/72 hrs	1	3–N
Improved Razors	NA	+8,500¥	6/72 hrs	1	3–N
Retractable Razors	.2	9,000¥	5/72 hrs	1	3–N
Hydraulic Jacks	.75 + (.25 per Rating)	Rating x 5,000¥	5/6 days	1	Legal
Internal Air Tank	.25	1,200¥	4/5 days	1.5	Legal
Tracheal Vent	.1	750¥	4/5 days	1.5	Legal
Jolt-alert	.1	1,500¥	4/48 hrs	1.5	Legal
Magnetic System	.3	2,800¥	6/7 days	2	Legal
Move-by-Wire					
Rating 1	2.5	250,000¥	8/10 days	2.5	3P–R
Rating 2	4	500,000¥	12/20 days	3	3P–R
Rating 3	5.5	1,000,000¥	18/30 days	3	3P–R
Rating 4	7	2,000,000¥	20/45 days	3.5	3P–R
Muscle Replacement (Maximum Rating 4)	Rating	Rating x 20,000¥	4/4 days	1	5P–Q
OXSYS Cybergill	.75	12,500¥	5/72 hrs	1.75	Legal
Reaction Enhancer (per point, Maximum 6)	.3	60,000¥	6/7 days	2	6P–R
Retractable Climbing Claws	.3	10,000¥	5/72 hrs	1.5	6P–N
Simrigs					
Baseline Cyberware Simrig	2	300,000¥	2/5 days	1	Legal
Full-X Cyberware Simrig	2	500,000¥	6/12 days	3	Legal
Simlink (Rating 1–10)	.6	70,000¥ + (Rating x 10,000¥)	3/5 days	1.5	Legal
Skillwires	.2 x Rating	Max Total MP x Max Rating x 500¥	(Rating)/10 days	1	Legal
Smartlink	.5	2,500¥	3/36 hrs	1	5P–N
Smartlink-2	.5	3,500¥	6/48 hrs	2	5P–N
Smartlink Subsystems					
Induction Pad	.1	200¥	4/48 hrs	1.5	5P–N
Eye Display	.1	300¥	4/48 hrs	1.5	Legal
Limited Simsense Rig	.1	1,000¥	4/48 hrs	1.5	5P–N
Personalized Smartlink Safety	—	200¥	4/48 hrs	1.5	Legal
Range Finder	.1	2,000¥	8/48 hrs	1.5	5P–N
Standard Processor	.2	1,000¥	4/48 hrs	1.5	5P–N
Smartlink-2 Proc.	.2	2,000¥	6/48 hrs	2	5P–N
Spur	.1	7,000¥	3/72 hrs	1	3–N
Retractable Spur	.3	11,500¥	5/72 hrs	1	3–N
Vehicle Control Rigs					
Level 1	2	12,000¥	6/48 hrs	1	6P–N
Level 2	3	60,000¥	8/48 hrs	1.25	6P–N
Level 3	5	300,000¥	8/48 hrs	1.5	5P–N
Voice Modulator	.2	45,000¥	2/24 hrs	1	Legal
Increased Volume	—	10,000¥	2/24 hrs	1	Legal
Playback	.2	40,000¥	4/48 hrs	1	Legal
Secondary Pattern	—	30,000¥ + (Rating x 20,000¥)	6/7 days	2	3–Q
Tonal Shift	—	25,000¥	2/24 hrs	1	Legal
Wired Reflexes					
Level 1	2	55,000¥	4/8 days	1	5P–Q
Level 2	3	165,000¥	4/8 days	1	4P–Q
Level 3	5	500,000¥	8/14 days	1	3–R
Reflex Trigger	+.2	+13,000¥	As wired reflexes	As wired reflexes	4P–Q
Stepped Reflex Trigger Modification	—	+25%	As wired reflexes	As wired reflexes	4P–Q

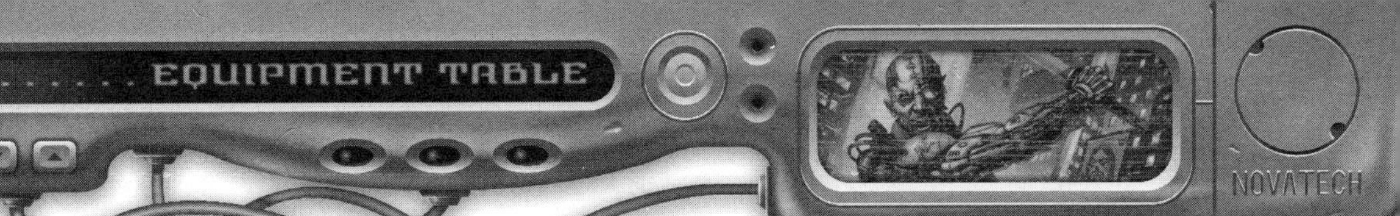

CYBERLIMBS

OBVIOUS LIMBS

OBVIOUS LIMBS	Essence	ECU*	Cost	Concealability	Availability	Street Index	Legality
Hand	.35	2	20,000¥	—	3/4 days	1	Legal
Lower Arm	.65	4	40,000¥	—	4/4 days	1	Legal
Lower leg	.65	8	40,000¥	—	4/4 days	1	Legal
Full Arm	1	10	75,000¥	—	4/4 days	1	Legal
Full Leg	1	20	75,000¥	—	4/4 days	1	Legal
Hook Hand	.1	—	30¥	—	1/6 hrs	1	Legal
Kid Stealth Legs (ea.)	1	10	100,000¥	—	6/2 wks	2	Legal
Peg Legs							
Knee Length	.2	—	50¥	—	1/6 hrs	1	Legal
Hip Length	.4	—	120¥	—	1/6 hrs	1	Legal
Skull	.75	2	35,000¥	—	6/4 days	1	Legal
Torso	1.5	7	90,000¥	—	6/4 days	1	Legal

* This refers to the ECU available in each limb.

SYNTHETIC LIMBS

SYNTHETIC LIMBS	Essence	ECU*	Cost	Concealability	Availability	Street Index	Legality
Foot	.35	1	25,000¥	10	3/4 days	1	Legal
Hand	.35	1	25,000¥	10	3/4 days	1	Legal
Lower Arm	.65	2	50,000¥	9	4/4 days	1	Legal
Lower Leg	.65	4	50,000¥	9	4/4 days	1	Legal
Full Arm	1	5	100,000¥	8	4/4 days	1	Legal
Full Leg	1	10	100,000¥	8	4/4 days	1	Legal
Skull	.75	1	55,000¥	10	6/4 days	1	Legal
Torso	1.5	3	120,000¥	8	6/4 days	1	Legal

* This refers to the ECU available in each limb.

CYBERLIMB ENHANCEMENTS

	Essence	ECU**	Cost	Concealability	Availability	Street Index	Legality
Body Plating							
Ballistic Armor (per point)	—	.5	2,500¥	–.5	8/2 wks	1	Legal
Impact Armor (per point)	—	.5	4,000¥	–.5	8/2 wks	1	Legal
Ablative Armor (per point)	—	1	7,000¥	–1	12/3 wks	2	4P–Q
Built-in Device	Varies	Varies	Cost of device x 4	–Variable	Per device	Per device	Per device
Cyberarm Gyromount	—	4	40,000¥	–1/–6	10/3 wks	2	4P–R
Cyberhand Safety	—	.5	800¥	—	3/36 hrs	1.5	Legal
Cyber Holster	.1	4	5,000¥	10	4/48 hrs	1	5P–N
Cyberskates	—	2	1,000¥	–5	3/24 hrs	1	Legal
Retractable	—	4	2,500¥	–2	4/48 hrs	1	Legal
Direct Neural Interface	.1	.25	4,500¥	—	4/6 days	1	5P–Q
DNI Adaptation	—	—	Cost of device x 150%	—	—	—	Per device
Integrity Enhancement (per point)	—	1	30,000¥	–1	6/4 days	1.5	6P–N
Quickness Enhancement (per point)							
Full Limb (1–3 pts)	—	—	30,000¥	–.5	8/4 days	1.5	6P–Q
Full Limb (4+ pts)	.3	1	45,000¥	–1	8/4 days	1.5	6P–Q
Replacement Modification	—	1	+10%	—	+2/+2 days	2	Legal
Signal Booster	—	4	Rating x 15,000¥	–1	6/72 hrs	1.5	Legal
Smartgun Link	.25	.5	2,500¥	—	6/4 days	1.5	5P–N
Strength Enhancement (per point)							
Foot (1–3 pts)	—	—	20,000¥	–1	6/4 days	1.5	6P–Q
Full Limb (1–3 pts)	—	—	50,000¥	–1	6/4 days	1.5	6P–Q
Full Limb (4+ pts)	.4	1	75,000¥	–2	6/4 days	1.5	6P–R
Hand (1–3 pts)	—	—	20,000¥	–1	6/4 days	1.5	6P–Q
Lower Arm (1–3 pts)	—	—	35,000¥	–1	6/4 days	1.5	6P–Q
Lower Leg (1–3 pts)	—	—	35,000¥	–1	6/4 days	1.5	6P–Q
Telescoping Cyberlimb	—	3	10,000¥	–1	6/72 hrs	1.5	Legal
Weapon Mounts							
External Mount	—	3	5,000¥	–5	6/4 days	2	3P–R
Retractable	—	5	15,000¥	–2/–5	6/4 days	2	3P–R
Tracking Mount	—	5	25,000¥	–6	8/7 days	2	3P–R
Retractable	—	7	40,000¥	–3/–6	8/7 days	2	3P–R
Articulated Arm	—	7	110,000¥	—	12/24 days	2	2P–R
Retractable	1	7	200,000¥	–5/—	12/24 days	2	2P–R

** This refers to the ECU space each enhancement takes up.

CYBER WEAPONS

	Essence	Concealability	Ammo	Mode	Damage	Cost	Availability	Street Index	Legality
Cyber Dartgun	.3	10	5(m)	SA	—	1,000¥	8/7 days	2	6P–Q
Cyber Taser	.3	10	2	SA	10S Stun	2,000¥	6/4 days	1.5	5P–Q
Cyberguns (Fichetti Brand)									
Hold-out Pistol	.15	12	2(m)/6(c)	SS	4L	250¥	8/7 days	2	8P–Q
Light Pistol	.35	10	12(m)/12(c)	SA	6L	650¥	8/7 days	2	6P–Q
Machine Pistol	.4	8	12(m)/35(c)	SA/BF	6L	900¥	8/7 days	2	4P–Q
Heavy Pistol	.6	8	10(m)/10(c)	SA	9M	800¥	8/7 days	2	4P–Q
Submachine Gun	1	6	12(m)/24(c)	SA/BF	7M	1,800¥	8/7 days	2	3P–Q
Shotgun	1.1	6	10(m)/10(c)	SA	8S	1,200¥	8/7 days	2	4P–Q
External Clip Port	.1	–1	—	—	—	100¥	8/7 days	2	As gun
Laser Sight	.1	–1	—	—	—	700¥	8/7 days	2	Legal
Silencer	.2	–2	—	—	—	1,000¥	8/7 days	2	As gun
Sound Suppresser	.3	–3	—	—	—	1,500¥	8/7 days	2	As gun
Cybersquirt	.4	8	10/10(c)	SA	Special	1,400¥	8/6 days	2	5P–Q
External Clip Port	.1	–1	—	—	—	100¥	8/7 days	2	As gun
Eye Dart	.25	10	1	SS	Special	4,200¥	8/2 wks	2	7P–Q
Eye Gun	.4	9	1	SS	3L	6,400¥	6/1 wk	3	6P–Q

	Essence	Concealability	Ammo	Mode	Damage	Cost	Availability	Street Index	Legality
Fangs	.1	5	—	—	(STR +1)L	5,000¥	4/48 hrs	1	Legal
Extendable	.15	9	—	—	(STR + 1)L	8,000¥	5/48 hrs	1	5P–N
Horns	.1	—	—	—	(STR)M	12,000¥	4/48 hrs	1	Legal
Retractable	.25	8	—	—	(STR)M	16,000¥	5/48 hrs	1	5P–N
Oral Dart	.25	10	3	SS	Special	3,600¥	6/1 wks	2	6P–Q
Oral Gun	.4	9	4	SS	4L	5,600¥	6/72 hrs	3	6P–Q
Shock Hand	.25	5	12	—	8S Stun	1,300¥	6/4 days	2	4P–Q
Venom Sack (2 doses)	.05	—	—	—	—	500¥	4/48 hrs	2	4P–Q

BIOWARE

BASIC

	Bio Index	Availability	Cost	Street Index	Legality
Adrenal Pump					
Level 1	1.25	10/16 days	60,000¥	3	5P–R
Level 2	2.50	10/16 days	100,000¥	3	5P–R
Cat's Eyes	.2	4/6 days	15,000¥	1	Legal
Chemical Gland	.6	10/4 days	Special	3	5–Q
Digestive Expansion	1	6/10 days	80,000¥	2	Legal
Enhanced Articulation	.6	5/6 days	40,000¥	1.5	Legal
Extended Volume					
Level 1	.2	4/4 days	8,000¥	1	Legal
Level 2	.3	4/4 days	15,000¥	1	Legal
Level 3	.4	4/4 days	25,000¥	1	Legal
Metabolic Arrester	.6	6/8 days	20,000¥	1.5	Legal
Muscle Augmentation (per level)	.4	6/6 days	20,000¥	.9	4P–Q
Muscle Toner (per level)	.4	6/6 days	25,000¥	.9	4P–Q
Nephritic Screen	.4	4/4 days	20,000¥	1	Legal
Nictitating Membranes	.1	4/6 days	8,000¥	1	Legal
Orthoskin					
Level 1	.5	8/8 days	25,000¥	.8	5P–N
Level 2	1	8/8 days	60,000¥	.8	5P–N
Level 3	1.5	8/8 days	100,000¥	.8	5P–N
Pathogenic Defense	.2 per level	4/4 days	24,000¥	1.5	Legal
Platelet Factories	.4	5/8 days	30,000¥	1.5	Legal
Suprathyroid Gland	1.4	8/12 days	50,000¥	2.5	6P–Q
Symbiotes					
Level 1	.4	5/10 days	15,000¥	1	Legal
Level 2	.7	5/10 days	35,000¥	1	Legal
Level 3	1	5/10 days	60,000¥	1	Legal
Synthacardium					
Level 1	.2	4/10 days	6,000¥	1.5	Legal
Level 2	.3	4/10 days	15,000¥	1.5	Legal
Tailored Pheromones					
Level 1	.4	12/14 days	20,000¥	2	Legal
Level 2	.6	12/14 days	45,000¥	2	Legal
Toxin Extractor (per level)	.4	4/4 days	45,000¥	1	Legal
Tracheal Filter (per level)	.4	4/4 days	60,000¥	1	Legal
CULTURED					
Cerebral Booster					
Level 1	.4	6/14 days	50,000¥	2	Legal
Level 2	.8	6/14 days	110,000¥	2	Legal
Damage Compensators (per level)					
Level 1–2	.2	6/6 days	25,000¥	2.5	6P–N
Level 3–5	.2	10/6 days	50,000¥	2.5	6P–N
Level 6–9	.2	12/6 days	100,000¥	2.5	6P–N
Mnemonic Enhancer (per level)	.2	6/7 days	15,000¥	1	Legal
Pain Editor	.6	6/6 days	60,000¥	1.2	6P–N
Reflex Recorder					
Base Skill	.25	8/6 days	25,000¥	1.5	Legal
Specialization	.1	5/6 days	10,000¥	1.5	Legal
Sleep Regulator	.3	4/4 days	20,000¥	1	Legal
Synaptic Accelerator					
Level 1	.4	6/12 days	75,000¥	2	5P–Q
Level 2	1.0	6/12 days	200,000¥	2	5P–Q
Thermosense Organs	.5	10/12 days	25,000¥	2	Legal
Trauma Damper	.4	6/8 days	40,000¥	2	6P–N
COSMETIC					
Chloroplast Skin	.2	6/8 days	10,000¥	2	Legal
Clean Metabolism	.2	4/4 days	10,000¥	1	Legal
Dietware	.2	4/4 days	10,000¥	1	Legal
Hair Growth	.1	4/4 days	2,000¥	1	Legal
Scent Glands	.1	4/4 days	5,000¥	1	Legal
Sensitive Skin	.2	6/6 days	10,000¥	2	Legal
Skin Pigmentation	.1	6/6 days	5,000¥	1	Legal

CHEMISTRY

APPLIED CHEMTECH COMPOUNDS

	Availability	Cost	Street Index	Legality
Acid (per dose)	(Rating)/6 days	Rating x 500¥	2	6P–X
Carcerands (per dose)	4/10 days	100¥ per day	2	Legal
Dikote	6/14 days	1000¥ per 100 cm^2	2	Legal
DMSO (per dose)	2/12 hrs	10¥ + chemical cost	1.5	Legal

	Availability	Cost	Street Index	Legality
Freeze Foam (per liter)	2/12 hrs	20¥	1	Legal
Solvent (per liter)	2/12 hrs	5¥	1	Legal
FAE Bomb (per kilo)	12/72 hrs	Rating x 500¥	5	2–J
Insecticide (per liter)	Always	10¥	1	Legal
Oxygenated Flourocarbons—P4MO Treatment (5 liters)	4/48 hrs	4,000¥	1	Legal
Plastisteel-7 Catalyst	10/48 hrs	500¥	1	Legal
Ruthenium Polymers	5/14 days	10,000¥ per m^2	2	Legal
Imaging Scanner	5/14 days	5,000¥	2	Legal
Slap Patch	6/72 hrs	50¥+chemical cost	2	Legal
Slip Spray (per liter)	4/48 hrs	100¥	1	Legal
Splat Glue (per liter)	6/72 hrs	100¥	1	Legal
Solvent (per liter)	2/12 hrs	5¥	1	Legal
Spray Foam Explosive can	10/48 hrs	Rating x 30¥	2	4–J
Thermite (per kg)	12/14 days	500¥	2	4P–U
Burning Bar	14/21 days	1,000¥	2	3P–U

CHEMTECH APPLICATION GEAR

	Concealability	Ammo	Mode	Damage	Weight	Cost	Availability	Street Index	Legality
Cascade	4	100/20(c)	SA	Special	5.5	1,800¥	12/14 days	2	6P–F
Dart Weapons									
Pistol	7	5(c)	SA	Special	1.5	600¥	6/2 days	2	Legal
Rifle	4	10(c)	SA	Special	3.25	1,700¥	8/2 days	2	Legal
Dart Rounds (per 10)	8	—	—	See rules	.15	200¥	4/48 hrs	2	Legal
ELD-AR	4	50(c)	SA/BF	4L Stun	4.5	950¥	9/7 days	2	Legal
Paint Rounds (per 10)	8	—	—	See rules	.15	5¥	2/24 hrs	1	Legal
Splat Gun	4	2(m)	SS	Special	3	600¥	9/7 days	2	Legal
Spray Tank	4	20	SS	Special	5	100¥	3/12 hrs	1	Legal
Splash Grenade	5	—	—	Special	.25	50¥	8/4 days	2	3–J
SuperSquirt II	7	20/20(c)	SA	Special	2	800¥	9/14 days	1.5	6P–E

HAZMAT GEAR

	Availability	Cost	Street Index	Legality
Gas Mask and Air Tank	4/12 hrs	1,000¥	1	Legal
Hazmat Suit	6/1 wk	5,000¥	1.5	Legal
X-E Suit	8/2 wks	15,000¥	2	Legal

DRUGS (EFFECTS)

	Vector	Speed	Damage	Addict.	Tolerance	Edge	Fix Factor
ACTH	Inhalation	Immediate	—	—	3	10/—	—
Anabolic Steroids	Ingestion, injection	—	—	3P	—	10/10	1 wk
Arsenic	Ingestion	1D6 hrs	10D	—	1	20/—	—
Deepweed	Ingestion, Inhalation	Immediate	—	7P	2	5/20	1 wk
Gemini	Injection	1 min	—	6M	—	2/20	3 days
Jazz	Inhalation	Immediate	—	4M/5P	2	2/8	3 days
Kamikaze	Inhalation	Immediate	—	5P	2	2/10	2 days
Long Haul	Injection	10 min	—	2M	2	10/10	2 wks
Psyche	Ingestion	10 min	—	4M	2	10/20	1 wk
Street Drugs							
Bliss	Inhalation, injection	1 Turn	—	5M/5P	2	2/30	2 days
Burn	Ingestion	10 min	3D Stun	2M	2	20/100	1 day
Cram	Ingestion, inhalation	10 min	—	4M	2	5/50	2 days
Nitro	Inhalation	1 Turn	4D	5M/8P	3	2/5	3 days
Novacoke	Inhalation, injection	1 Turn	—	6M/5P	2	3/50	2 days
Zen	Inhalation	5 x D6 min	—	3M	2	5/50	2 days

PHARMACEUTICAL COMPOUNDS (EFFECTS)

	Vector	Speed	Damage
Atropine	Injection	Immediate/15 min	7D
CS/Tear Gas	Contact or inhalation	1 Combat Turn	Special
Cutters	Injection	2 min	9M
Cyanide	Ingestion, inhalation, injection	Immediate or 1 min	7D
Fugu-5	Ingestion or injection	Immediate	3D
Fugu-6	Ingestion or injection	Immediate	6D
Fugu-8	Ingestion or injection	Immediate	8D
Gamma-scopolamine	Injection	Immediate	10D Stun
Green Ring 3	Contact or inhalation	Immediate	8S
Green Ring 8	Contact or inhalation	Immediate	10S
Hyper	Inhalation or injection	Immediate	6S Stun
Laés	Injection	Immediate	Special
MAO	Injection	Immediate	12L Stun
Narcoject	Injection	Immediate	6D Stun
Nausea Gas	Inhalation	5 Combat Turns	Special
Neuro-stun VIII	Contact or inhalation	1 Combat Turn	6S Stun
Neuro-stun IX	Contact or inhalation	1 Combat Turn	6S Stun
Neuro-stun X	Contact or inhalation	1 Combat Turn	8S Stun
Pepper Punch	Contact or inhalation	1 Combat Turn	12L Stun
Seven-7	Contact or inhalation	1 Combat Turn	10D

DRUGS AND PHARMACEUTICAL COMPOUNDS (PURCHASING, PER DOSE)

	Availability	Cost	Street Index	Legality
ACTH	5/12 hrs	100¥	1	Legal
Anabolic Steroids (per dose)	4/12 hrs	40¥	1	Legal
Arsenic (per dose)	4/12 hrs	40¥	1	Legal
Atropine (per dose)	5/12 hrs	600¥	1	Legal
CS/Tear Gas (per dose)	4/36 hrs	10¥	1	Legal
Cyanide (per dose)	3/48 hrs	360¥	1	4P–X
Fugu-5 (per dose)	4/72 hrs	10,000¥	.5	3–X
Fugu-6 (per dose)	5/1 wk	20,000¥	.5	3–X
Fugu-8 (per dose)	8/2 wks	30,000¥	.5	3–X
Gamma-scopolamine	8/2 wks	300¥	3	3–X
Green Ring 3 (per dose)	14/2 wks	500¥	5	2–K
Green Ring 8 (per dose)	16/2 wks	800¥	5	2–K
Hyper (per dose)	4/24 hrs	180¥	.9	4P–X
Jazz (per dose)	8/4 days	40¥	3	4P–X
Kamikaze (per dose)	5/4 days	50¥	5	3P–X
Laés (per dose)	21/21 days	1,000¥	2	Legal
Long Haul (per dose)	6/6 days	500¥	2	Legal
MAO (per dose)	5/36 hrs	280¥	2	4P–X
Narcoject (per dose)	3/48 hrs	150¥	1	Legal
Nausea Gas (per dose)	4/48 hrs	10¥	2	8P–X
Neuro-stun VIII (per dose)	4/24 hrs	20¥	1.5	6P–X
Neuro-stun IX (per dose)	6/36 hrs	20¥	2	6P–X
Neuro-stun X (per dose)	8/48 hrs	30¥	2	6P–X
Pepper Punch (per dose)	2/4 hrs	5¥	1	Legal
Psyche (per dose)	8/72 hrs	500¥	2	Legal
Seven–7 (per dose)	20/2 wks	1,000¥	5	2–K
Street Drugs				
Bliss	5/48 hrs	15¥	2	5–X
Burn	2/30 min	5¥	1	Legal
Cram	4/12 hrs	20¥	1	6P–X
Nitro	6/48 hrs	100¥	1	4–X
Novacoke	3/12 hrs	20¥	1	6–X
Zen	3/6 hrs	5¥	1	8–X

MAGICAL COMPOUNDS

	Vector	Speed	Duration
Animal Tongue	Ingestion	Immediate	Essence + 1D6 hrs
Deepweed	Ingestion or Inhalation	Immediate	Essence + 1D6 hrs
Immortal Flower	Ingestion	Immediate	Essence + 1D6 hrs
Little Smoke	Inhalation	Immediate	Essence + 1D6 hrs
Rock Lizard Blood	Ingestion	Immediate	Essence + 1D6 hrs
Spirit Strength	Ingestion	Immediate	Essence + 1D6 hrs
Witch's Moss	Ingestion	Immediate	Essence + 1D6 hrs

NANOTECHNOLOGY

NANO-IMPLANTS

	Essence	Cost	Availability	Street Index	Legality
Nanite Facilitator	.3	9,000¥	10/1 mo	2	Legal
Nanite Hive	.7	80,000¥	18/2 mo	4	4P–R
Nano-Biomoniter Systems					
CrashCart Med-Alert	1	100,000¥	8/2 wks	1.5	Legal
Guardian Angel	1.2	130,000¥	12/1 mo	4	4P–R

NANOWARE

	Nanite Type	Cost	Availability	Street Index	Legality
Bioware Regenerator	Fixed Transient	10% of implant cost	10/2 wks	2	Legal
Carcerand-Plus					
	Free-floating	30,000¥	12/2 wks	2	Legal
	Transient	7,000¥	10/1wk	2	Legal
Cutters (per dose)	Transient	20,000¥	20/1 mo	5	2–Y
Cyberware Repair Unit	Fixed Transient	10% of implant cost	8/2 wks	1.5	Legal
Fingerprint Mappers	Transient	Rating x 5,000¥	12/1 mo	2	5P–Y
Gemini (per dose)	Transient	20,500¥	14/48 hrs	3	2–Y
Gremlins	Transient	20,000¥	14/2 wks	3	2–Y
Nanite Hunters	Transient	20,000¥	16/3 wks	3	4–Y
Nanosymbiotes	Free-floating	70,000¥	12/1 wk	2	Legal
Nanotattoos	Free-floating	5,000¥	8/2 wks	3	Legal
Nantidotes					
	Free-floating	500¥ x toxin's cost	10/2 wks	2	Legal
	Transient	200¥ x toxin's cost	8/1 wk	2	Legal
Oxy-rush	Transient	10,000¥	8/2 wks	2	Legal
Retinal Tailors	Transient	Rating x 6,000¥	12/1 mo	2	5P–Y
Taggants					
Etchers	Transient	5,000¥	6/1 wk	1.5	Legal
Markers	Free-floating	10,000¥	8/2 wks	2	Legal

NANOGEAR

	Conceal	Weight	Availability	Cost	Street Index	Legality
Monowire (per meter)	8	—	24/14 days	2,000¥	3	1–K
Nanoscanner	6	1	(Rating)/1 wk	Rating x 5,000¥	2	8P–U
Savior Advanced Medkit	—	4	6/1 wk	1,500¥	2	Legal
Savior Supplies	8	—	6/1 wk	300¥	2	Legal
Smart Corrosives (per dose)	—	—	12/1 mo	7,000¥	3	3P–Y

A
Acids, 111
ACTH (adrenocorticotropic hormone), 64, 117
Addiction, 108–9
  code, 108
  effects, 109
  quitting, 109–10
  rating, 108
  recovery and, 110
  withdrawal and, 110
Adrenal pump, 63–64, 78–79
AG Chemie, chemistry and, 104
Alchemy, 104
Ambulances, 138–39
Anabolic steroids, 117–18
Animal tongue, 122-23
Antidote, 106
Applied compounds, 111–15
Ares Macrotechnology
  Ares Arms, 115
  cyberware and, 12
  nanotechnology and, 89–90
Arsenic, 118
Articulated arm, 40, 41
ASIST converter, 19
Atropine, 118
Attribute
  damage, 129
  failure, 129–30, 133
  stress repair, 131
Auto-injector, 25, 55
Aztechnology, 54, 62–63, 92
  cyberware and, 12
  nanotechnology and, 88
  optical chips by, 105

B
Balance augmenter, 13, 84
Balance tail, 25
BattleTac
  cyberlink, 22
  cyberware and, 42-44
  drone networks and, 44
  Fire Direction Data Manager (FDDM) system, 23, 44
  Inter-Vehicle Information System (IVIS), 23, 44
  Small Unit Tactics Skill and, 48
  tactical computer modification, 22
Better-Than-Life chips, 102, 121–22
Biogene, 54, 63
Bio Index, 77, 78, 149–51
Biomonitor cyberware, 25–26, 91
Biosystem overstress, 62
Bio-tattoos, 76
Biotechnology, 60, 62–63
Biotech Skill, 133, 135–36
  surgical planning and, 145
  surgical tests and, 146
  unconsciousness revival and, 131–32
Bioware, 63–72, 76–79
  Awakened and, 78
  basic, 63–72
  compatibility, 78–79
  cosmetic, 62, 76
  critters and, 79
  cultured, 72–75, 77
  damage, 128
  drawbacks, 62, 77–78
  effects of installing, 77
  excessive, 78
  failure, 128
  First Aid modifiers, 133
  grades, 62, 76–77
  implanting, 60, 62
  installation, 148
  removal, 148
  stress repair, 130–31
  used, 62, 77
Bioware regenerator, 91–92
Black clinics, 142
Bliss, 121–22
Body compartments, 26–27
Body part replacement, 148
Body parts, 139–40
Body plating, 35, 36, 37
Bodyware, 11
Bone lacing, 27, 84
Brainware, 11
Brightlight eye units, 15
Burn, 121–22

C
Carcerand-plus, 92
Carcerands, 92, 111
Cascade rifle, 115
Catastrophic clonic seizure syndrome (CCSS), 25, 31
Cat's eyes, 64, 79
Cerebral booster, 72
Chemical analyzer, 13, 84, 107
Chemical gland, 64–65
Chemical immunity, 84
Chemistry, 101
  applied compounds, 111–15
  applied industrial, 101–2
  basics, 101, 107–10
  drug rules, 105–7
  magical compounds, 122–23
  players in, 104–5
Chemistry tools, 107–8
Chemsuits, 105
Chemtech application gear, 115–17
Chipjack, 26
  expert driver, 19
  multi-slot, 21
Chloroplast skin, 76
Chronic dissociation syndrome (CDS), 59
Clean metabolism, 76
Climbing claws, retractable, 31
Cloned body parts, 140
Communications cyberware, 11, 18–19
Concealability, 79, 145, 150
  body compartments, 27
  cyberguns, 41
  cyberlimb, 35
  eye datajack, 13
  monowire, 95
  obvious implant, 149
  optical scanning link and, 15
  subdermal display, 26
Consciousness, 131–32
Corrosives, 111
Cosmetic bioware, 76, 146
Cosmetic surgery, 132, 146, 147, 149
Cram, 121–22
Cranial remote decks, 23–24
CrashCart, 12, 87
CrashCart Med-Alert, 91
Critters
  bioware and, 79
  cyberware and, 44
Cross Applied Technologies, 91
  biotechnology and, 63
  cyberware and, 12
  nanotechnology and, 88
CS/tear gas, 118
Cutters, 92
Cyanide, 118
Cyberarm gyromount, 36–37
Cyberdecks, cranial, 19–20
Cybereyes, 16–17, 76
  modification limits, 44
  single, 44
Cyberfins, 27–28
Cyberguns, 41
Cyberhand safety, 37
Cyber holster, 37
Cyberlegs, "Kid Stealth," 37–38
Cyberlimbs, 11, 32–36
  accessories, 36–41
  cyberware compatibility, 32–33
  enhanced articulation and, 79
  integrity enhancement, 39
  multiple enhancements, 35
  muscle enhancements, 79
  orthoskin, 79
  partial, 39
  weapon mounts, 40–41
Cyberlink, BattleTac, 22
Cybermancy, 50, 52, 54–56
  access to, 54
  advantages of, 52
  cancer and, 59
  delta clinics and, 53
  drawbacks to, 52
  long-term effects of, 59
  magical ritual, 55–56
  rules, 54
  social, Karma penalties, 58
  surgery, 55, 146
  surgery side effects, 56–58
Cyberskates, 38
Cyberskull, 28, 35, 36
Cybersquirt, 41–42
Cybersurgery, 54, 55
Cybersystem damage, 127
Cyber taser, 42
Cybertorso, 28, 35, 36
Cyberware, 13, 90, 148, 149
  accessories, systems, 45
  availability, 45
  bodyware, 25–32
  brainware, 19-23
  direct neural interface, 8, 10
  Essence and, 10
  failure, repair, 128, 147
  general rules, 42–49
  grades of, 10–11, 36, 44–45
  installation, 147
  interconnectivity, 10
  magic and, 47
  power players in, 12-13
  power sources, 11–12
  reflex enhancements, 45–46
  repair kit, 92
  riggerware, 22–25
  senseware, 13–18
  signature and, 47
  social interaction and, 48
  stress repair, 130, 147
  system damaged, 127–28
  triggers, 48
  upgrade, 147
  upkeep, 131
  used, 45, 124
Cyberweapons, 41–42
Cyberzombies, 57, 127

D
Damage compensators, 72
Dartgun, 41, 105, 111, 116
Data compactor, 20
Data filter, 20
Data lock, 20
Datajack, 10, 26, 46
Debeers-Universal Omnitech, 105
Deepweed, 123
Delta clinics, 53–54
Dermal armor damage, 133–34
Dermal plating
  cosmetic bioware and, 79
  orthoskin, 79
Dermal sheathing, 28, 84
  cosmetic bioware and, 79
  nanites and, 84
  orthoskin, 79
Diagnosis processor, 26
Dietware, 76
Digestive expansion, 65–66, 76, 79
Dikote, 111
Dimethyl sulfoxide (DMSO), 41–42, 111–12, 115, 116
Direct neural interface (DNI), 8, 10, 14, 22, 28, 38, 39
DocWagon, 13, 139, 140, 141, 142
Dosage, 105
  additional 106–7
Draco Foundation, 88–89
Drugs, 102
  effects, 105–7, 116, 117
  exposure to, 105–6
  rules, 105–7

E
ELD-AR rifle, pellets, 113, 115
Emergency care, 142–43
Encephalon, 20–21, 48
Enhanced articulation, 66, 79
Envirosealed armor, 105–6
Equipment capacity, 35–37
  cyberlimb, 35–36
  cyber replacement, 37
Essence, 10, 84
  addiction and, 109
  cost, 149
  cybermancy and, 58
  cybersurgery and, 55
  cyberware and, 10, 45
  death and, 50,52
  drug recovery and, 110
  Index, 62, 77, 78
  Loss, 5–6, 149
  nanotechnology and, 84
  reduction, 150
  Signature and, 47
  slots, 127, 150
Etchers, 94, 95
Exhalation spray, 64, 65
Extended volume, 66, 79
External weapon mount, 40
Eye dart, 15, 16
Eye datajack, 13
Eye gun, 15, 16
Eye laser systems, 13–15
  laser designators, 14
  laser microphone, 14
  tool laser, 15
Eye light systems, 15
Eye weapons, 15–16

F
Fang implant, 42
Fingerprint mappers, 92–93
Fingerprint, synthetic, 27
First Aid, 132–3, 136
Fix Factor, 108
Fix, getting a, 109
Flex hands, 28–29
Foot anchor, 29
Freeze foam, 112
Fuel-air explosives, 112–13

G
Gaeatronics, 90
Gas spectrometer, 13
Gemini, 93
Genetique, 88, 92
Global positioning system, internal, 17, 18
Green Ring 3, 118–19
Green Ring 8, 119, 121

Gremlins, 93
Guardian Angel, 91, 133

H

Hacking Pool
- encephalon and, 20–21
- math subprocessor unit and, 21

Hair growth, 76
Handheld spray tank, 112
Hazmat Gear, 106, 116, 119
Headware, 11, 28
Hook hand, 39
Horn implant, 42
Hospitals, 138
Hydraulic jacks, 29
Hyper, 119

I

Immortal flower, 123
Induction datajack, 21
Insecticides, 113
Interconnectivity, 10, 22, 46
Internal air tank, 29, 127
- OXSYS cybergill and, 31

Internal voice mask, 18–19
Invoked memory stimulator (IMS), 21, 52, 55, 58, 59

J-K

Jazz, 119
Jolt-alert, 29–30
Kamikaze, 119–20
Karma hazing, 57, 59

L

Laés, 120
Little smoke, 123
Lockpick gun, 10, 27
Lockpicks, 27
Lone Star, 119, 141
Long haul, 120

M

Magic
- bioware and, 79
- cybermancy resistance to, 56–57
- cybermantic, 55–56
- cyberware and, 47
- healing and, 131, 136
- Loss, 109, 151

Magical compounds, 104, 122–23
Magnetic system, 30
MAO (monoamine oxidase), 64, 120
Markers, 95
Math subprocessor unit, 21
Matrixware, 11
Med-Alert System, 87
Medical care
- bioware stress, 131
- finding, 140–44
- healing with, 134
- nonemergency, 143
- provider, 140–44

Medical diagnosis, 144–45
Medical facilities, 138
Medical gear, 136, 138–40
Medical profile, 140, 144–45
Medical telepresence gear, 138, 139
Medicine Skill, 136, 145–46
Medkits, 136, 138
Metabolic arrester, 66–67, 91
Microscopic vision, 17
Mitsuhama Computer Technologies, 93, 121
- chemistry and, 104–5
- cyberware and, 12
- nanotechnology and, 87, 88

Mnemonic enhancer, 72–73, 79
Monofilament, 84
Monowire, 95
Move-by-wire system, 30–31
Multi-slot chipjacks, 21
Muscle augmentation, 67
Muscle toner, 67

N

Nanite facilitator, 90–91, 99, 147
Nanite hive, 91, 100
Nanite hunters, 93
Nanites, 84
- direct control of, 97
- industry and, 85
- loss of, 99–100
- reprogrammable, 96–97
- shutting down, 97–98
- thermographic detection of, 100
- wound healing and, 85

Nano-biomonitor systems, 91
Nanodrones, 96–97
Nanoscanner, 95
Nanosurgery, 133, 150
Nanosymbiotes, 93
Nanotattoos, 94
Nanotechnology, 80, 82
- computers and, 85
- Gear, 90–91, 95–100
- heavy industry, manufacturing and, 85
- human augmentation and medicine, 84–85
- limitations of, 85–86
- nanomachines, 82–83
- players in, 86-90
- rules, 96
- space and, 85

Nanoware, 90, 91–95, 98
- acquisition of, 98
- detection, 100
- excessive, 100
- fixed, 98–99, 147
- free-floating, 98–99
- installation of, 99
- legality, 98
- maintenance, 100
- transient nanite treatments, 98, 99

Nantidotes, 94
Nausea gas, 120
Nephritic screen, 67
Neuro-stun gases, 120–21
Nictitating membranes, 67–68, 79
Nitro, 121, 122
Novacoke, 121, 122
Novatech Incorporated
- cyberware and, 13
- nanotechnology and, 90

O

Olfactory booster, 17
Optical scanning (optiscan) link, 14–15
Oral slasher, 17
Oral weapons, 17
Organ culture, growth, 136
Organic body parts, 139
Organic damage, 129, 130
Orientation system, 17, 18, 22
Orthoskin, 68, 84
- cyberlimbs, 79
- dermal plating, sheathing, 79

Overdosing, 107, 109
Oxygenated fluorocarbons, 113
Oxy-rush, 94
OXSYS cybergill, 31

P

P4MO, 113
Pain editor, 73-74, 131
Pathogenic defense, 68
Peg leg, 39–40
Pepper punch, 106, 121
Personalized Smartlink safety (PSS), 32
Pharmaceutical compounds, 102, 104, 117–22
Plastisteel-7 catalyst, 113
Platelet factories, 68–69
Proteus AG, 63
Psyche, 121
Pueblo Corporate Council, 53, 90

R

Range finder, Smartlink,32
RAS override, 15, 21–22
Reflex recorder, 74, 79
Reflex trigger, stepped modification, 32
Remote control encryption module (RCEM), 24
Renraku Computer Systems
- cyberware and, 12
- nanotechnology and, 87
- Seattle Arcology, 53, 80, 82, 86, 87, 92

Replacement limbs, 39
Respirators, 106
Retinal tailors, 94
Rigger decryption module, 24–25
Rigger protocol emulation module, 25
Riggerware, 11
Rock lizard blood, 123
Router, 10, 22, 46
Ruthenium polymers, 114

S

Saeder-Krupp, 89
- biotechnology and, 63
- chemistry and, 104
- cyberware and, 13
- nanotechnology and, 87, 88

Savior advanced medkit, 95–96, 133
Scars, 132–33, 149
Scent glands, 76
Senseware, 11
Sensitive skin, 76
Seven-7, 121
Shiawase Corporation, 54, 91
- biotechnology and, 12, 62, 95
- chemistry and, 105
- nanotechnology and, 87

Shock hand, 42
Signal booster, cyberlimb, 40
Skin pigmentation, 76, 79
Slap Patches, 116
Sleep regulator, 74
Slip spray, 114
Small Unit Tactics, 22, 23, 47–48
Smart corrosives, 96
Smartlink system, 46
- subsystems, accessories, 32

Smartlink-2, 31
Spatial recognizer, 18
Speed
- drug, 105
- magical compounds, 122
- period, 106–7

Spirit strength, 123
Splash grenade, 113
Splat glue, 114, 116
Splat gun, 116
Spray foam explosive, 114
Spray tank, 116
Street drugs, 102, 104, 121–22
Stress
- Attribute dice and, 131
- automatic, 31
- bioware, 77, 128
- correction, 147
- cosmetic bioware, 76
- Level, 126
- maintenance, 130–31
- Point, 45, 124, 126
- Point removal, 150
- repair, 131, 147
- Test, 126 127, 150
- using, 131

Subdermal display, 26, 91
Subdermal speakers, 19
Substance abuse, 108–10
Superflash, 15
SuperSquirt II, 115
Suprathyroid gland, 69, 79
Surgery, 5, 135, 136, 143, 144, 146, 148
- bioware, 62
- costs, 151
- cybermancy side effects, 56–58
- skills for, 135–36
- tools, 136

Surgical option, 144, 146, 148–50
Surgical planning, preparation, 145–46
Surgical procedures, 136
Symbiotes, 69–70
Synaptic accelerator, 74–75, 79
Synthacardium, 70

T

Tactical computer, 22
Taggants, 85, 94–95
Tailored pheromones, 70–71
Tamanous, 63
Task Pool, 48
- chipjack expert driver, 19
- encephalon and, 20

Tear gas, 118
Telescoping cyberlimbs, 40
Therapeutic surgery, 130, 131, 147, 148
Thermite, 114–15
Thermosense organs, 75
TLE-x, 30-31
Tolerance, 108
- acquiring, 109
- Rating, 110

Toxin extractor, 71
Tracheal filter, 71–72, 79
Tracking weapon mount, 40, 41
Transducer, 14, 19
Transimplant surgery, 136, 147–48
Transys Neuronet, 12, 63
Trauma damper, 75–76
Trauma surgery, 148, 151

U

Ultrasound vision, 18
Unconscious revival, 131–32
United Oil Industries, 105
Universal Omnitech, 12, 90
- biotechnology and, 62
- nanotechnology and, 88

V

Valkyrie module, 139, 140
Vector, 105
Venom sack, 42
Visibility modifiers, 49
Vision systems
- multiple, 49
- use, 48-49

Voice mask, internal, 18–19

W

Witch's moss, 123
Withdrawal, 110
- forced, 109, 110

Wound effects, 126–30, 134, 150
- deadly, 129–30
- Stress and, 124

Wuxing, Incorporated, 53, 54
- cyberware and, 13
- nanotechnology and, 90

X-Z

X-E suit, 119
Yakashima
- biotechnology and, 63
- chemistry and, 105

Yamatetsu, 88, 90, 91
- biotechnology and, 63
- cyberware and, 12
- nanotechnology and, 86, 87

Z-IC splash grenades, 117
Zen, 121
Zeta-ImpChem, 104